THE WORLD'S MOST BEAUTIFUL CG CHARACTERS

EXOTIQUE 3™

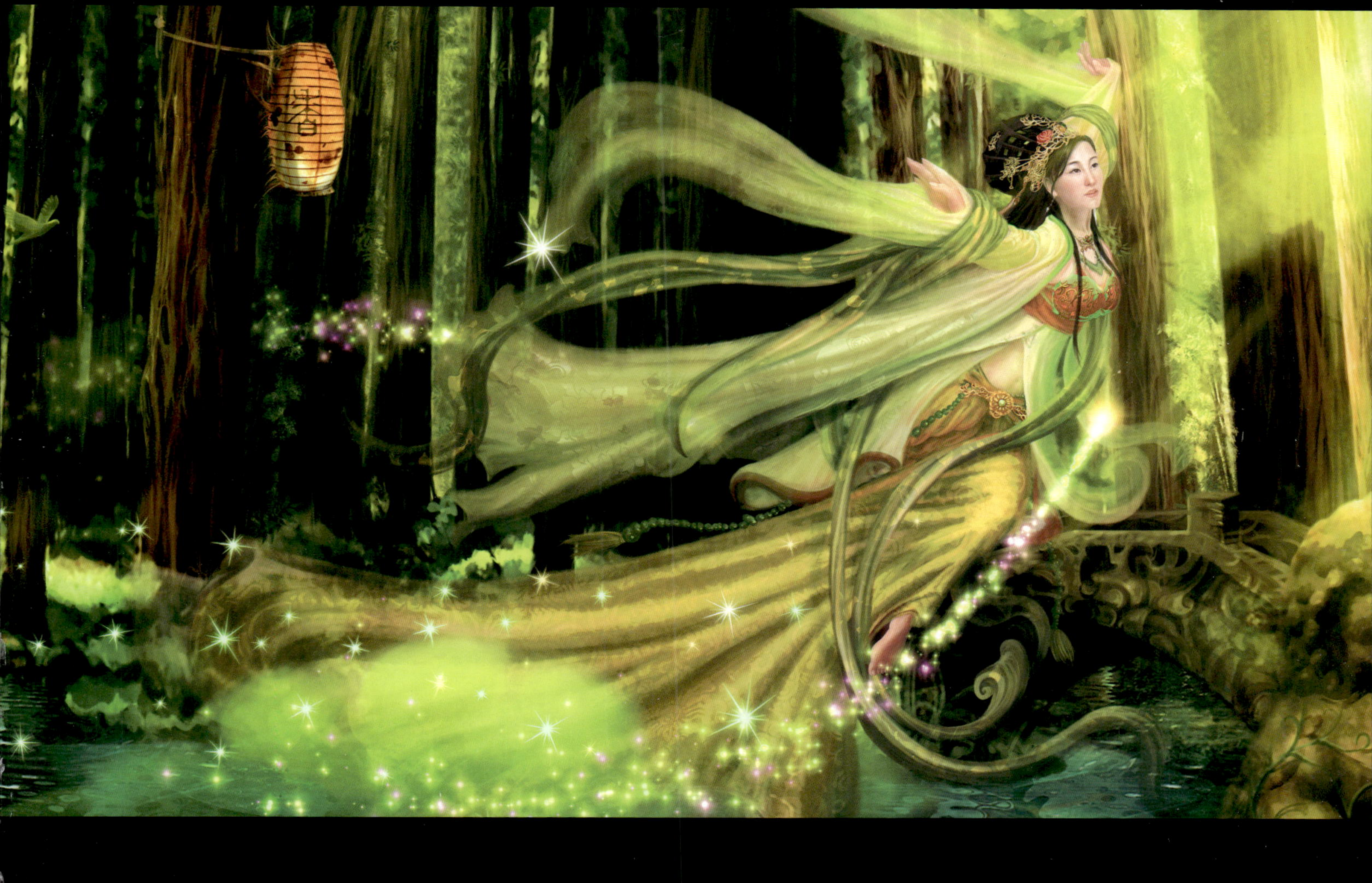

Edited by

Daniel Wade & Paul Hellard

EXOTIQUE 3™

Published
by
Ballistic Publishing
Publishers of digital works for the digital world
135 Gilbert St
Adelaide, SA 5000
Australia
www.BallisticPublishing.com
Correspondence:
info@BallisticPublishing.com

First Edition published in Australia 2007 by Ballistic Publishing

Softcover Edition ISBN 978-1-921002-45-8
Special Edition ISBN 978-1-921002-44-1

Managing Editor
Daniel Wade

Assistant Editor
Paul Hellard

Art Director
Mark Snoswell

Design & Image Processing
Lauren Stevens

Printing and binding
Everbest Printing (China)
www.everbest.com

Partners
The CGSociety (Computer Graphics Society)
www.CGSociety.org

Also available from Ballistic Publishing

d'artiste Character Modeling 2	ISBN 978-1-921002-35-9
Creative ESSENCE: The Face	ISBN 978-1-921002-36-6
EXPOSÉ 5 Softcover	ISBN 978-1-921002-39-7
EXOTIQUE 2 Softcover	ISBN 978-1-921002-34-2
EXOTIQUE Softcover	ISBN 978-1-921002-26-7

Visit www.BallisticPublishing.com
for our complete range of titles.

Cover image credits

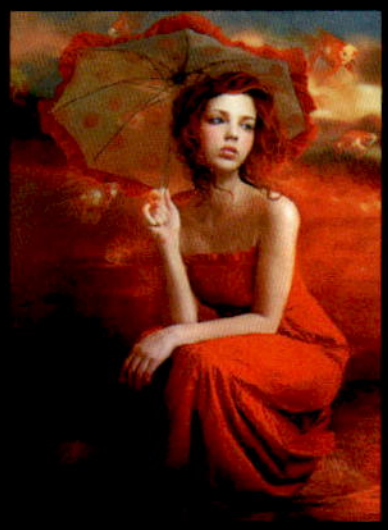

Umbrella sky
Painter, Photoshop
Client: ImagineFX magazine
Marta Dahlig, POLAND
[Front cover: EXOTIQUE 3 Softcover edition], 68-69

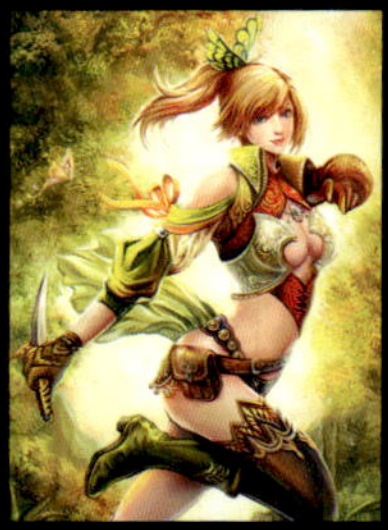

Little thief in the forest
Photoshop
Fan Yang, USA
[Back cover: EXOTIQUE 3 Softcover edition], 183

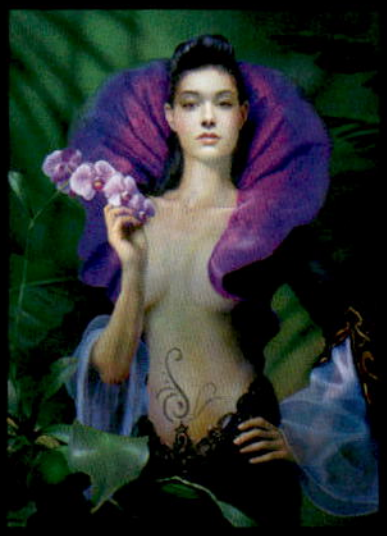

Purple Orchid
Photoshop
Drazenka Kimpel, USA
[Cover: EXOTIQUE 3 Special Edition], 19

EDITORIAL

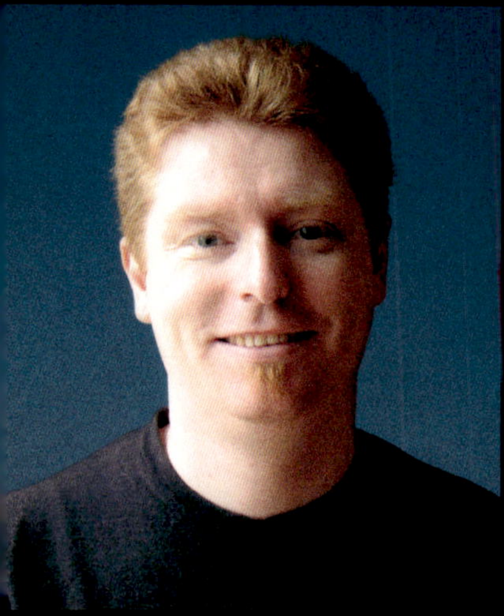

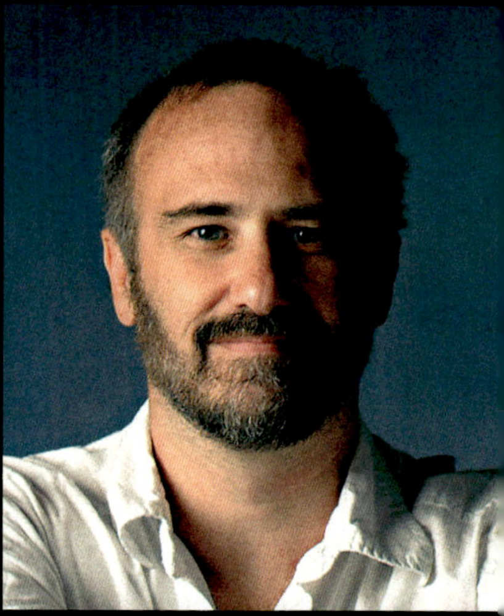

Daniel Wade | Managing Editor & Mark Snoswell | Publisher

Once limited to portraits and cartoon characters, character artists are no longer restricted in either their medium or where their characters can appear. Every film or game project requires character artists from the initial concepts through to realizing them in 3D space. 2D artists start with the idea of the character, fixing them within a moment in time to either tell a story in a single frame or to begin a 3D character's life. 3D character artists can take on the roles of sculptor, makeup artist, stylist, or animator in the service of creating believable characters. Regardless of the stage at which they are involved, character artists can be found working on blockbuster movies, TV shows, games, or in traditional mediums like books, comics, or even on canvas.

While the digital tools now allow us to create realistic digital humans, the fertile imagination and honed artistic eye of an artist is required to conceive and execute works of art which are the basis of these characters. Today's artists design, model, compose, texture, light and render their work. Everything must be executed well and work in harmony to achieve the best result possible. More than ever before, the digital artist must be aware of all the elements that combine to make an appealing and inspiring image. Natural talent and a good eye need to be augmented by a deep understanding of the subject, medium, light interactions and techniques.

EXOTIQUE 3 pays homage to the imagination and creative talents of these digital artists from all around the world. The third book in the series brings together the world's most beautiful CG characters in genres from science fiction, fantasy, and anime, to photorealism and stylized realism. EXOTIQUE was conceived as a vehicle for the truly great character artwork that overflowed from our EXPOSÉ annuals. Just three years later EXOTIQUE now stands beside EXPOSÉ as the industry's best collection of character art. The quality of entries for EXOTIQUE 3 made the selection of artwork a significant challenge and we recommend visiting the Ballistic Publishing web site to view the many worthy entries that narrowly missed out (www.BallisticPublishing.com/bsw/viewEntries.php). With just over 2,200 entries in total, one in seven images entered for EXOTIQUE 3 were successful. This meant we were able to squeeze another 23 pieces of artwork into EXOTIQUE 3 from 197 artists in 45 countries (up from 168 artists and 38 countries in EXOTIQUE 2). Another gratifying statistic was the 119 artists featured for the first time in a Ballistic publication. With the enormous talent in our online communities the EXOTIQUE series will continue to document the development of character art and the world's best examples of digital character art.

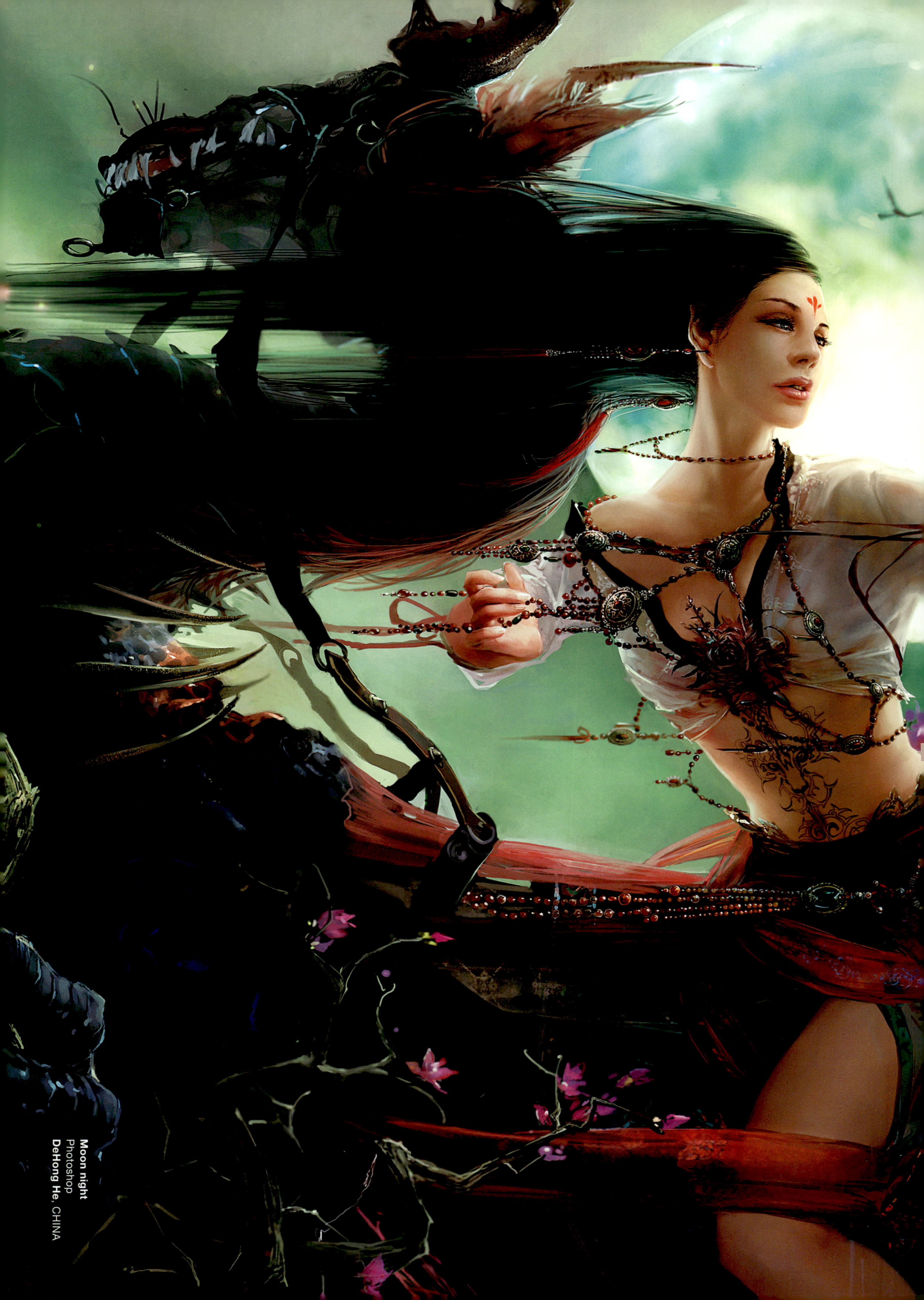

Moon night
Photoshop
DeHong He, CHINA

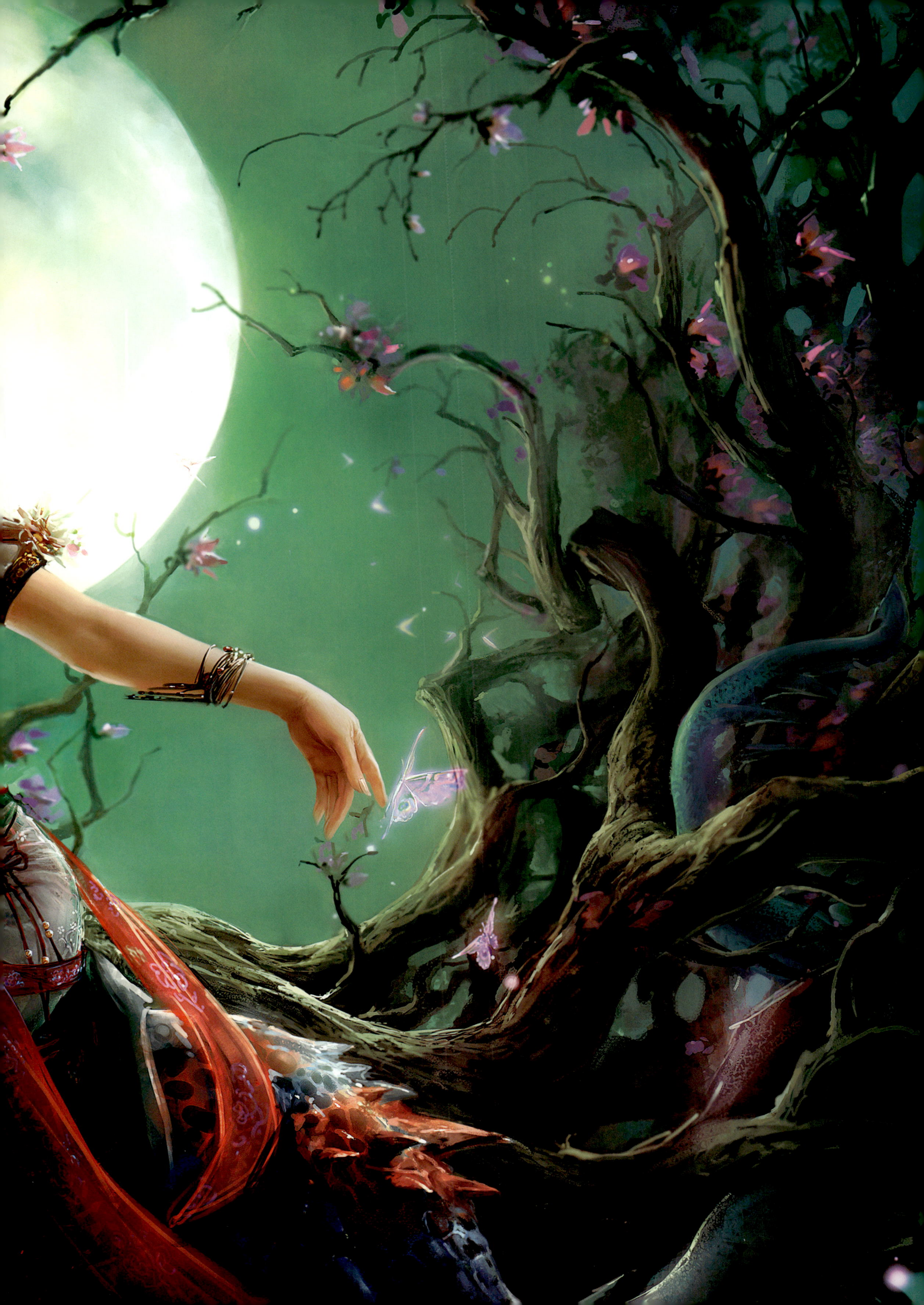

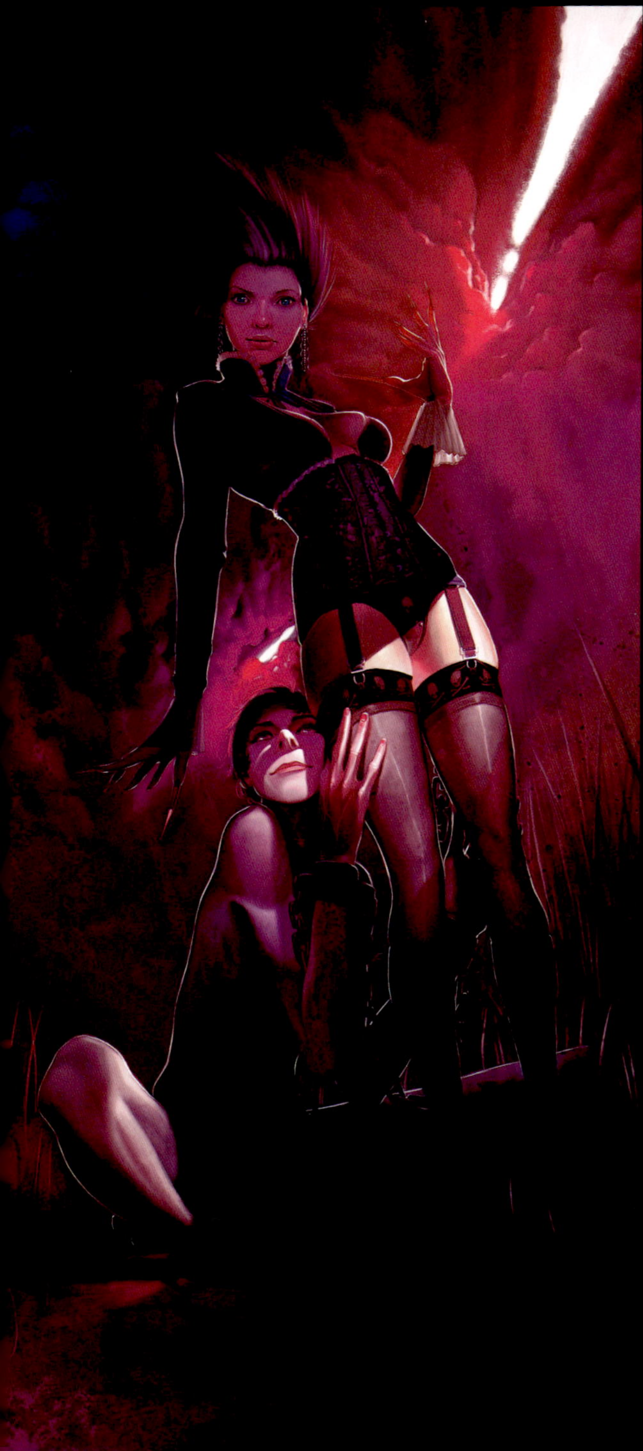

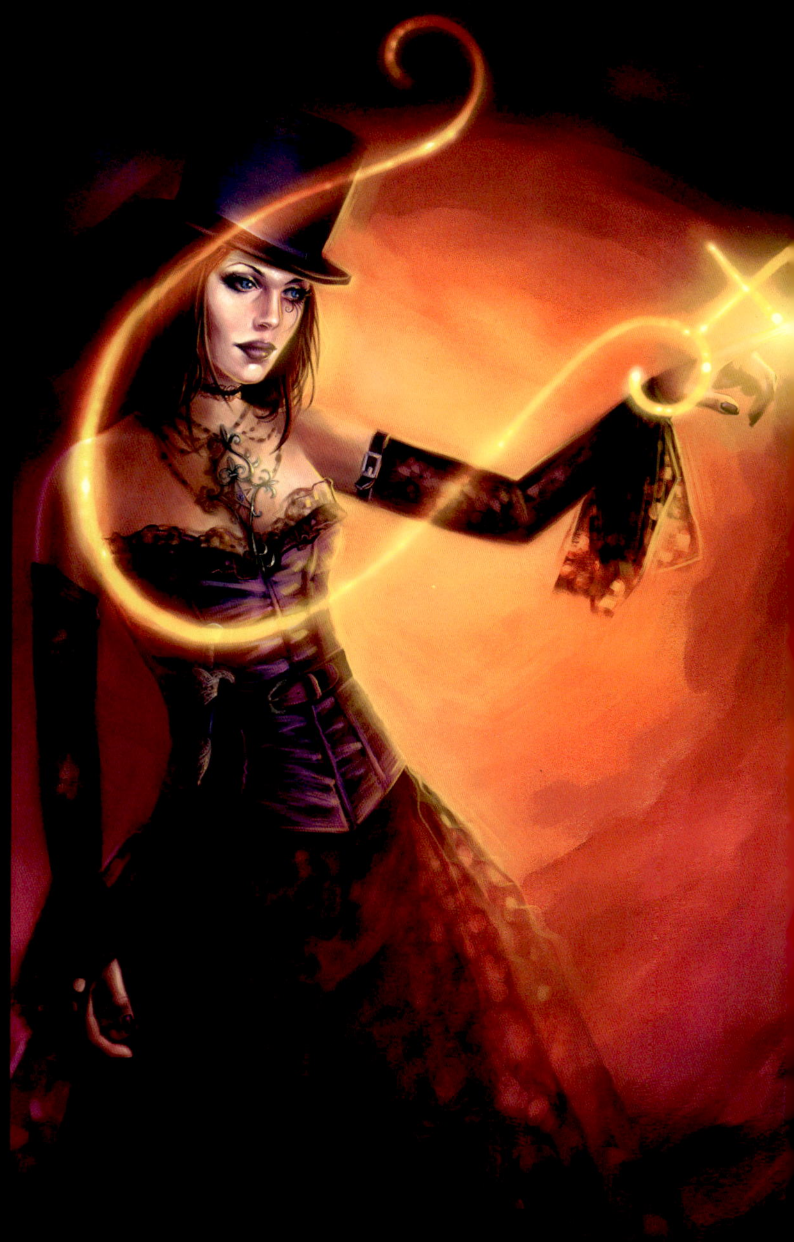

A lucky charm
Photoshop
Andrew Hibner, USA
[above]

Vex Harrow
Painter
Sanjana Baijnath, NEW ZEALAND
[above]

Brume
Photoshop, Painter
Melanie Delon, FRANCE
[right]

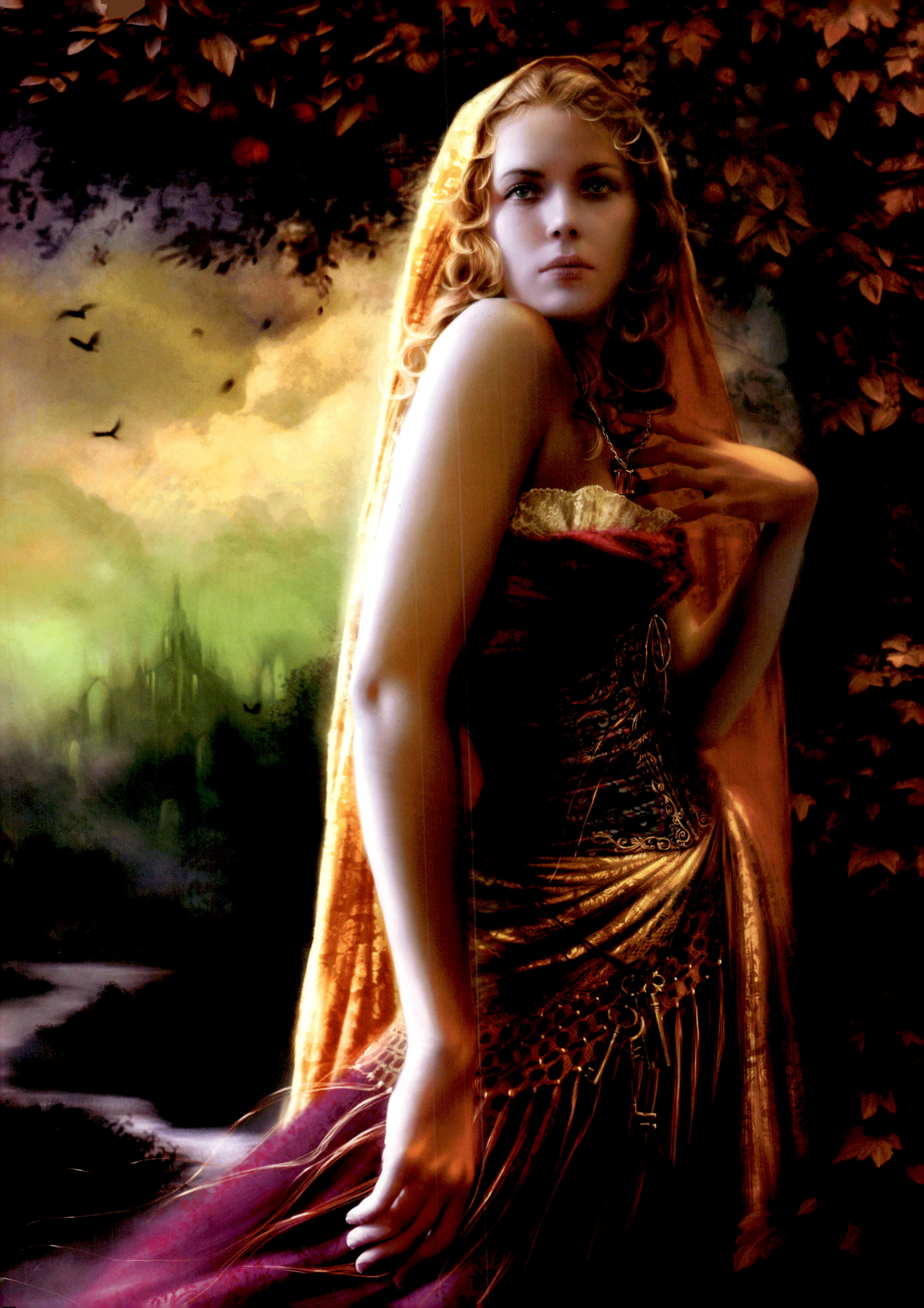

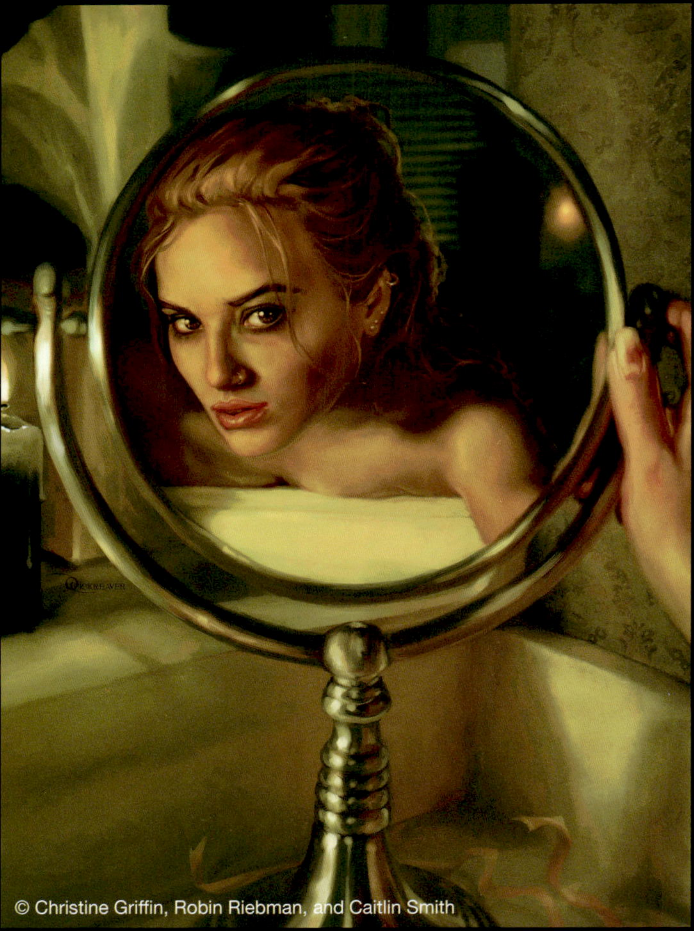

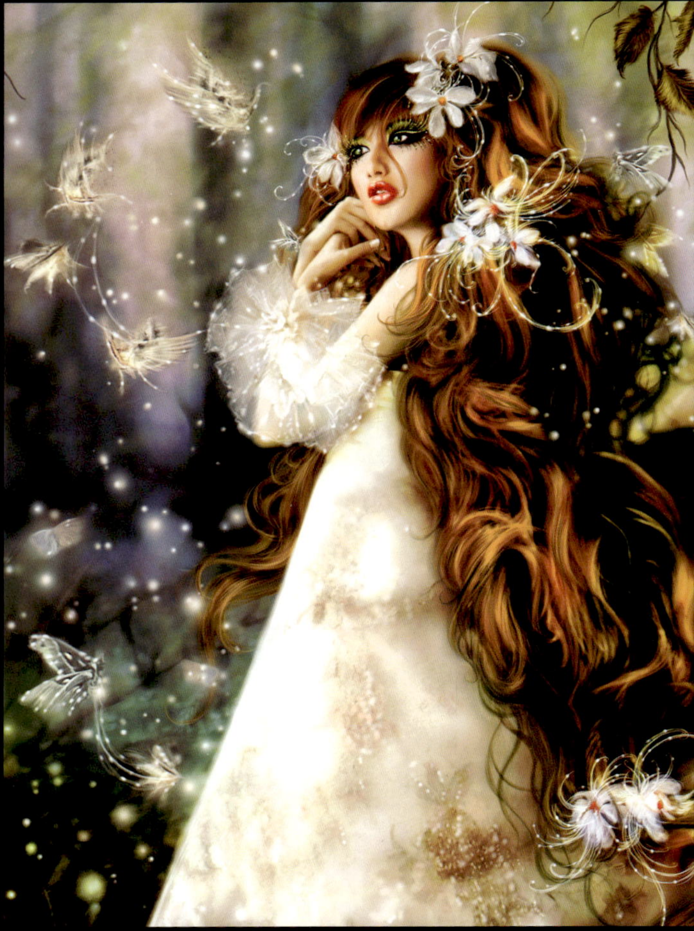

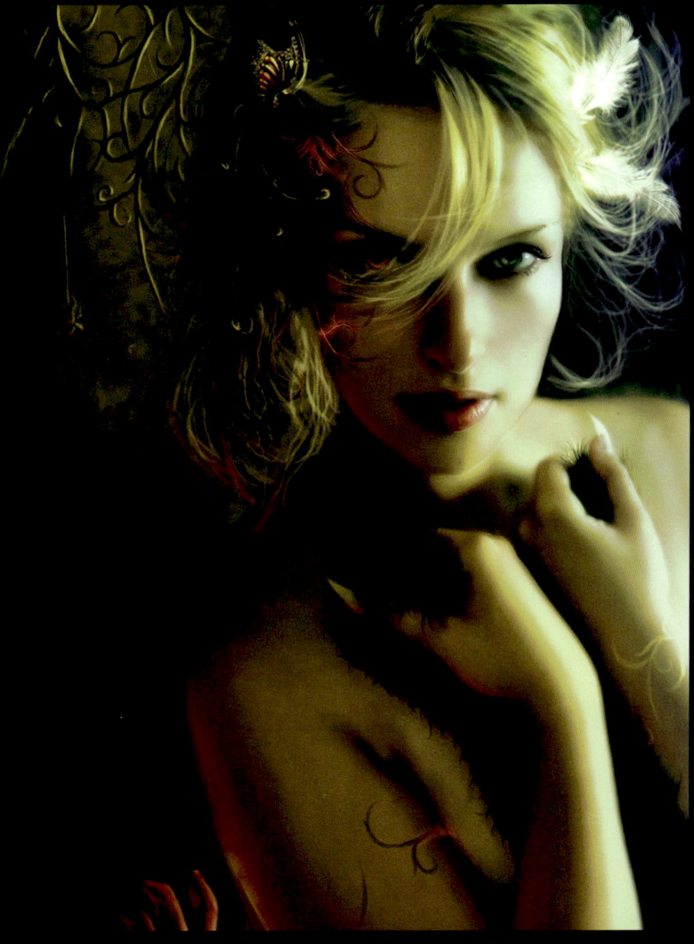

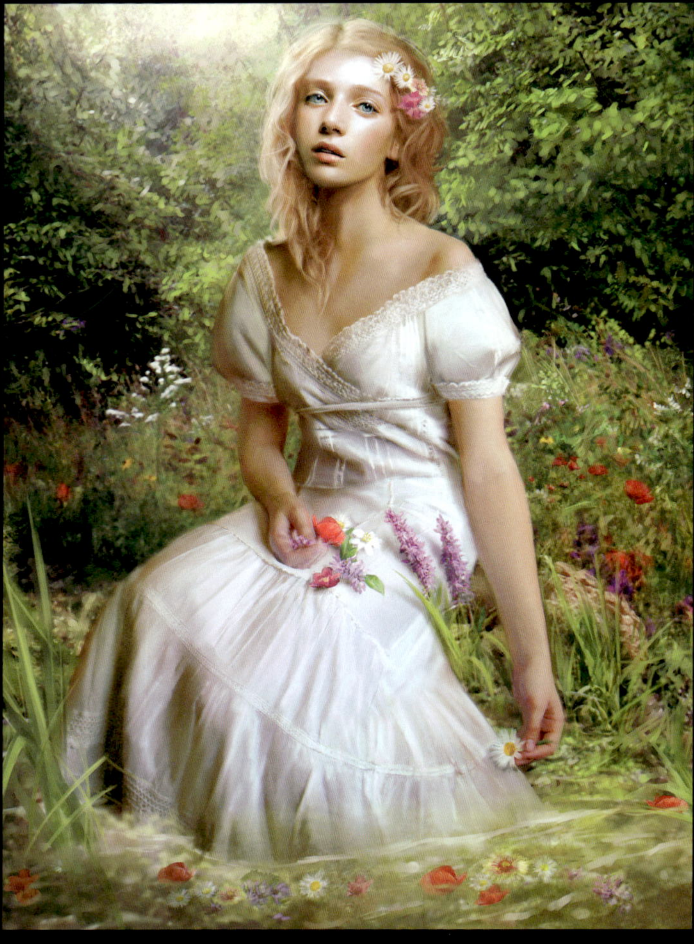

Jane
Painter, Photoshop
Christine Griffin,
USA
[top]

Malcanteth
Photoshop
Suzanne van Pelt,
NETHERLANDS
[above]

World-without-end hour
Painter
Katarina Sokolova,
UKRAINE
[top]

Ophelia
Painter, Photoshop
Client: ImagineFX magazine
Marta Dahlig, POLAND
[above]

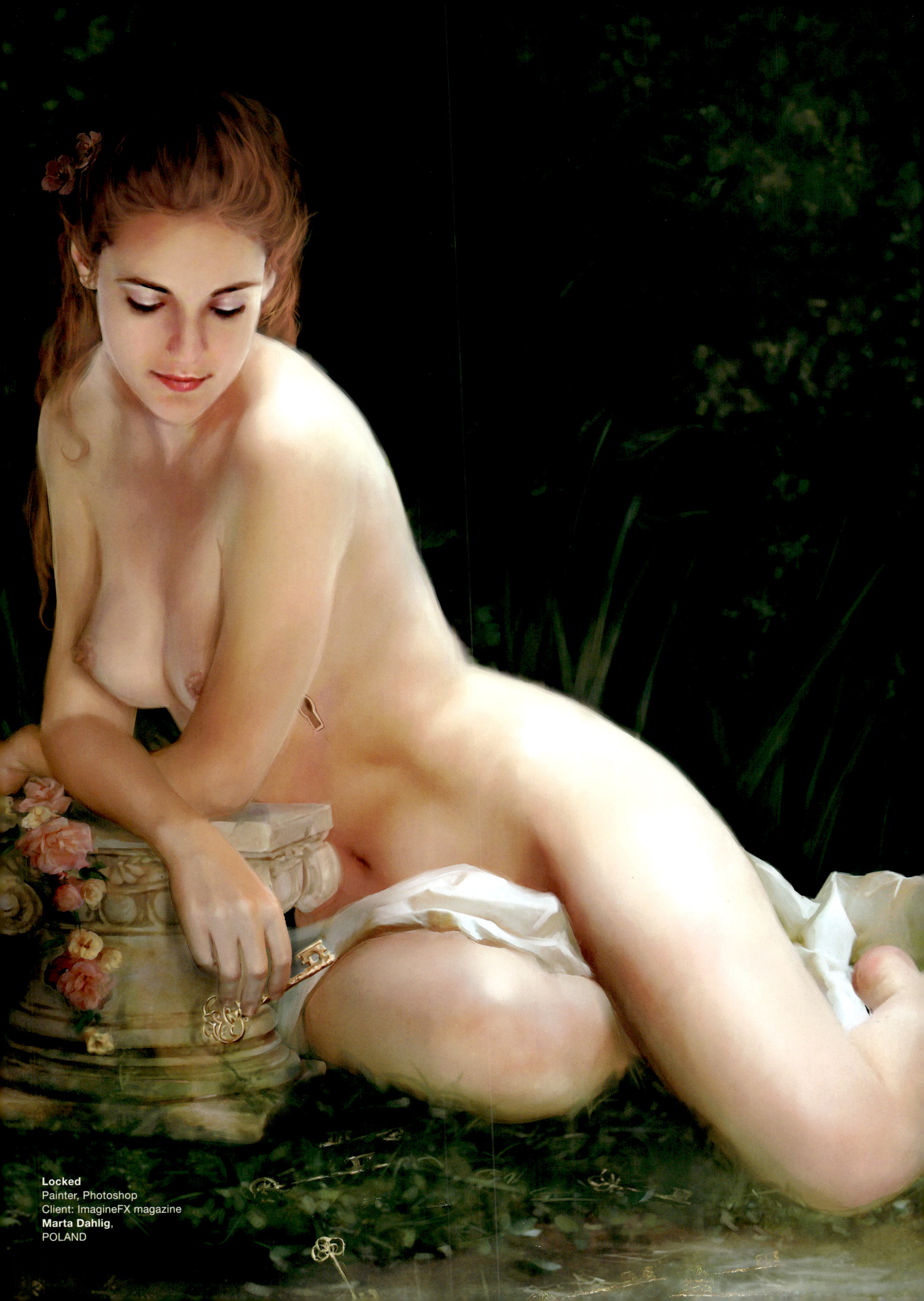

Locked
Painter, Photoshop
Client: ImagineFX magazine
Marta Dahlig,
POLAND

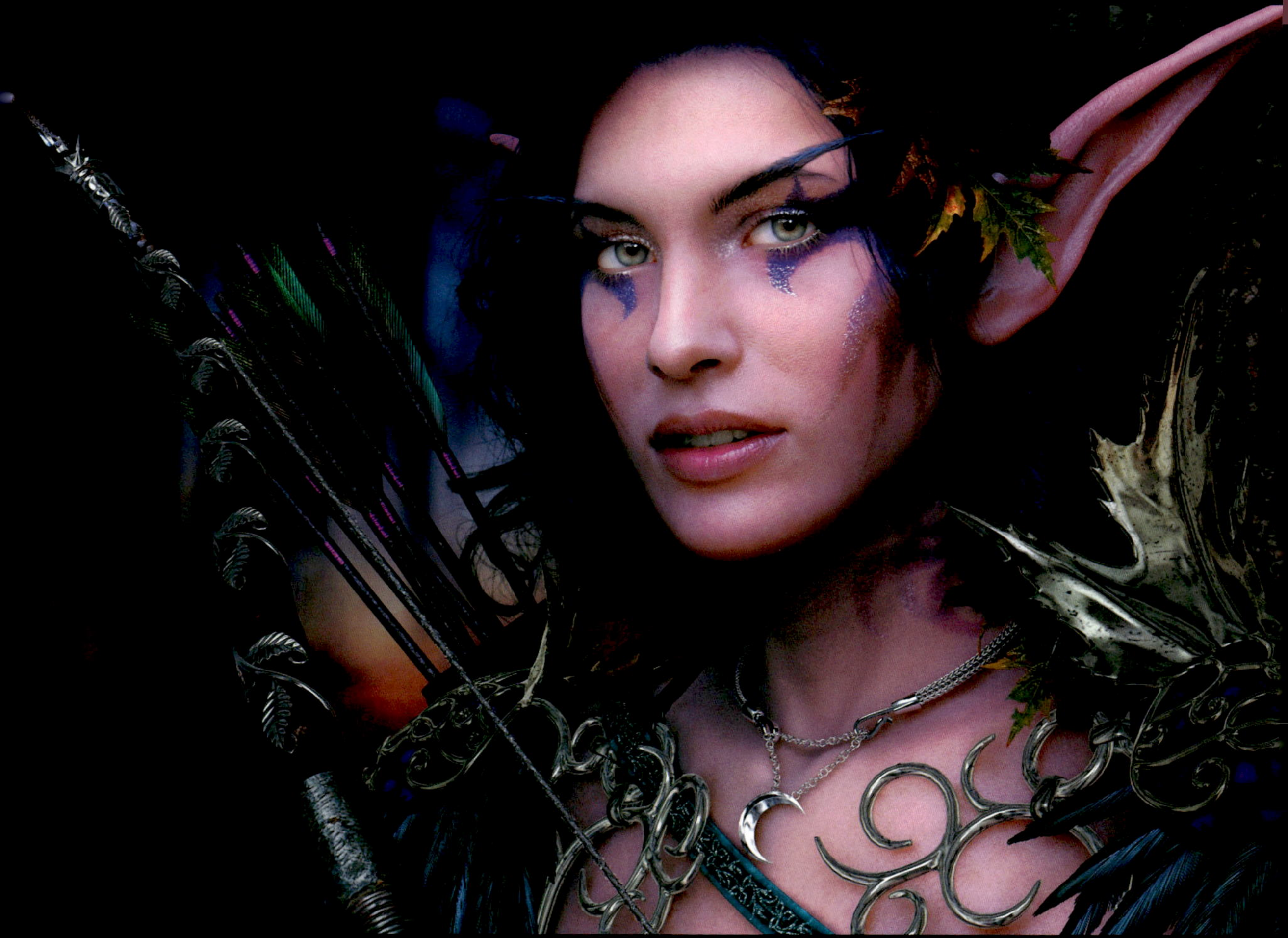

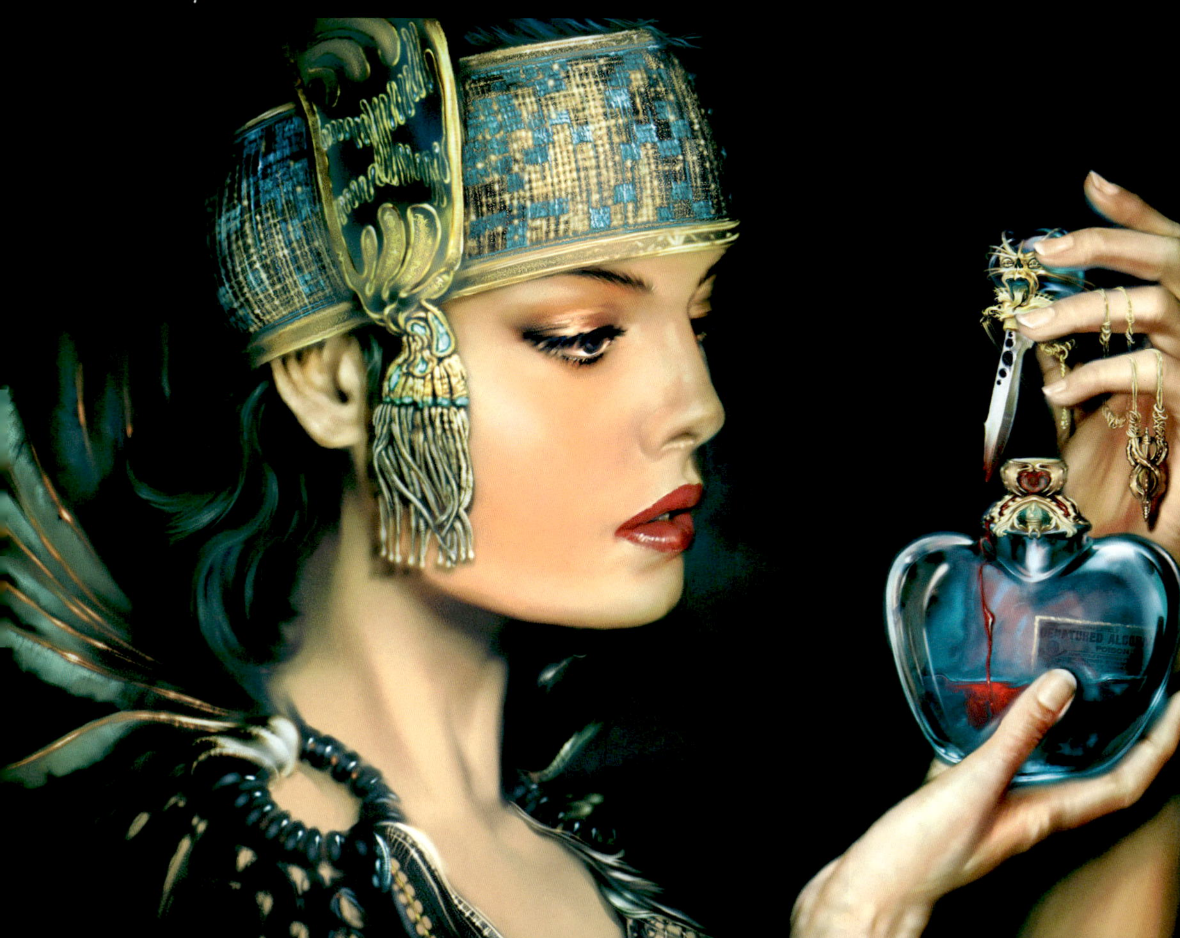

Night Elf
Maya
Max Kor, ISRAEL
[top]

Poisonous heart
Painter
Emile Noordeloos, NETHERLANDS
[above]

Peacock woman
3ds Max
Jiri Adamec, CZECH REPUBLIC
[right]

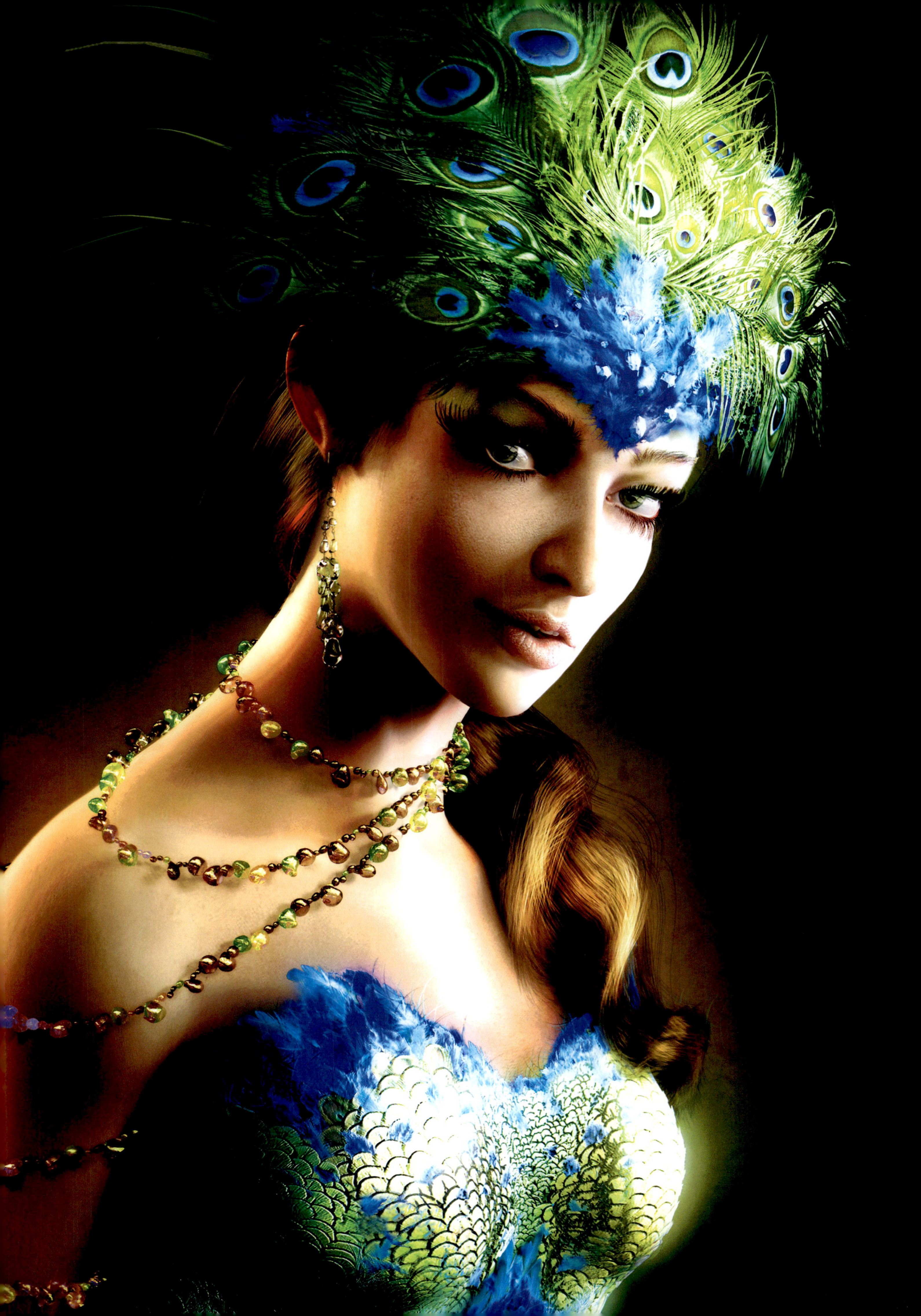

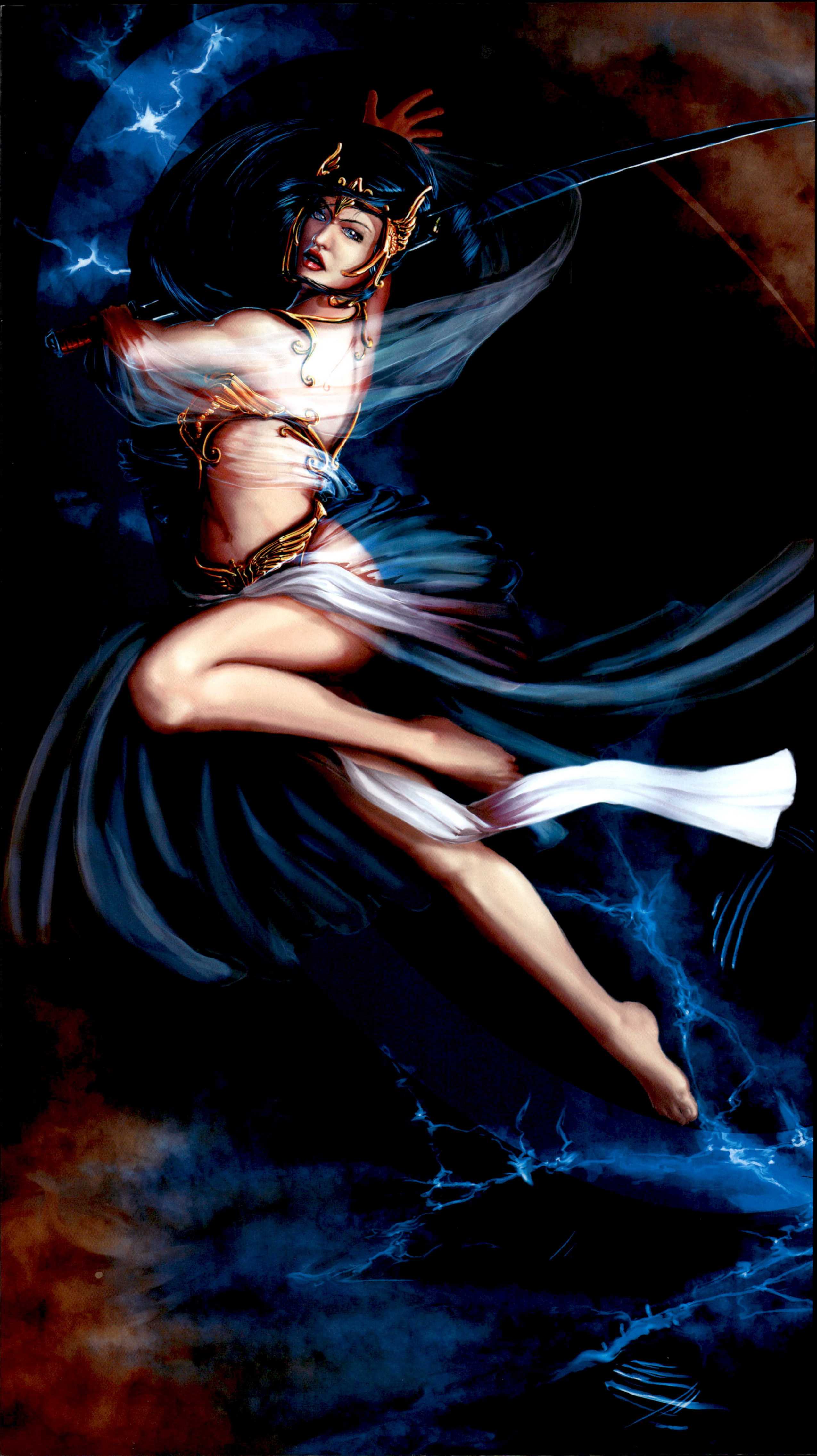

Valkyrie Nuevo
Photoshop
Chelsea Gaither, USA
[left]

Glory falls
Photoshop
Fan Yang, USA
[right]

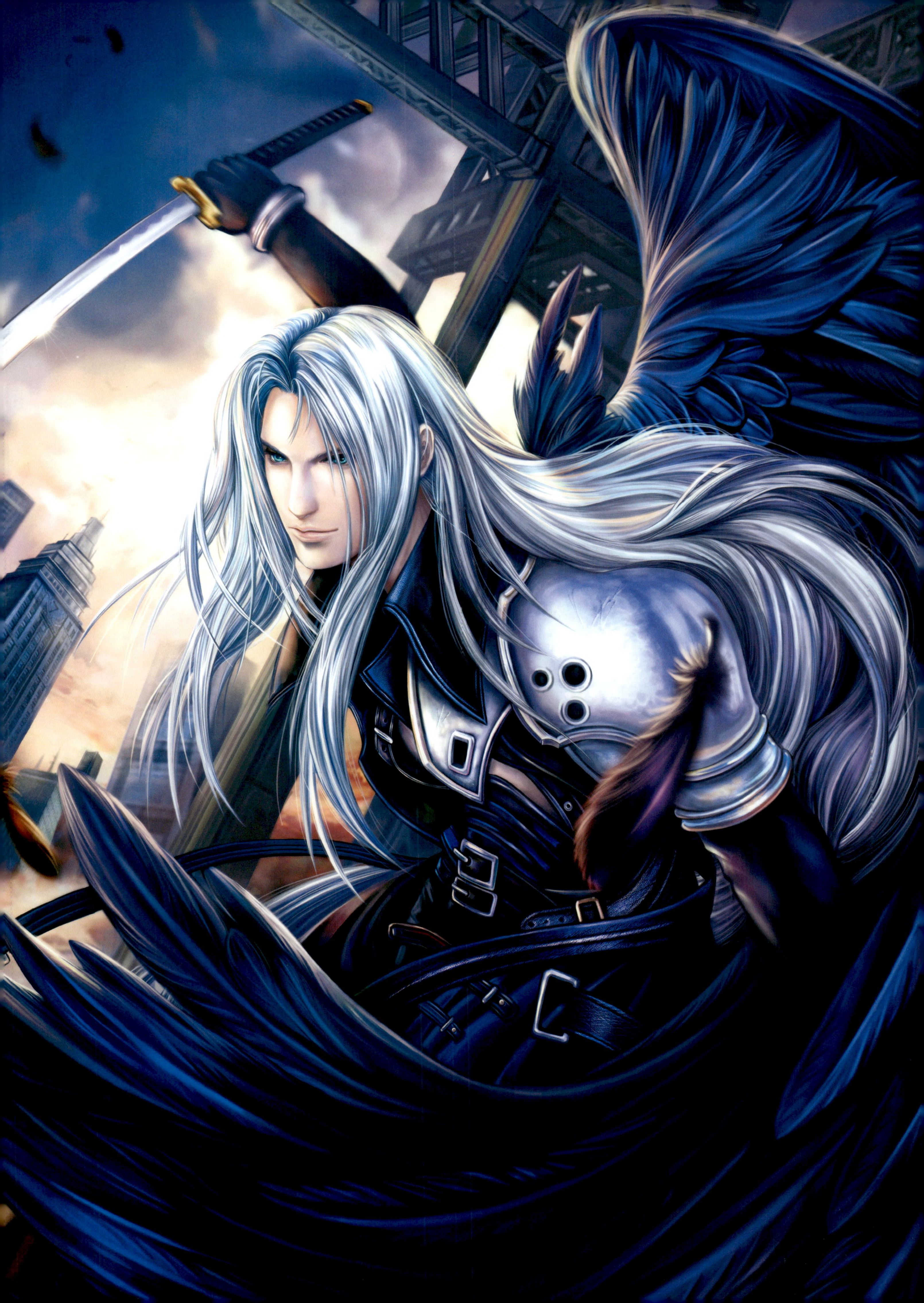

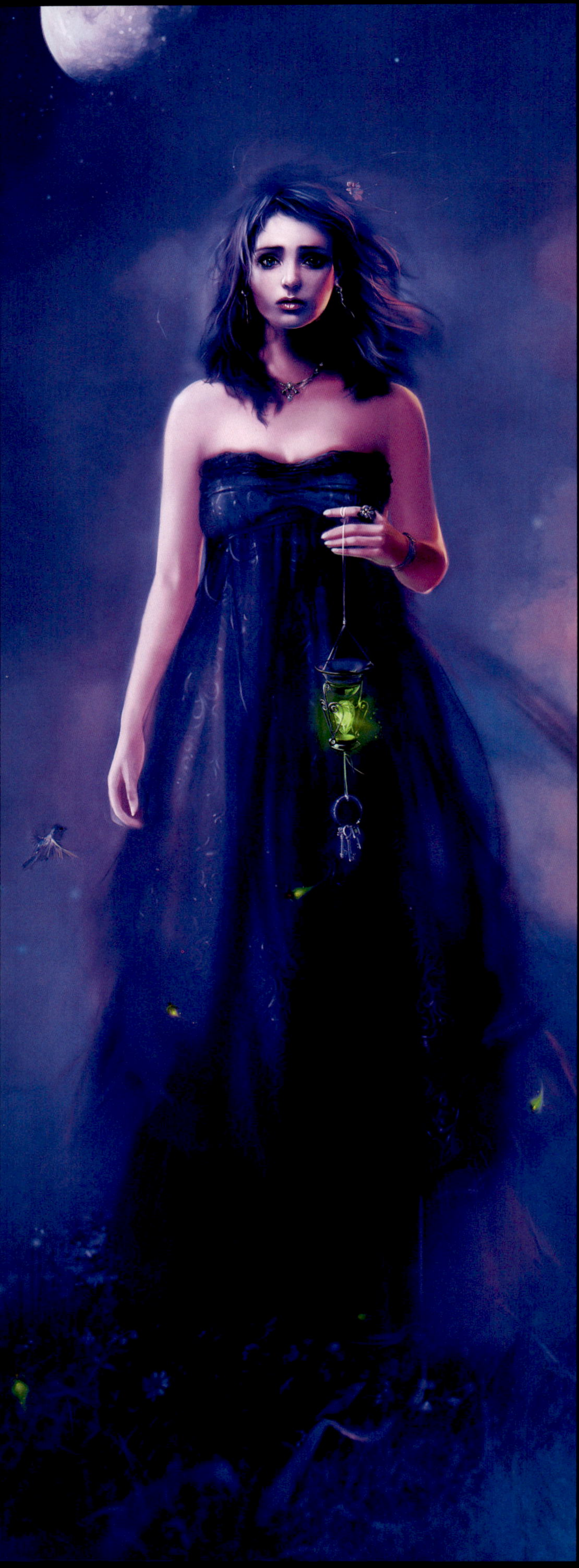

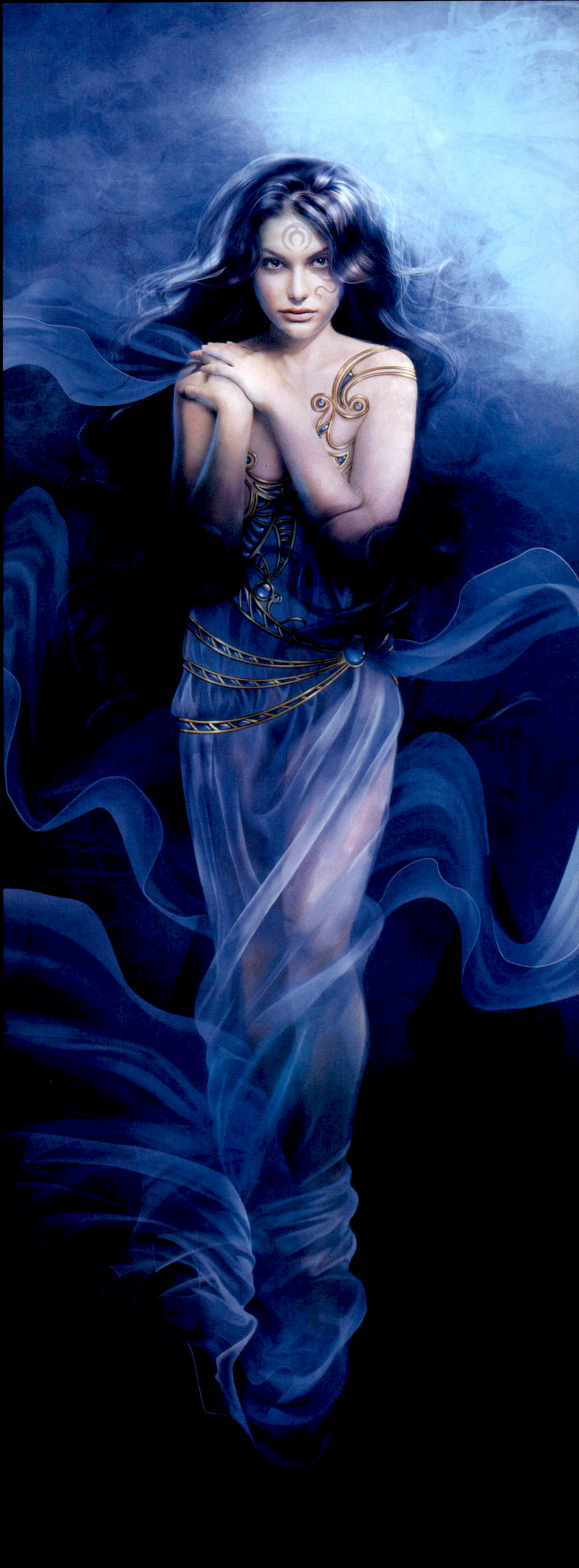

Hecate
Photoshop
Xiao Bing, CHINA
[above]

Indigo
Photoshop
Drazenka Kimpel, USA
[above]

The Intrigue of Goddess
Painter, Photoshop
Na Sun, CHINA
[right]

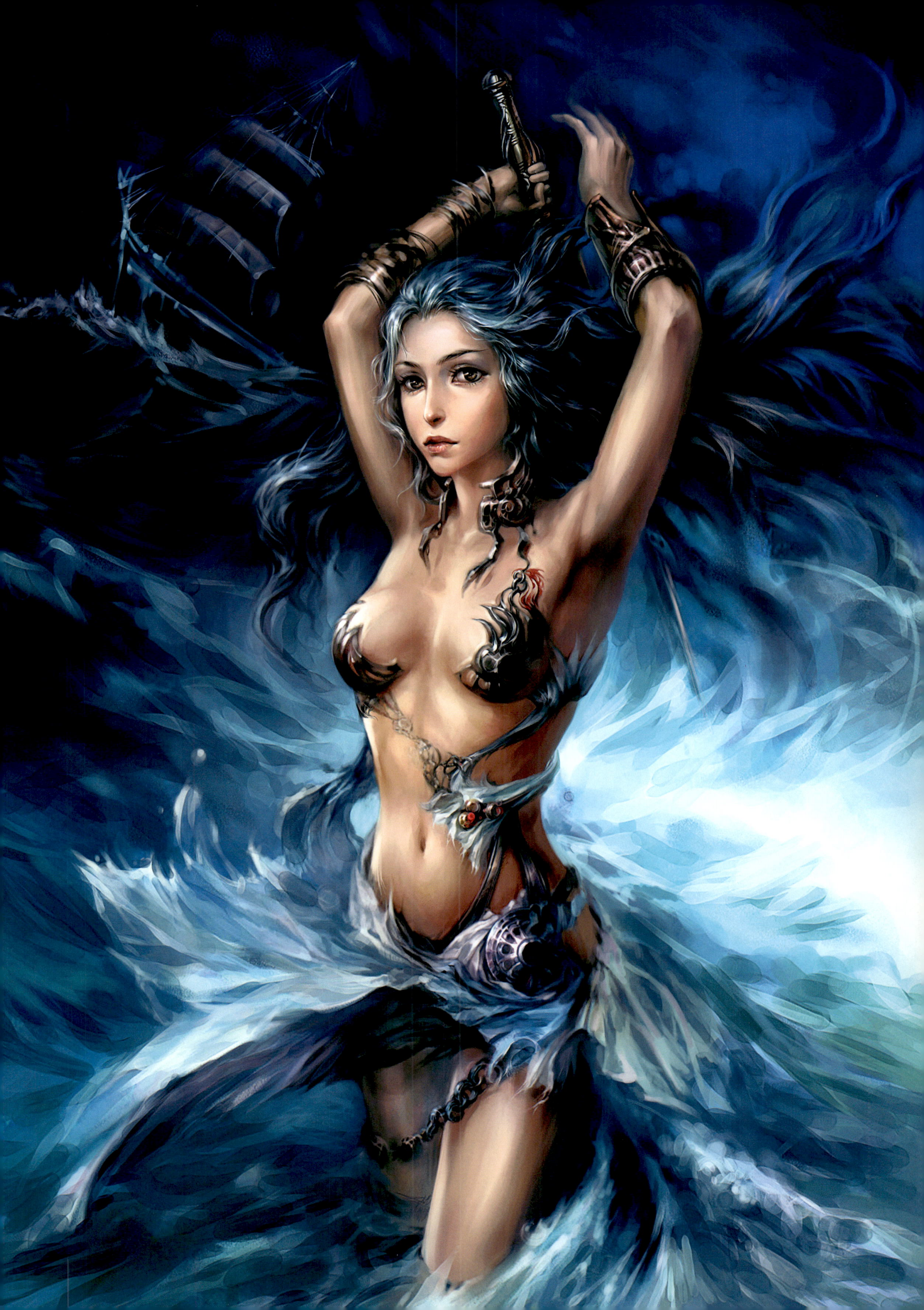

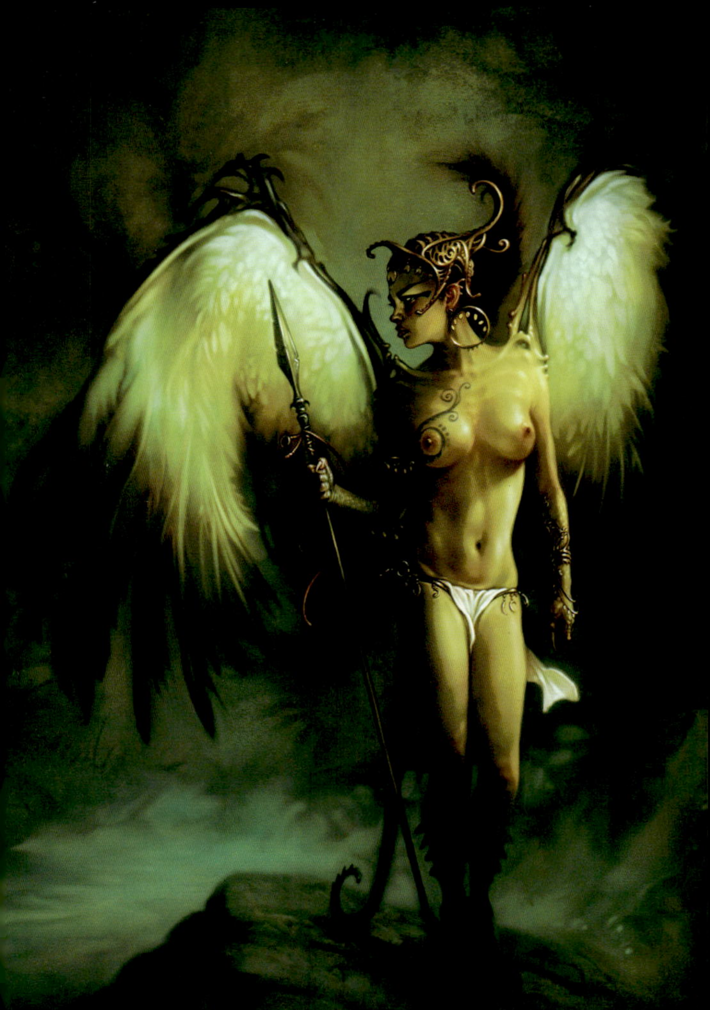

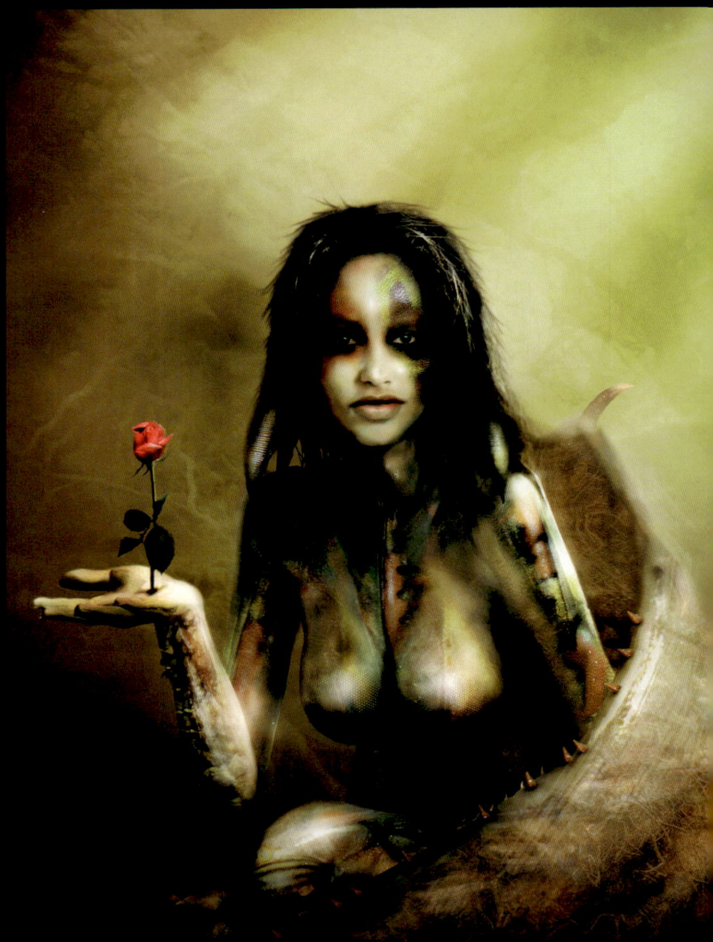

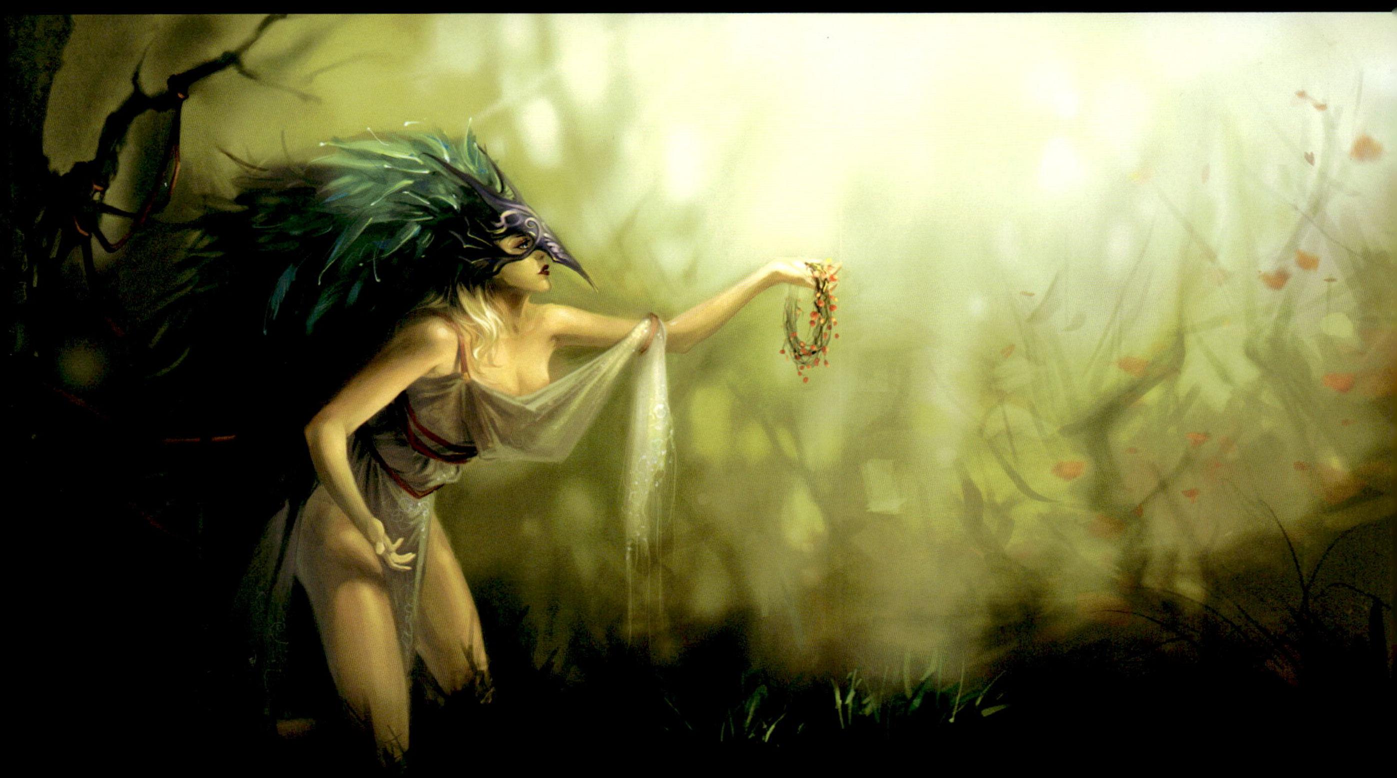

Seraph
Painter
Patrick J. Jones, AUSTRALIA
[top]

Mummer's dance
Photoshop
Mingjue Chen, USA
[above]

EarthRose
Photoshop, Painter
Paul Gerrard, GREAT BRITAIN
[top]

Follow me
Painter, Photoshop
Benita Winckler, GERMAN
[right]

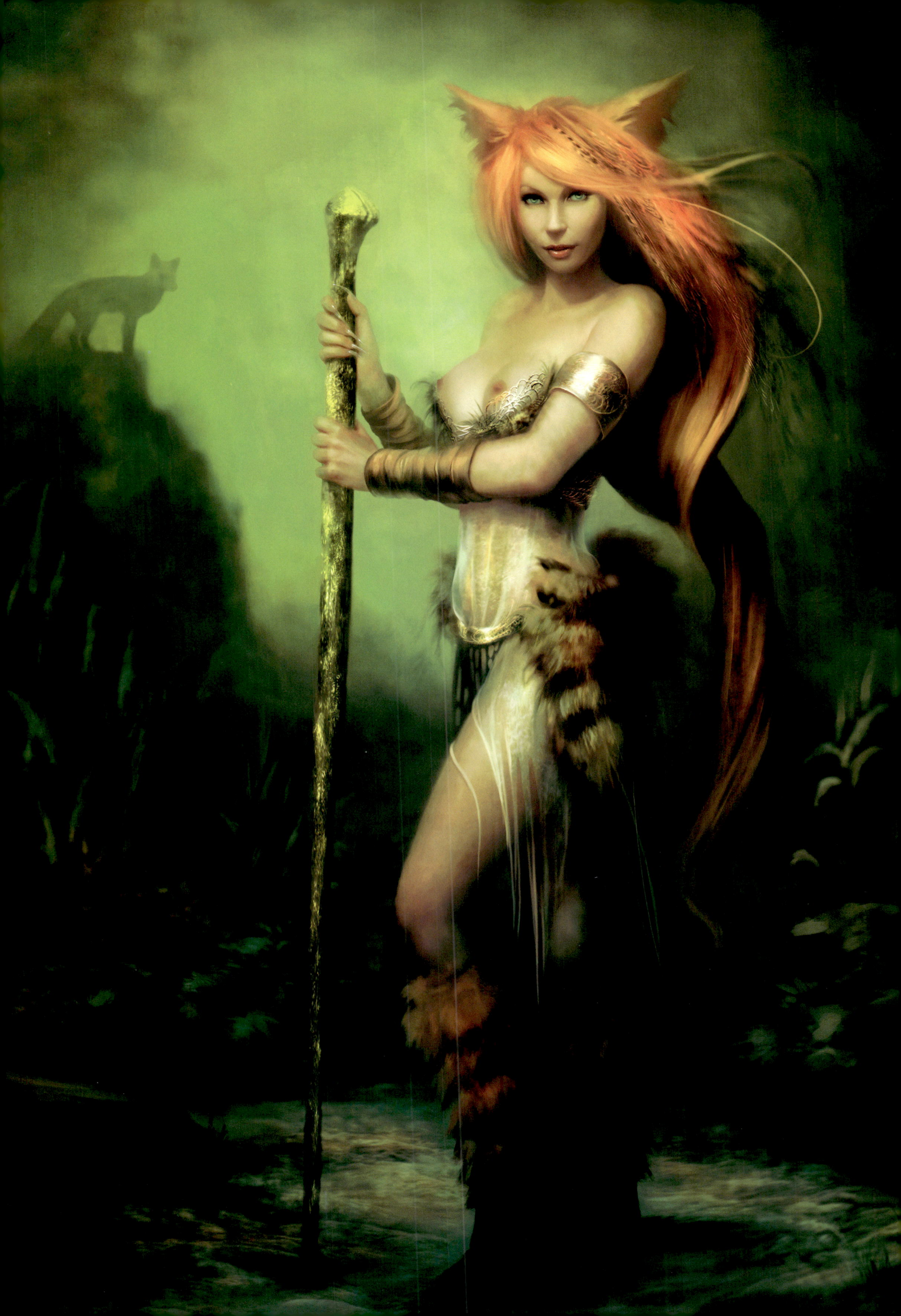

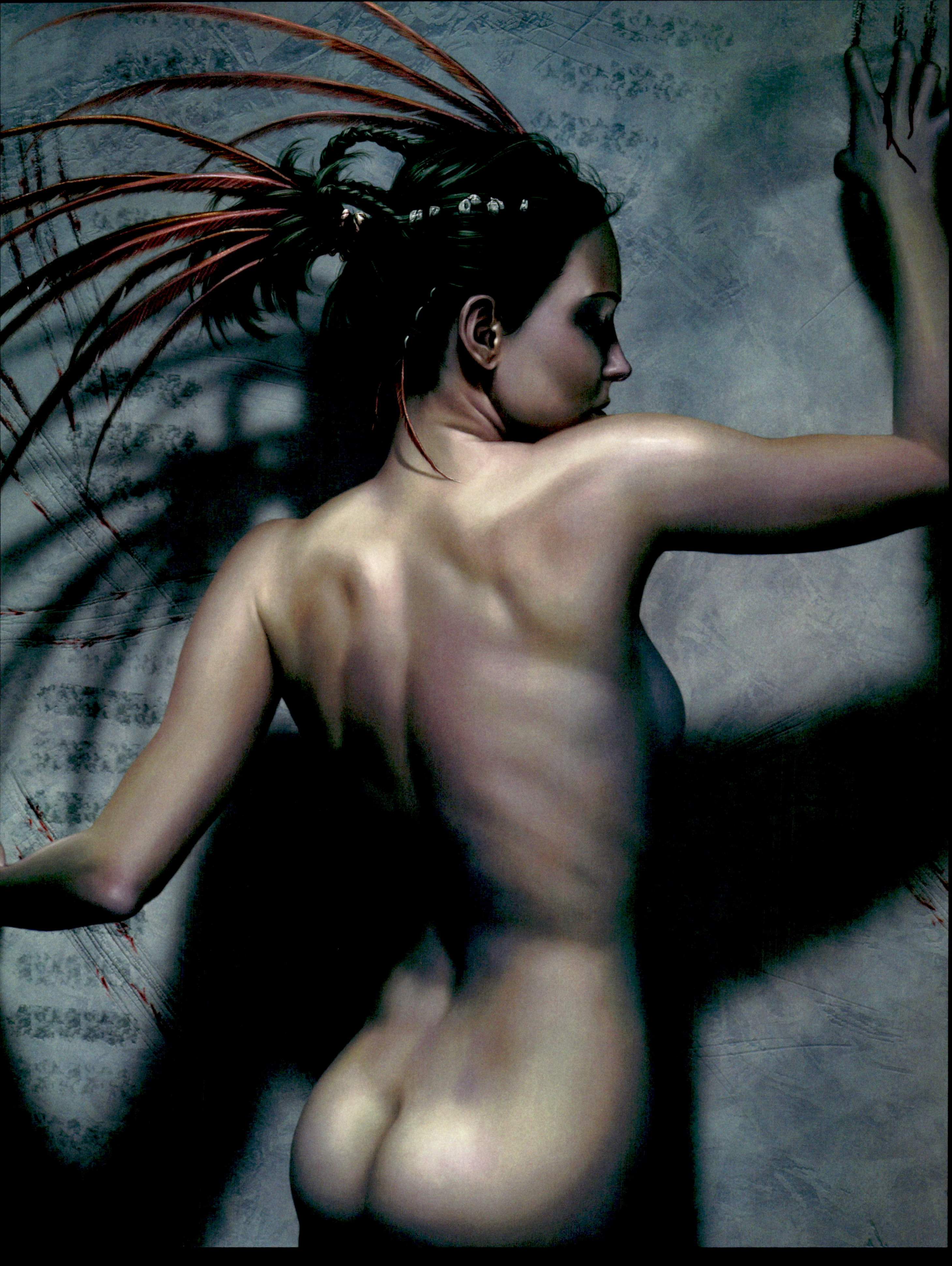

Wall
Photoshop
Henning Ludvigsen, NORWAY
[above]

Purple Orchid
Photoshop
Drazenka Kimpel, USA
[right]

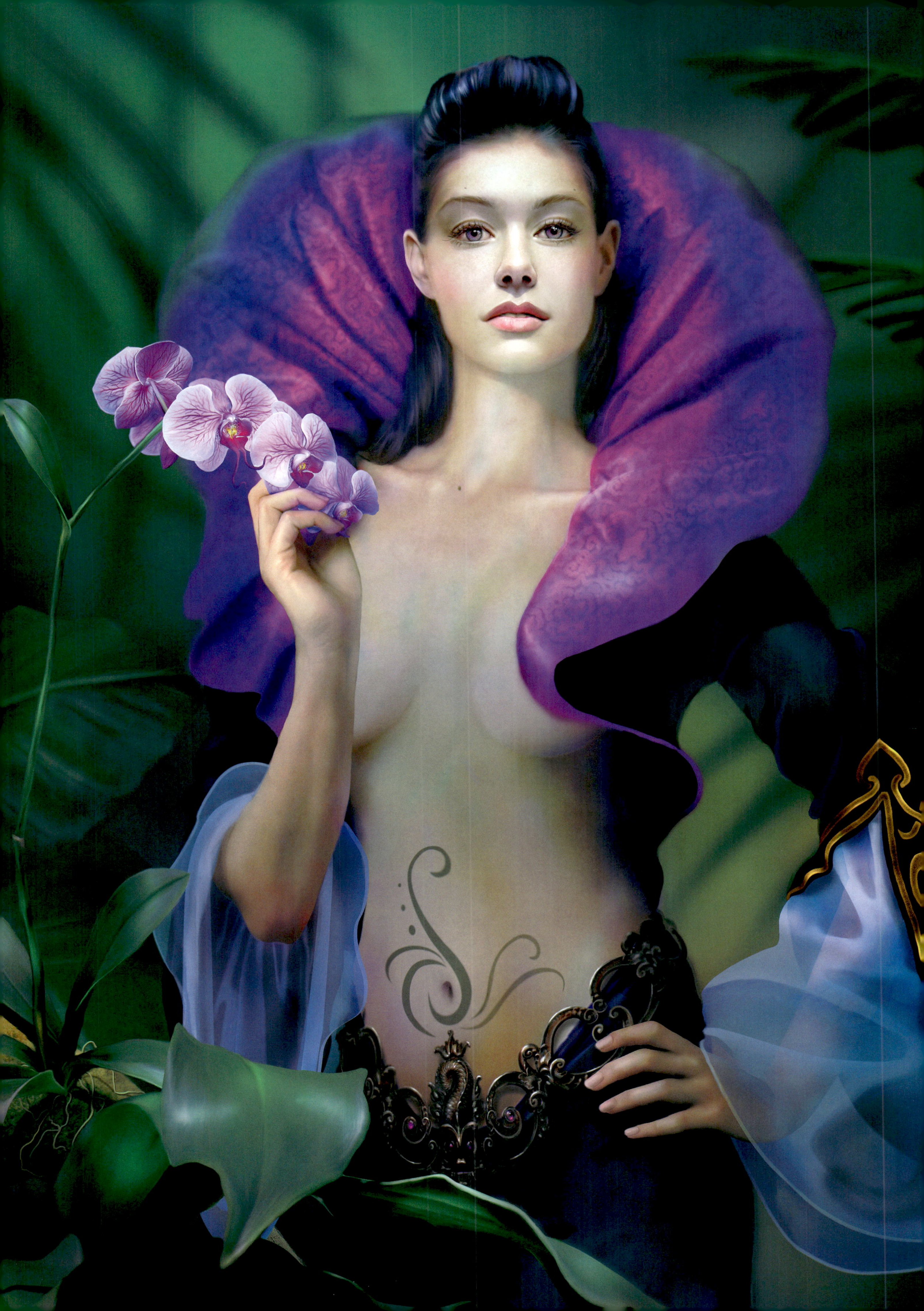

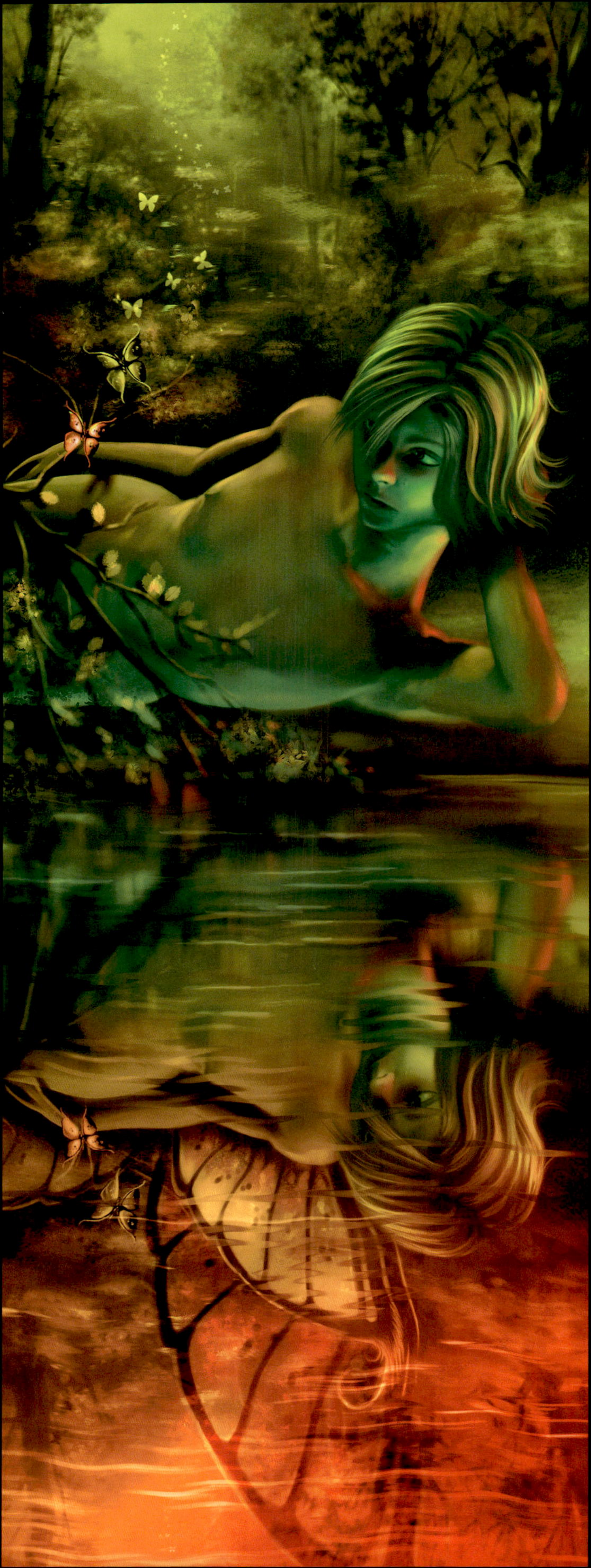

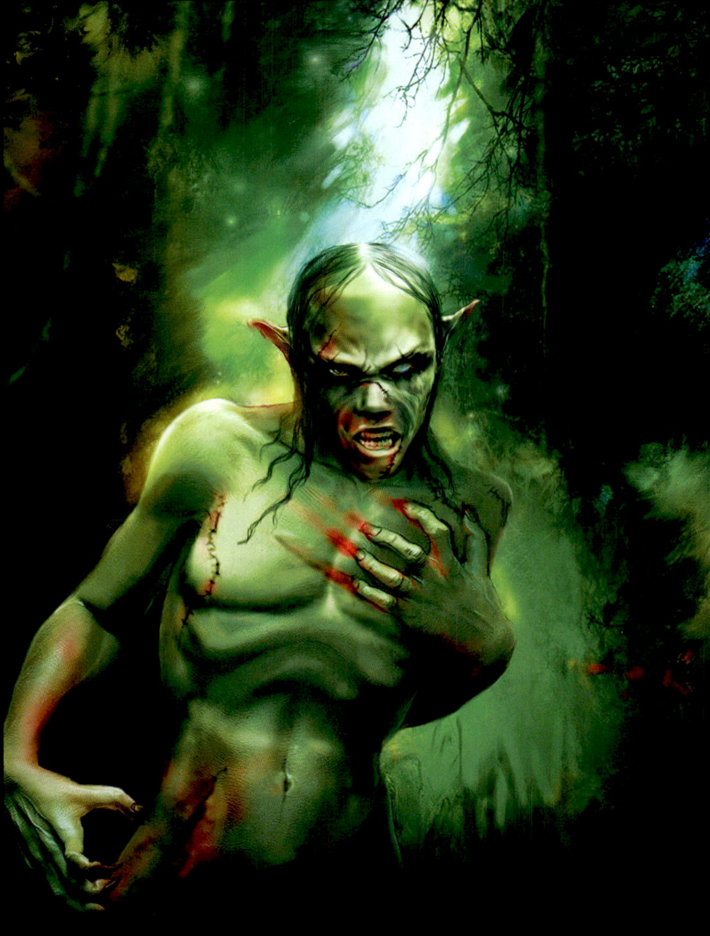

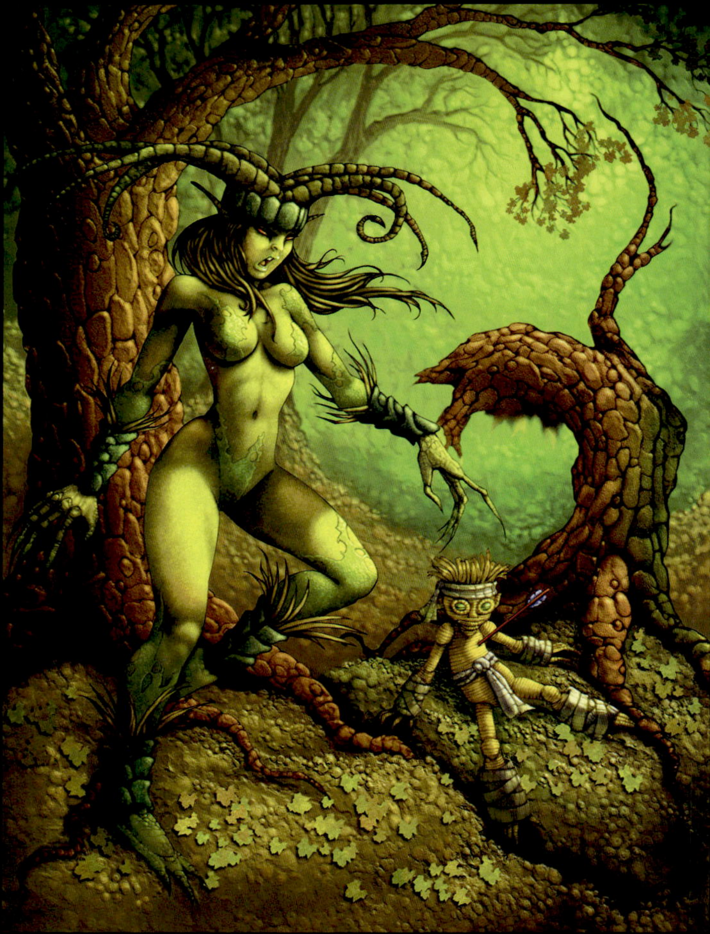

Dream comes true
Photoshop, Painter, Poser
Angelos Agiostratitis,
GREECE
[above]

Cave dweller
Photoshop, Painter
Dawn Austin, austinillustration,
HONG KONG
[top]

Battle Dryad
Photoshop, Painter
Alejandro Gutiérrez Franco,
MEXICO
[above]

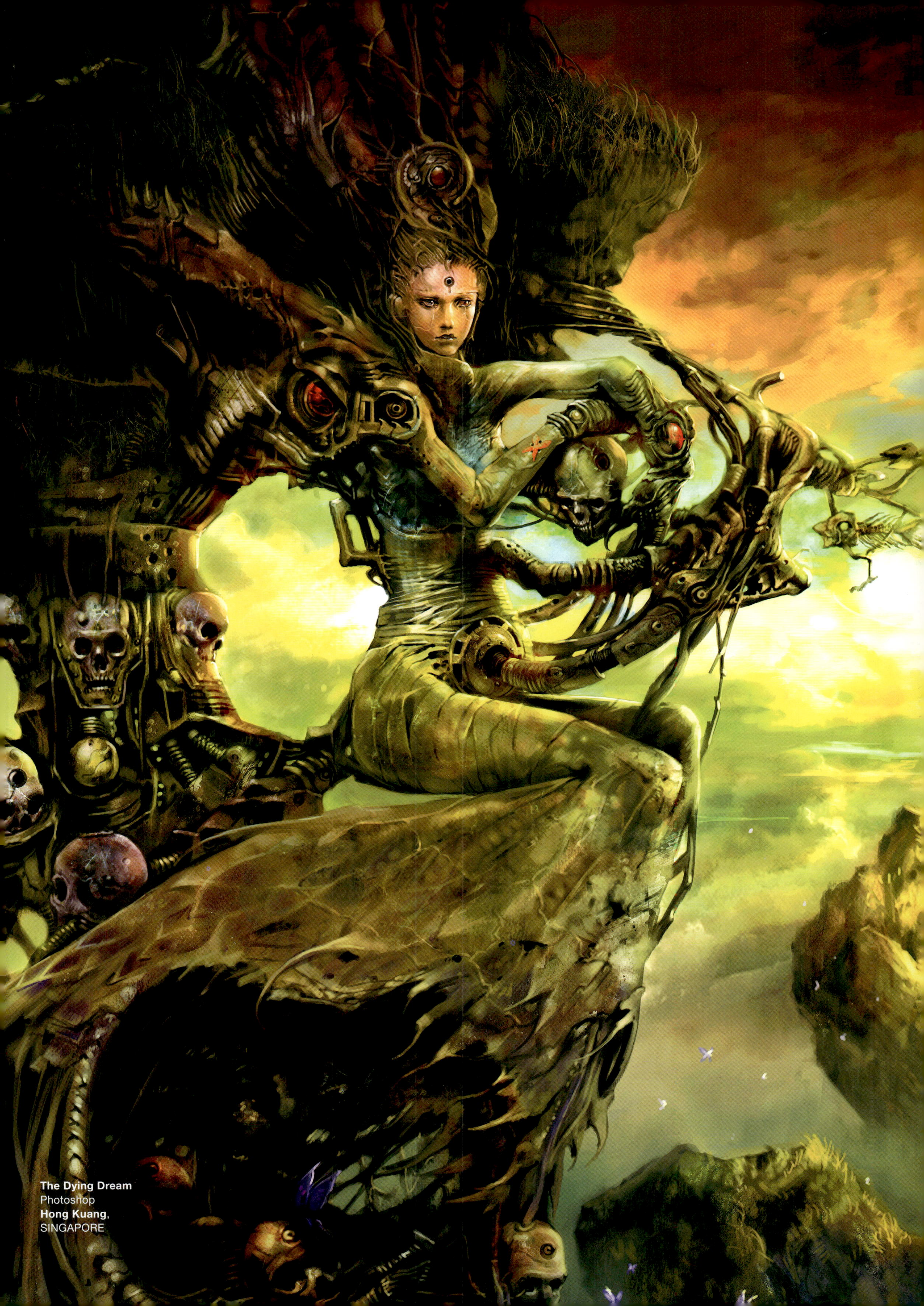

The Dying Dream
Photoshop
Hong Kuang,
SINGAPORE

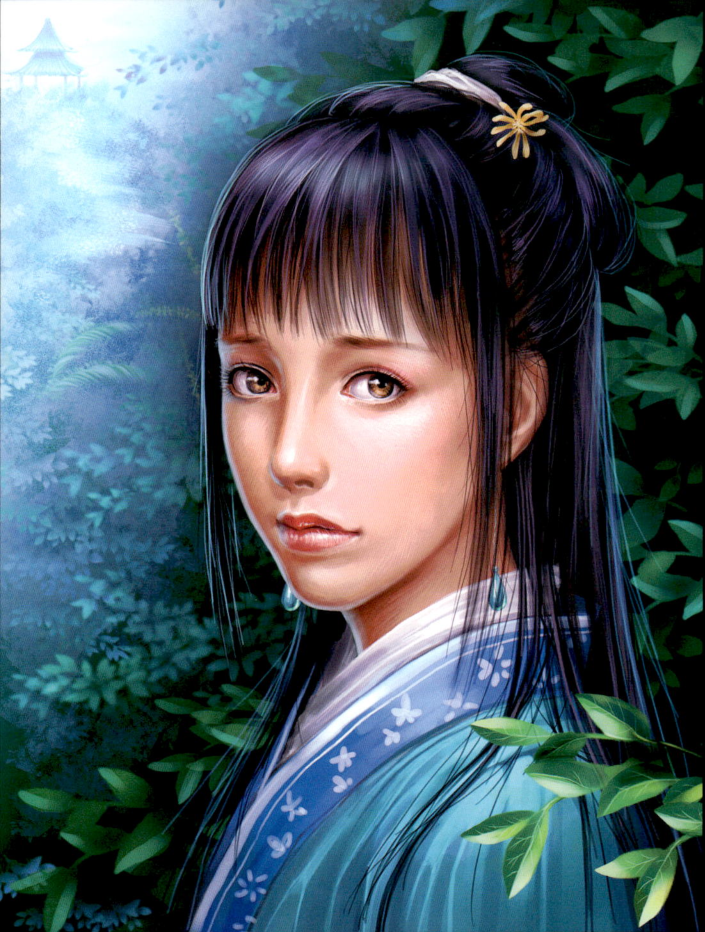

Sad 12
Photoshop
Hui Tian, CHINA
[top]

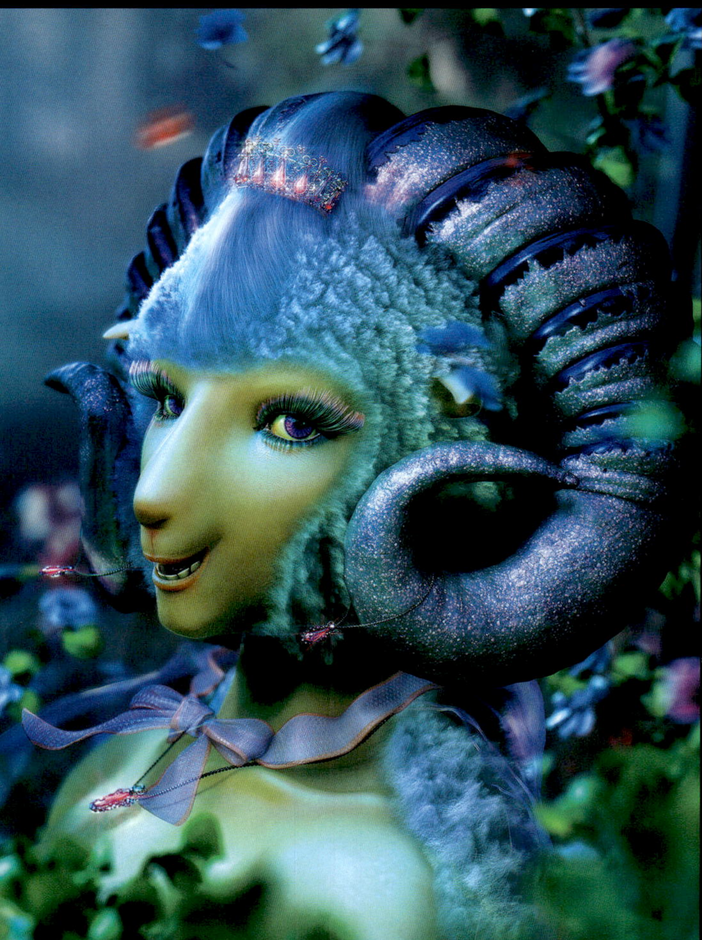

Princess Violet
Maya, mental ray, ZBrush, Shake
Jie Jiang (T.G.Jay), CHINA
[above]

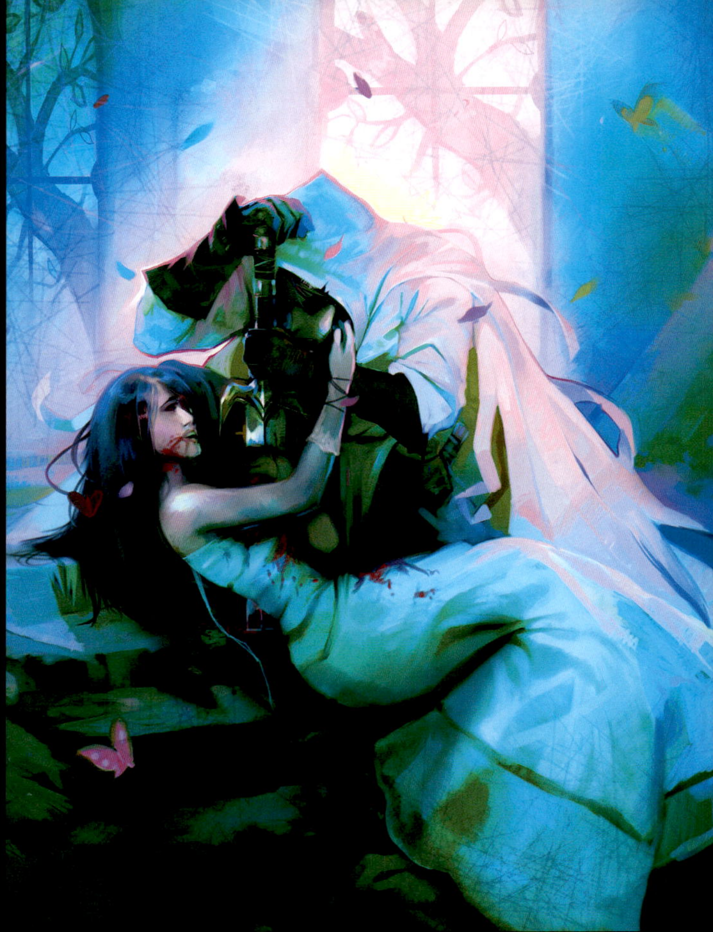

I forgive you
Painter, Photoshop
Corey Loving, USA
[top]

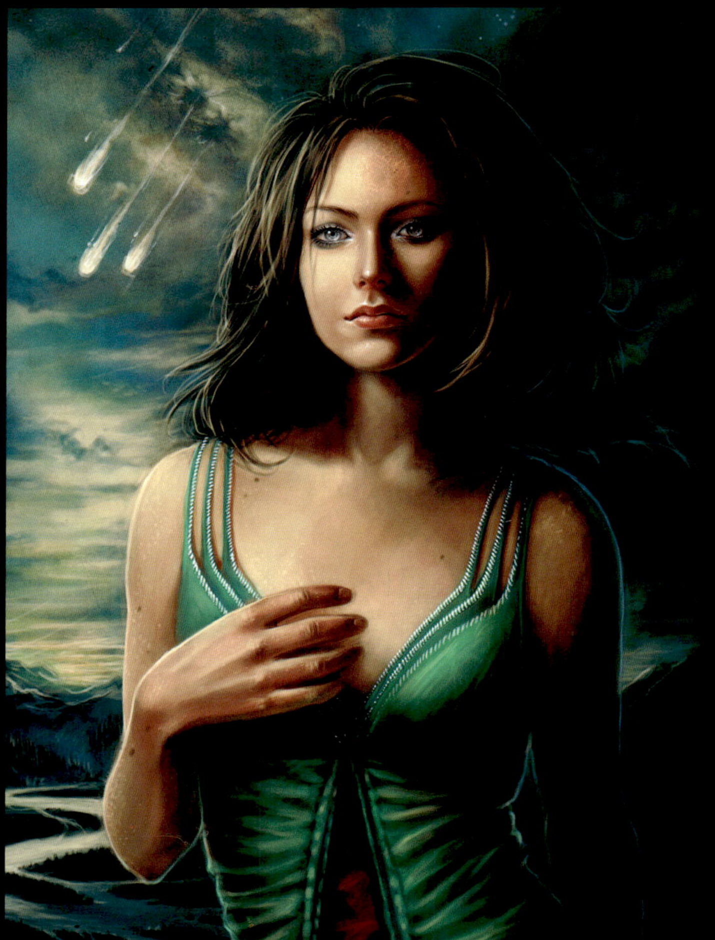

Wish
Photoshop
Sandra Kristin Steffensen, NORWAY
[above]

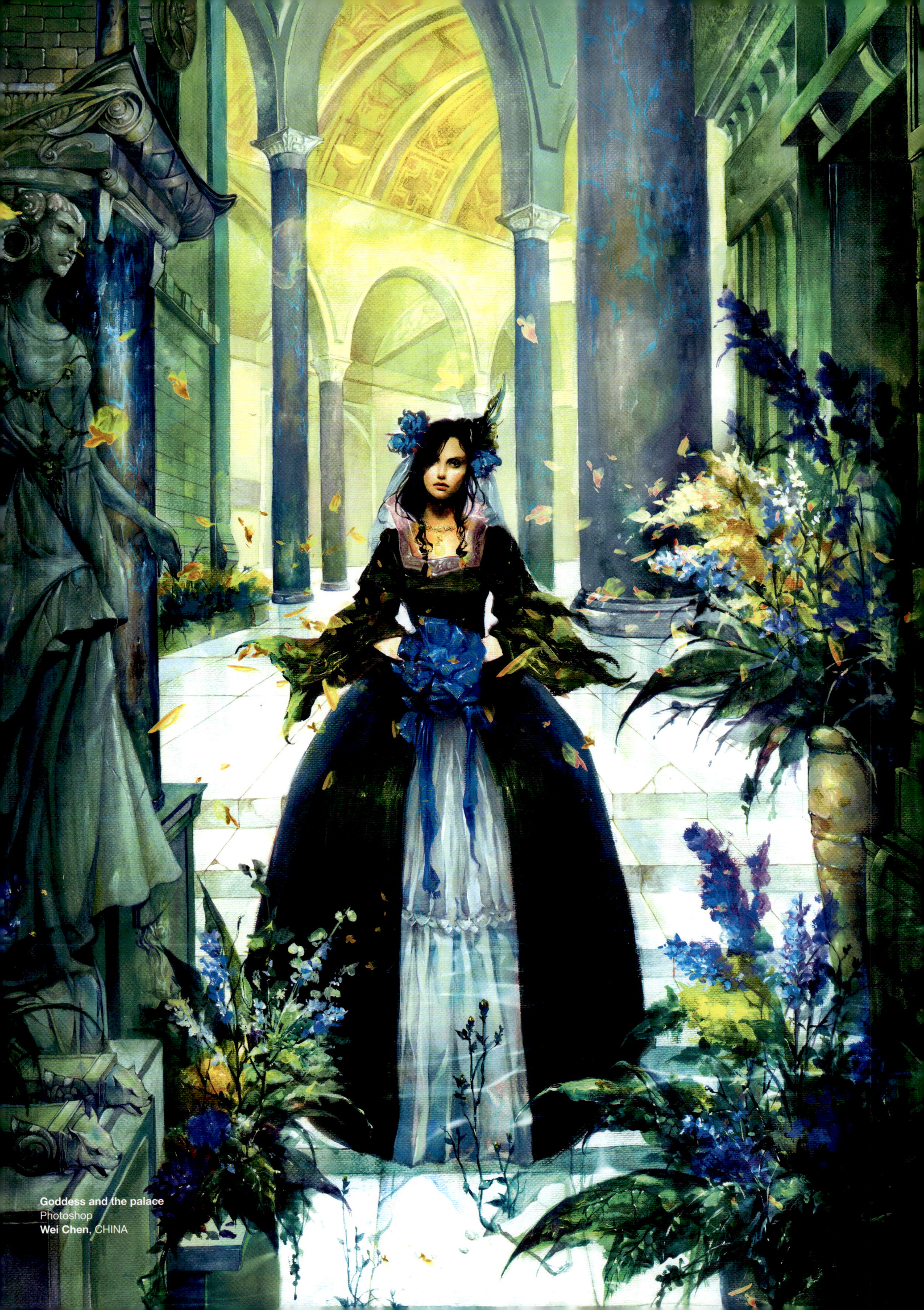

Goddess and the palace
Photoshop
Wei Chen, CHINA

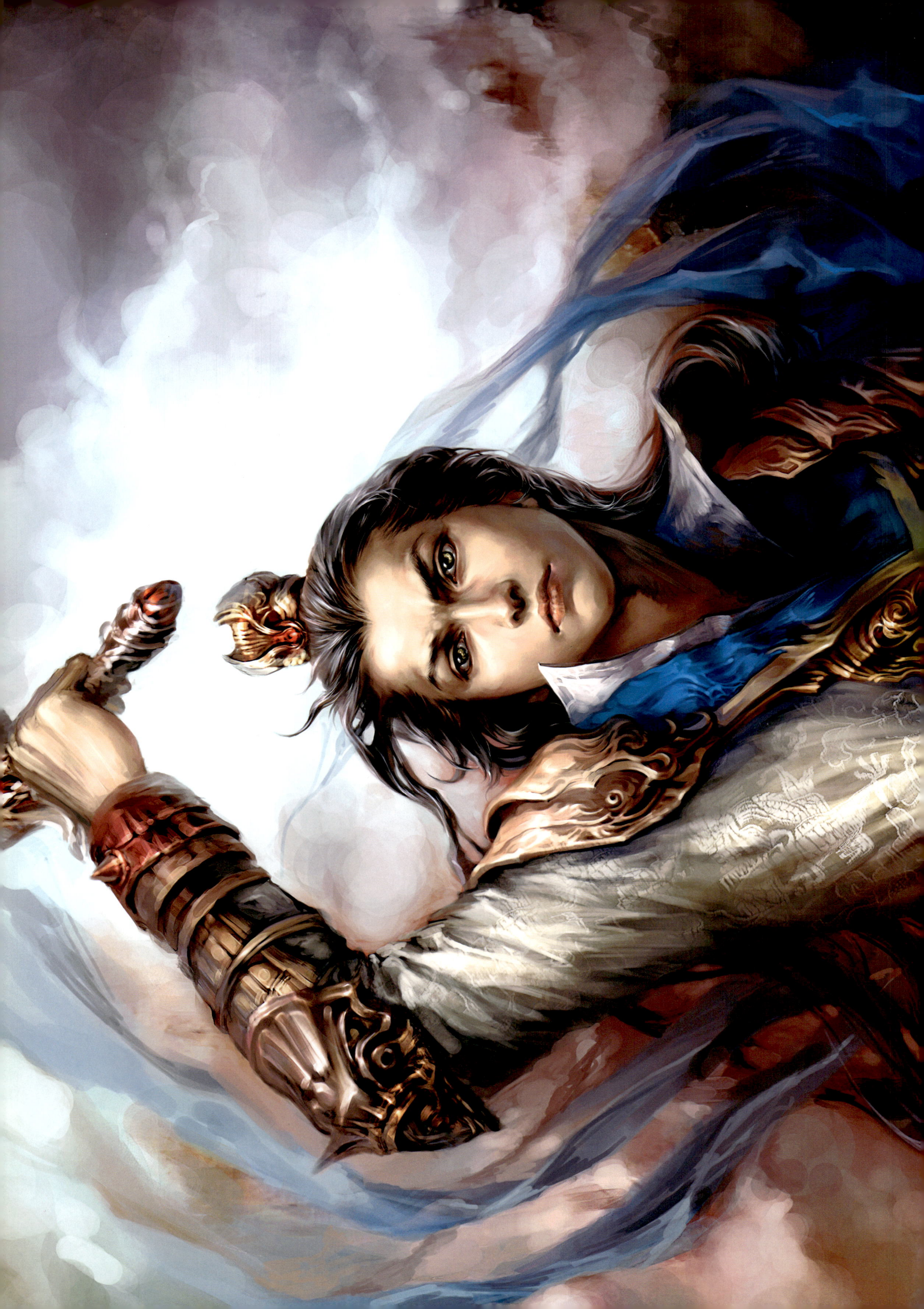

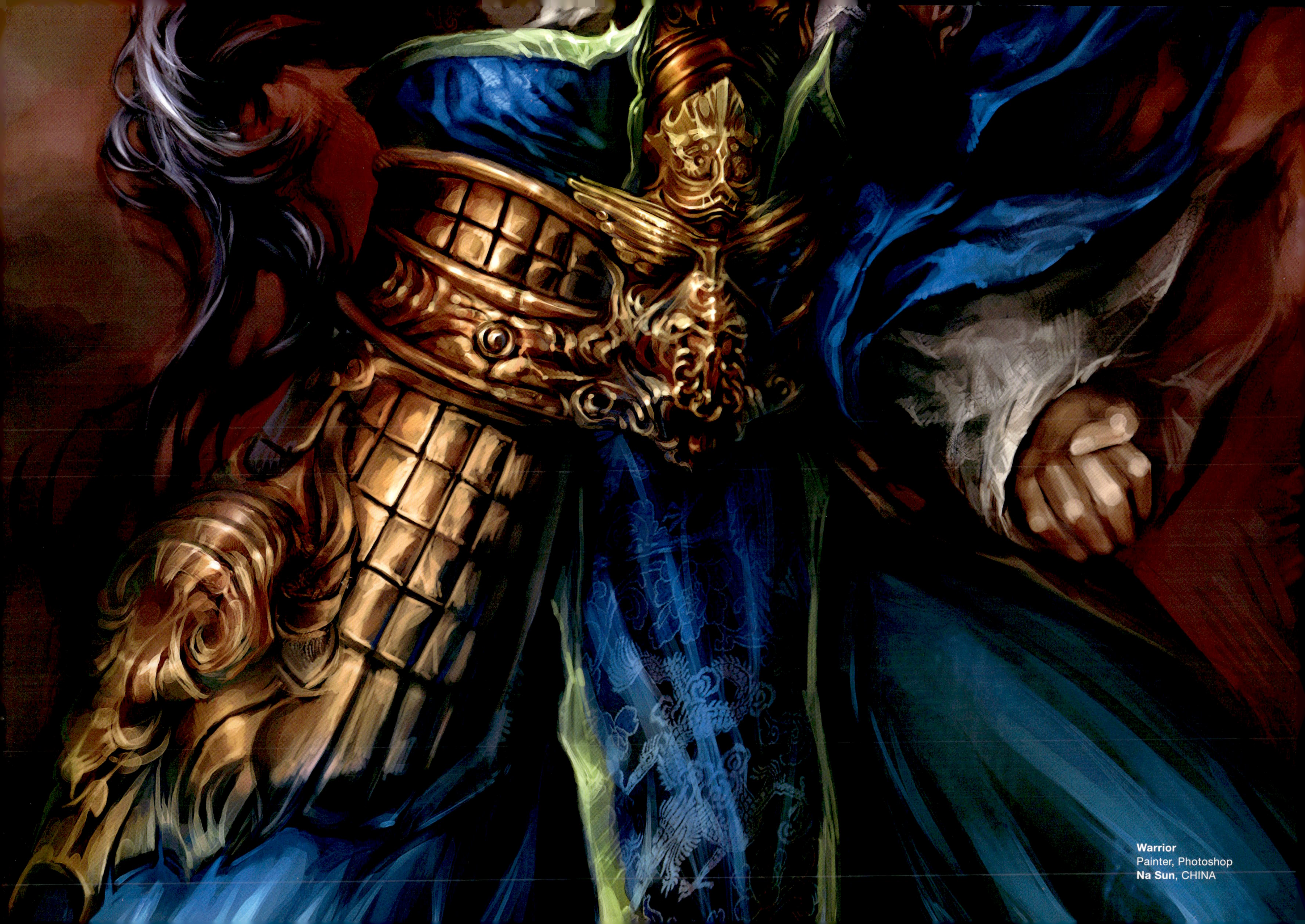

Warrior
Painter, Photoshop
Na Sun, CHINA

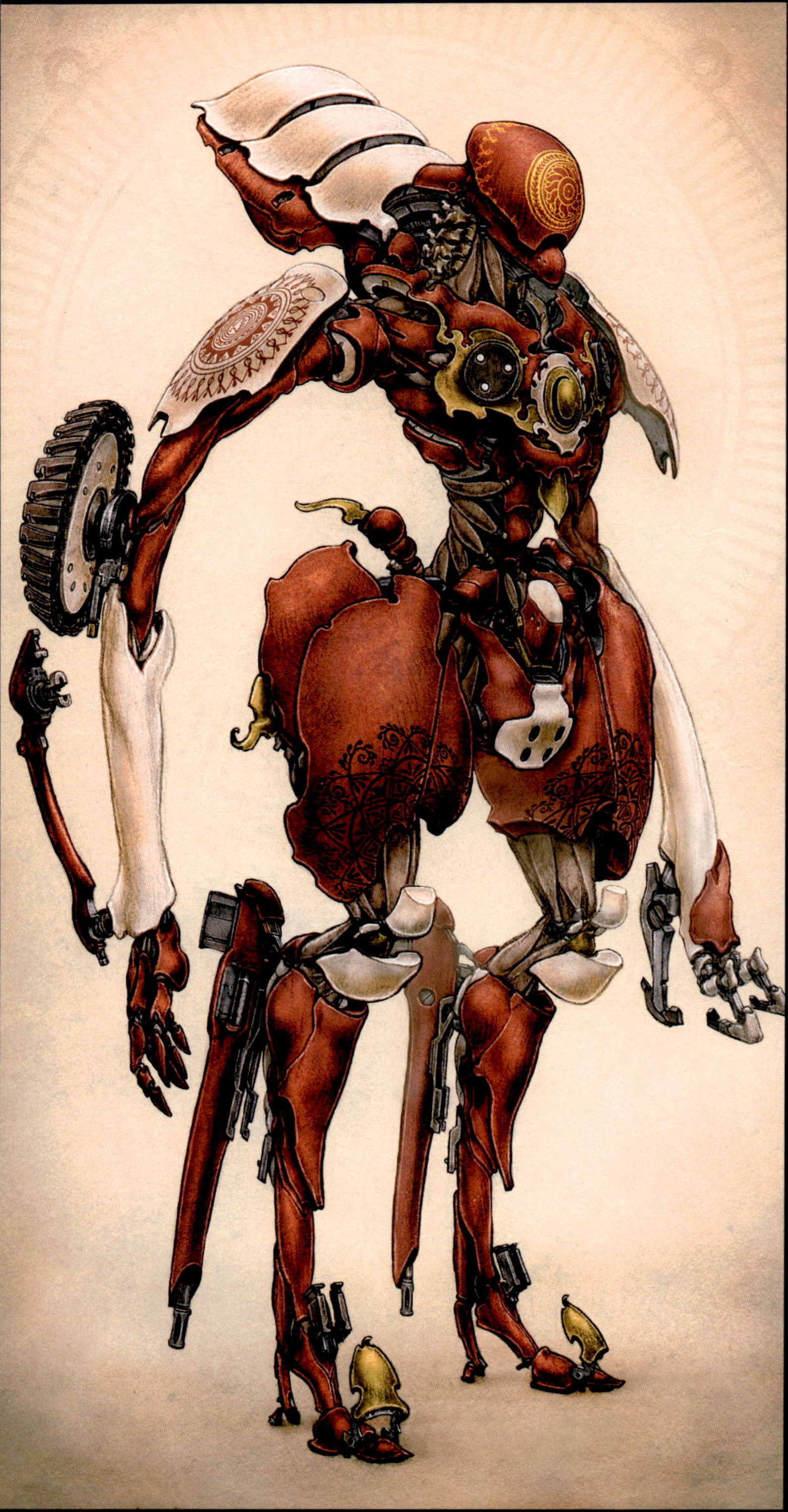

Dajjal
Photoshop
Client: Truemax
Keith Thompson, CANADA
[above]

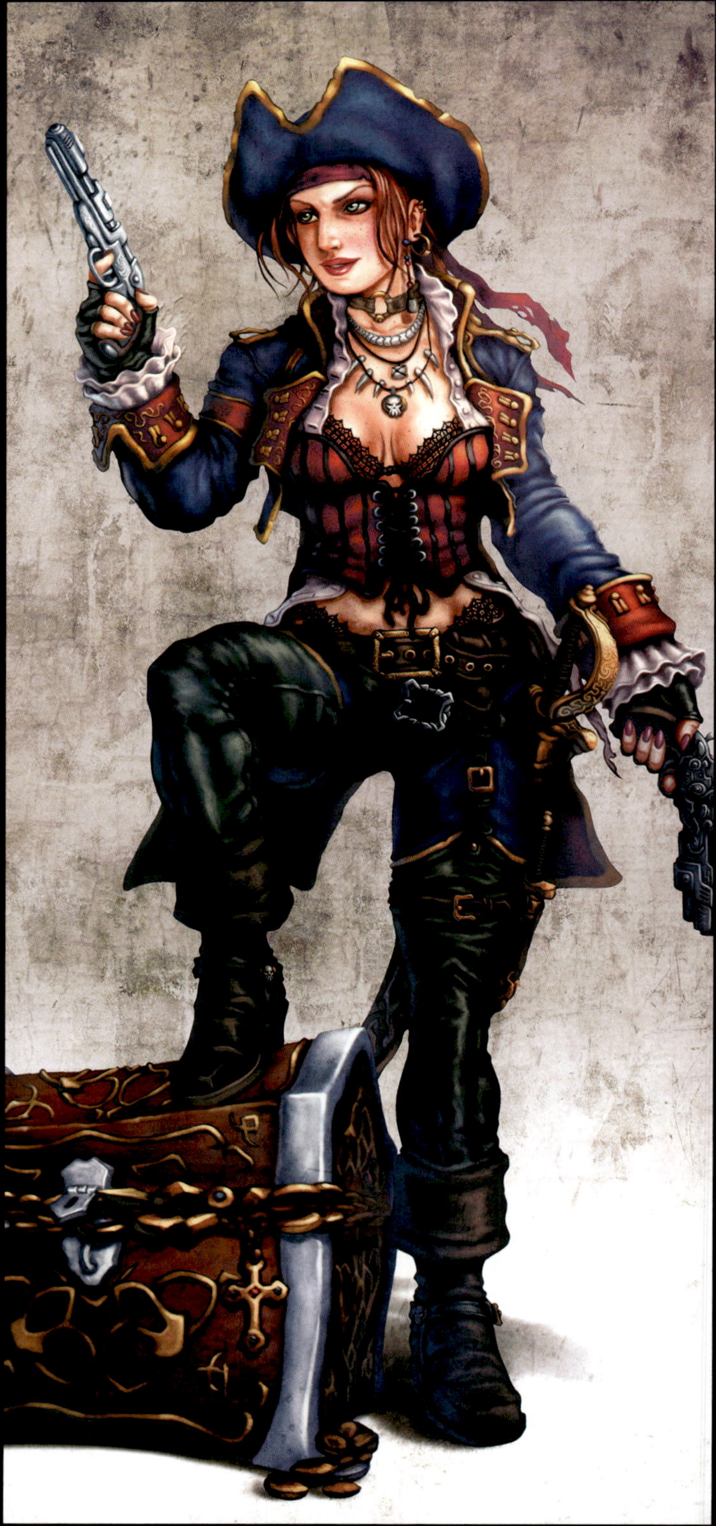

Victoria: Pirate Girl
Painter, Photoshop
Hector Moran, Streamline Studios, NETHERLANDS
[above]

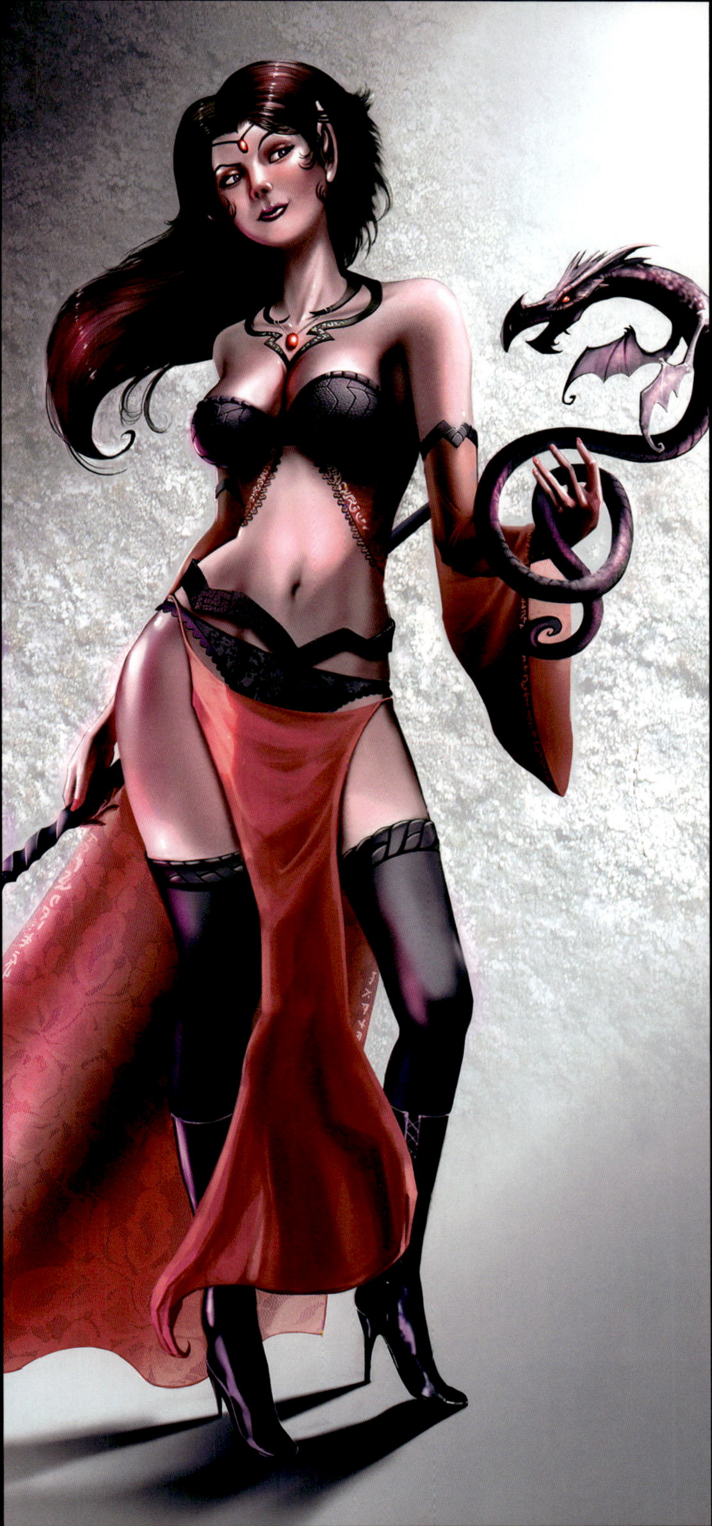

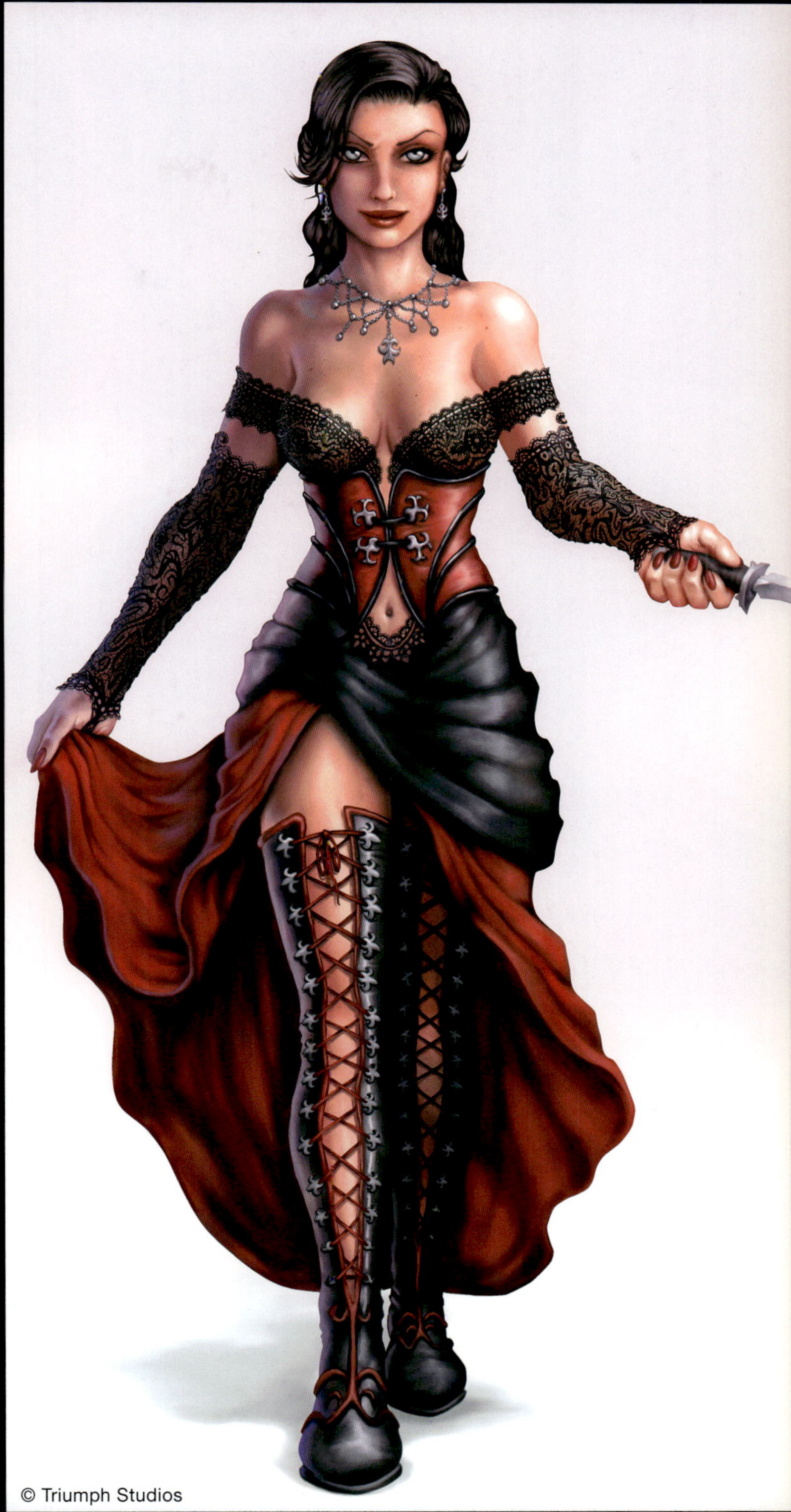

Onuwen the Dragon Queen
Photoshop, Painter
Kevin Chin,
USA
[above]

Velvet
Painter, Photoshop
Hector Moran, Streamline Studios,
NETHERLANDS
[above]

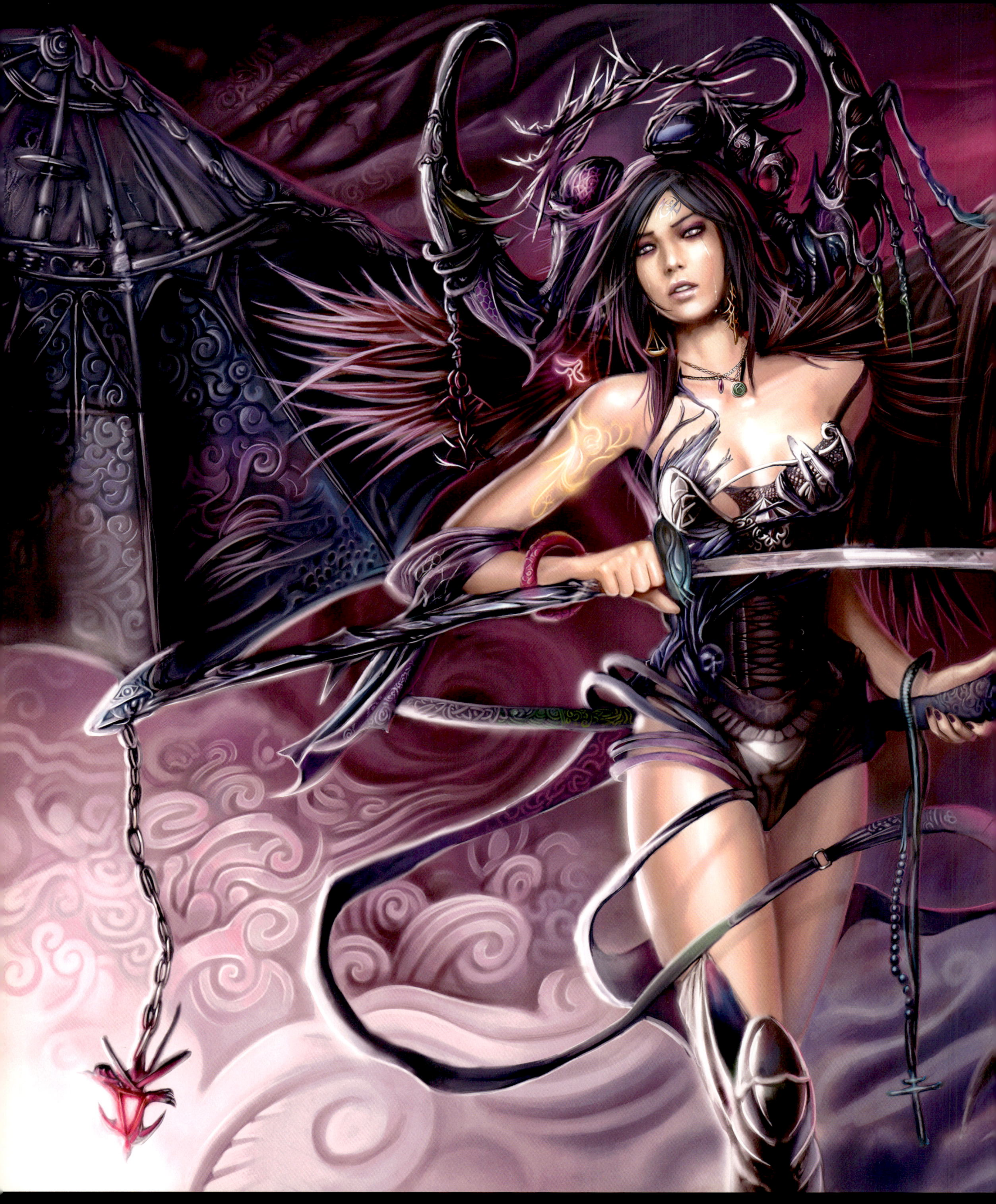

Reflection of Fate
Photoshop
Paul Kwon, USA
[above]

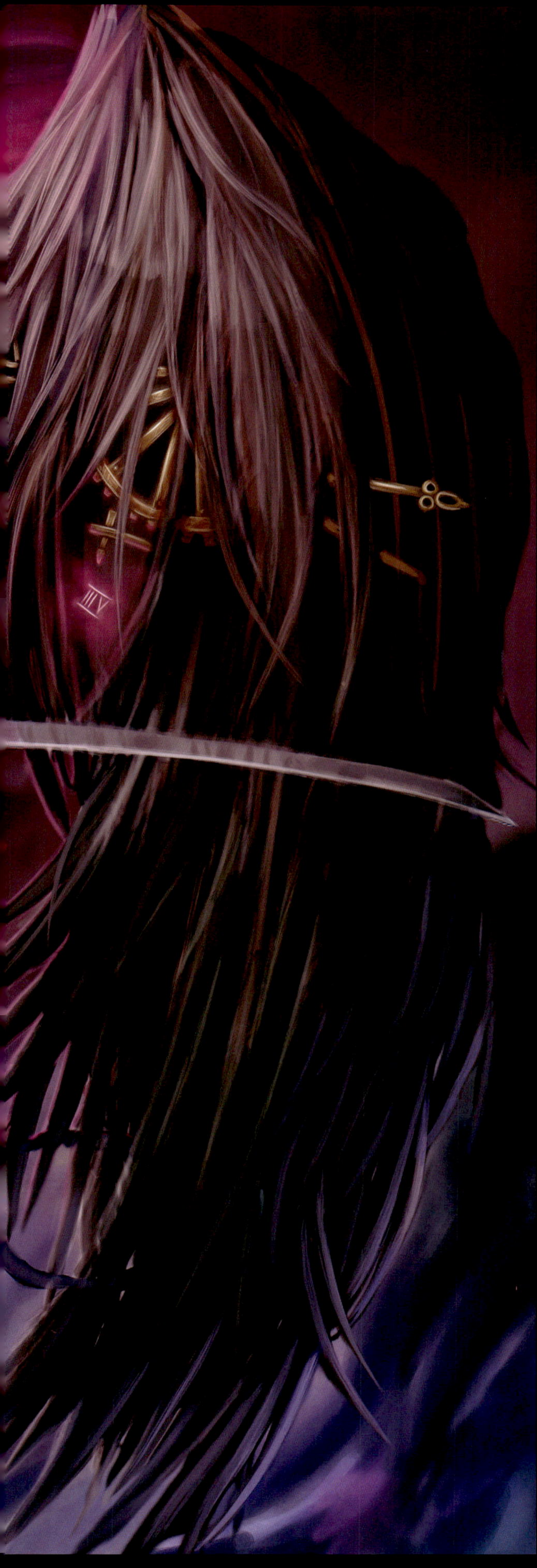

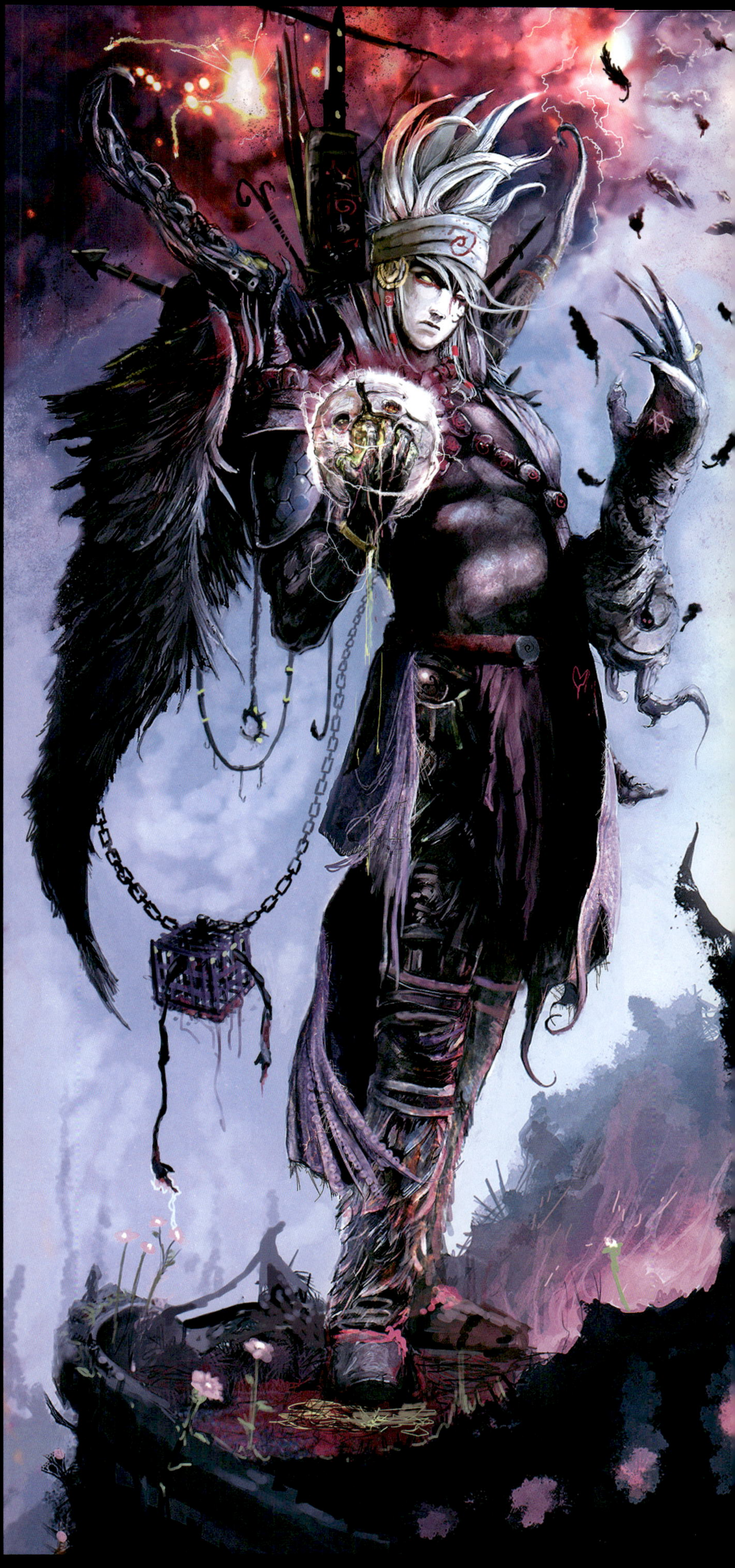

Love and hate, this is the keeper
Photoshop, Painter
Robin Olausson, SWEDEN
[above]

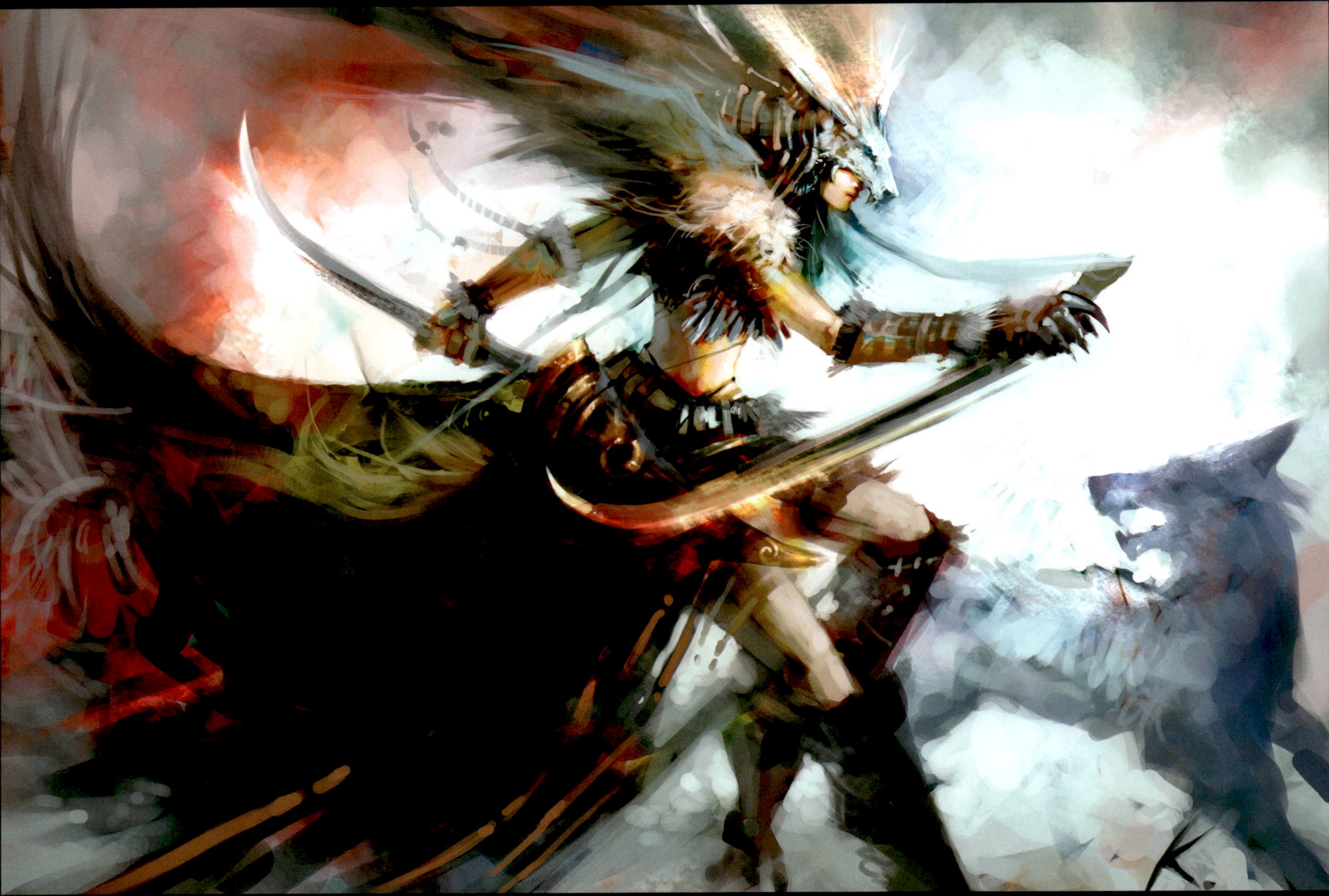

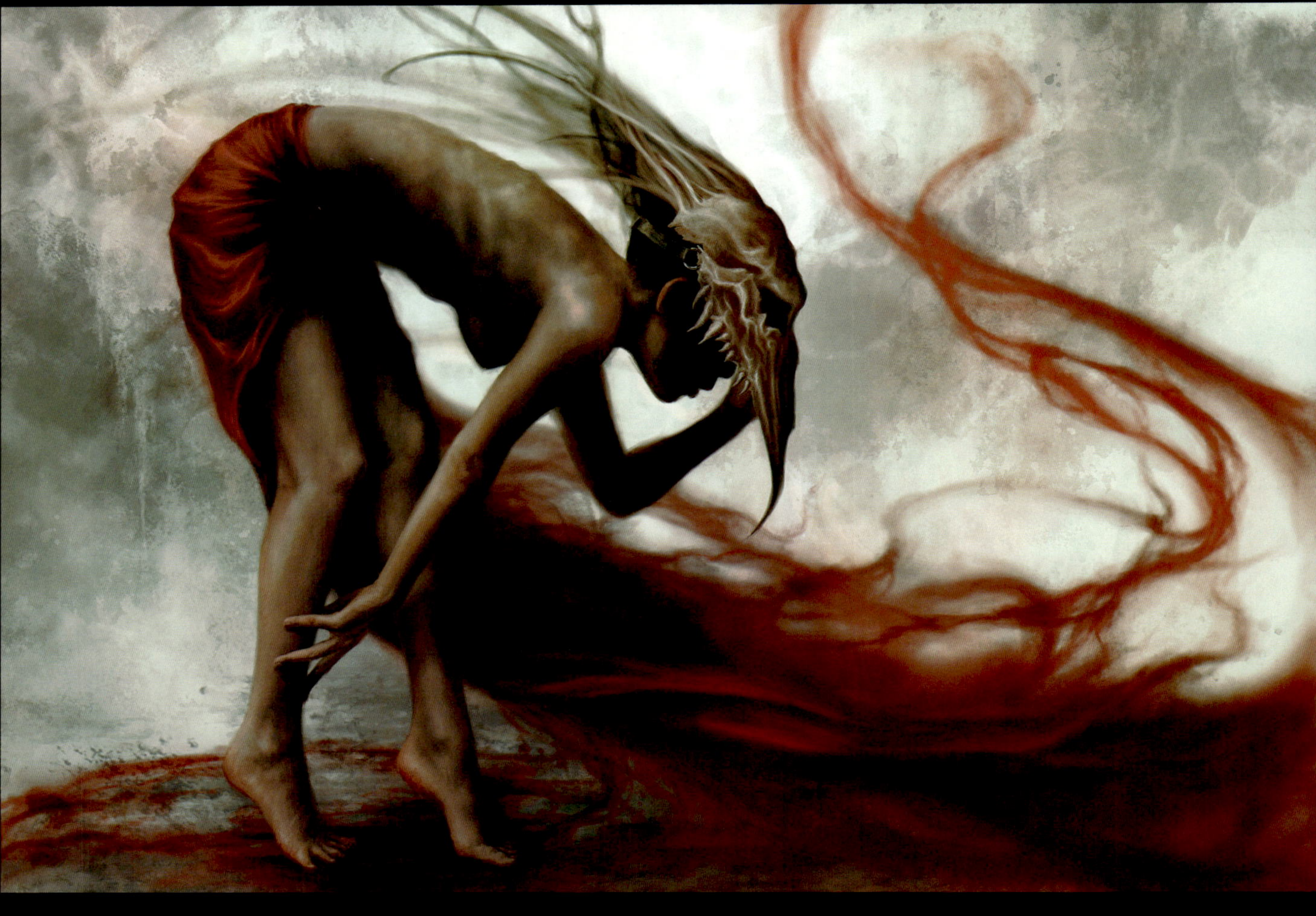

The girl of Wolf Rise
Photoshop
Xiao-chen Fu, CHINA
[top]

Bloodstone
Photoshop
Lauren K. Cannon, USA
[above]

First Snow
Photoshop
Marc Brunet, CANADA
[right]

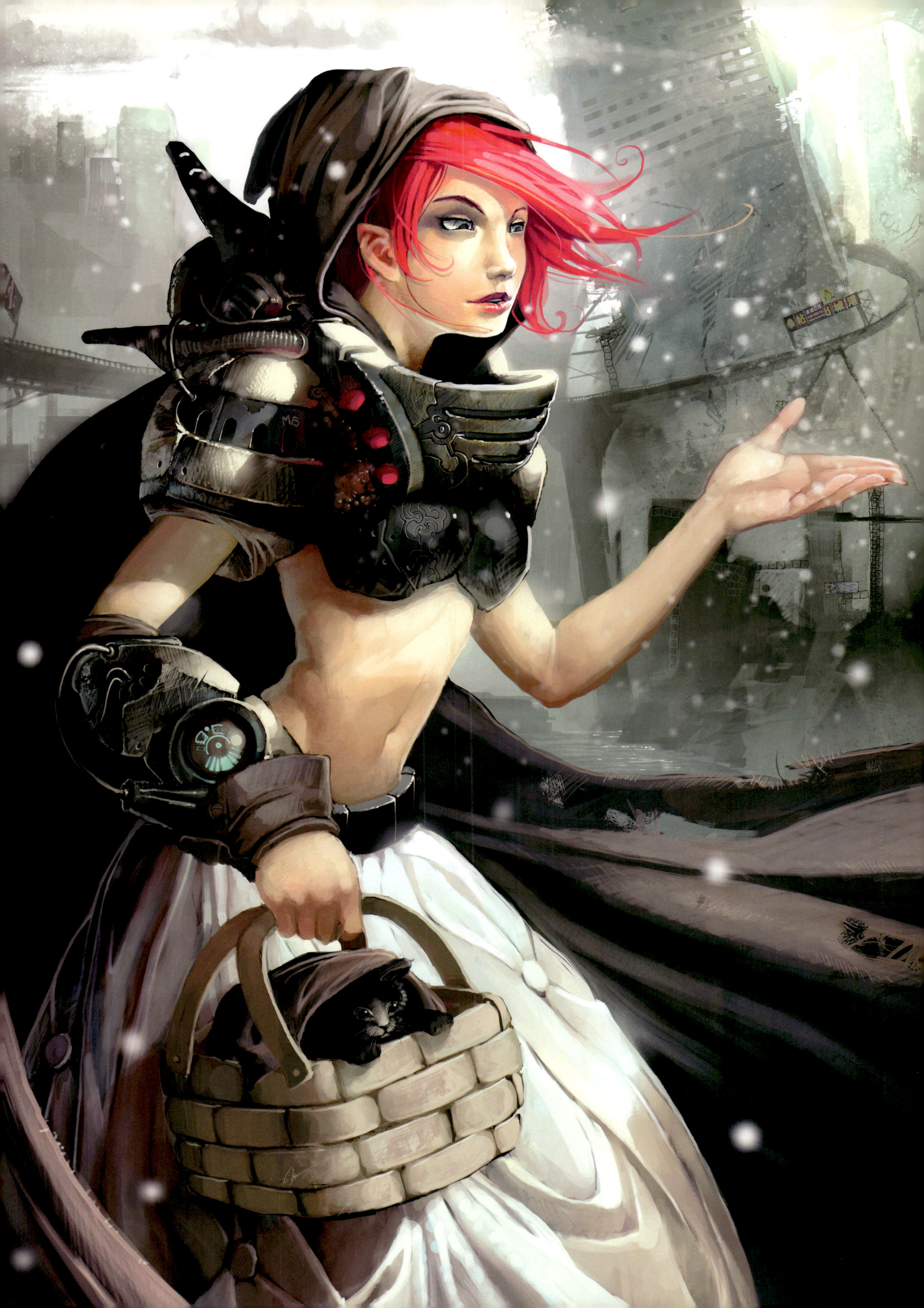

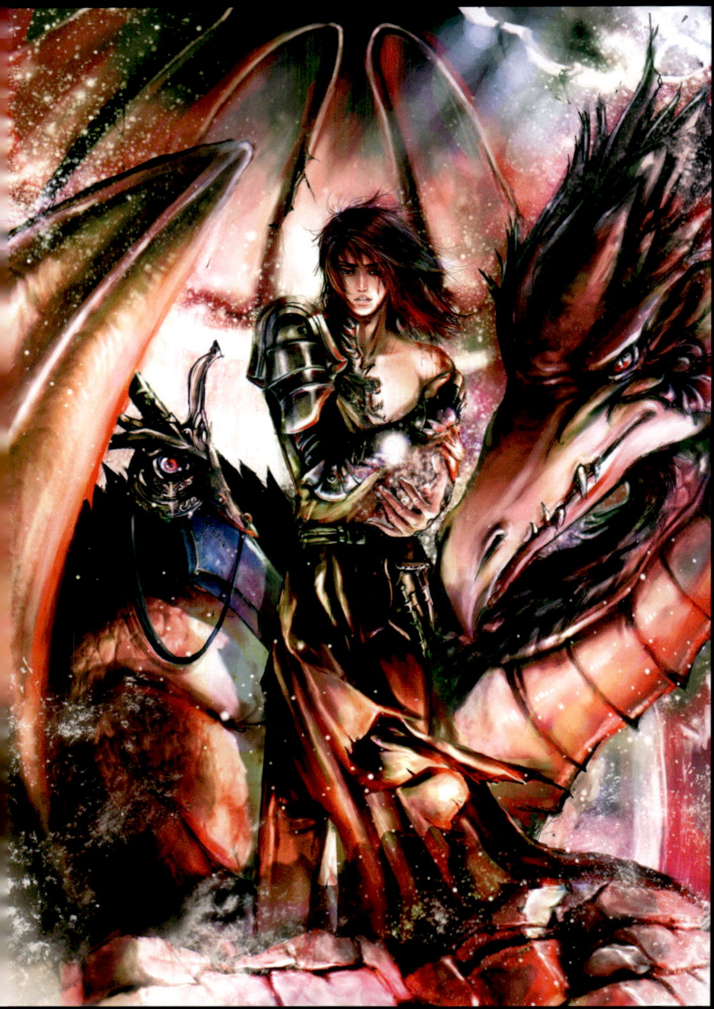

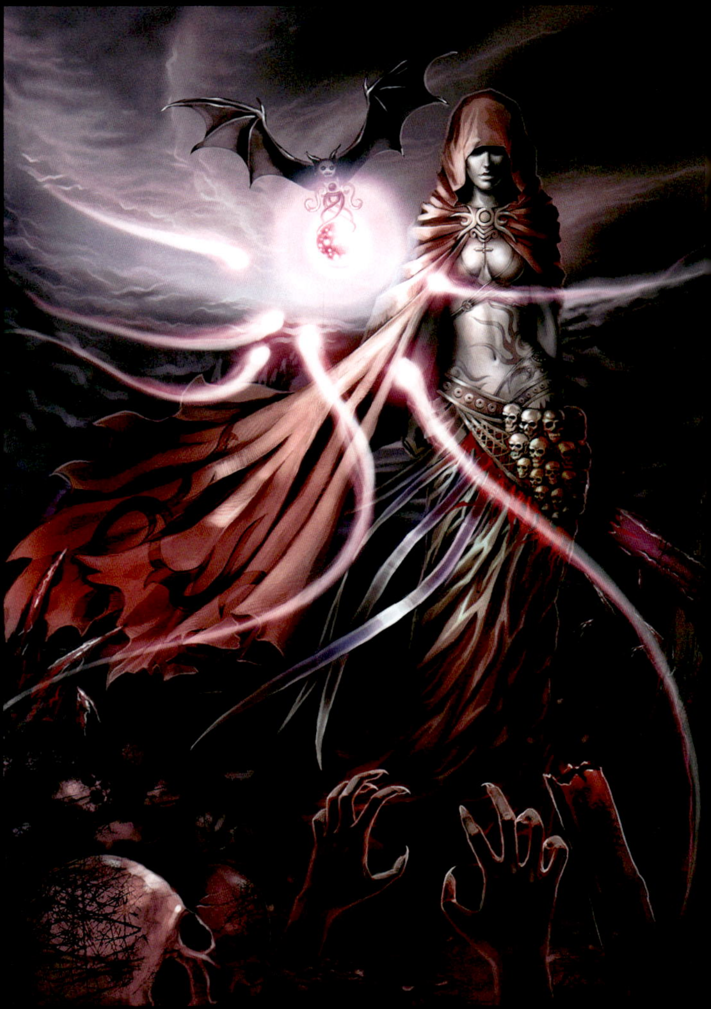

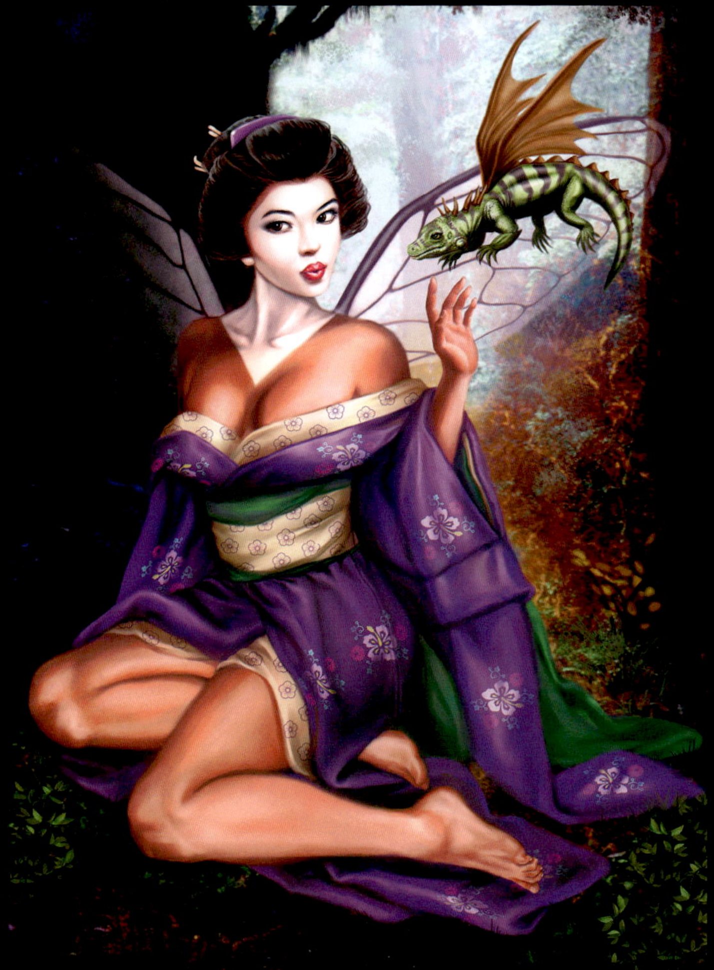

Farewell fireflies
Photoshop, Painter
Anggia Lestari, INDONESIA
[top left]

Soul siren
Photoshop
Hui Tian, CHINA
[above]

Geisha Faerie and Orson the Dragon
Painter, Photoshop
Sandra Chang-Adair, USA
[left]

Shusan
Photoshop
Hui Tian, CHINA
[right]

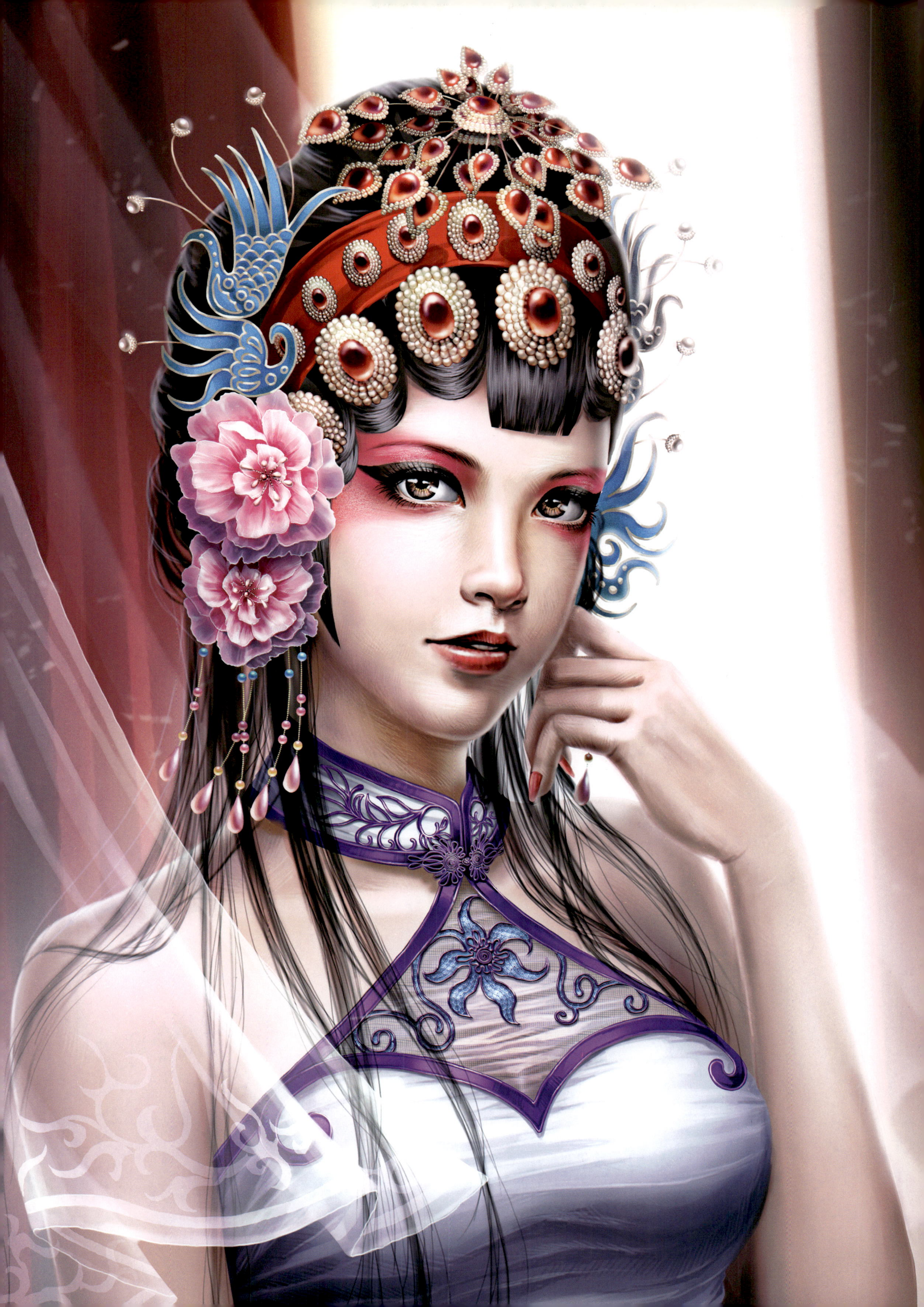

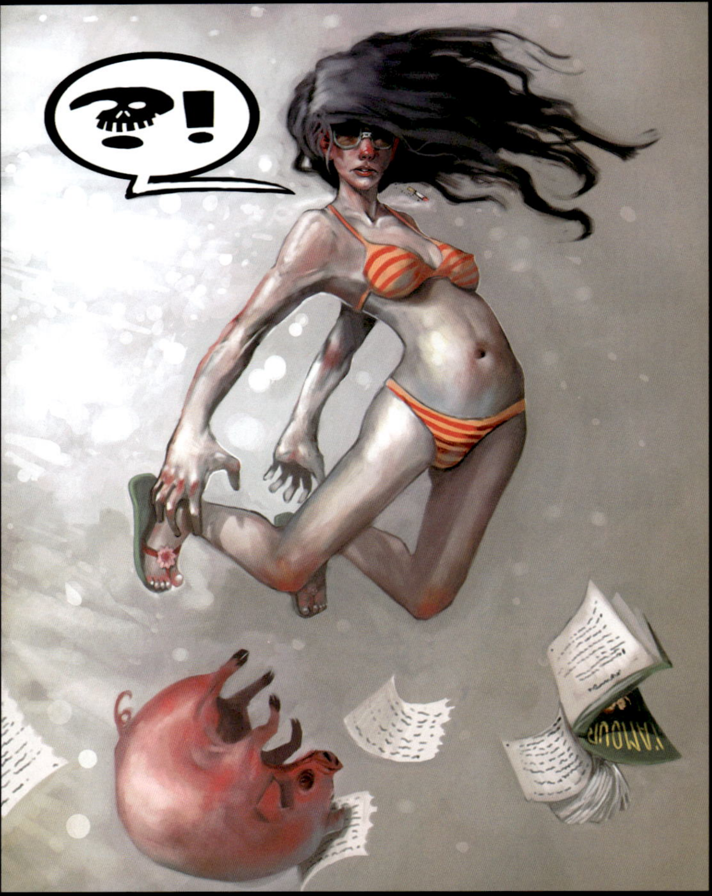

We're having freaky weather
Photoshop
Rudy Jan Faber, NETHERLANDS
[top]

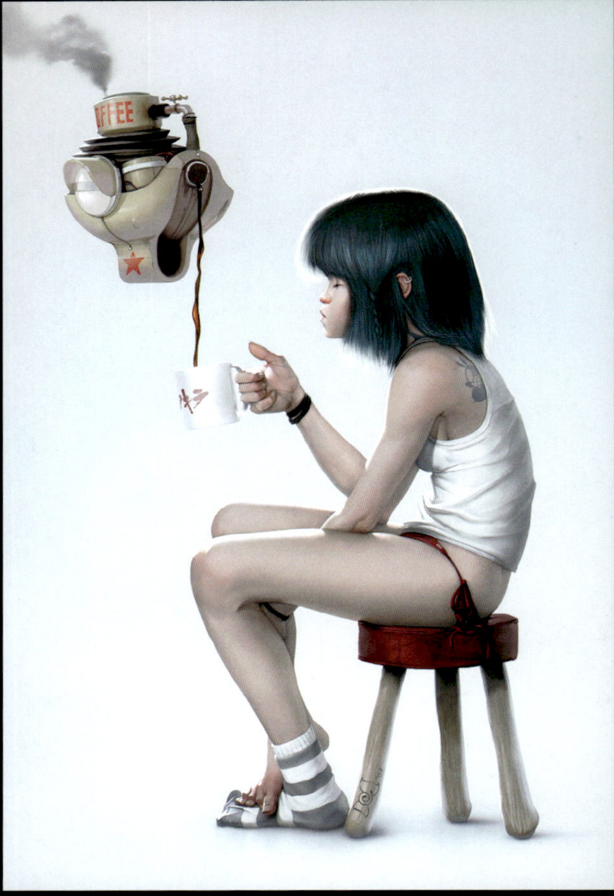

MuMorning
Photoshop
David Cabrera, SPAIN
[top]

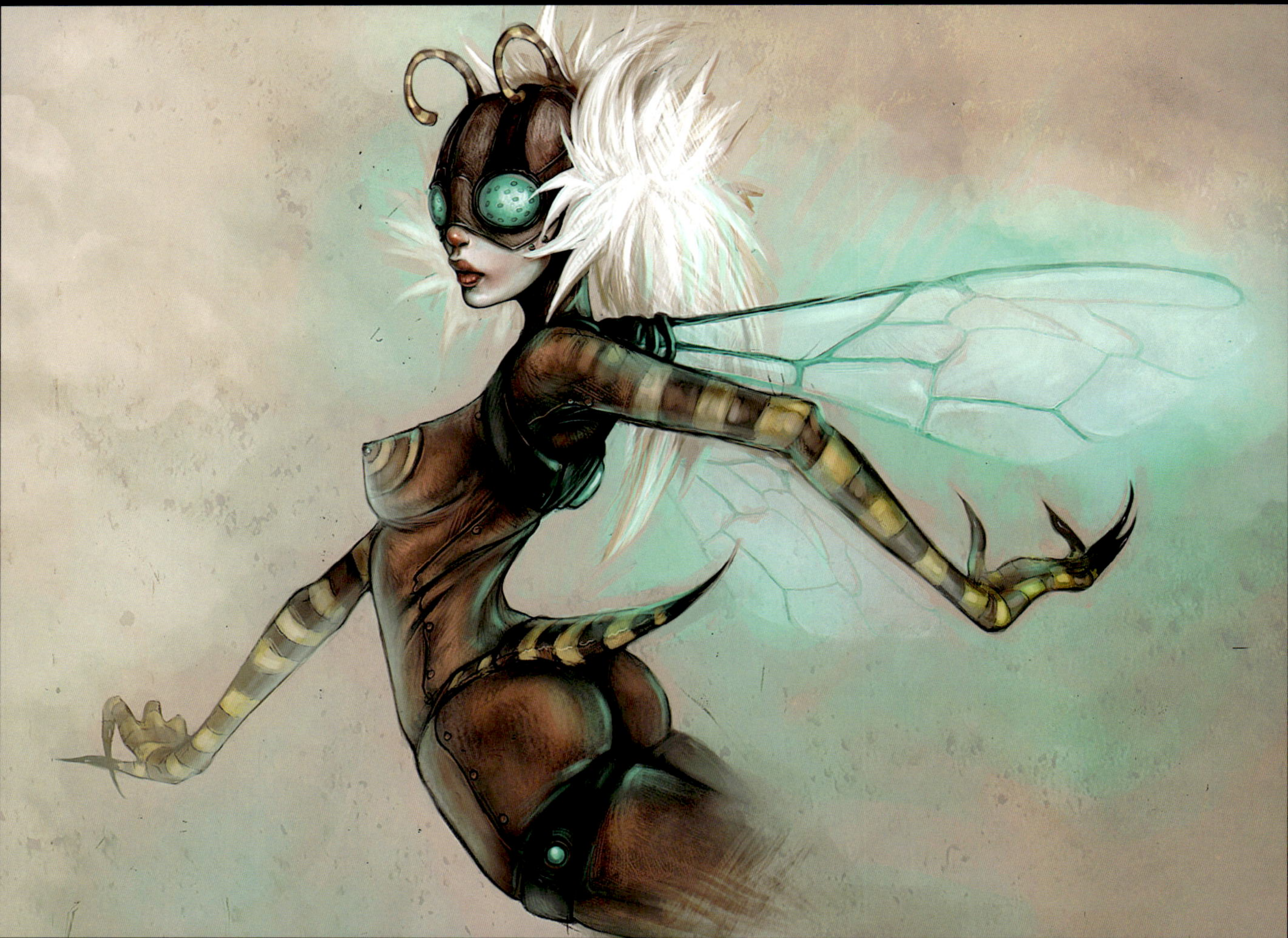

Hylaeus species
Photoshop
Daniela Uhlig, GERMANY
[above]

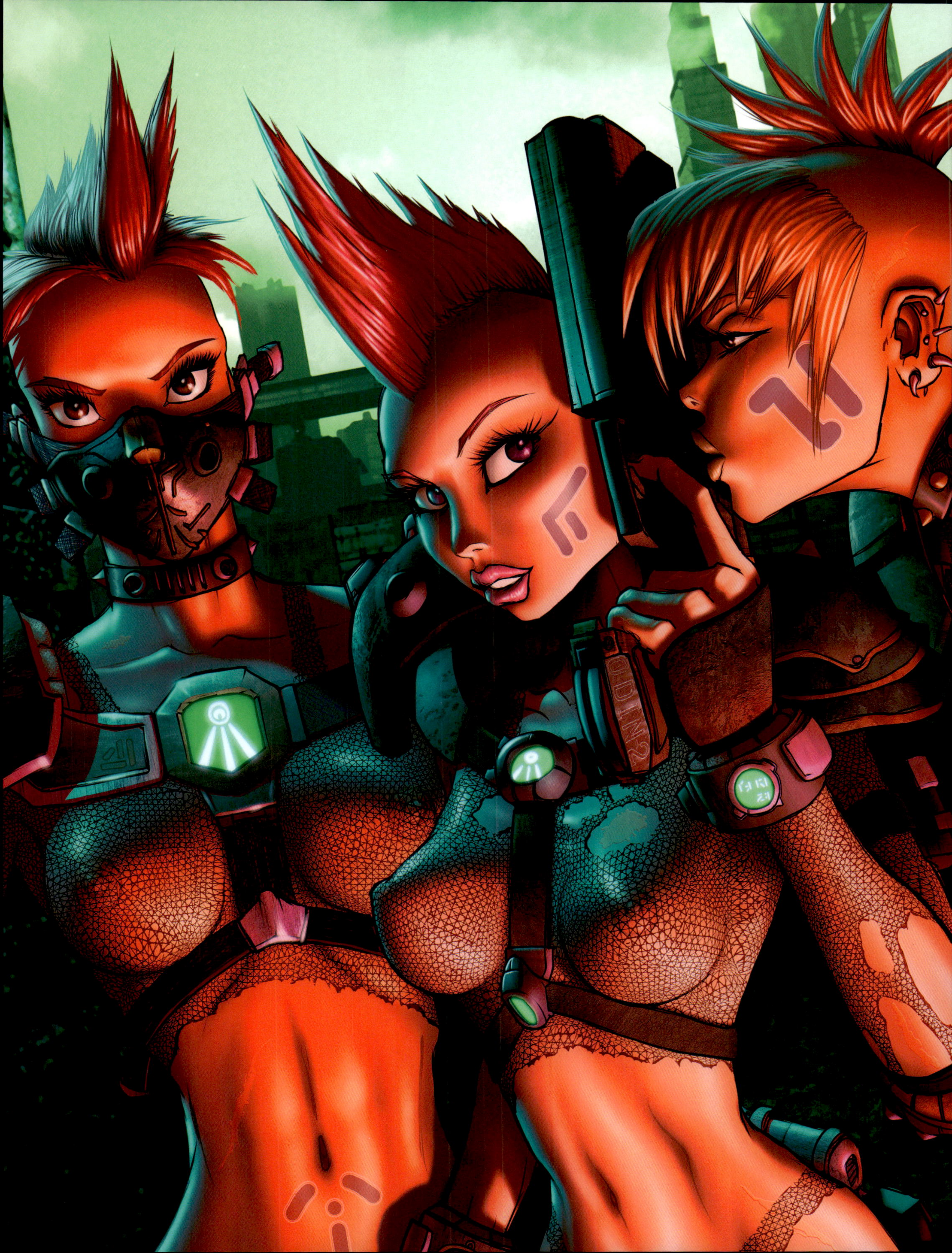

Electric boogaloo
SketchBook Pro, Photoshop, Vue d'Esprit
Jaysin and Embrio, DPI Studios,
CANADA

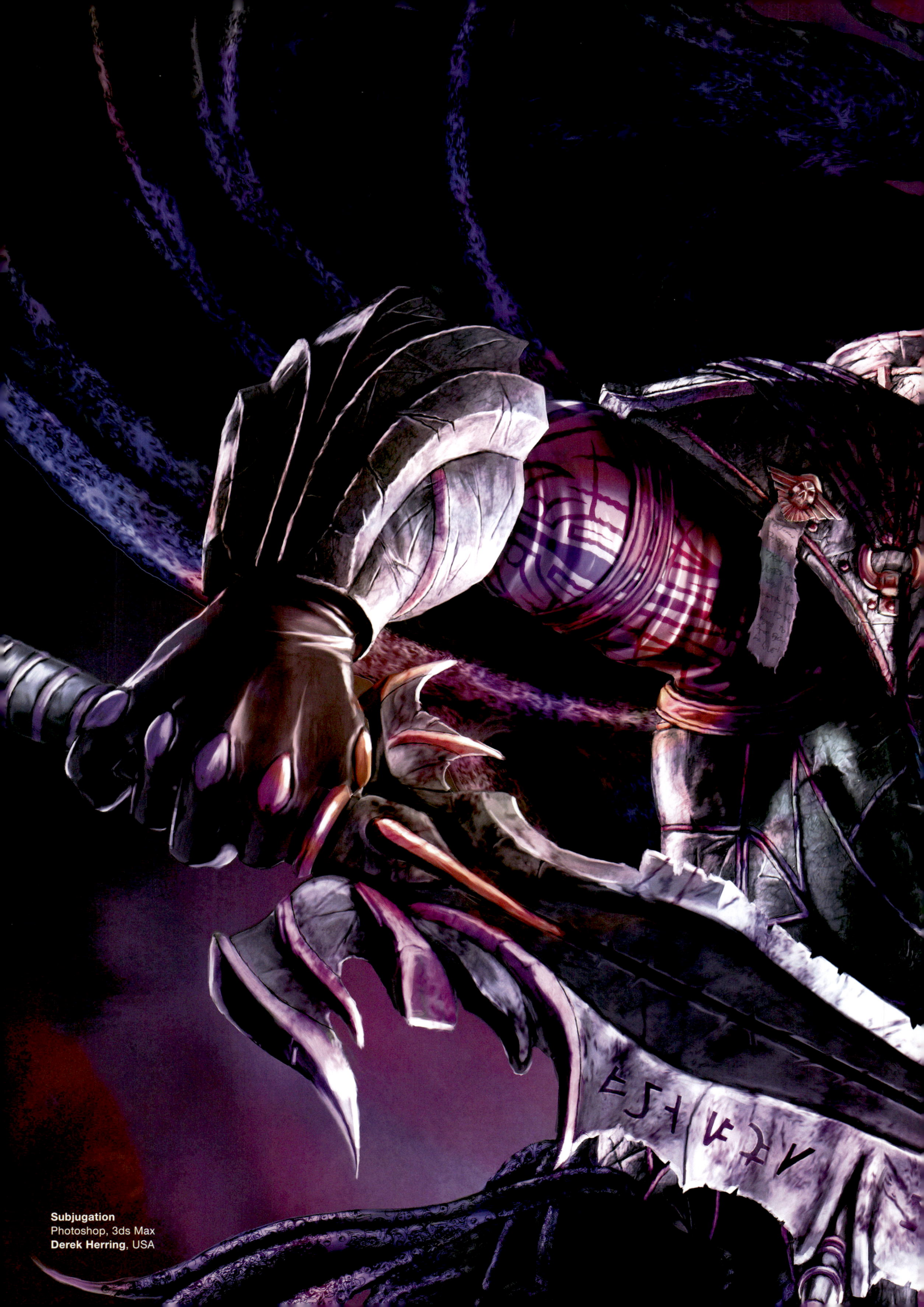

Subjugation
Photoshop, 3ds Max
Derek Herring, USA

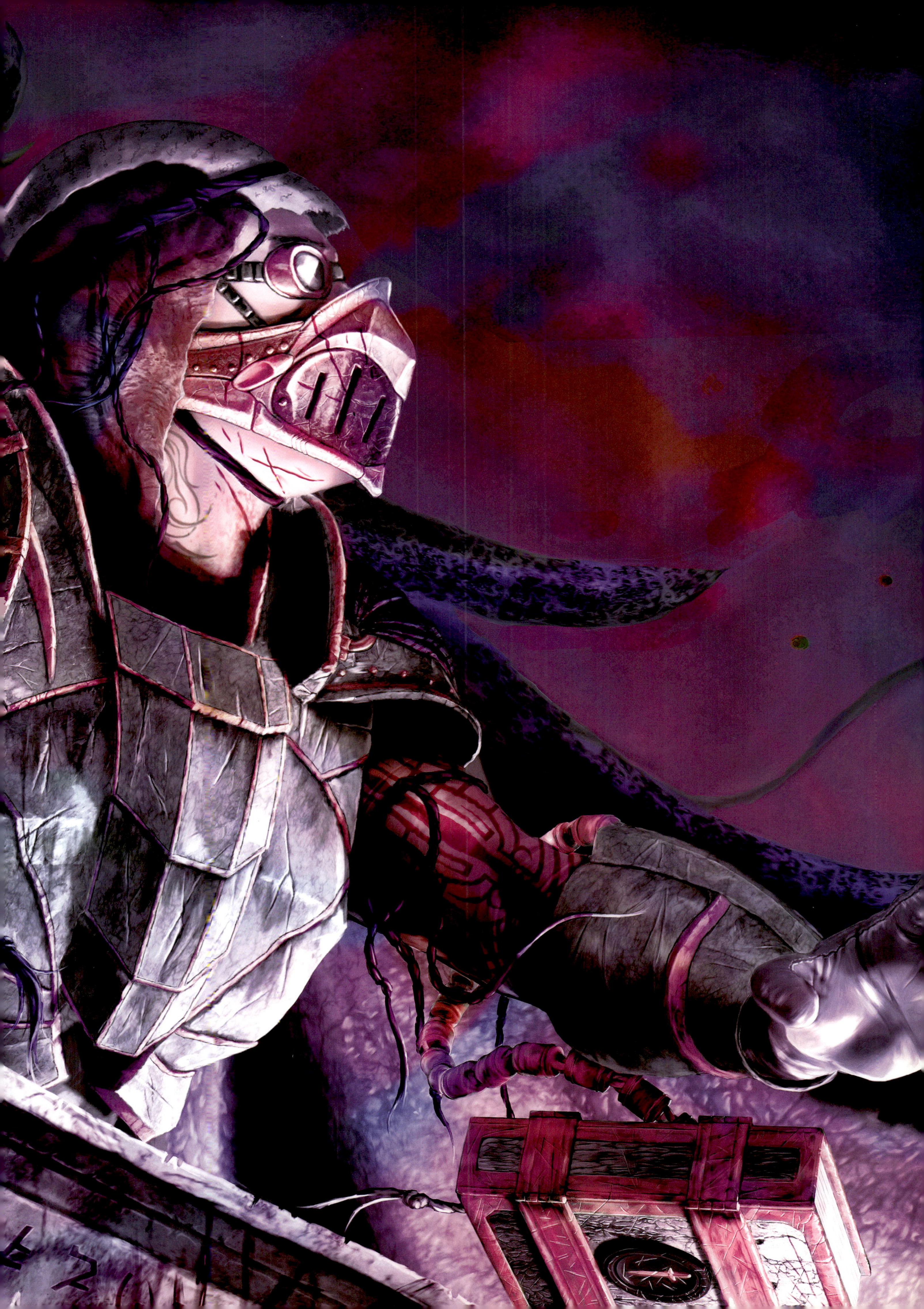

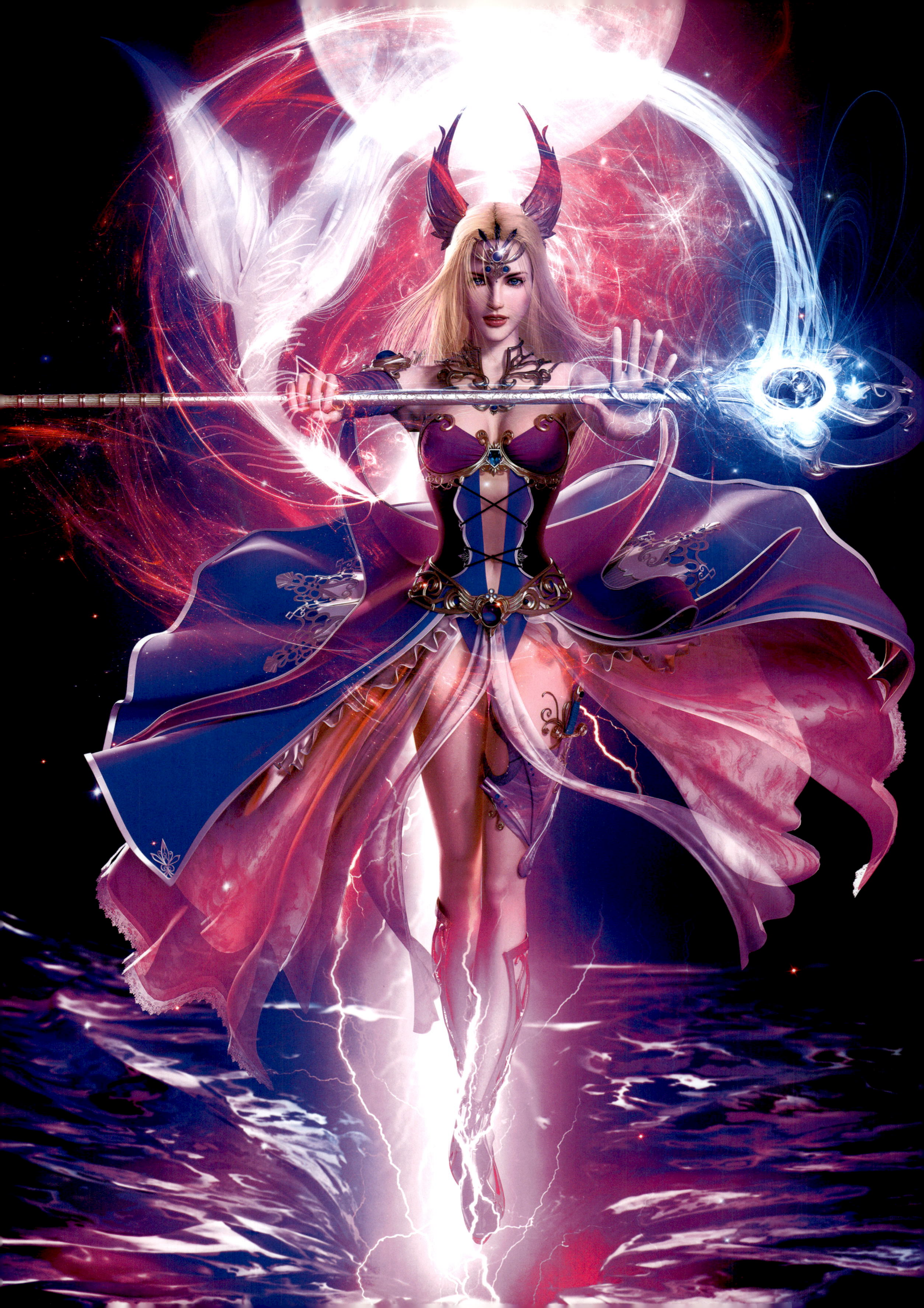

Rebirth of Elene
3ds Max
Client: ELSA
Soa Lee, KOREA
[left]

Eternal
Photoshop
Client: Deltavision
Kira Santa, HUNGARY
[right]

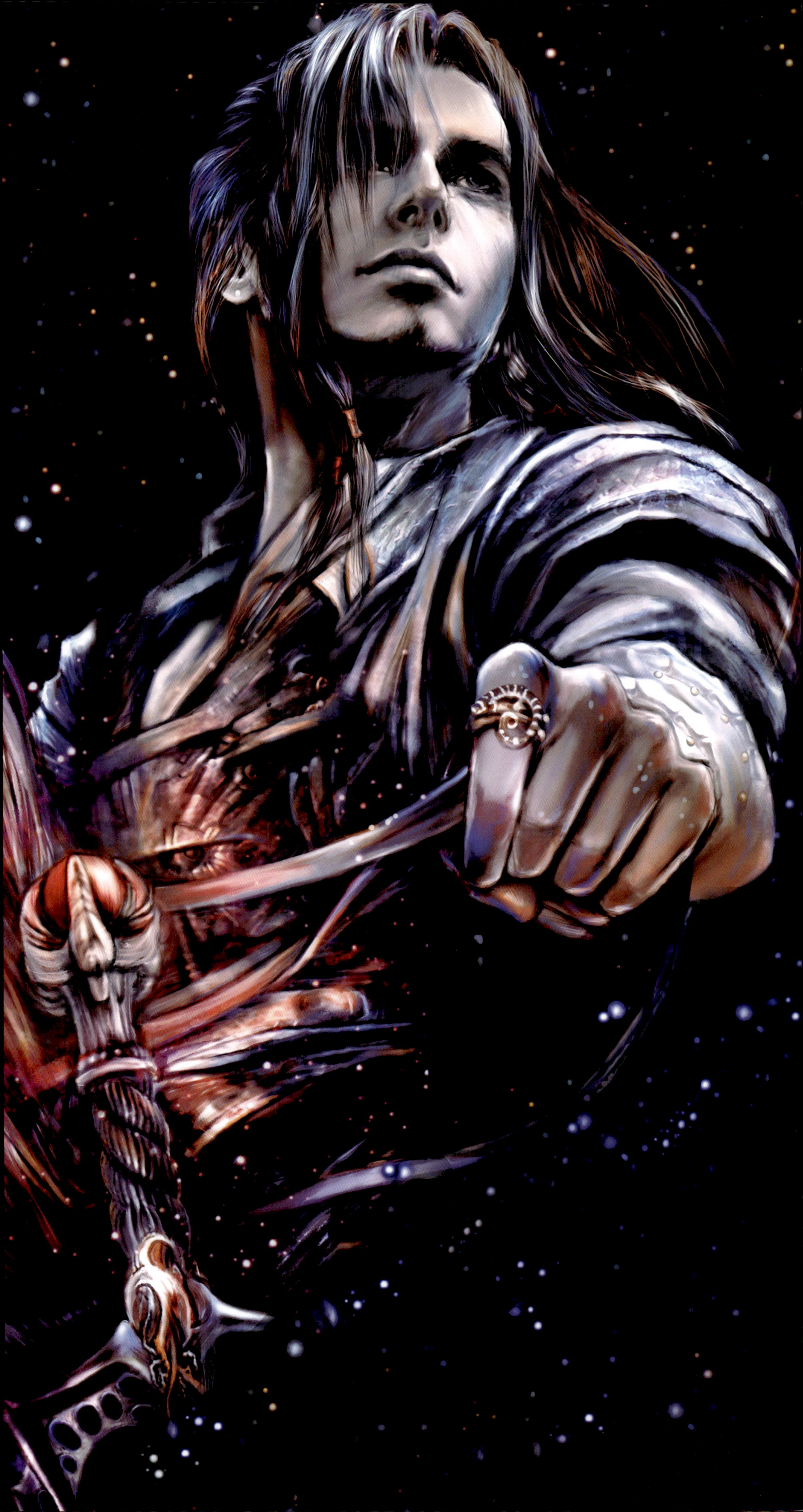

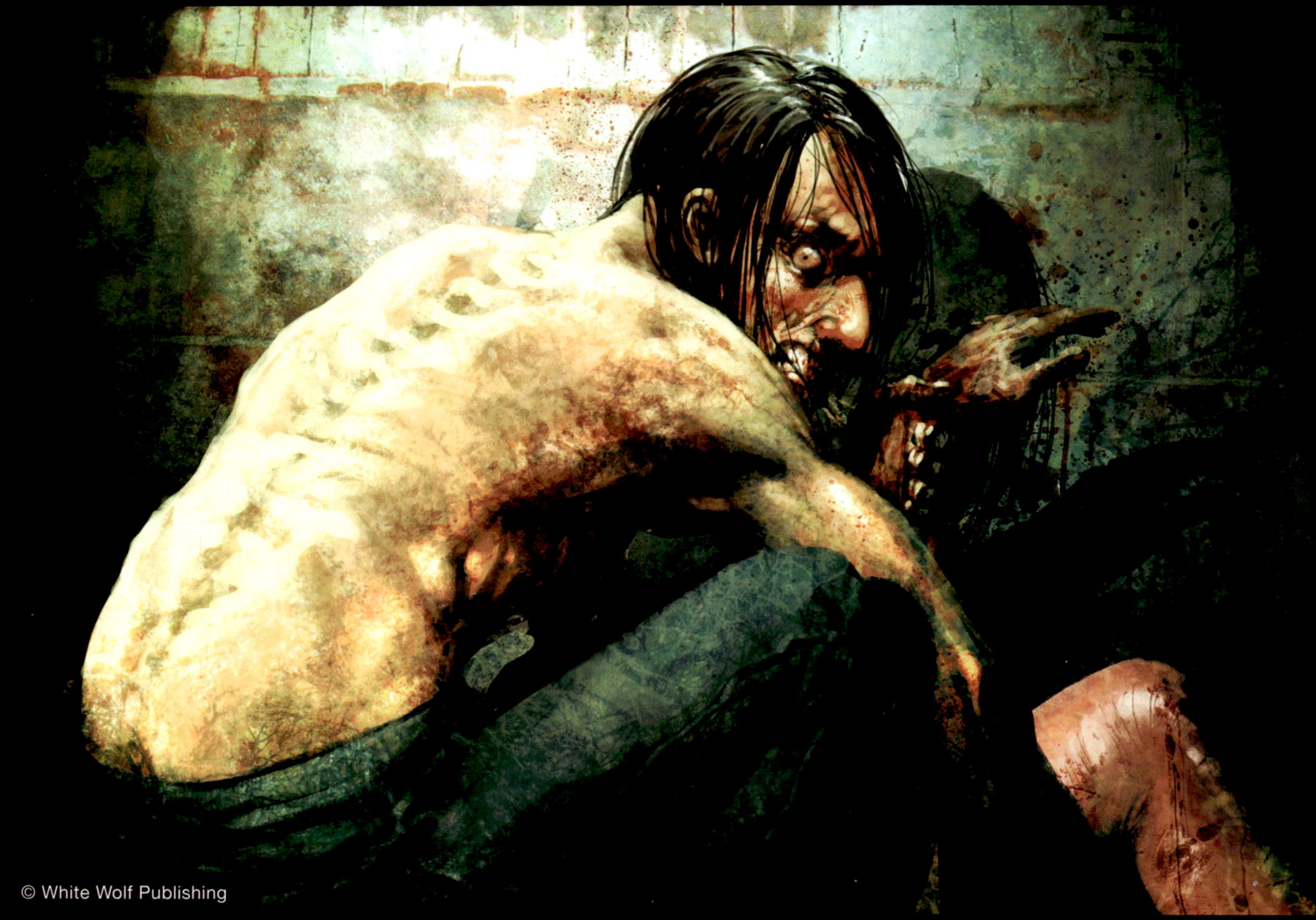

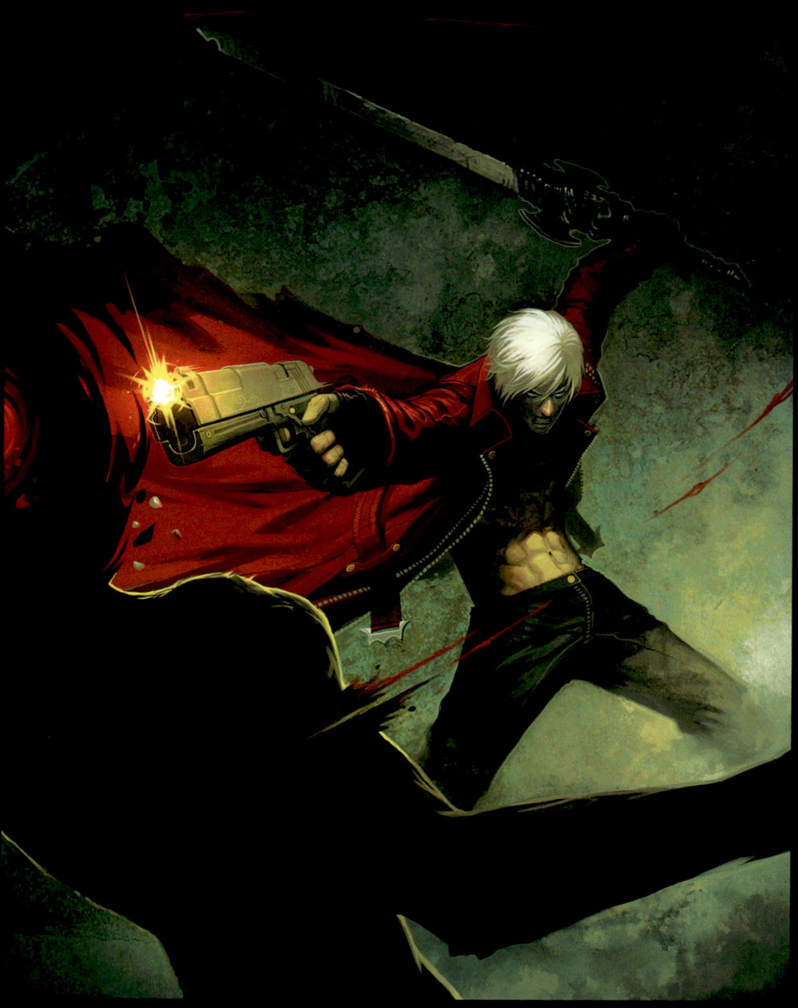

The pursuit
Photoshop
Tomasz Jedruszek, POLAND
[above]

Slash'n bang!
Photoshop
Andrew Hou, CANADA
[left]

Jaga
Photoshop
Michal Ivan, SLOVAKIA
[right]

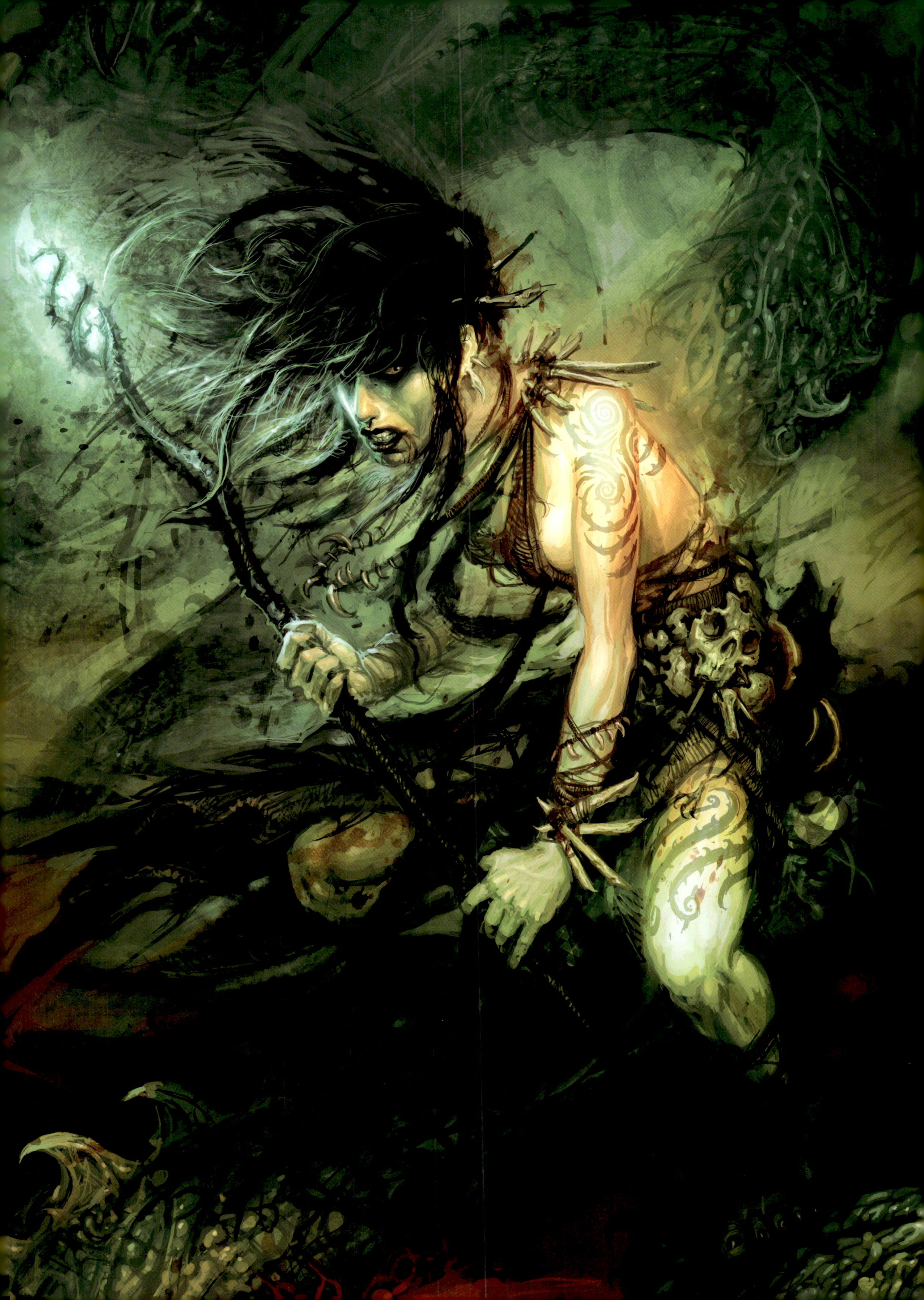

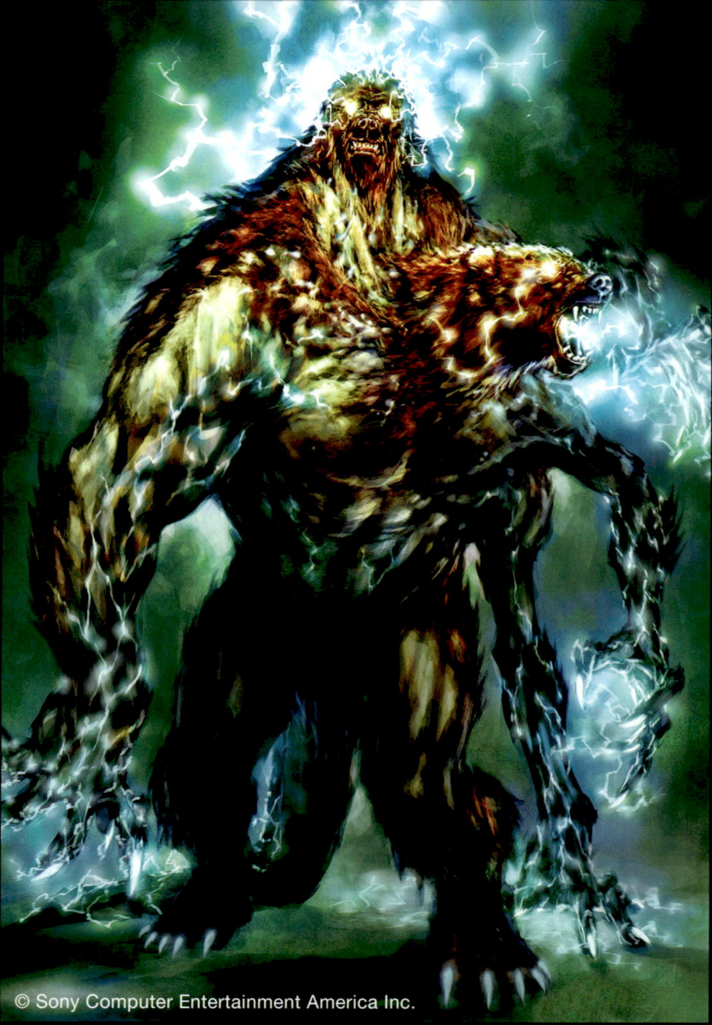

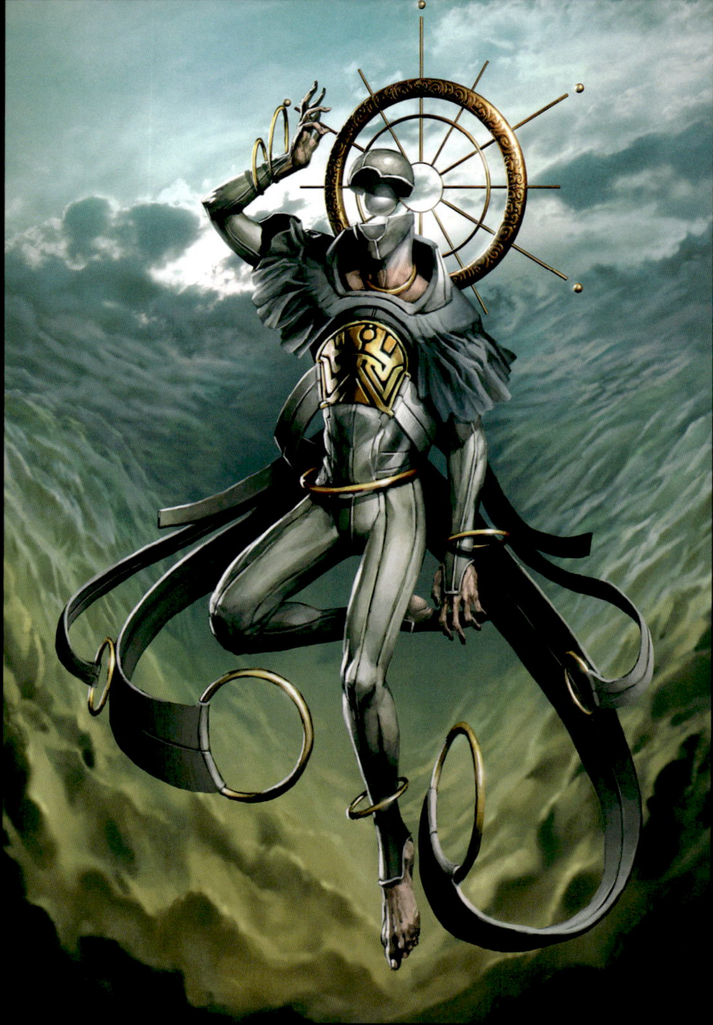

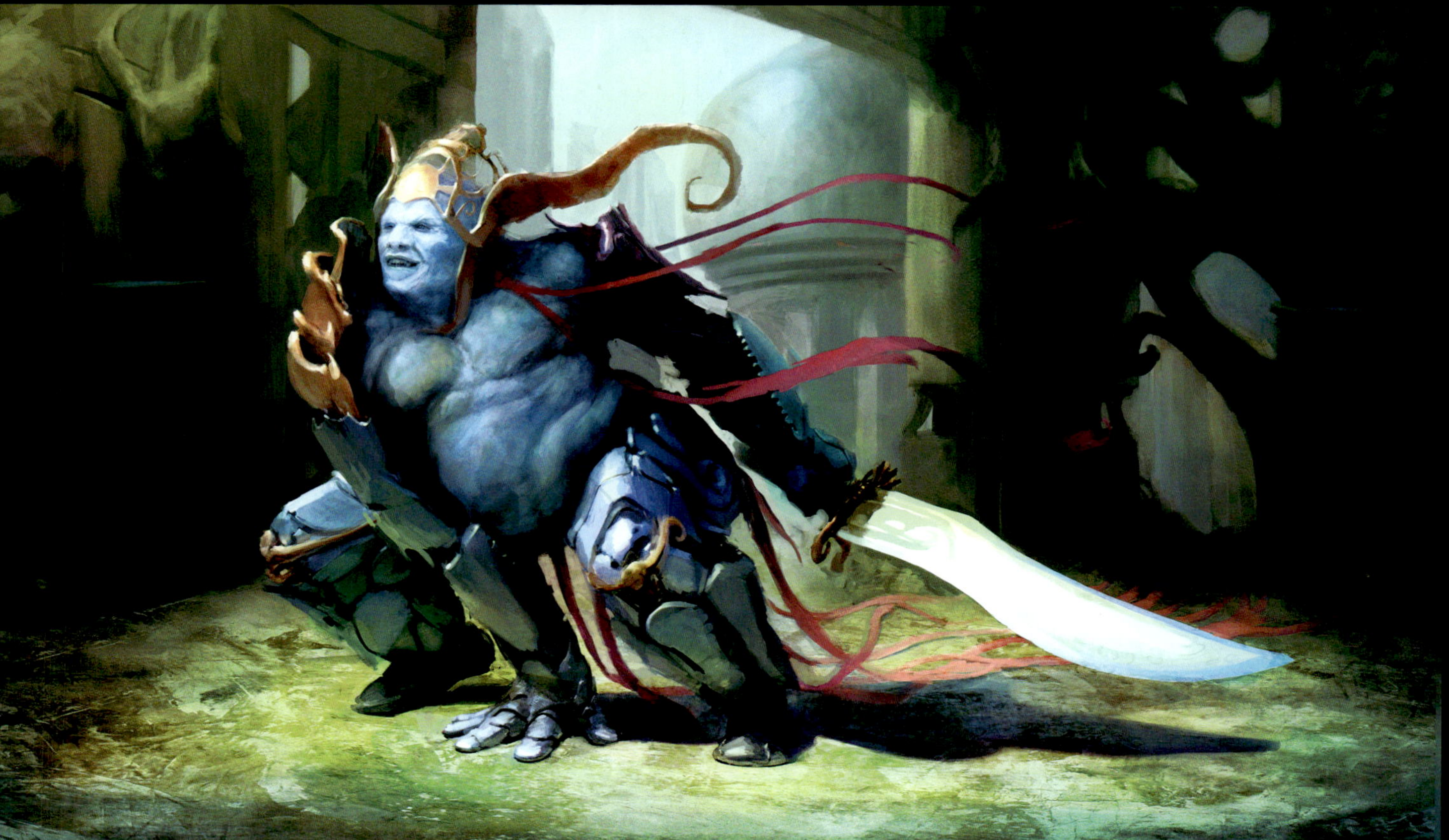

Coterus
Photoshop
Andy Park, SCEA, USA
[top]

Skelter Felter
Painter, Photoshop
Branko Bistrovic, CANADA
[above]

Sahaqiel
Photoshop, 3ds Max
Peter Mohrbacher, USA
[top]

The Avatar of the Great Enemy
Photoshop
Per Øyvind Haagensen, NORWAY
[right]

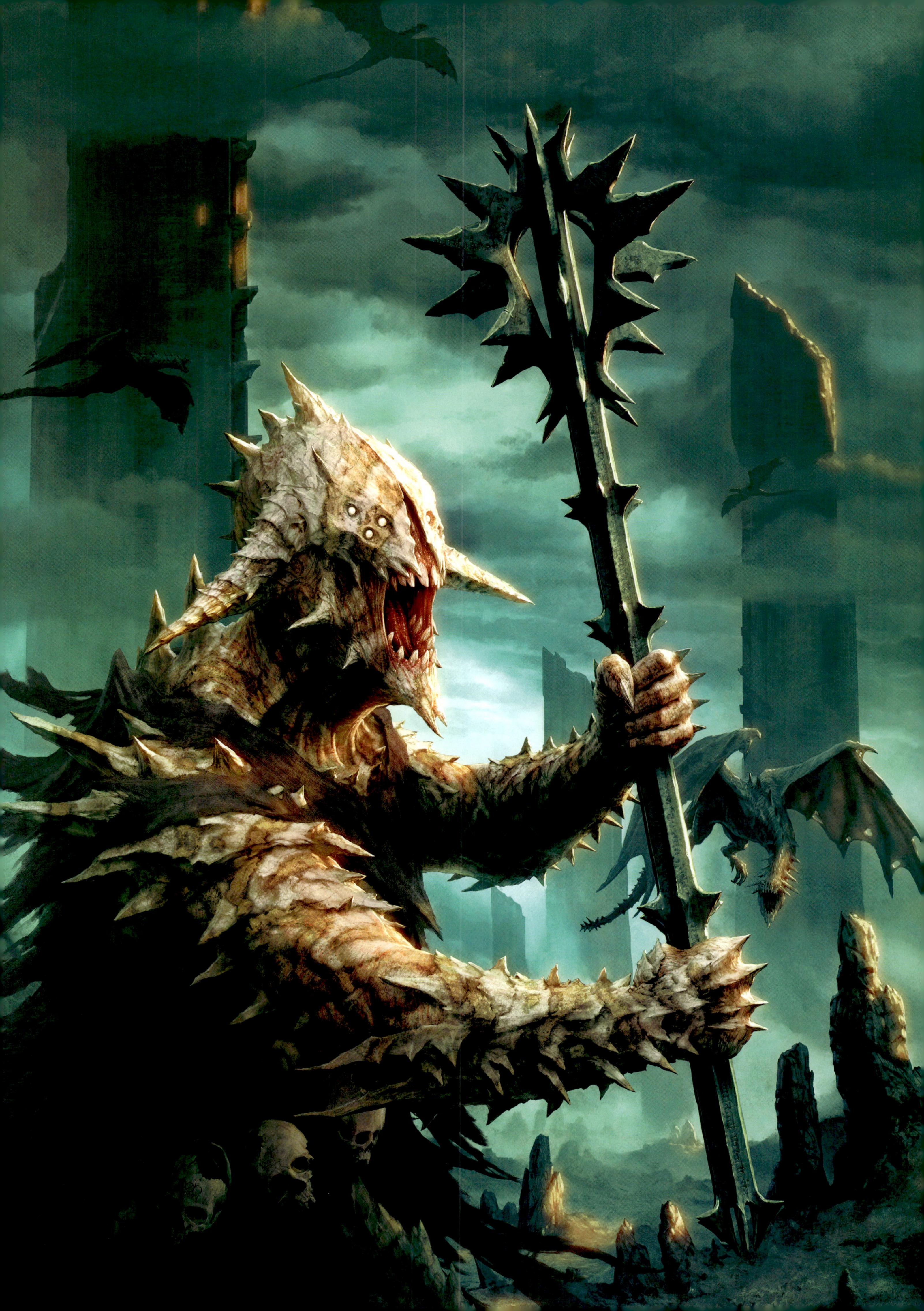

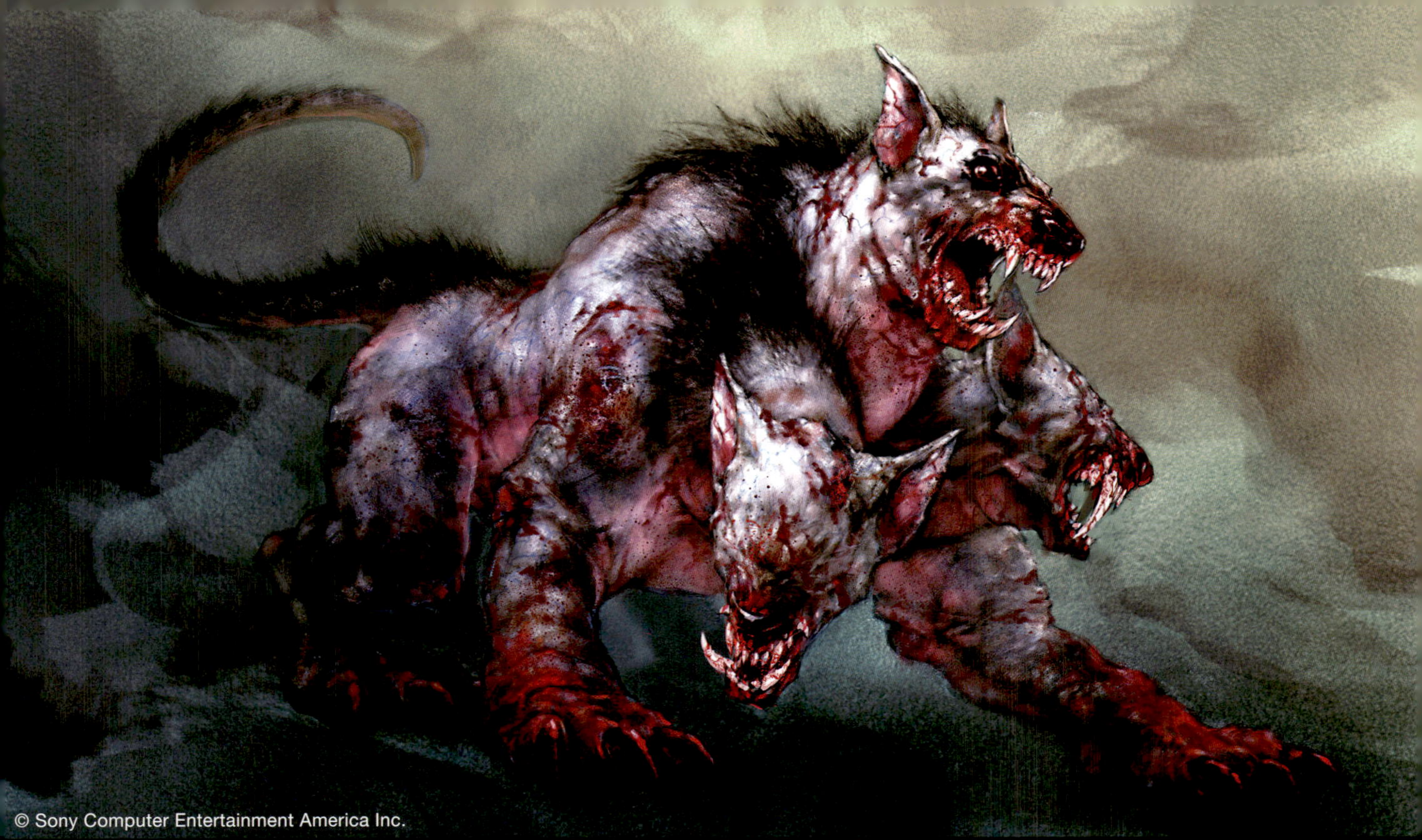

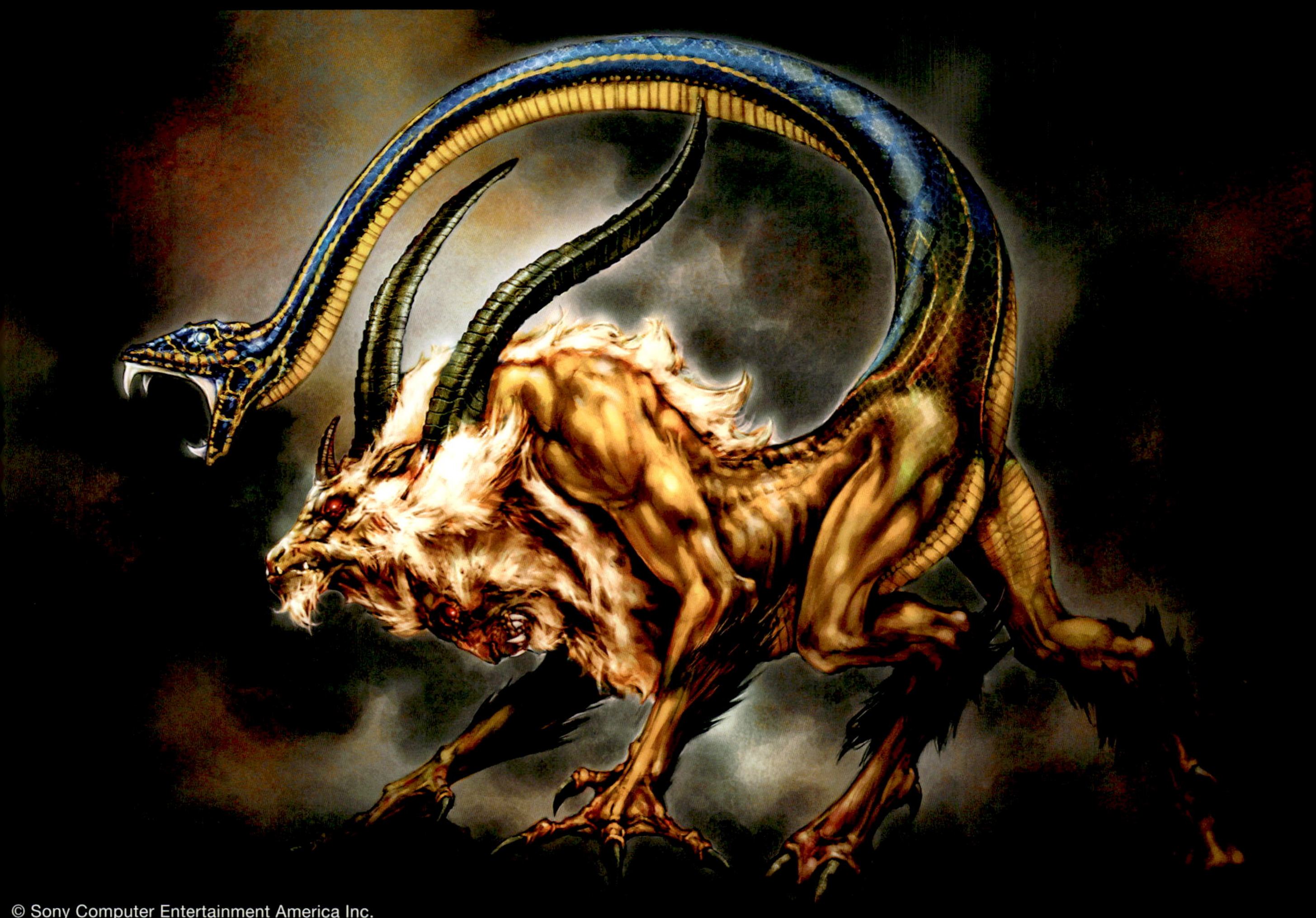

Mole Cerebus
Photoshop
Andy Park, SCEA, USA
[top]

Chimera
Photoshop
Andy Park, SCEA, USA
[above]

Beast from hell
Photoshop
Henryca Citra, frameworks studios, INDONESIA
[right]

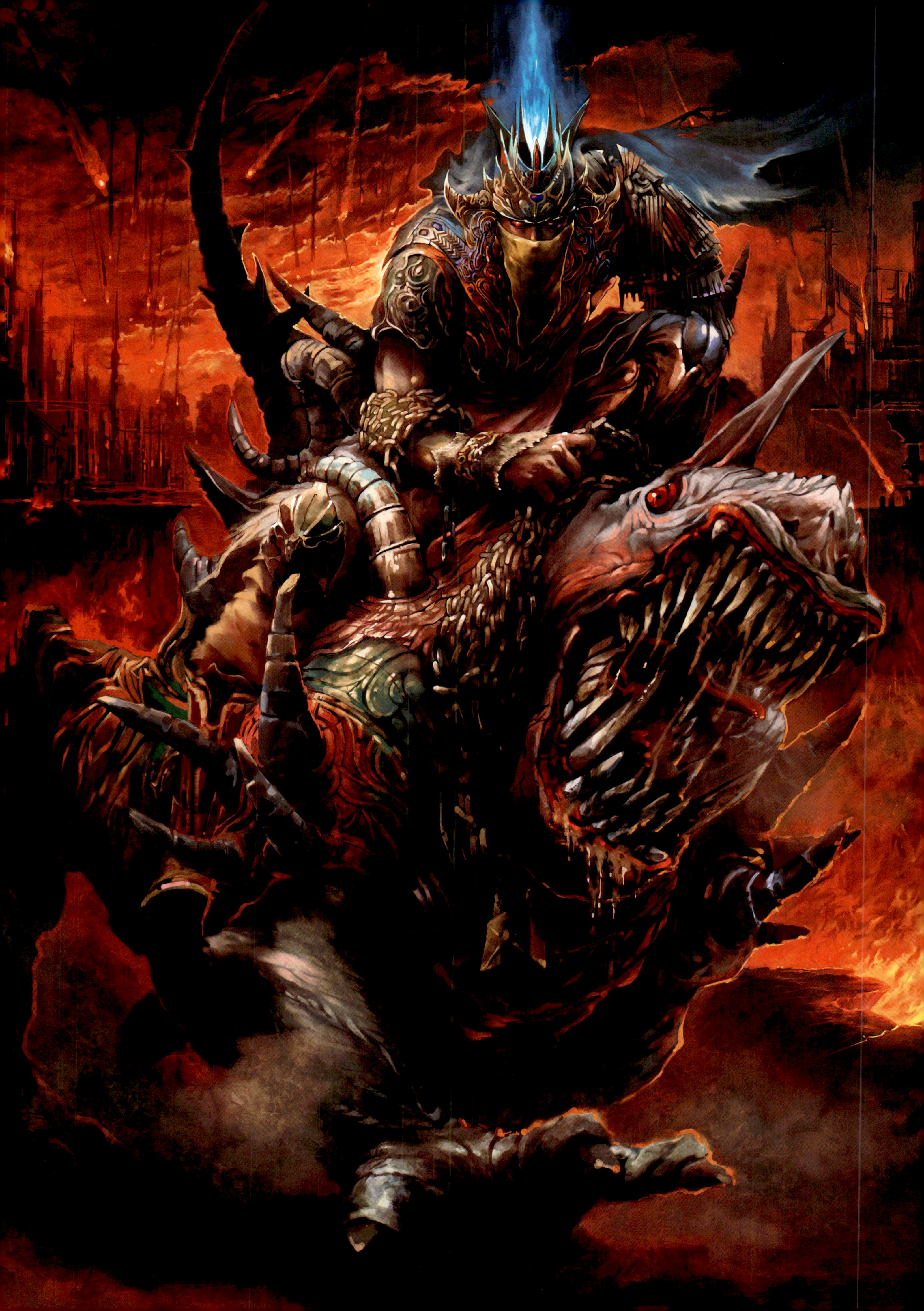

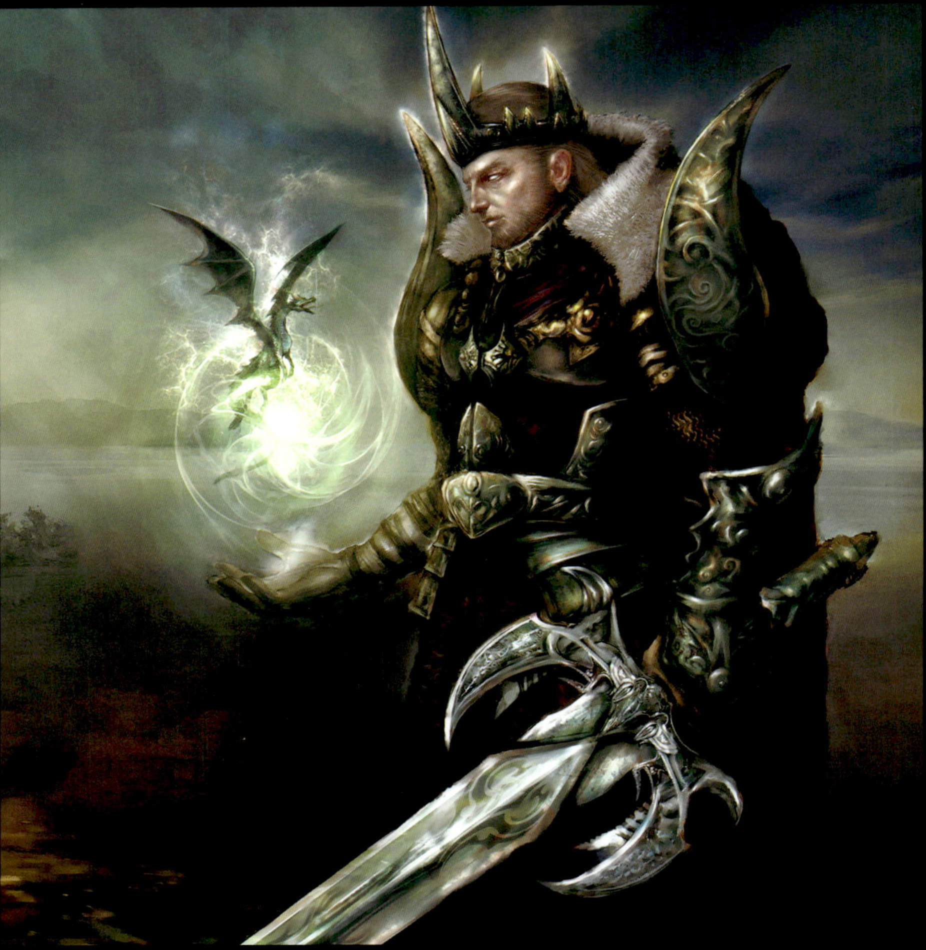

Dark Spell
Painter, Ph
Kyushik Sh
[left]

Barbarian
Softimagel
Photoshop
Helmet mo
Silvia Fuse
[right]

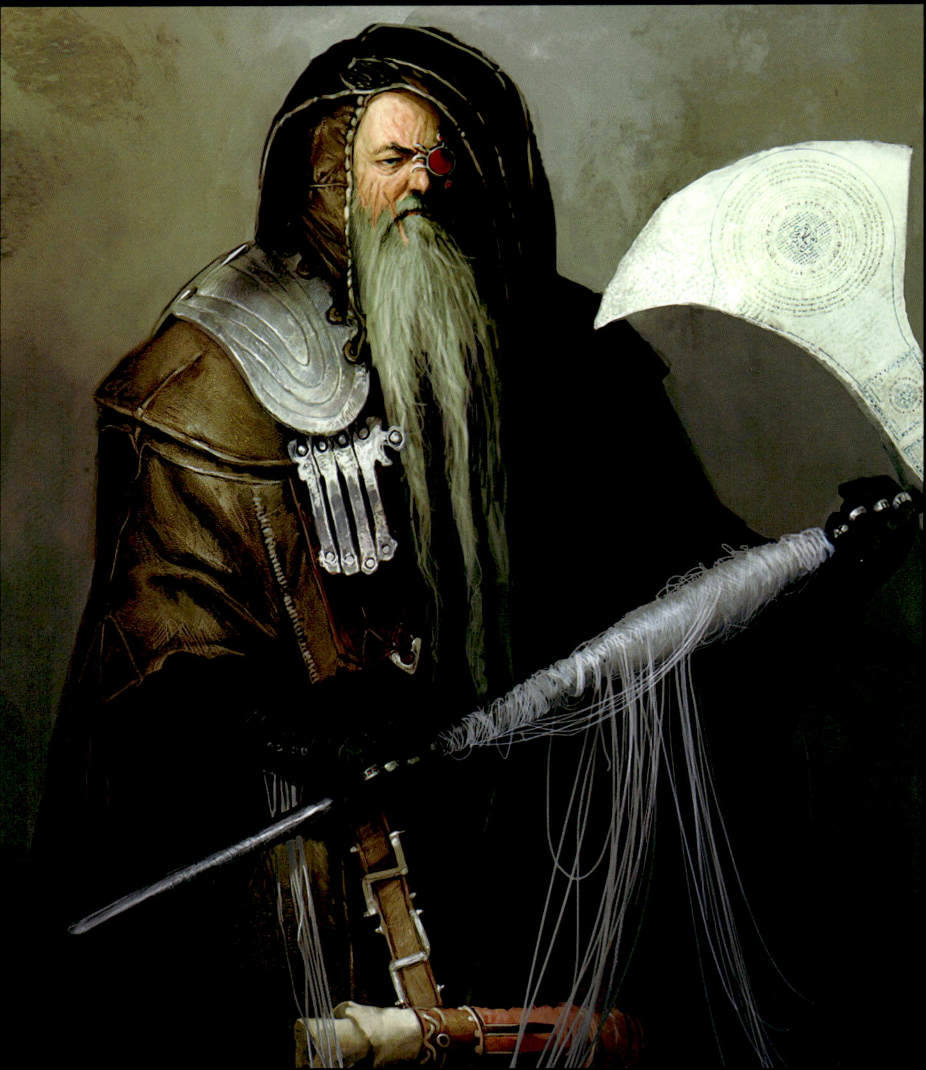

Ply spell
Photoshop
David Mun
SPAIN
[left]

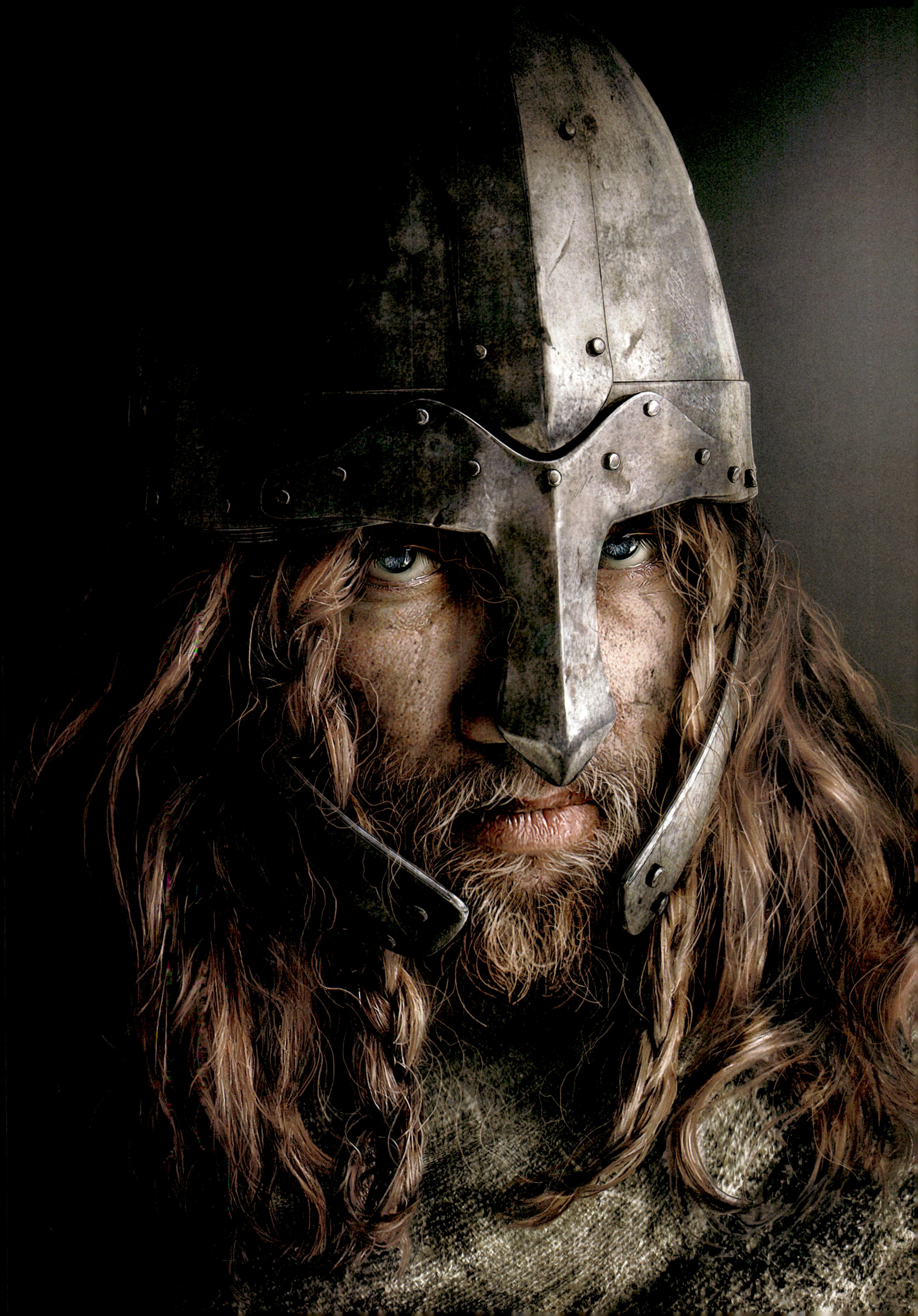

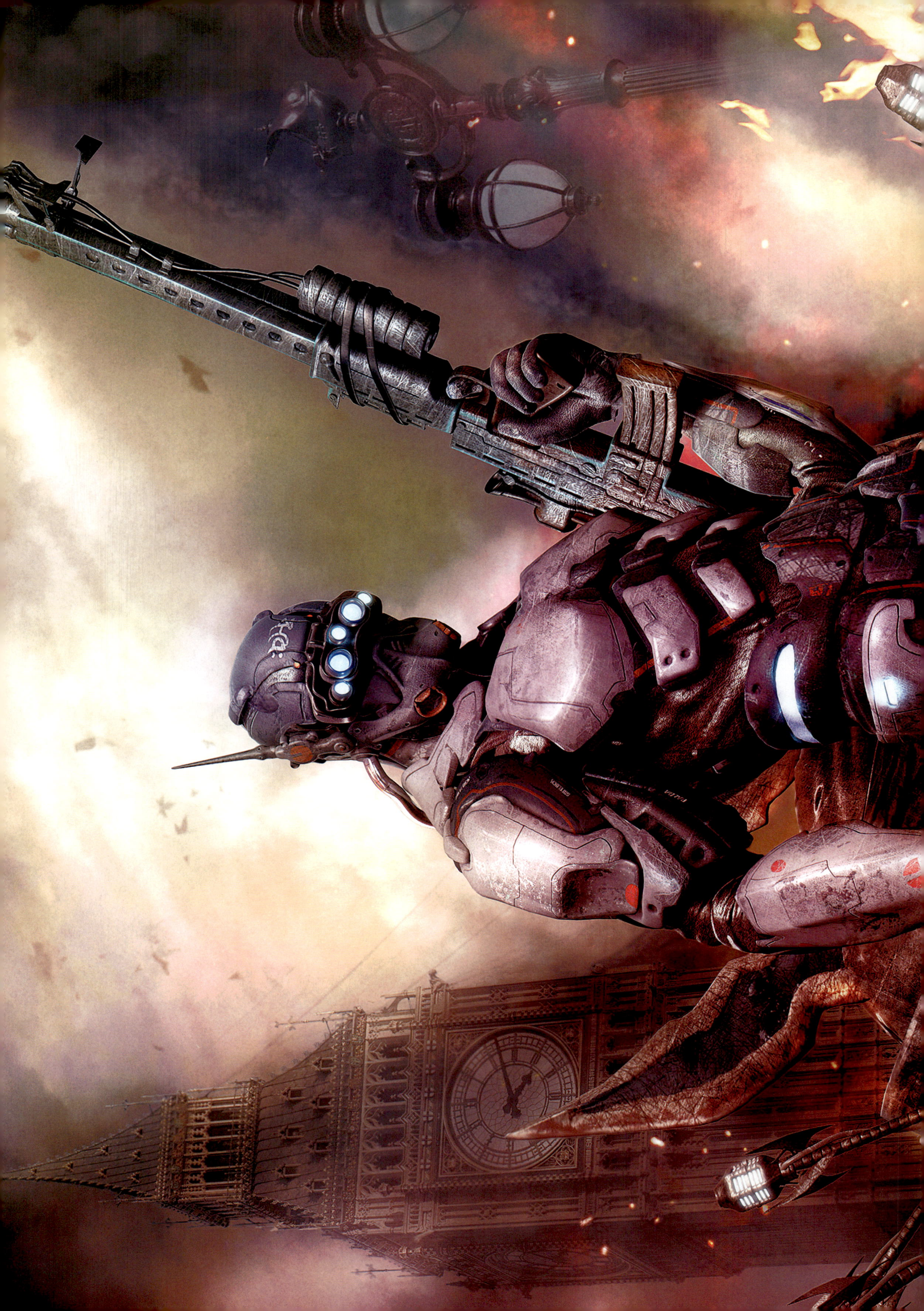

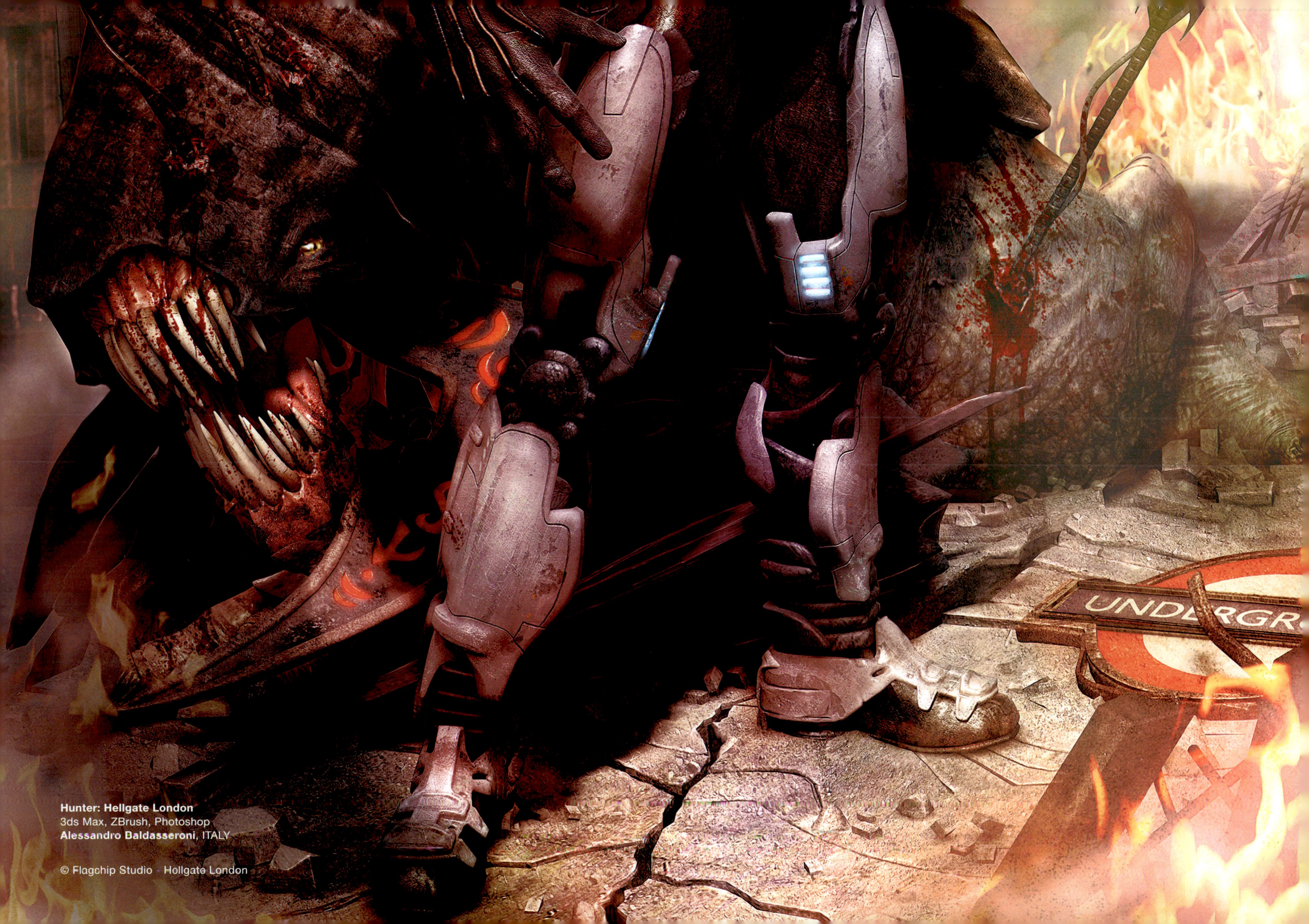

Hunter: Hellgate London
3ds Max, ZBrush, Photoshop
Alessandro Baldasseroni, ITALY

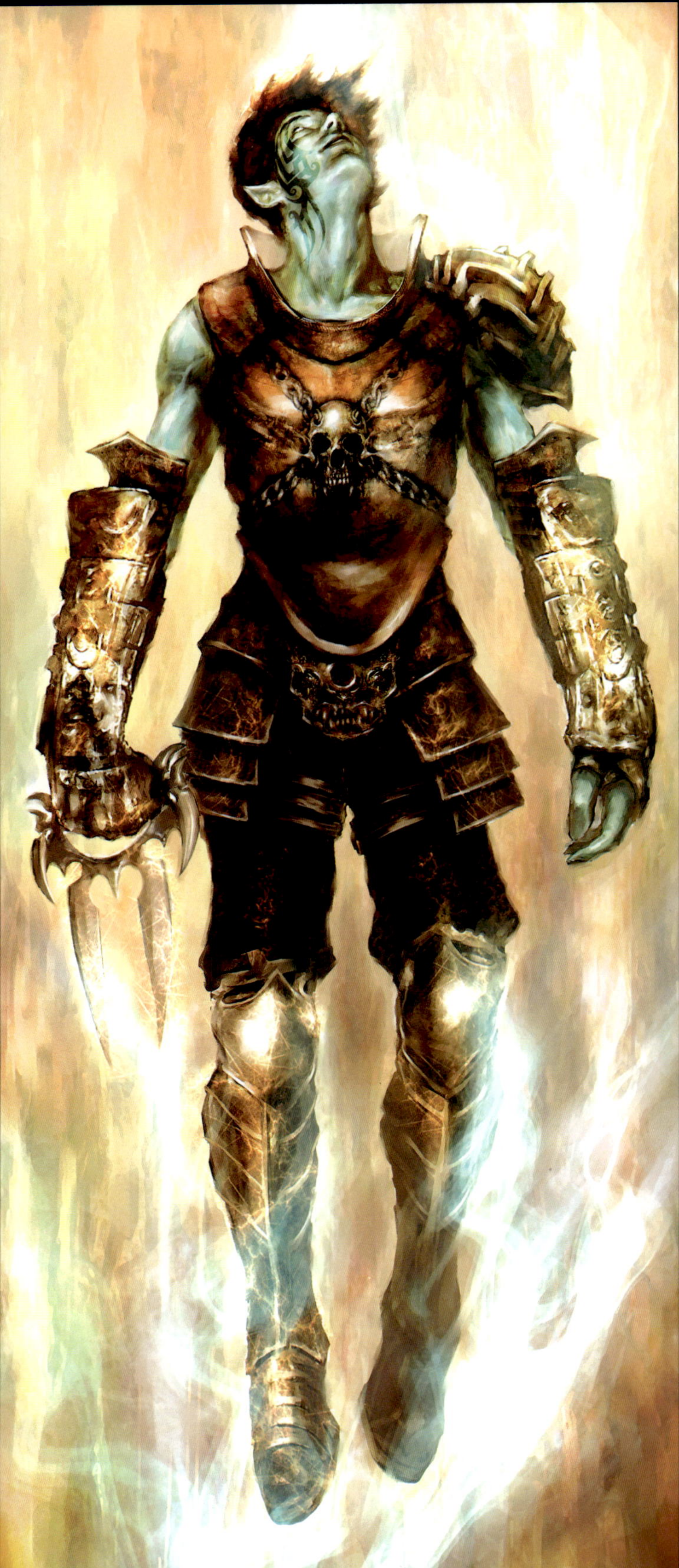

The Warrior
Painter, Photoshop
Kyushik Shin, USA
[above]

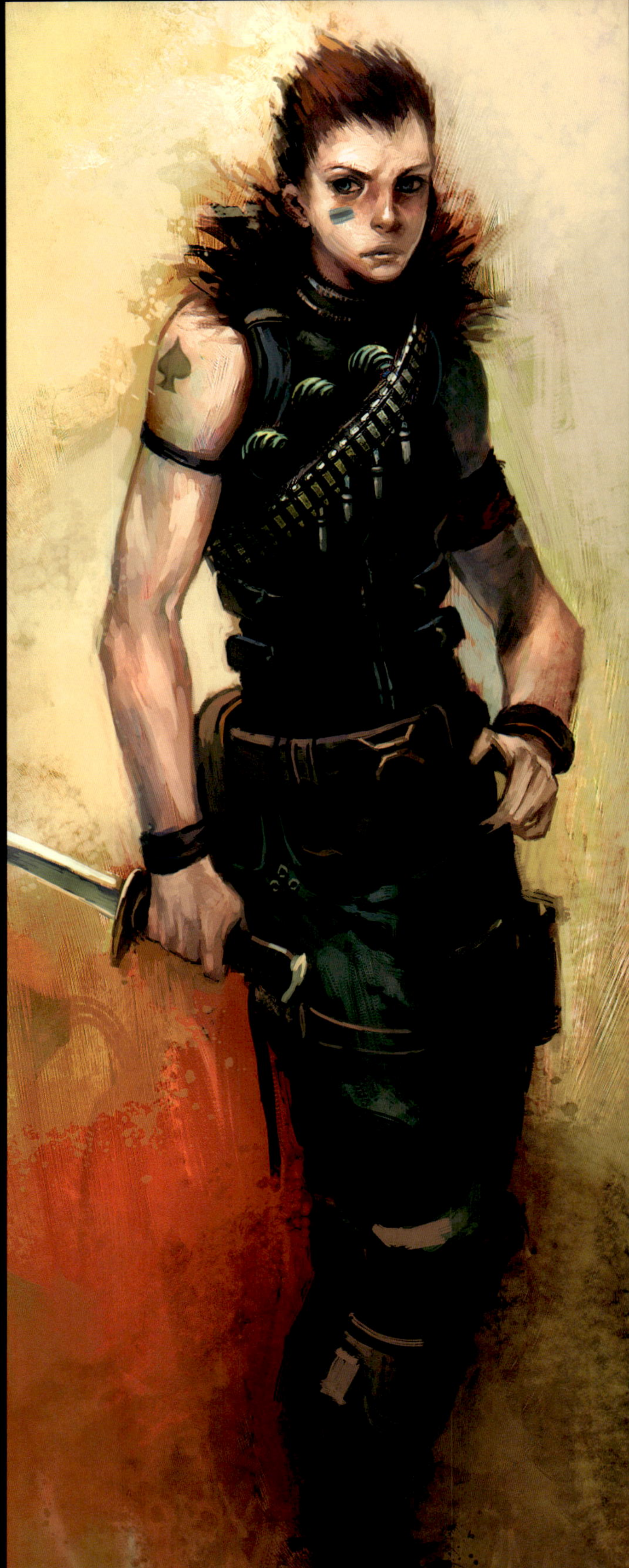

Ace
Photoshop, Painter
Leung Chun wan, HONG KONG
[above]

Blind invader
Photoshop
David Munoz Velazquez, SPAIN
[right]

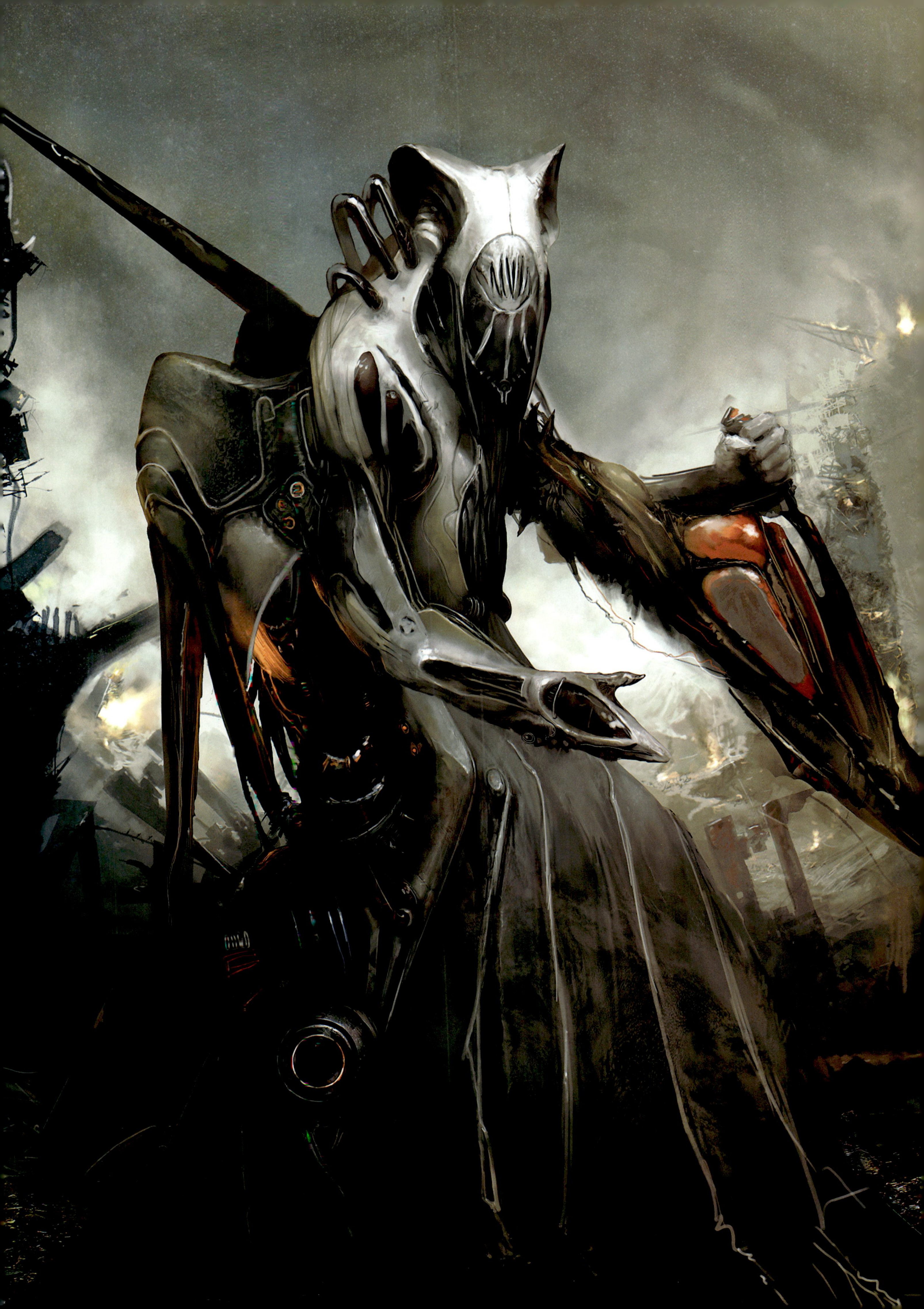

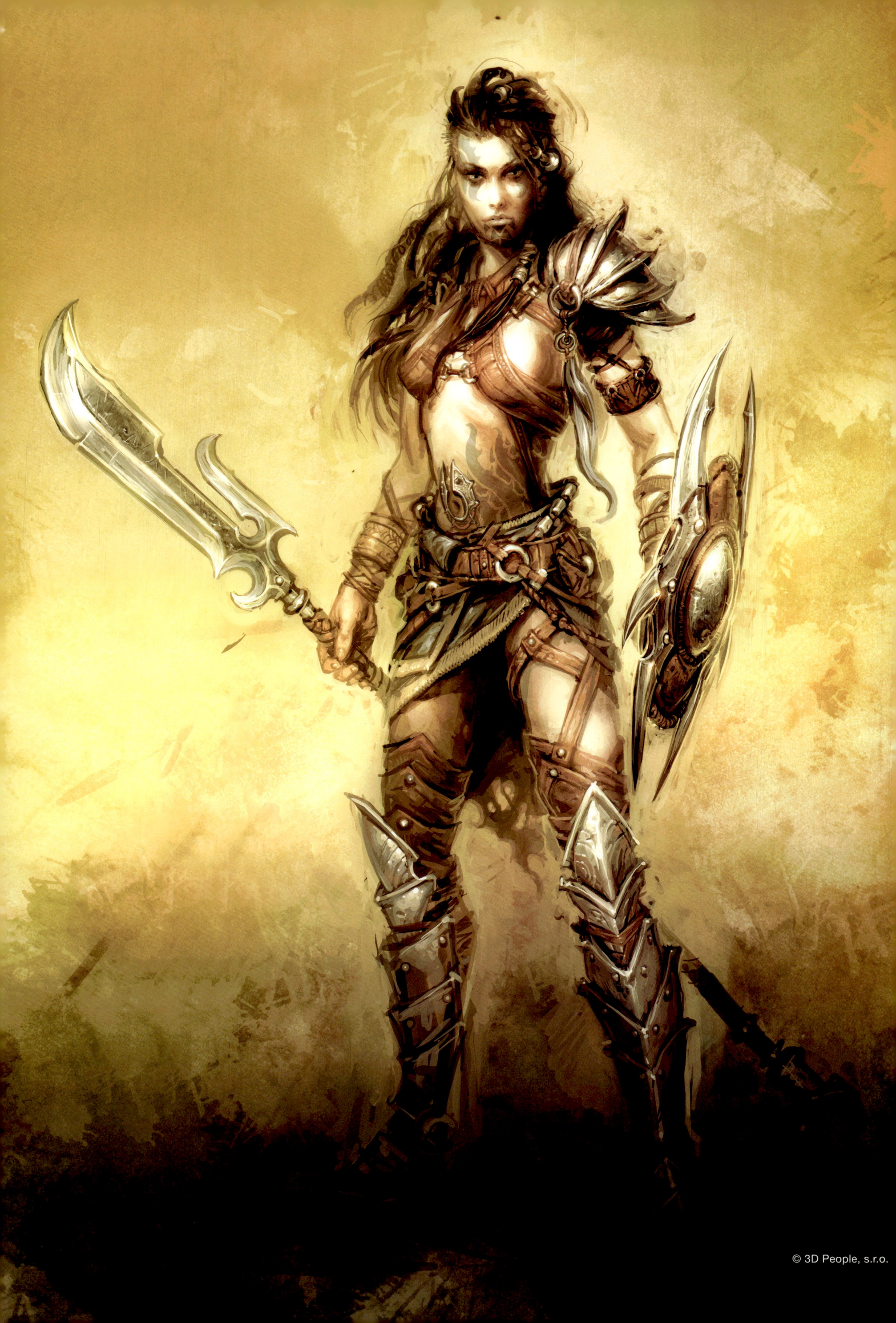

Warrior girl
Photoshop
Michal Ivan, SLOVAKIA
[left]

Melandru
Photoshop
Client: ArenaNet: GuildWars
Kekai Kotaki, ArenaNet, USA
[right]

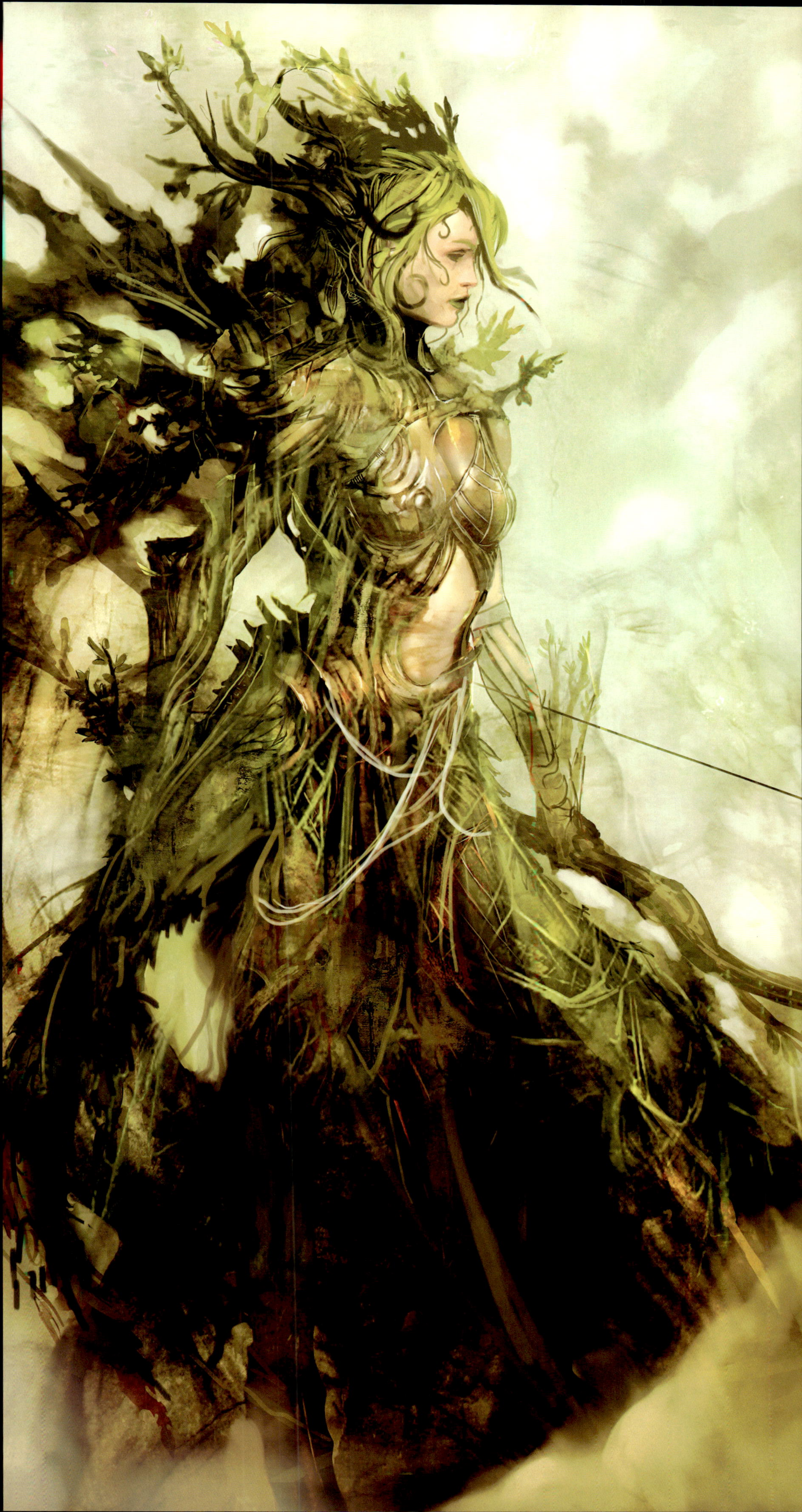

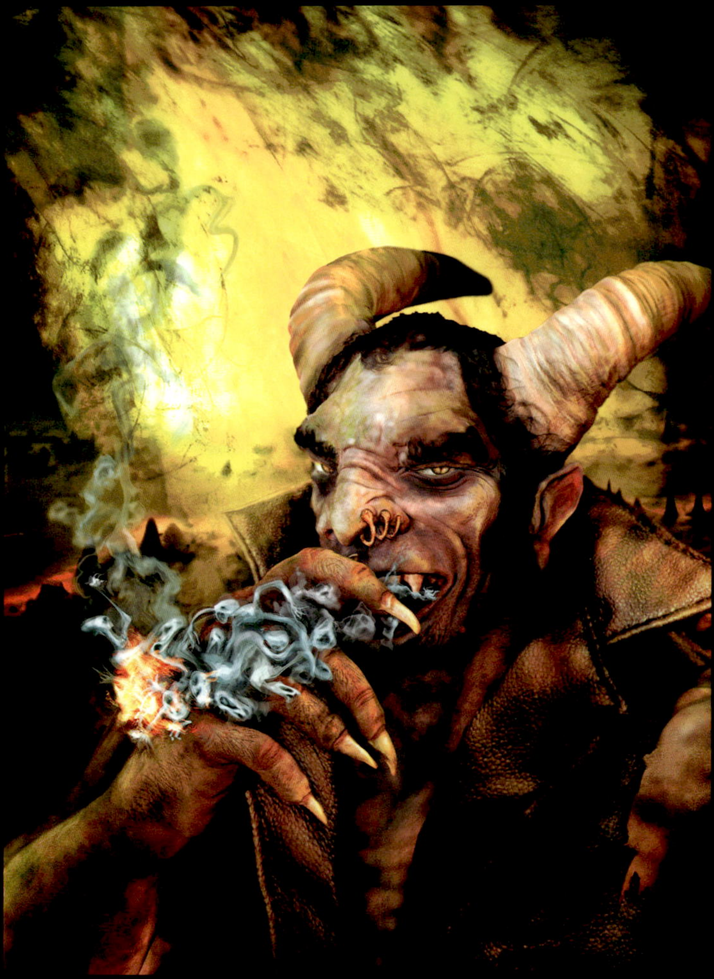

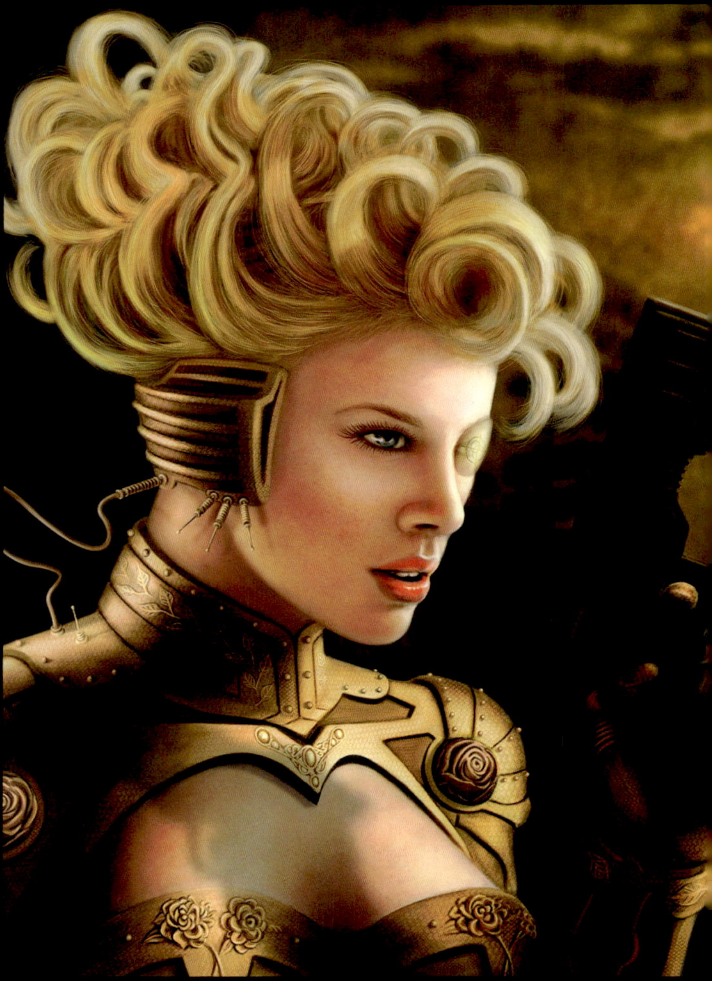

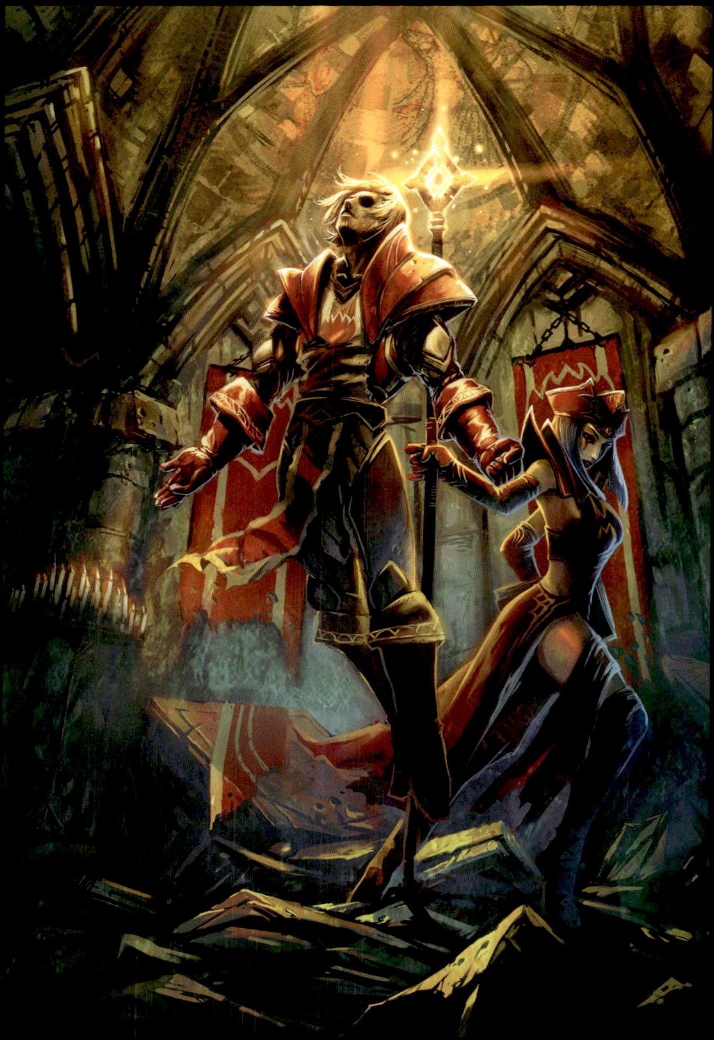

Daemon smoking souls
ZBrush, Photoshop
Juan Fernández, animastur, SPAIN
[top left]

Rosas de Oro
Photoshop
Jeffrey M. de Guzman, PHILIPPINES
[above]

Resurrection
Painter, Photoshop
Jian Guo, CHINA
[left]

Unleashed fury
3ds Max, ZBrush, Photoshop, VRay
Robin Benes, CZECH REPUBLIC
[right]

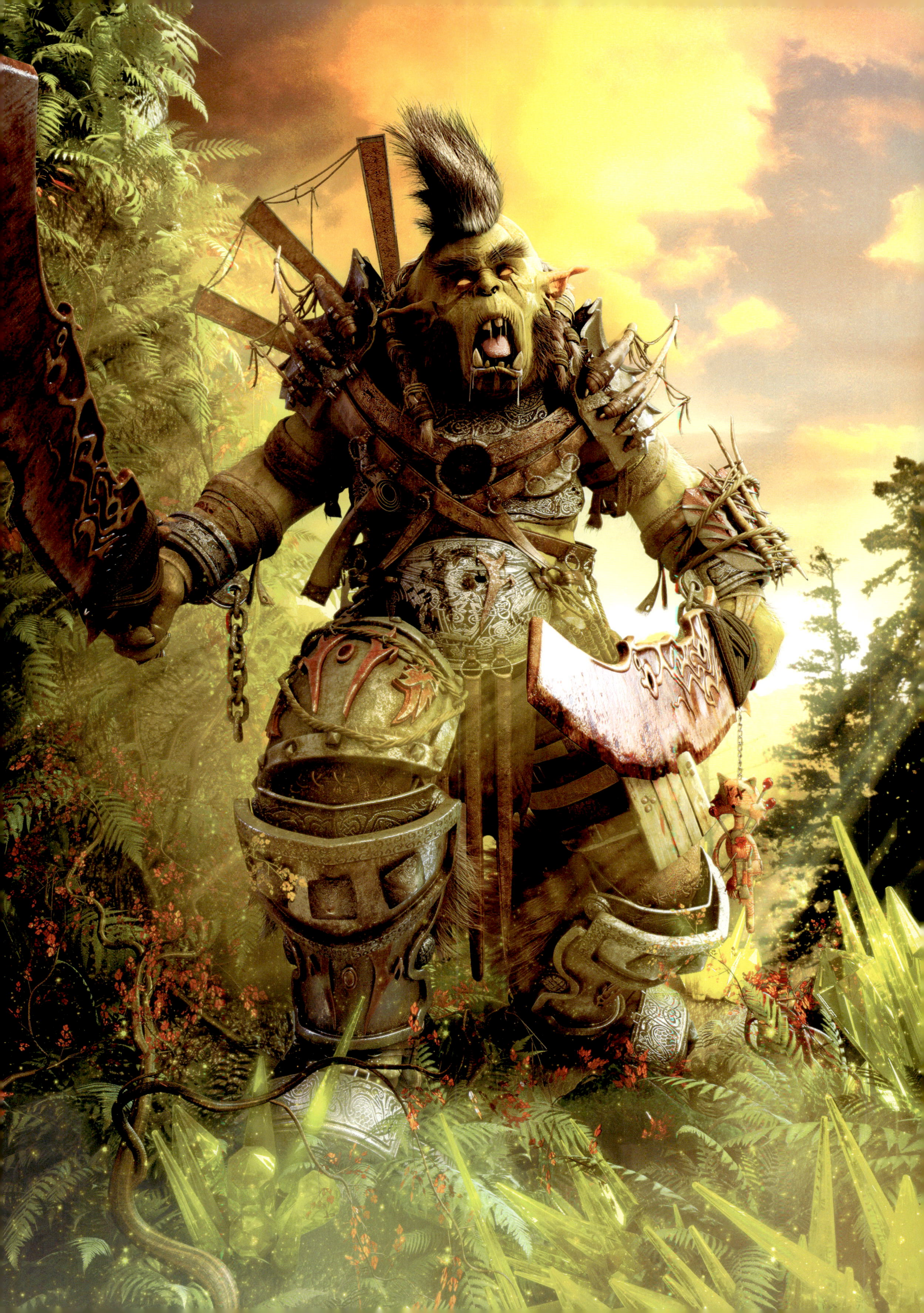

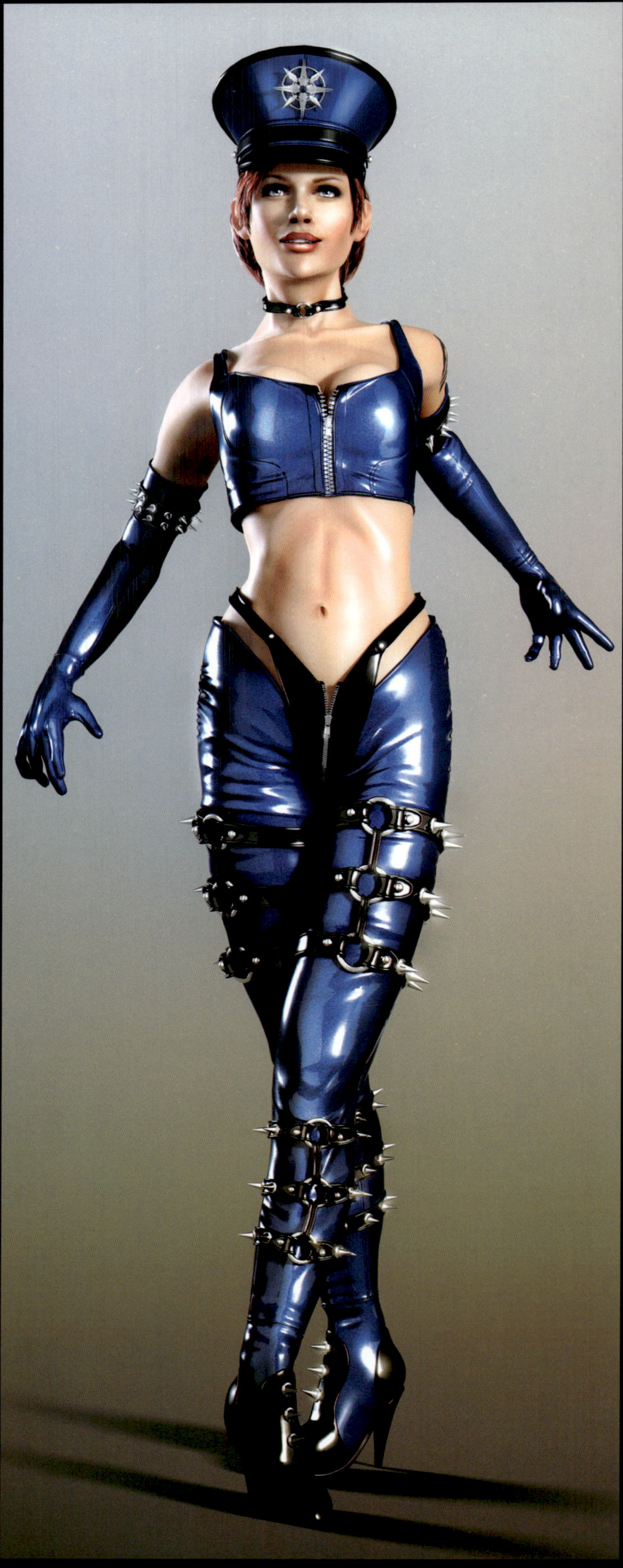

New Order
3ds Max, ZBrush, Photoshop
Plamen Iliev, BULGARIA
[above]

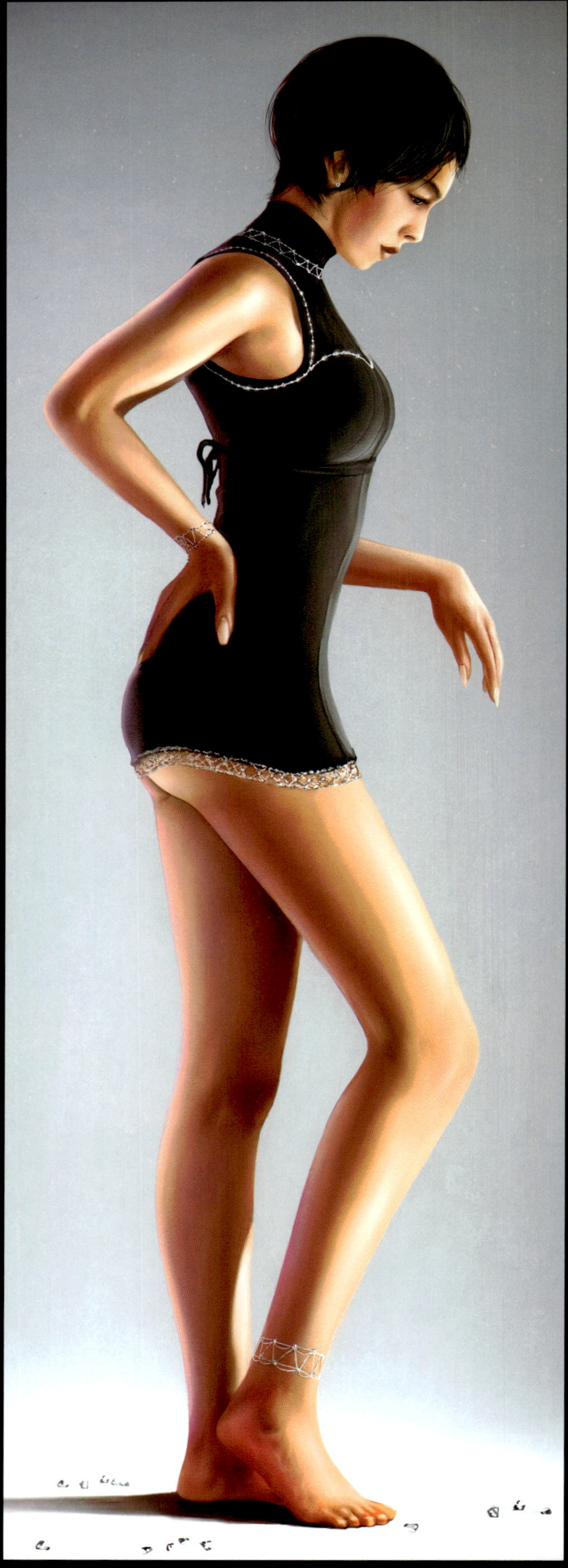

Precious Stone
Photoshop, Painter
Andreas Rocha, PORTUGAL
[above]

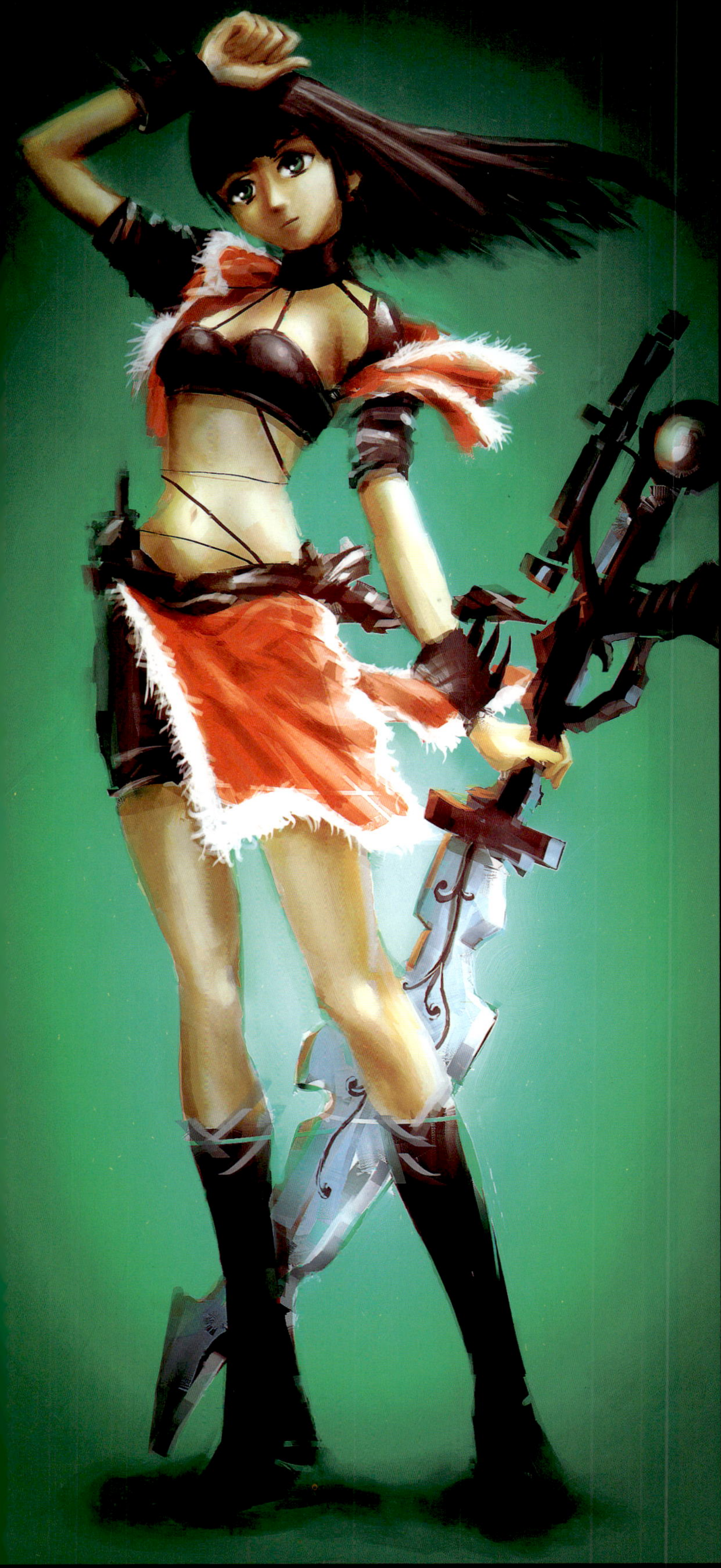

Blaster Mega
Photoshop, Painter
Raffy Encarnacion Dematawaran, PHILIPPINES
[above]

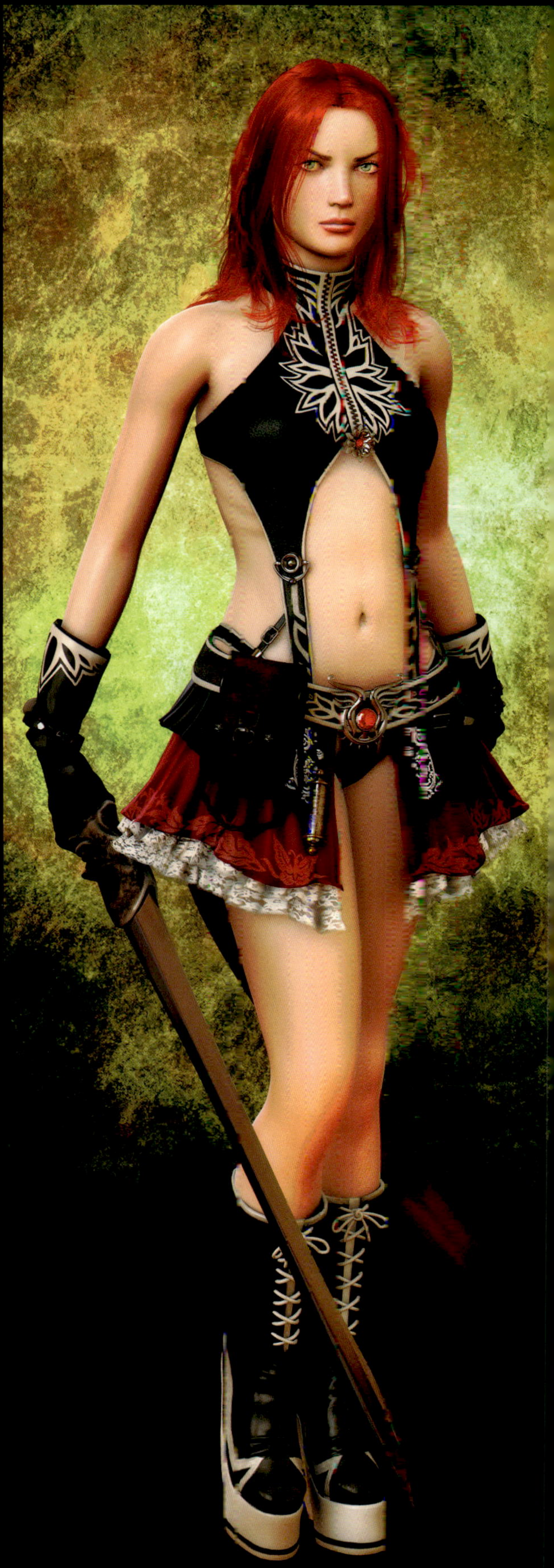

The Mistress of the Sword
3ds Max, BodyPaint 3D, Photoshop
Marc Tan, Insane Polygons, SINGAPORE
[above]

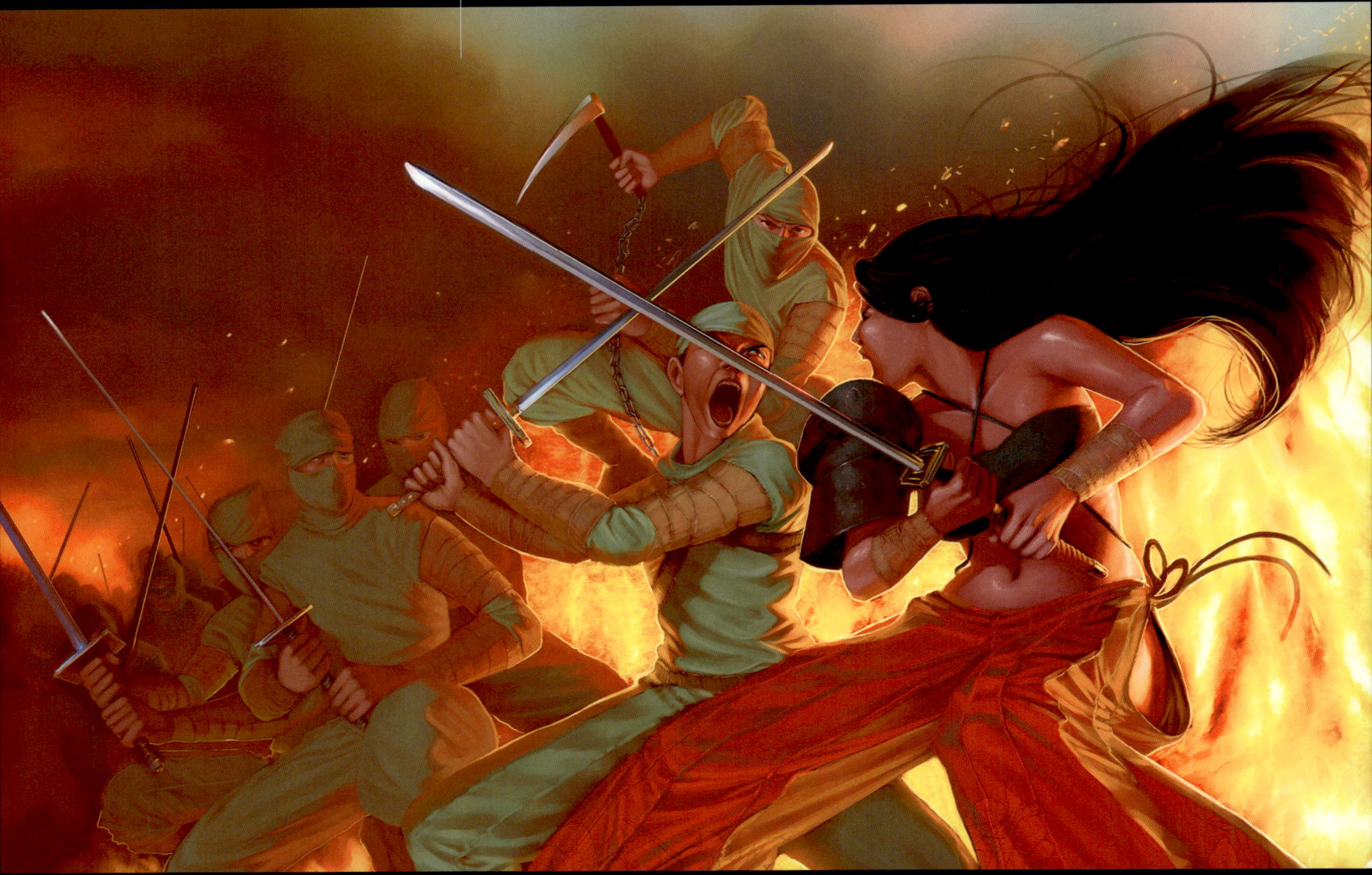

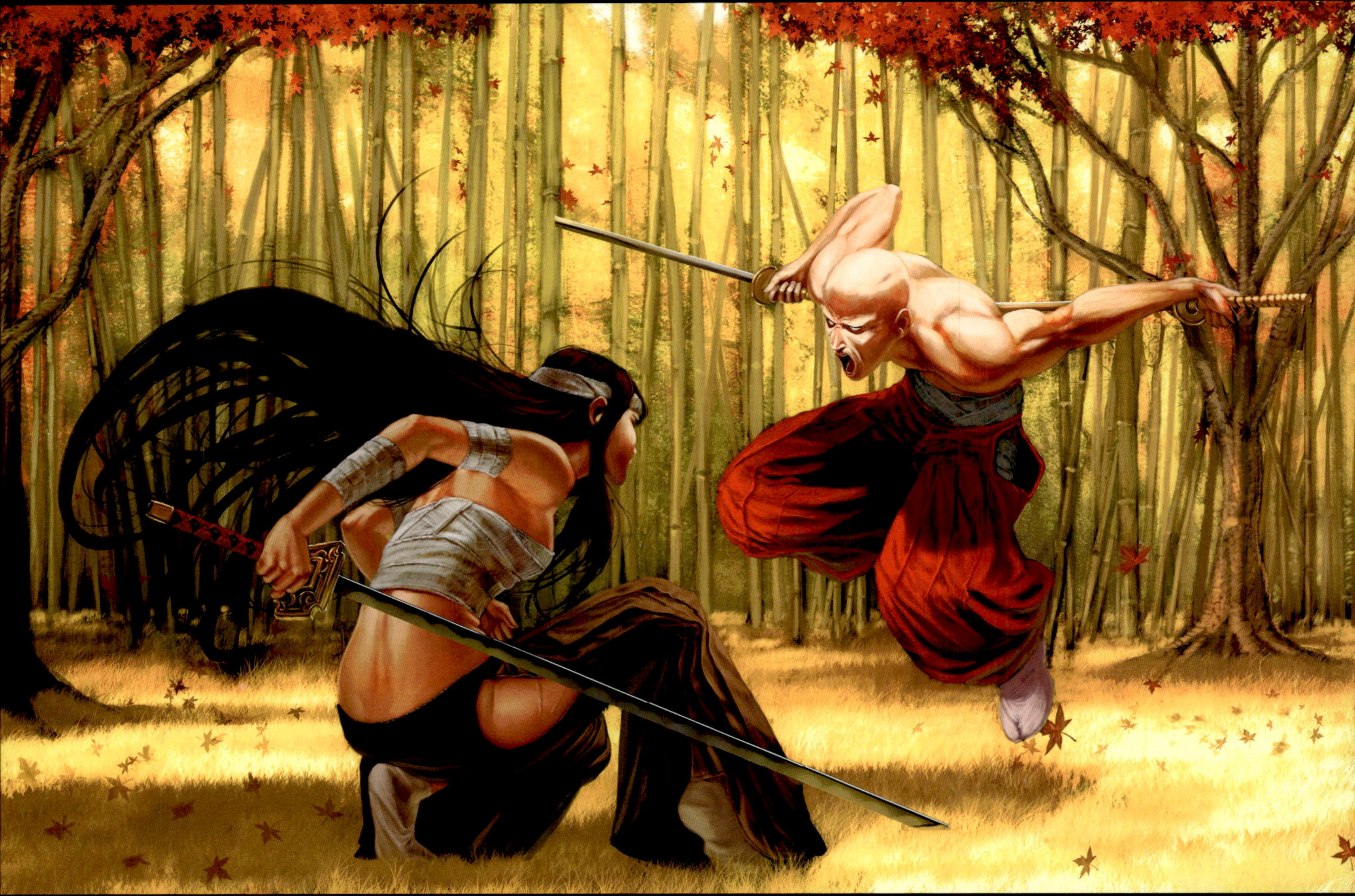

99
Photoshop
Dan Howard, USA
[top]

Full Tang
Photoshop
Dan Howard, USA
[above]

Warhammer
Photoshop
Jiansong Chen, LusioSoft Entertainment Co., Ltd, CHINA
[right]

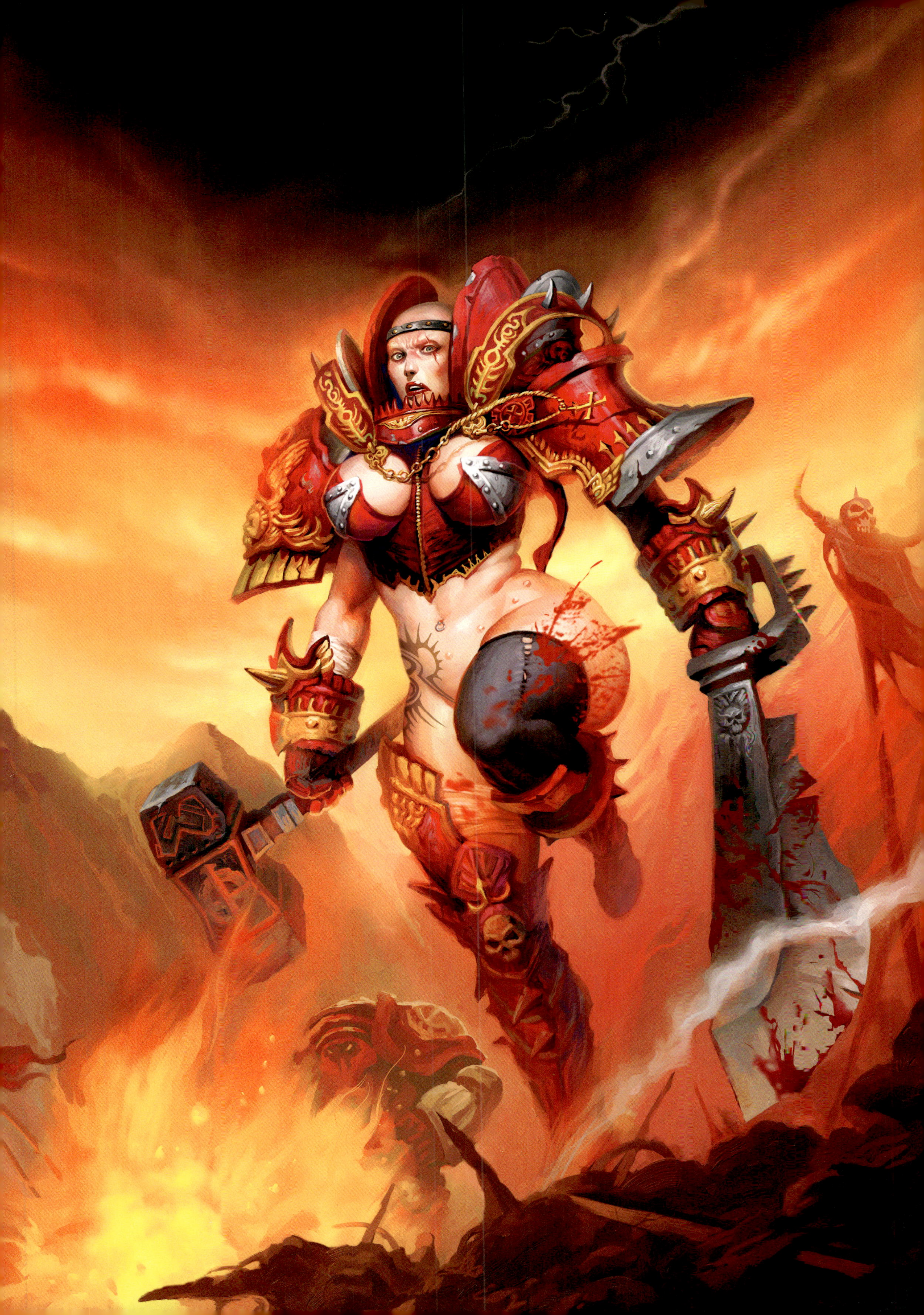

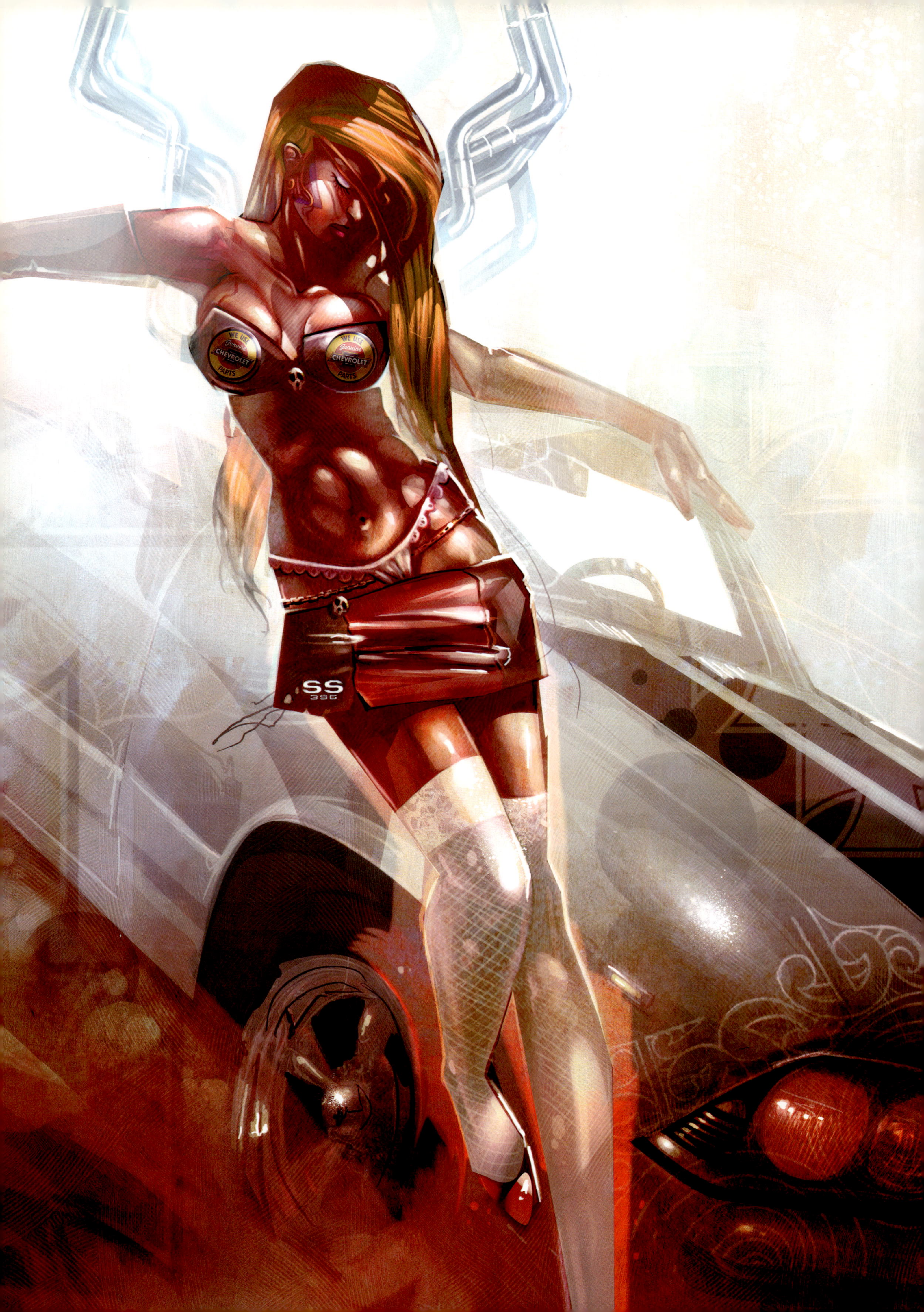
WE USE Genuine CHEVROLET PARTS
WE USE Genuine CHEVROLET PARTS
SS
396

Bigblock belle
Photoshop
Glen Angus, USA
[left]

Cosmic punch
Photoshop
Rafi Adrian Zulkarnain, INDONESIA
[right]

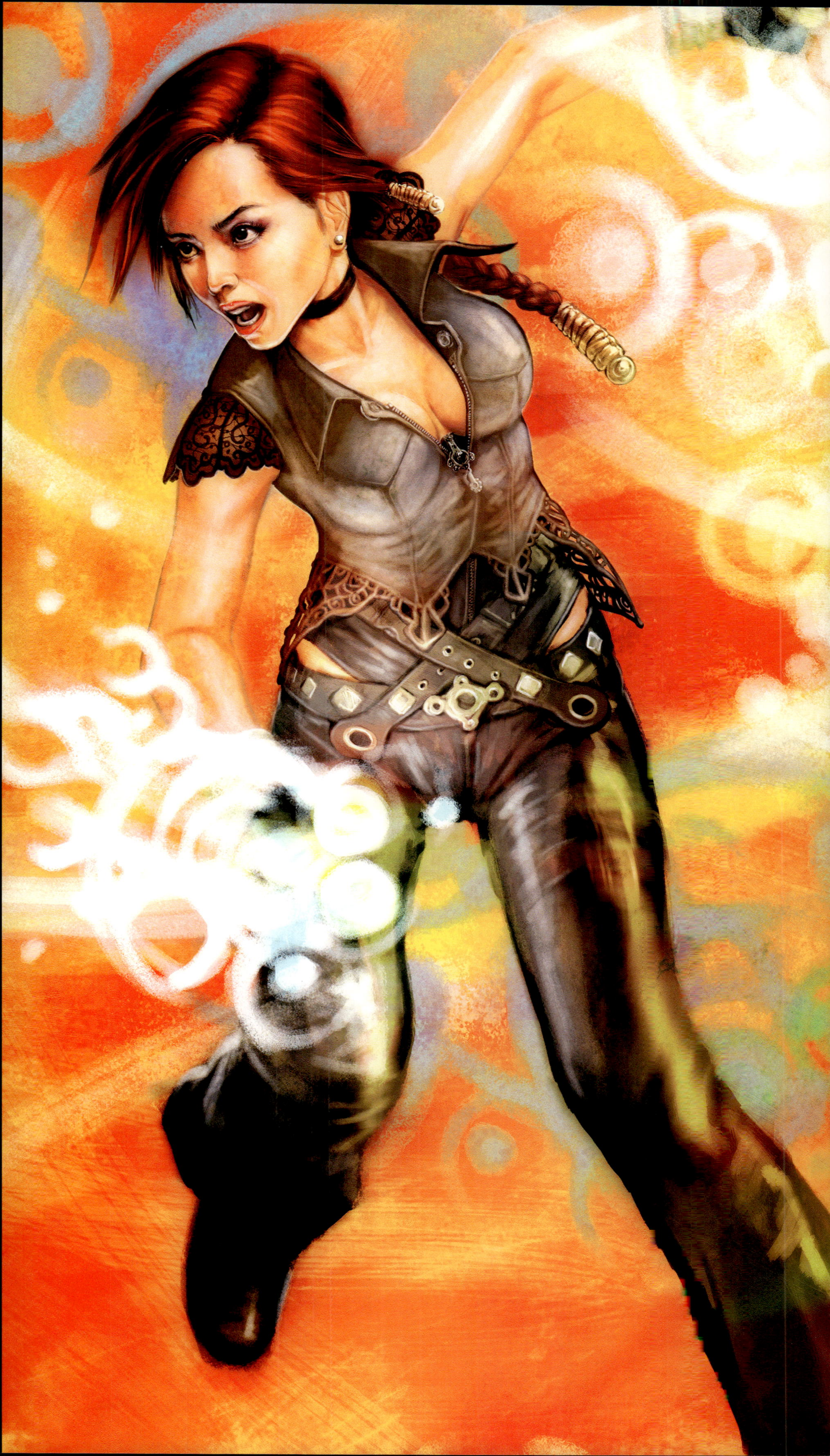

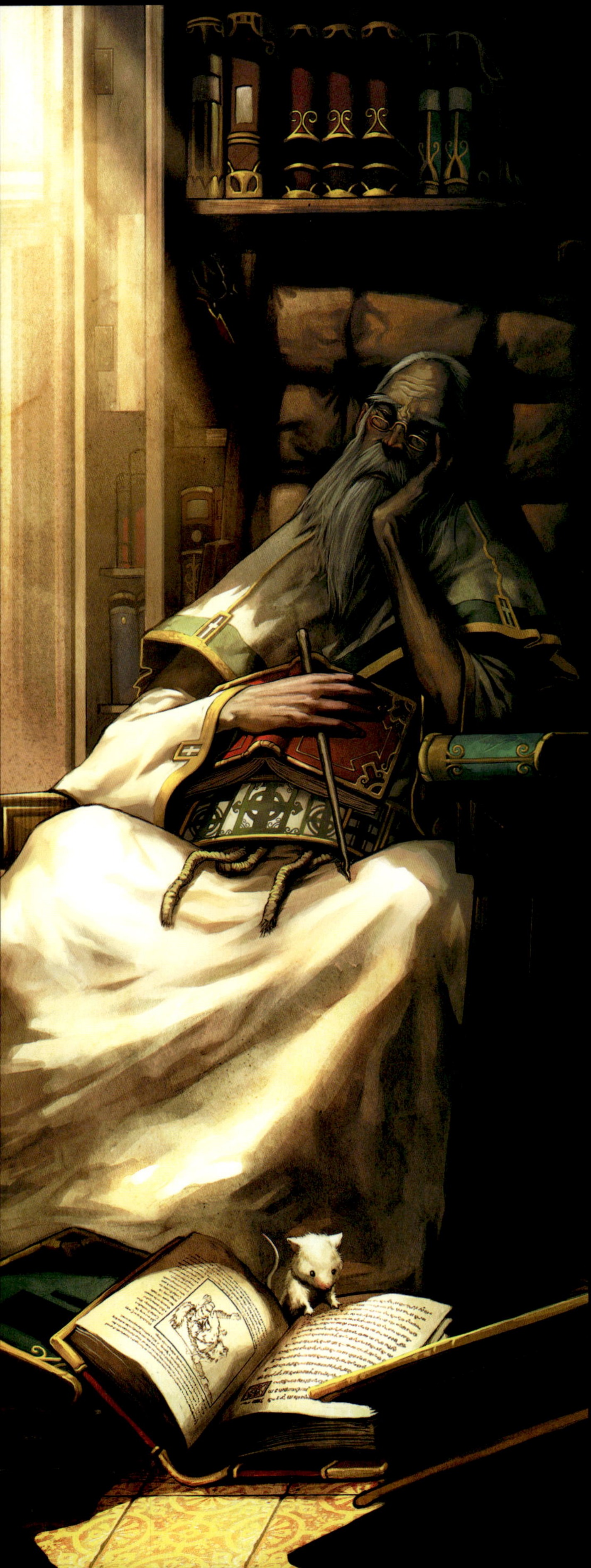

Sage's Nap
Photoshop
Client: Paizo Publishing
Andrew Hou, CANADA
[above]

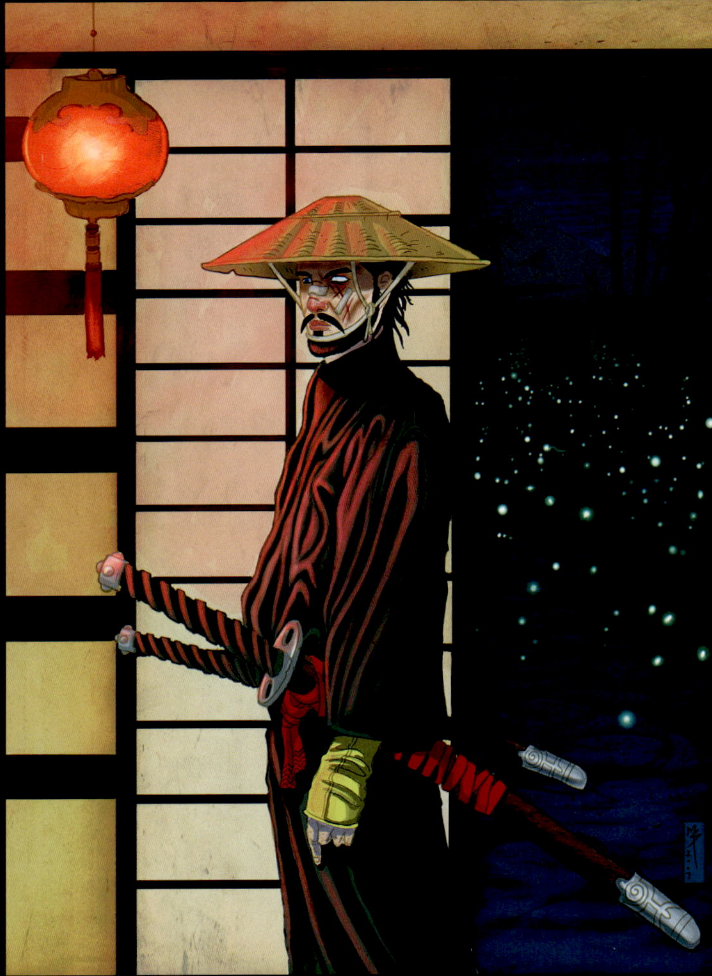

Vagabond
Pencil, Photoshop
Mack Sztaba, Eternal Concepts, CANADA
[top]

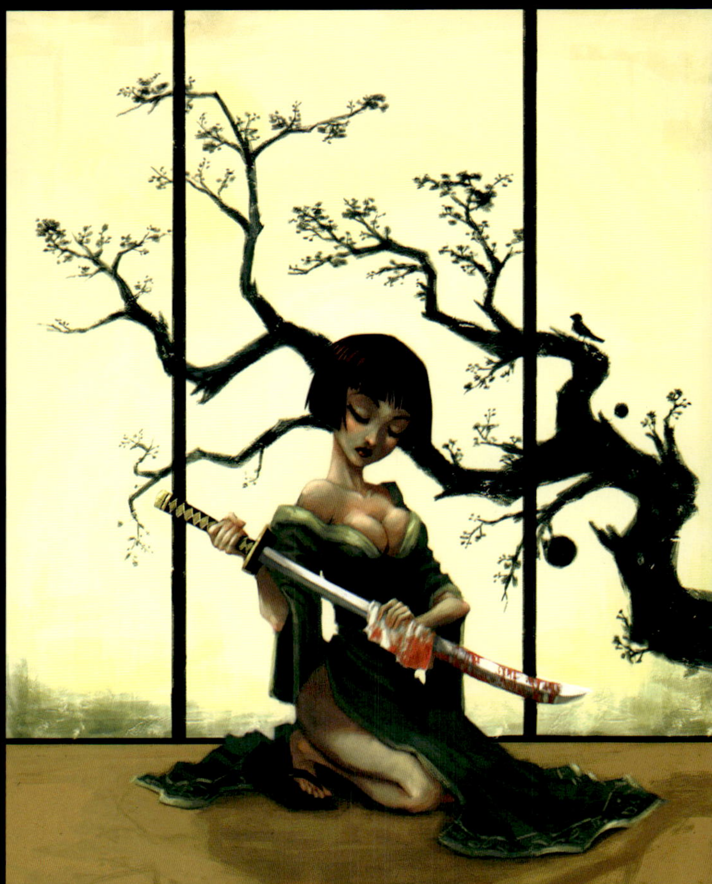

The assassin
Photoshop, Painter
Kei Acedera, CANADA
[above]

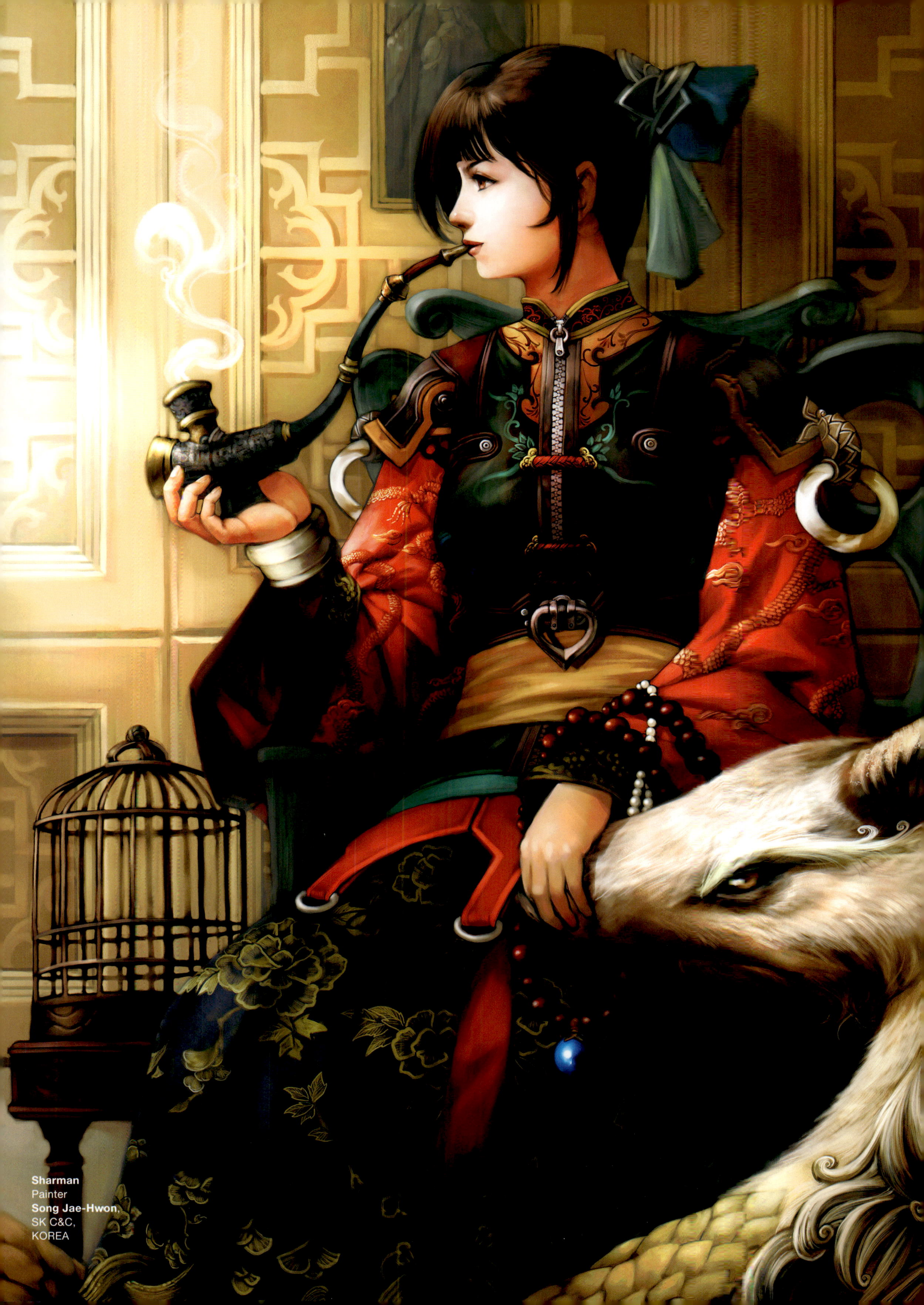

Sharman
Painter
Song Jae-Hwon,
SK C&C,
KOREA

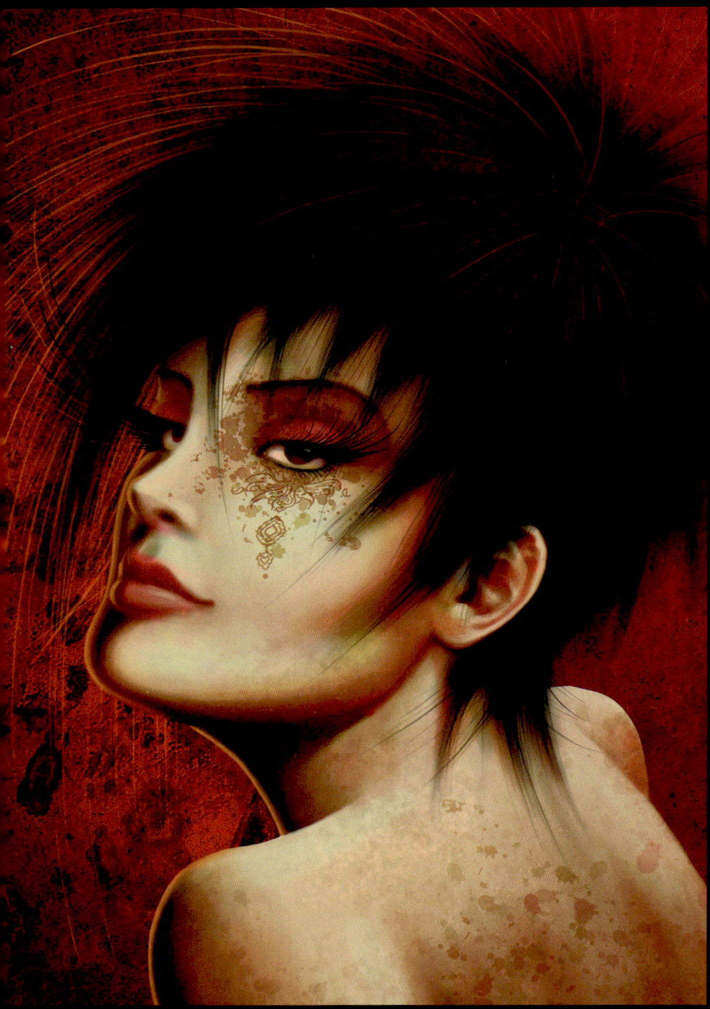

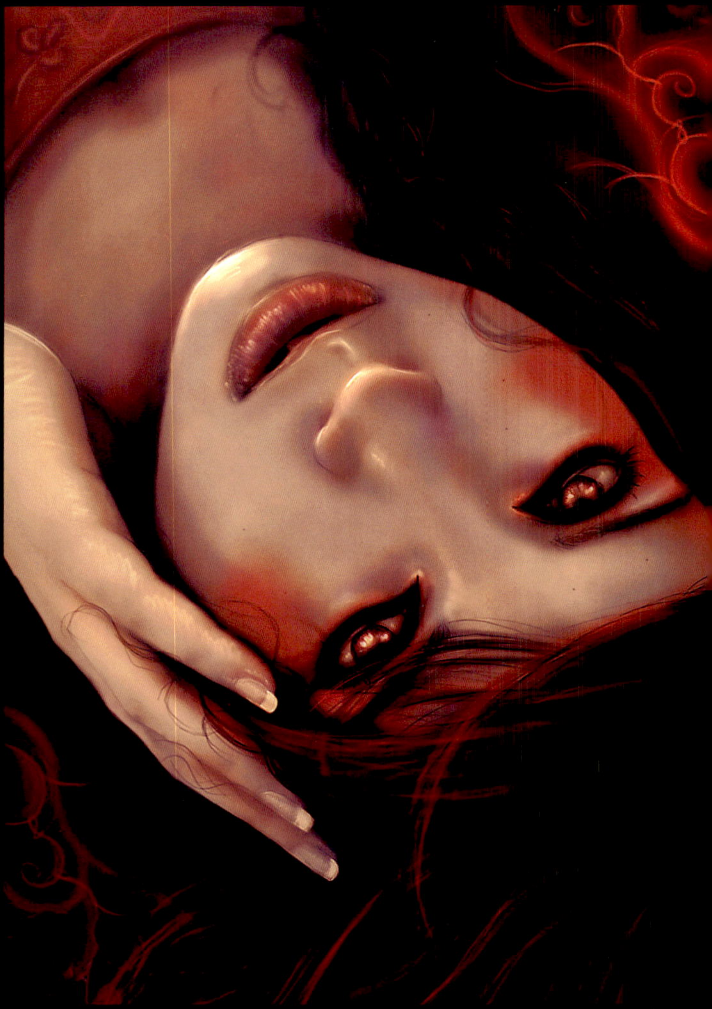

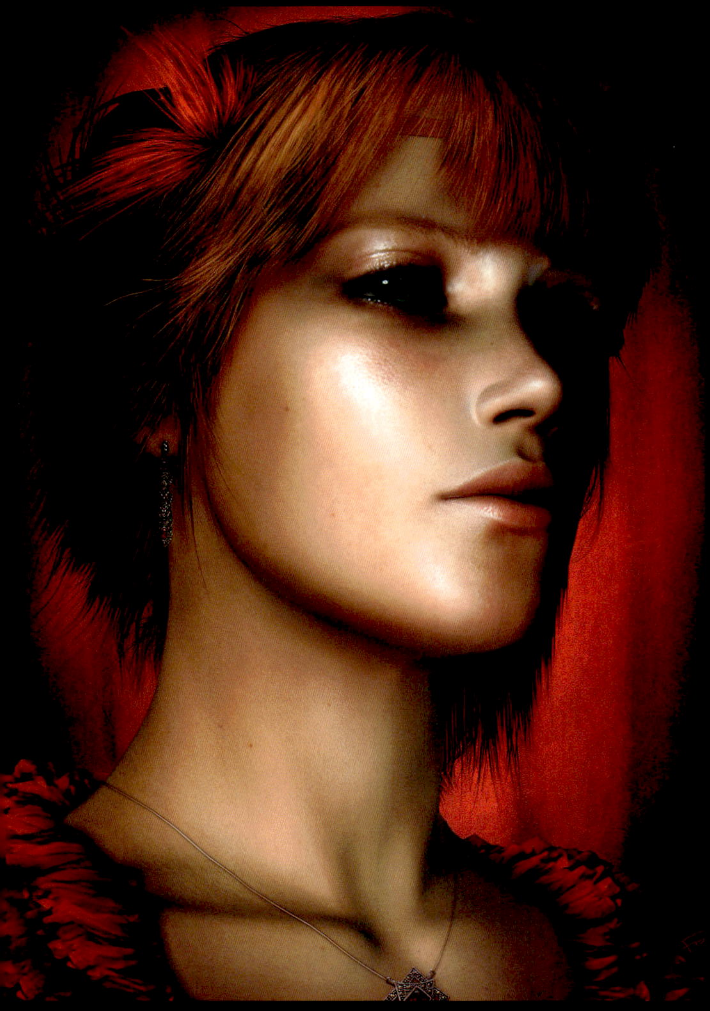

Dream of nightmares
Photoshop
Alireza Lotfalikhani, IRAN
[top left]

Liliana
Photoshop
Suzanne van Pelt,
NETHERLANDS
[above]

Red girl
3ds Max
Weiye Yin, CHINA
[left]

Chio chio san
Painter
Katarina Sokolova, UKRAINE
[right]

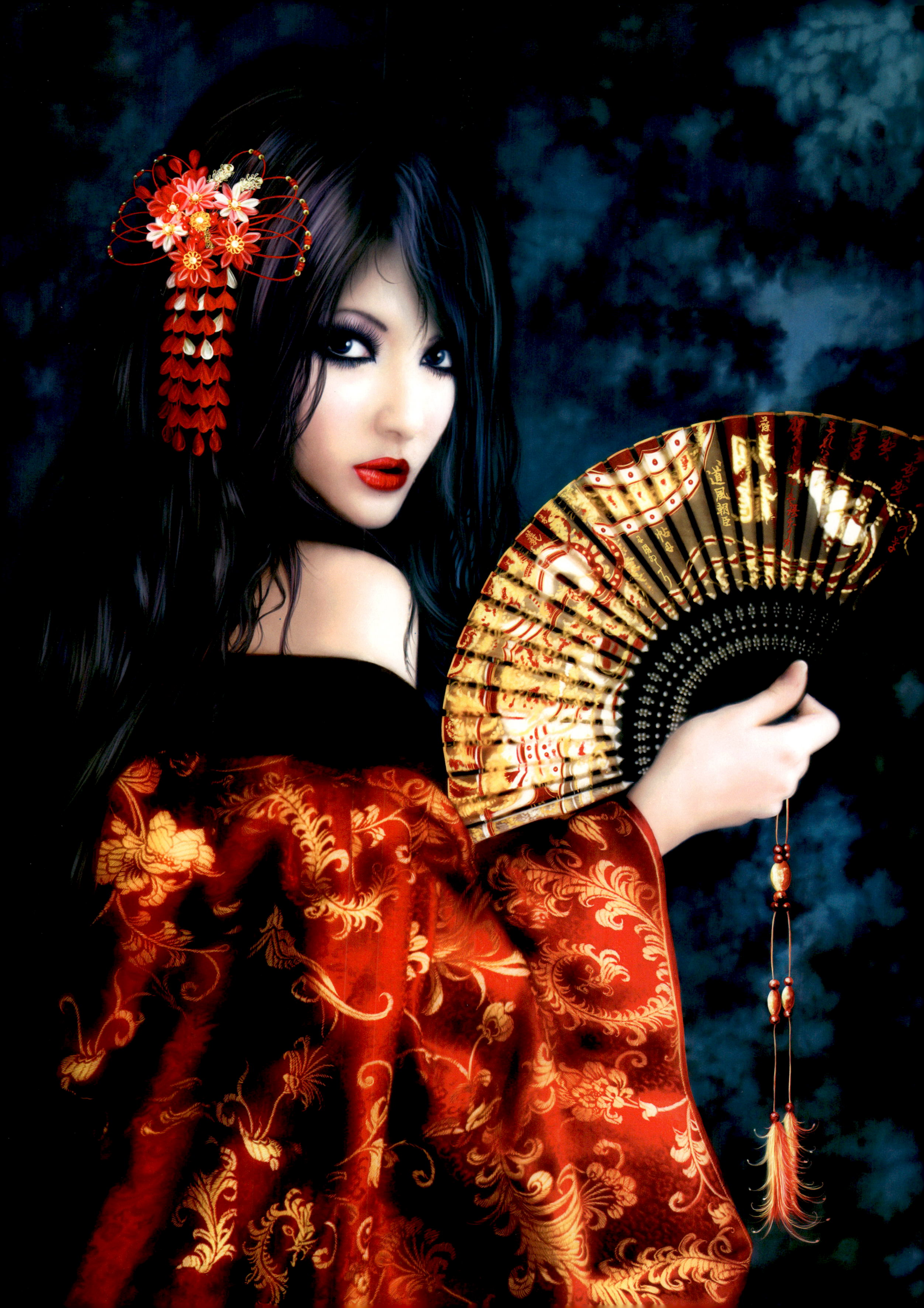

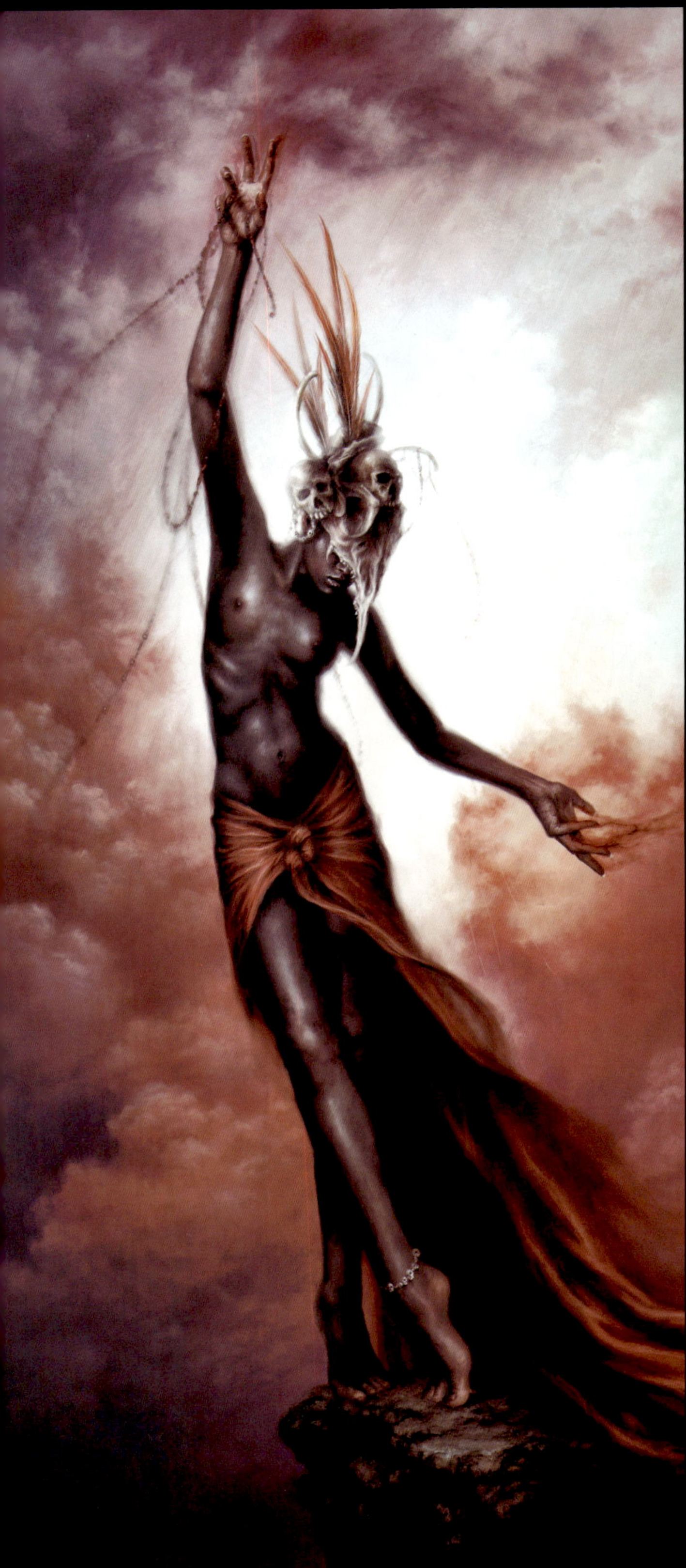

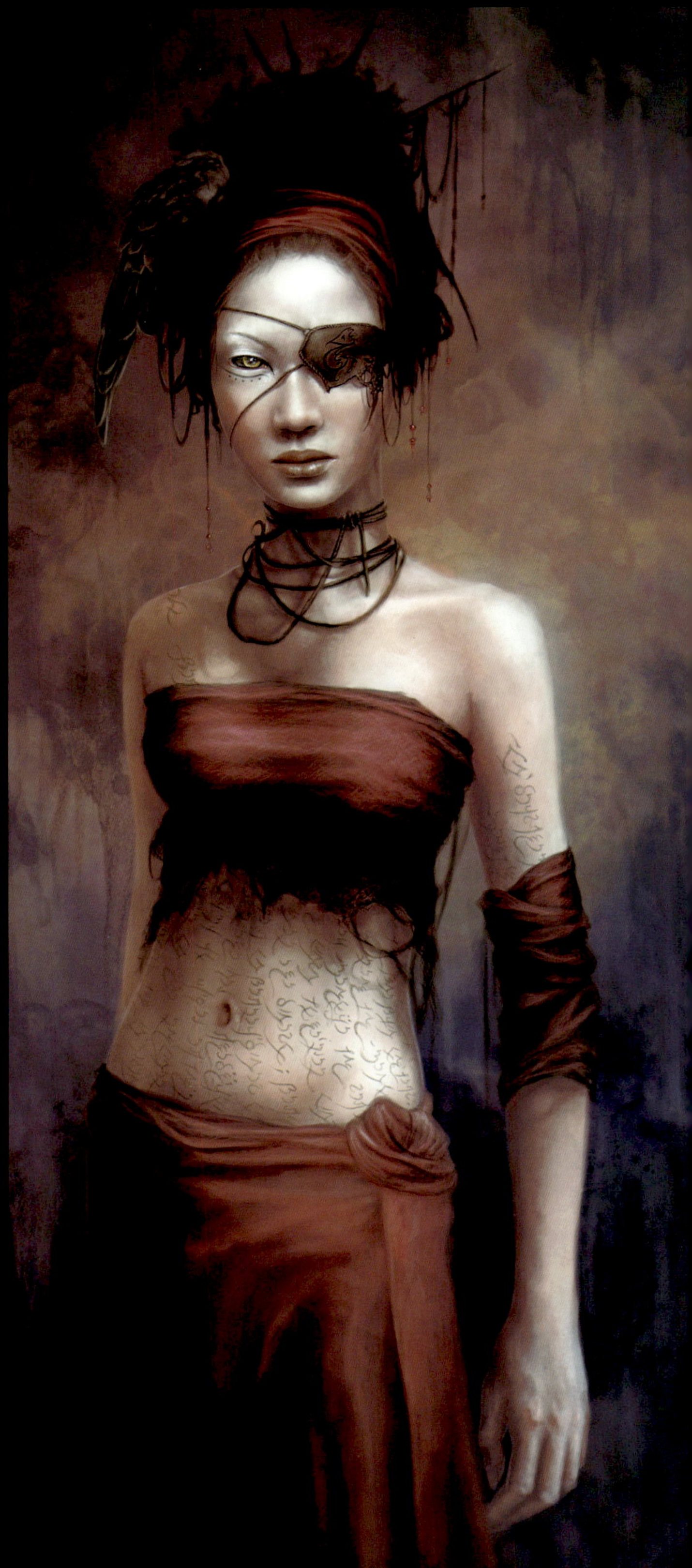

Heaven slain
Photoshop, Painter
Lauren K. Cannon, USA
[above]

Mhiet'e
Photoshop
Lauren K. Cannon, USA
[above]

Red Queen
Painter, Photoshop
Doris Mantair, NETHERLANDS
[right]

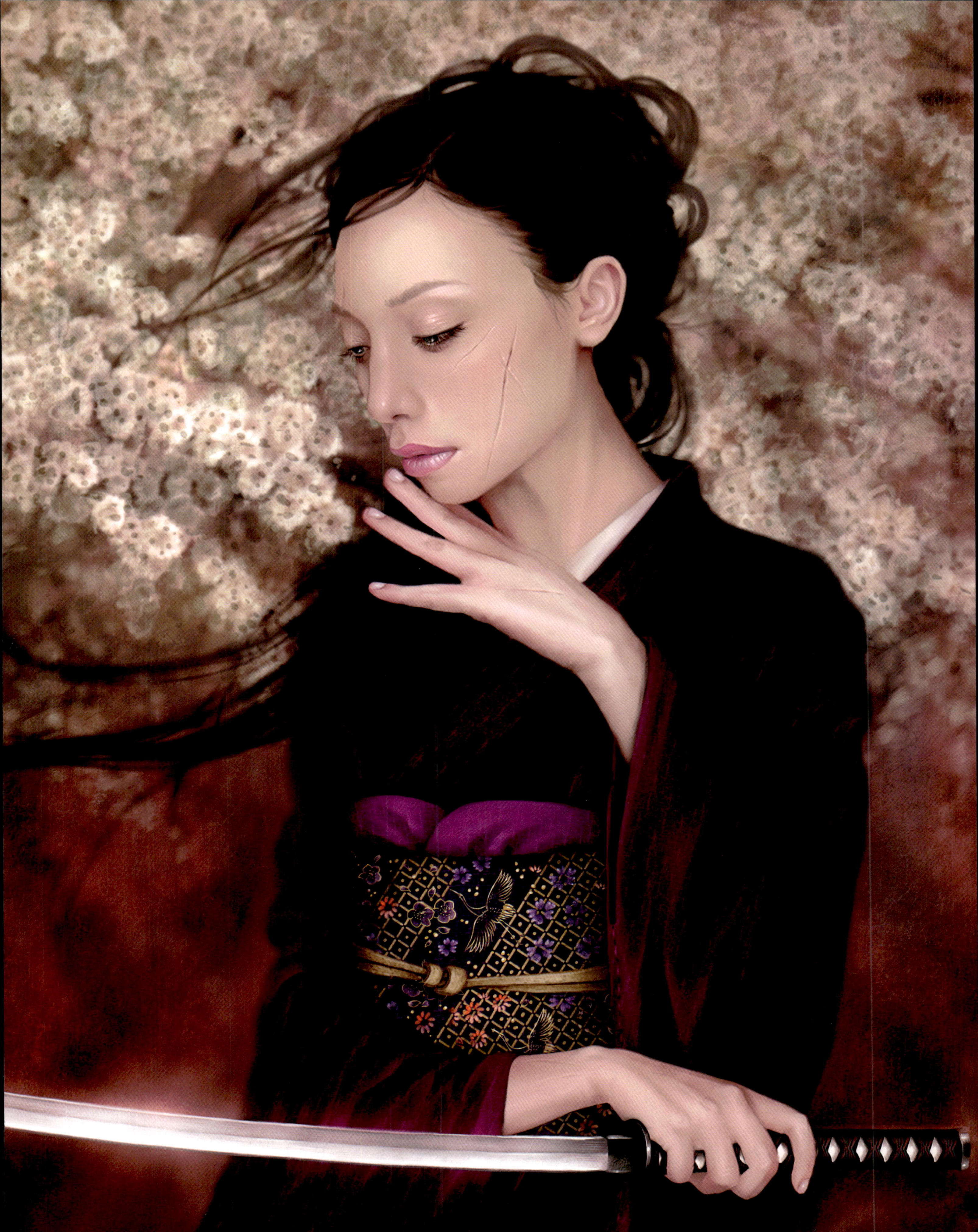

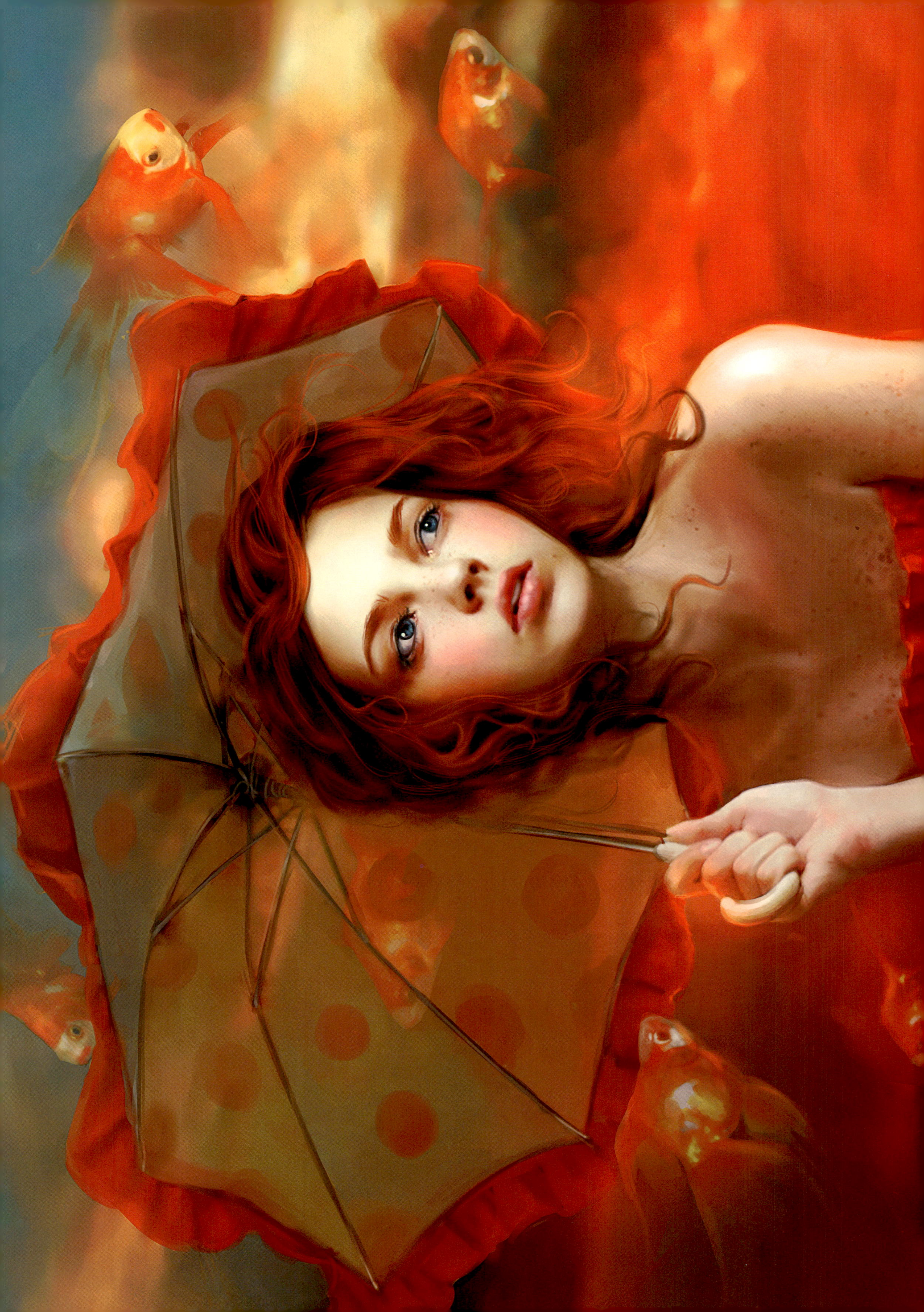

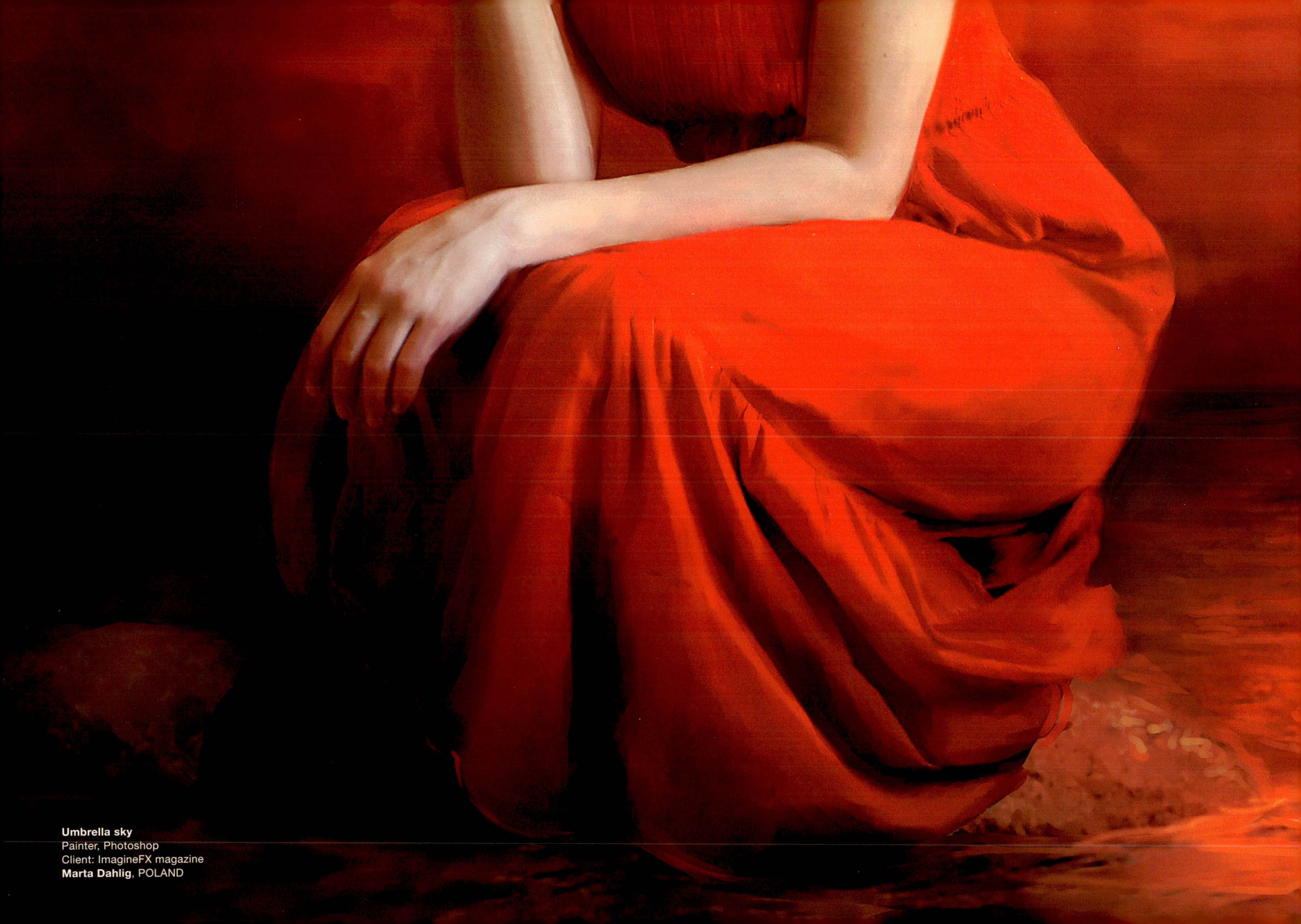

Umbrella sky
Painter, Photoshop
Client: ImagineFX magazine
Marta Dahlig, POLAND

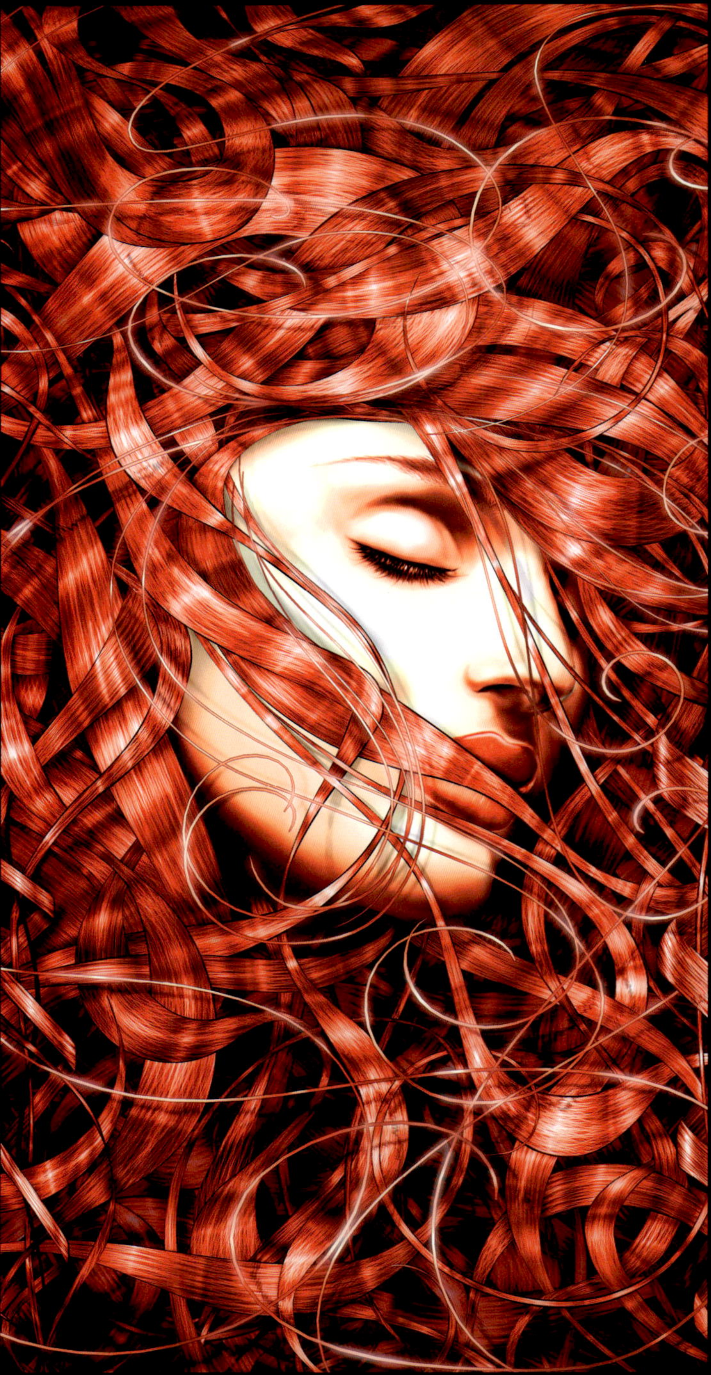

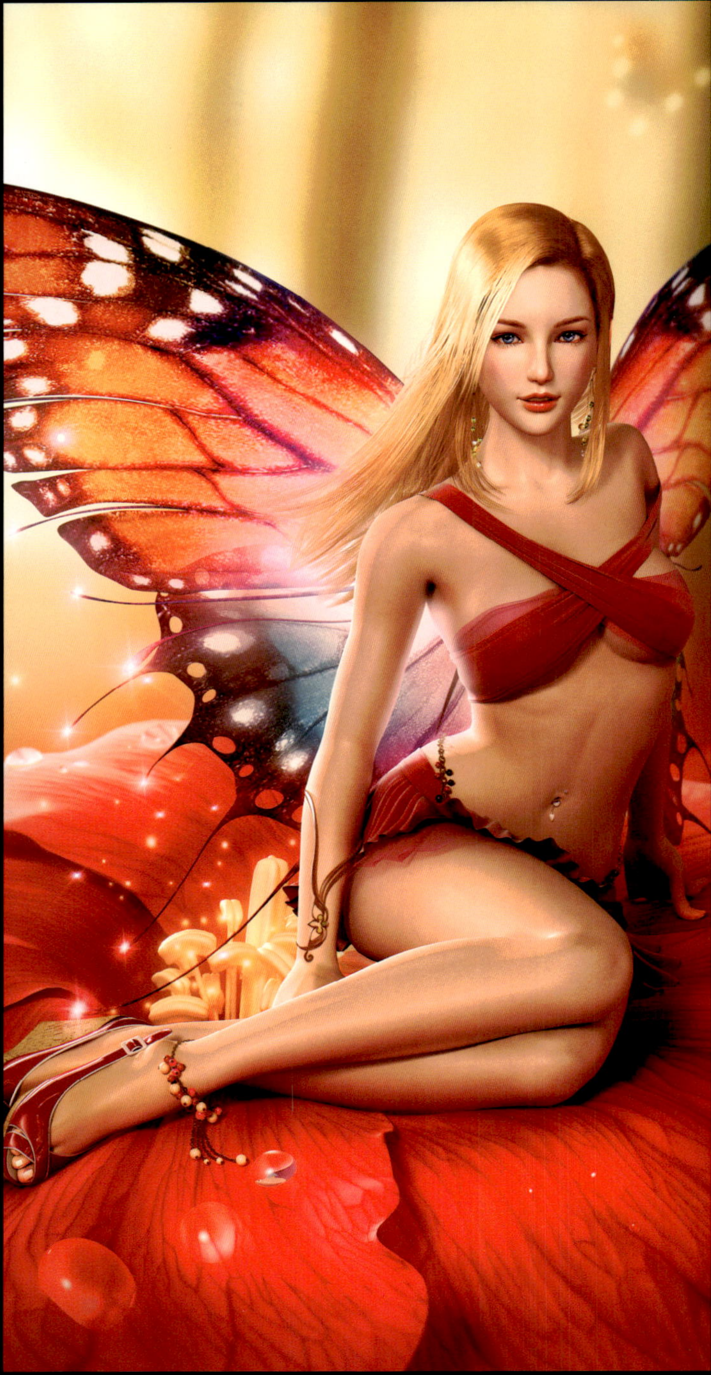

Muse
Photoshop
Val Aren, POLAND
[above]

A Fascinating Bloom
3ds Max, Photoshop
Client: Legend Footwear
Soa Lee, KOREA
[above]

Rose
Poser, Photoshop
Adriana Vasilache, ROMANIA
[right]

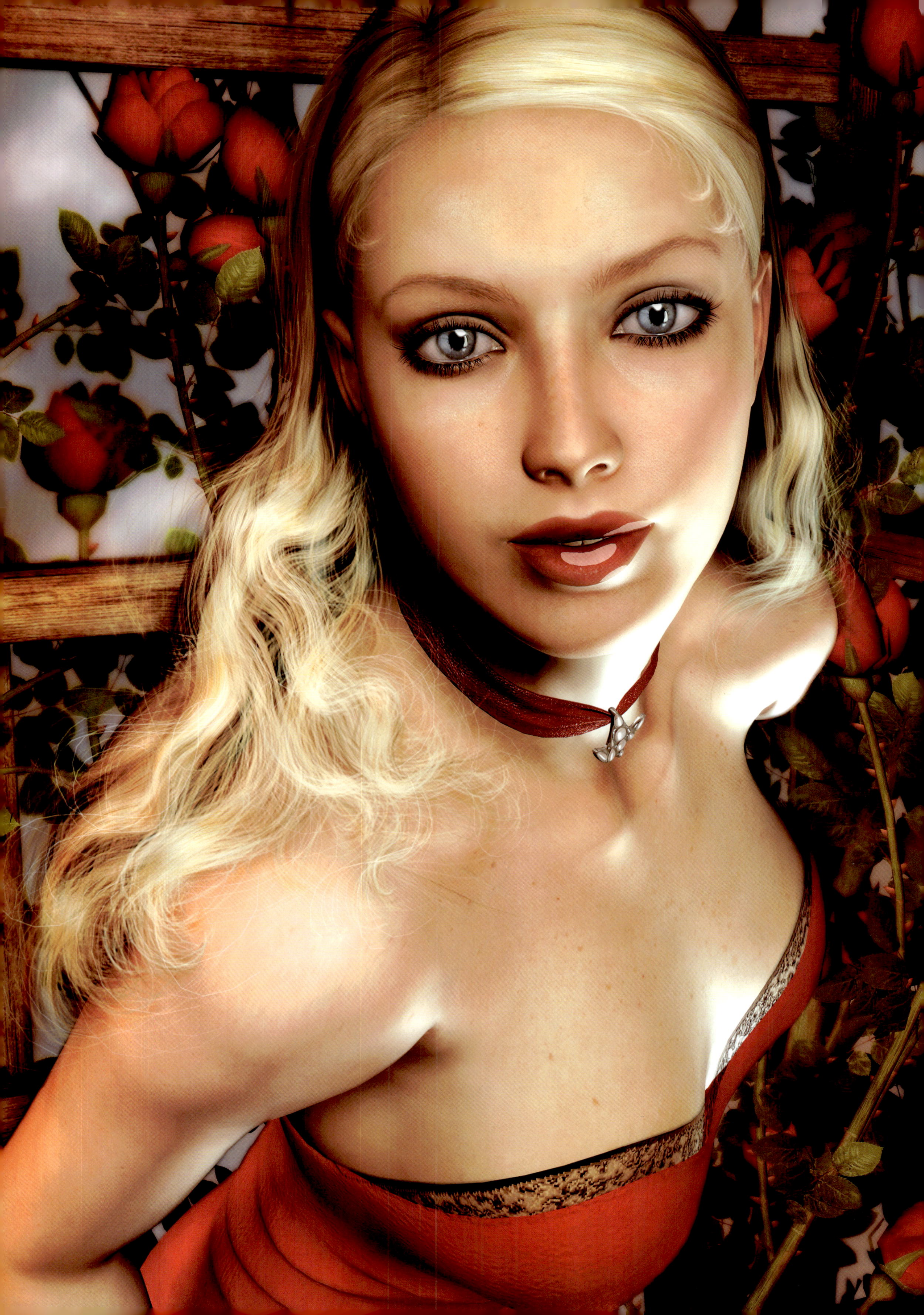

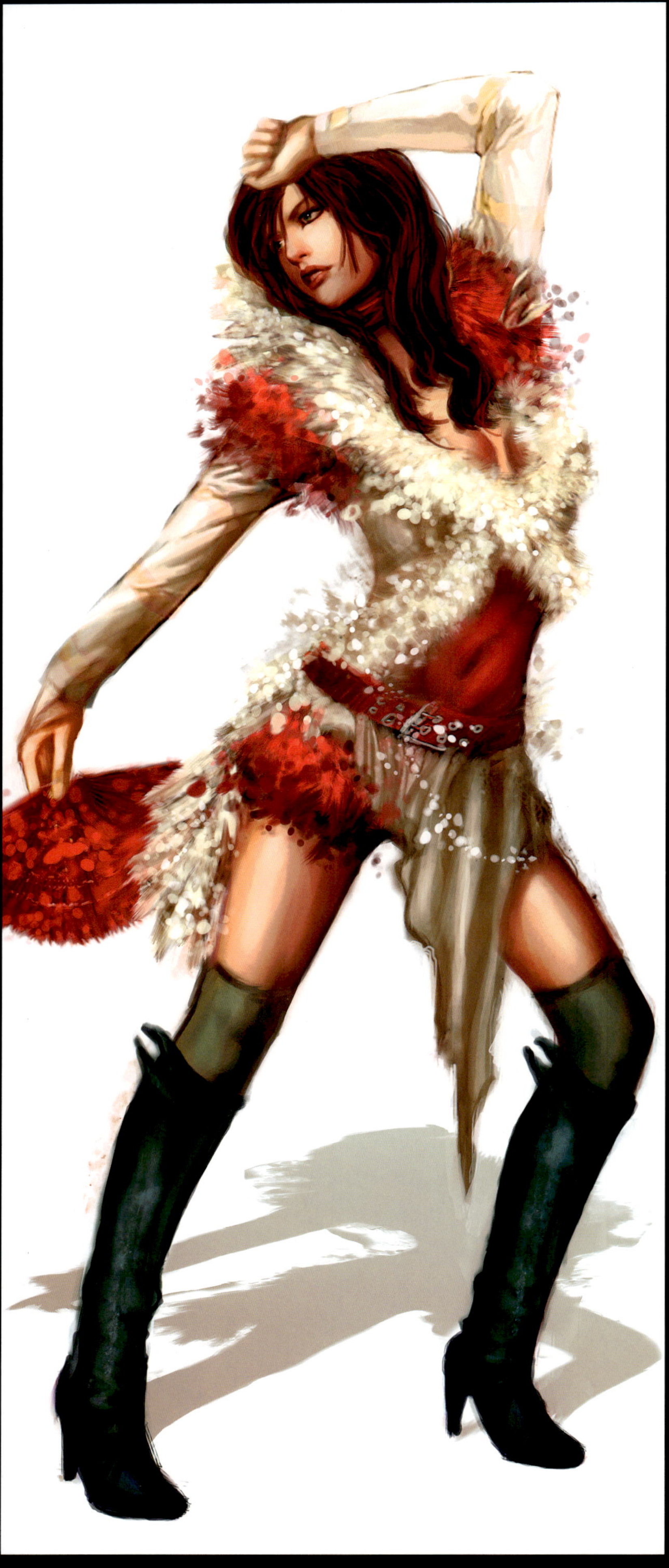

Fine lady
Photoshop
Ann-Christin Pogoda, GERMANY
[above]

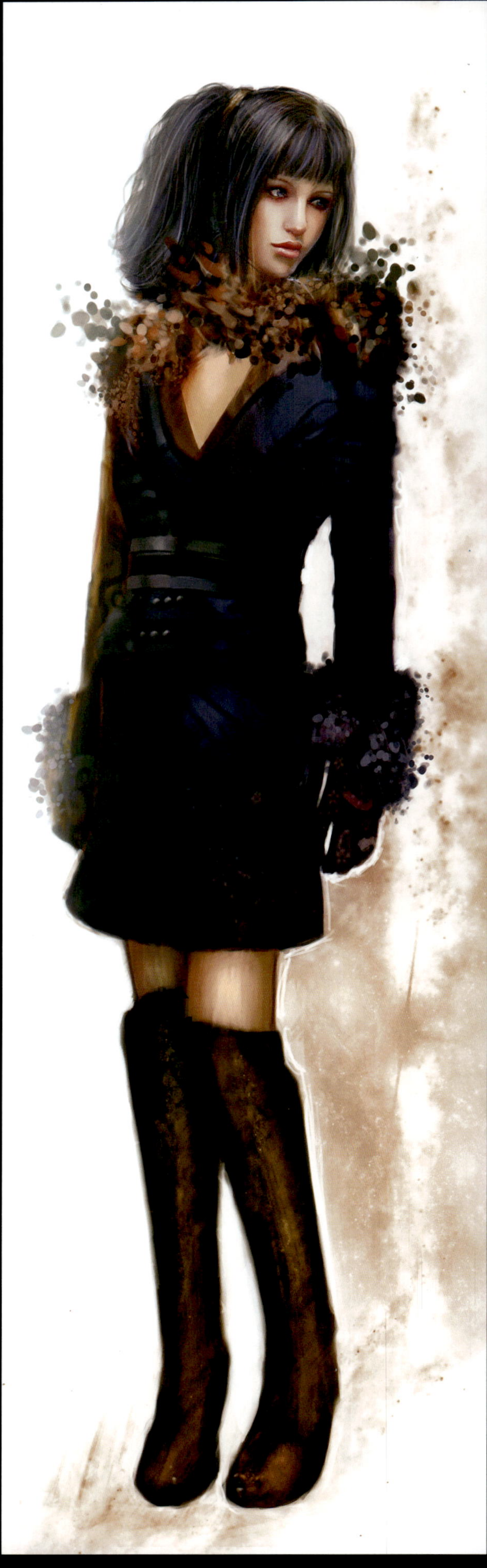

Honey
Photoshop
Ann-Christin Pogoda, GERMANY
[above]

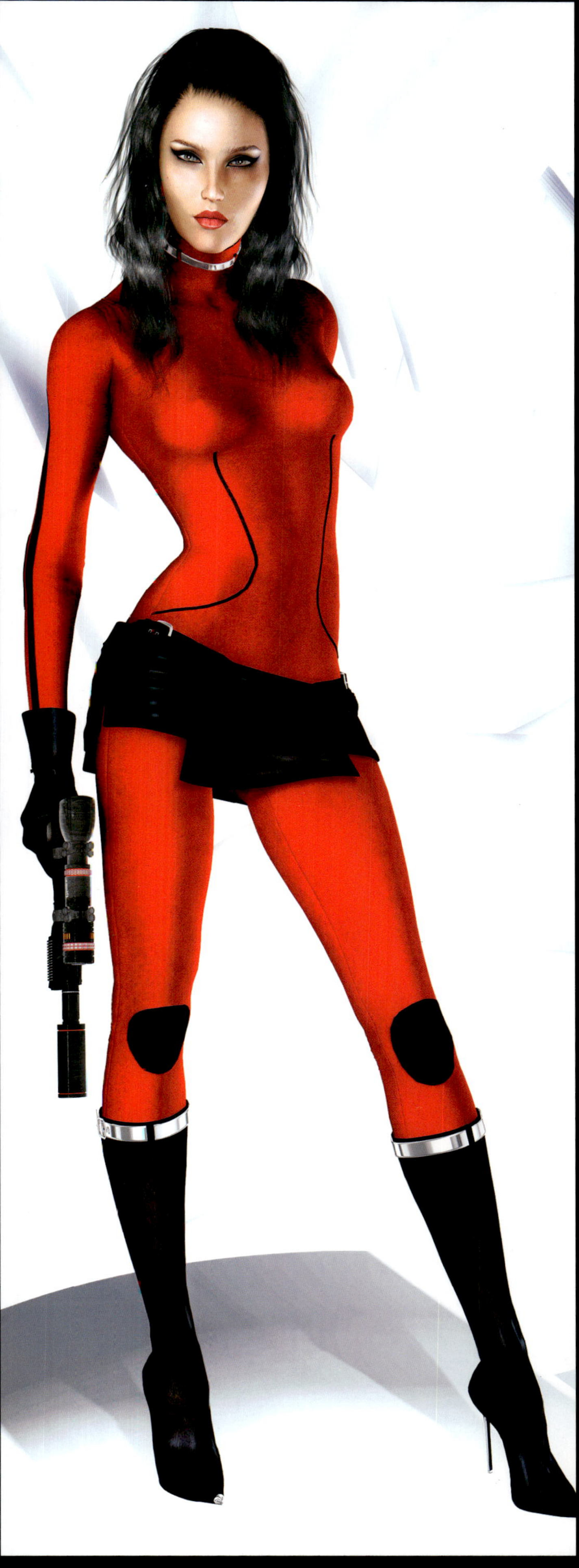

Loscil Venusian vixen
DAZ Studio, Photoshop
Matt 'Shimuzu' Smith, GREAT BRITAIN
[above]

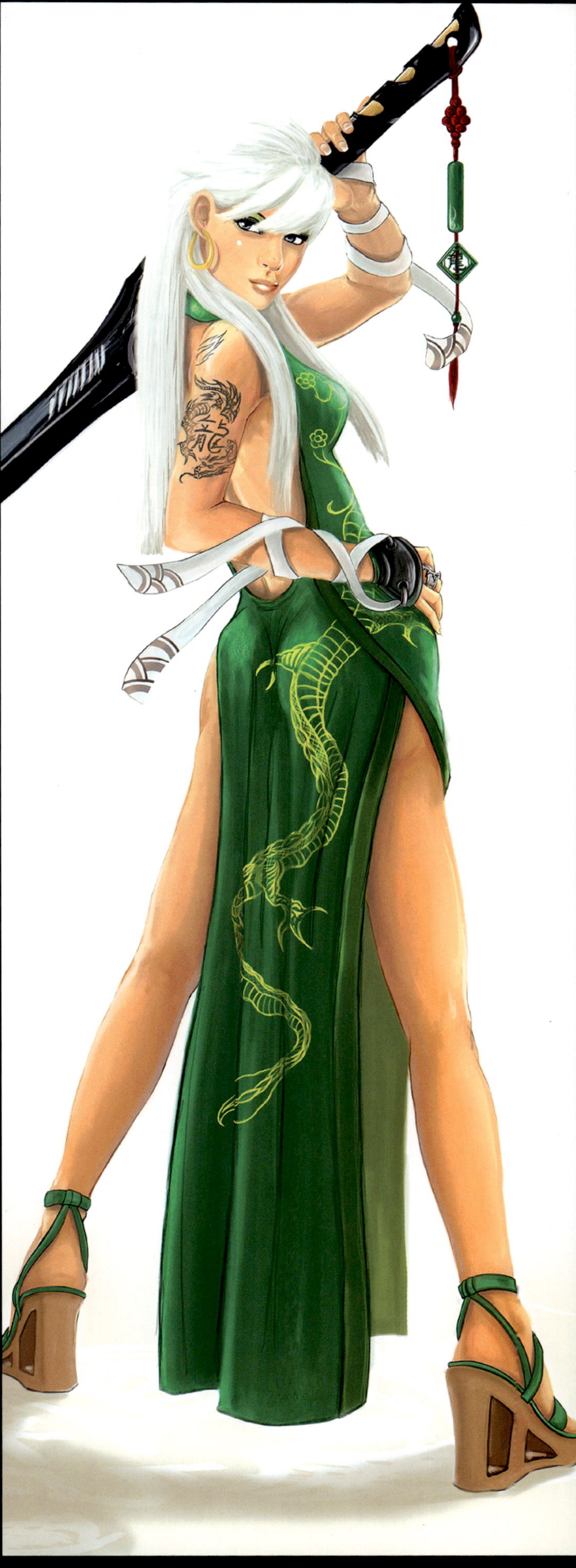

DragonsBlade
Photoshop
Jamie Wong, GREAT BRITAIN
[above]

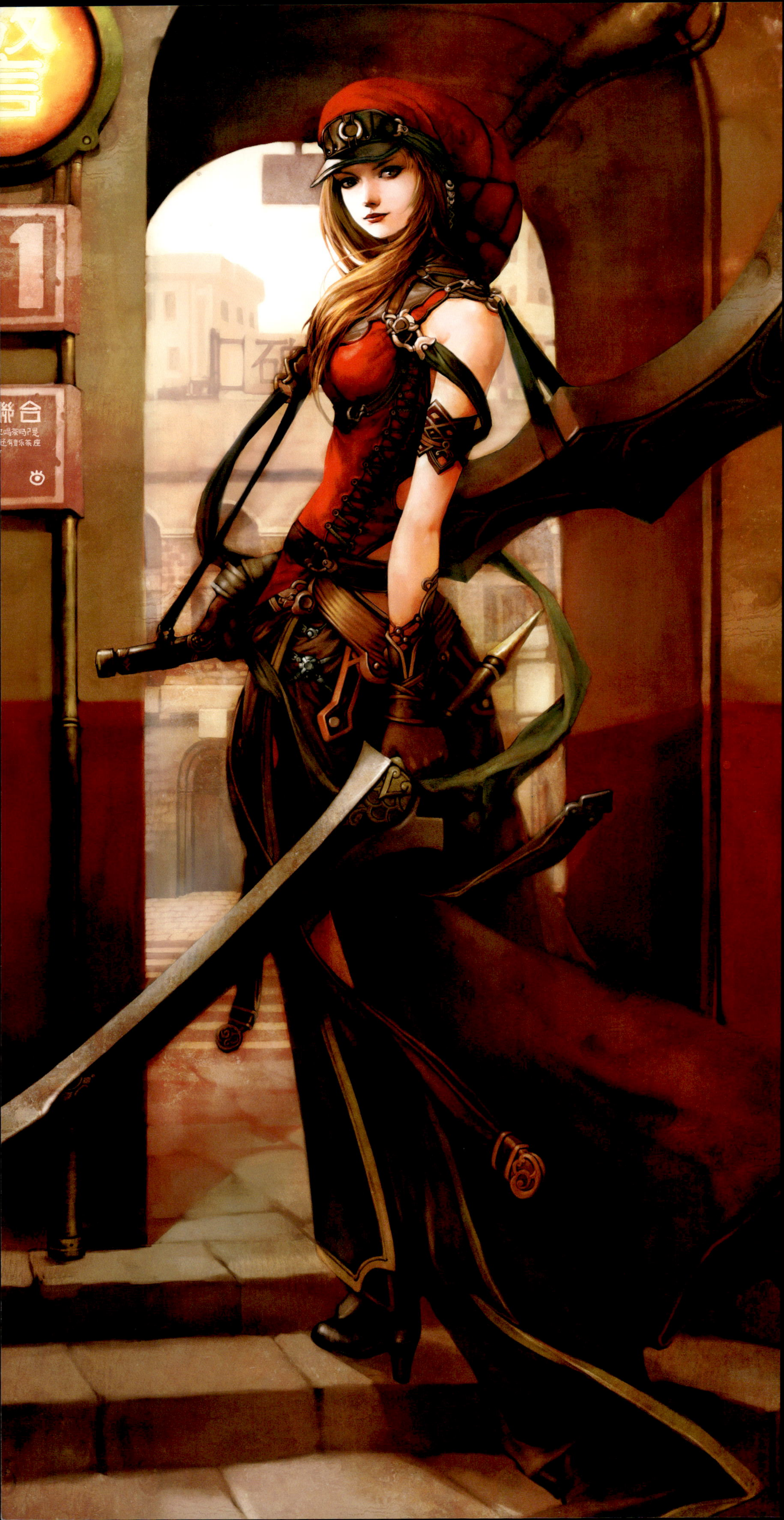

Amazon
Painter
Song Jae-Hwon, SK C&C, KOREA
[left]

Flight
Photoshop
Client: ImagineFX magazine
Hoang Nguyen, USA
[right]

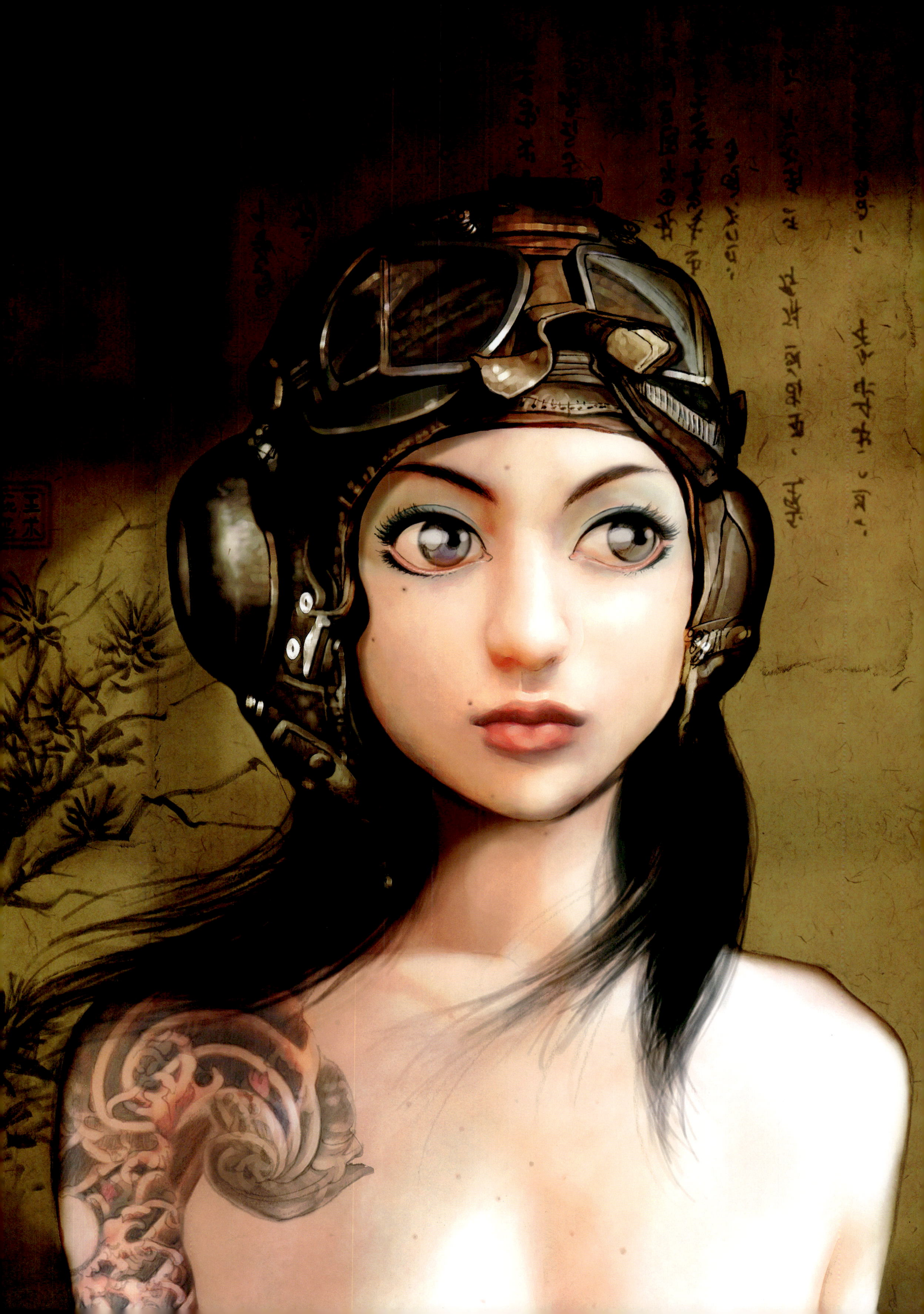

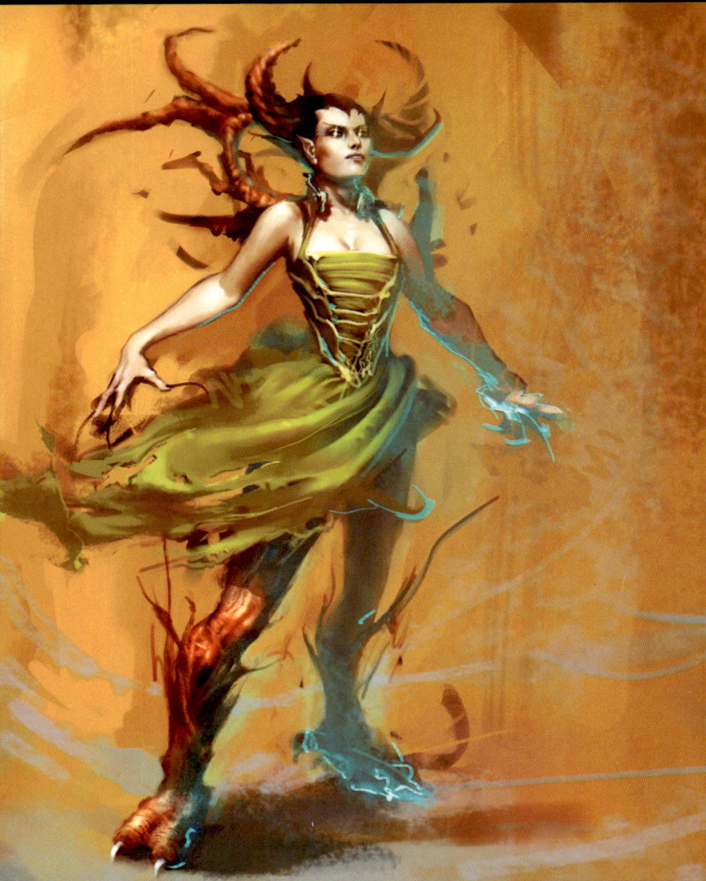

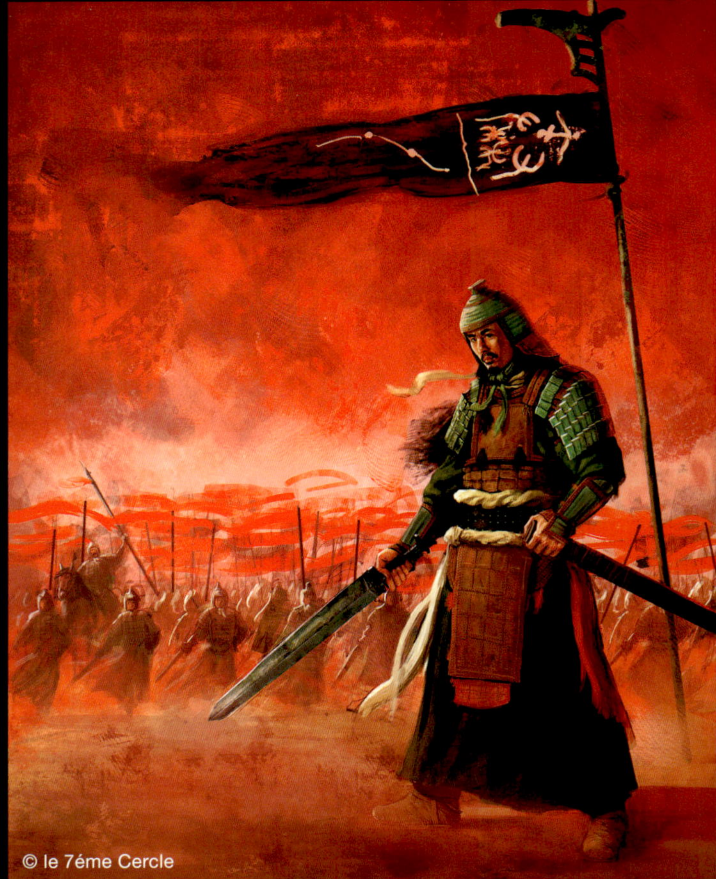

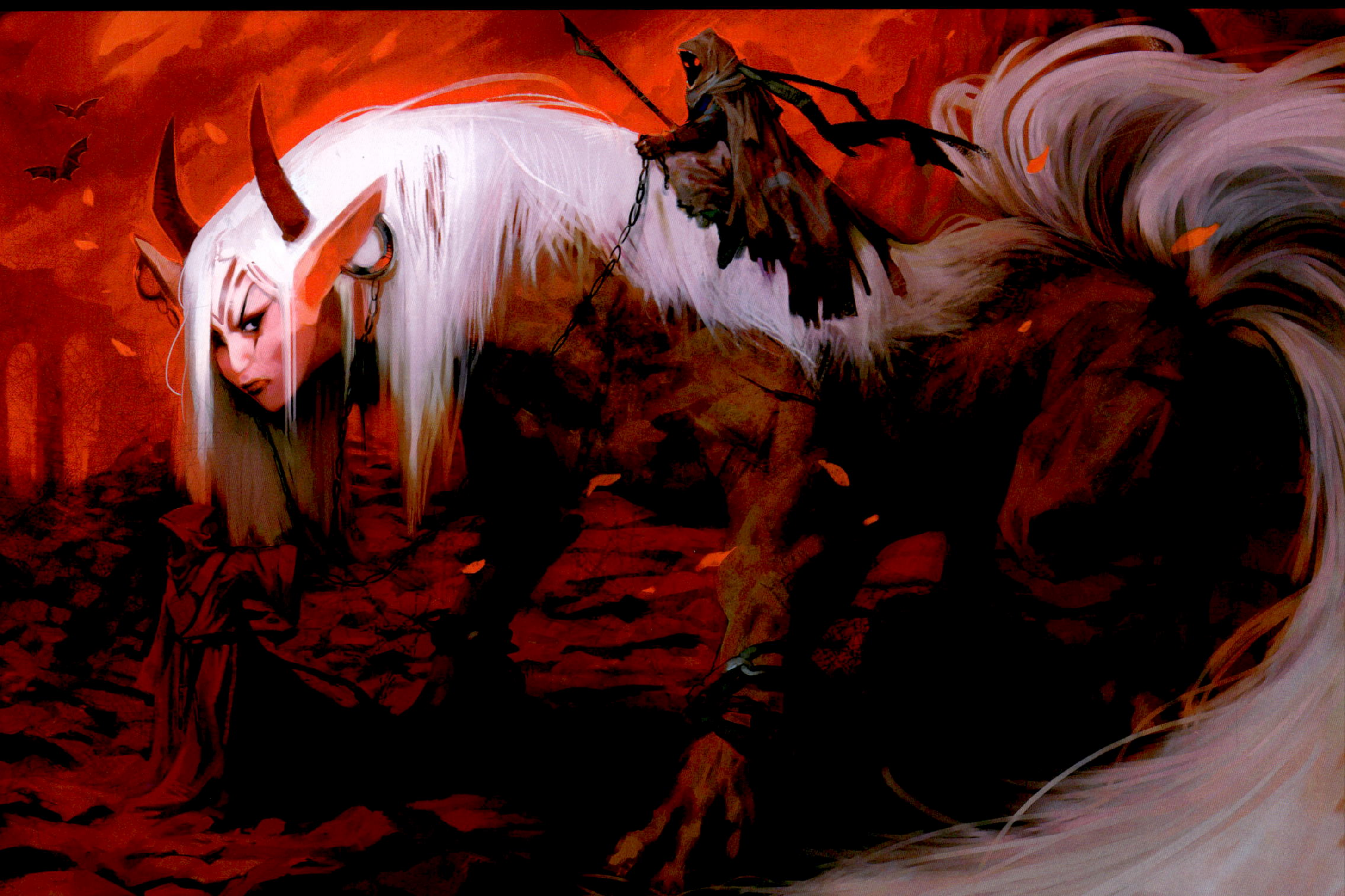

Zera
Photoshop
Camille Kuo,
TAIWAN
[top]

Tamed
Painter, Photoshop
Corey Loving,
USA
[above]

Art of war
Photoshop
Client: le 7éme Cercle
Marc Simonetti, FRANCE
[top]

Paladin
Painter, Photoshop
Wei Chen,
CHINA
[right]

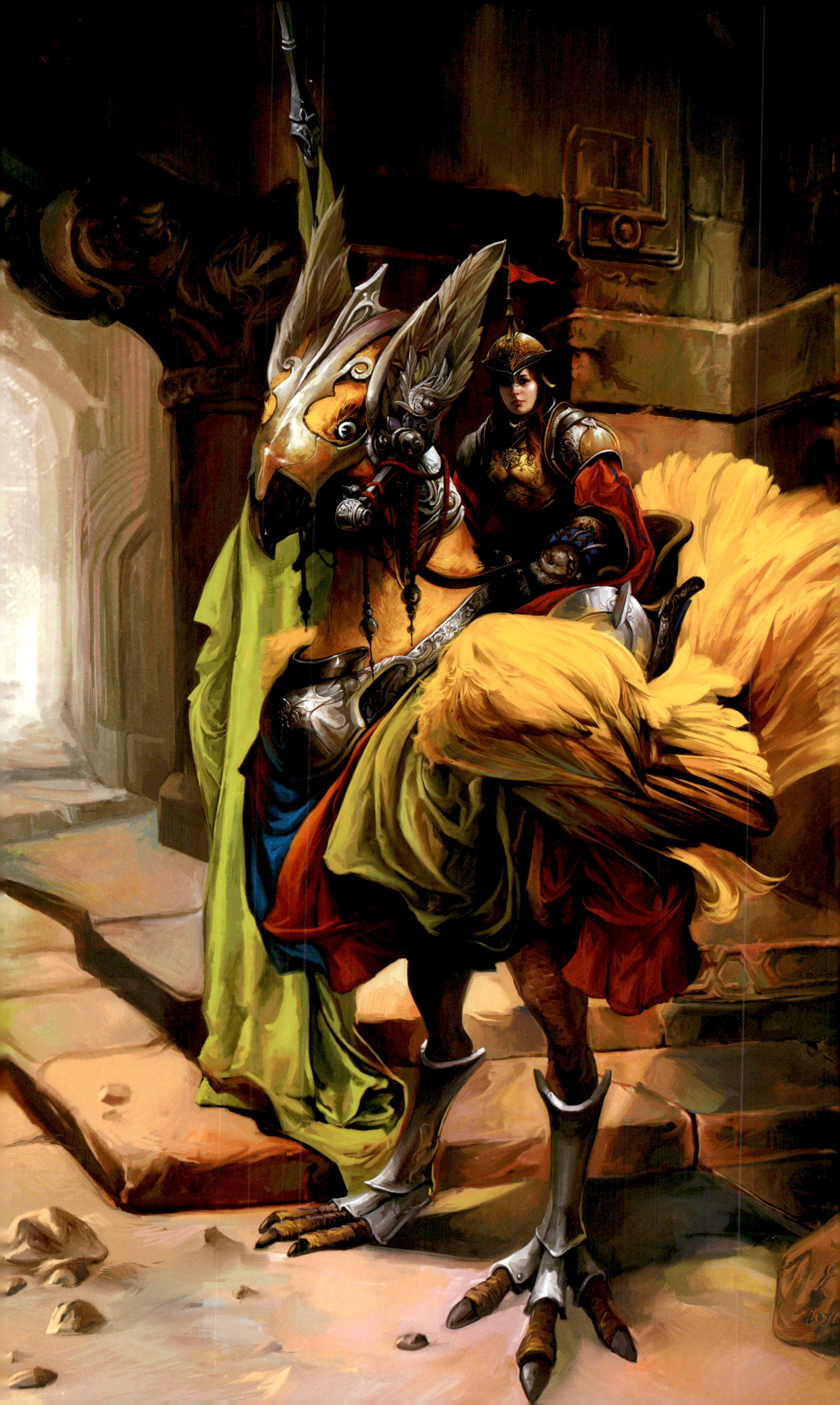

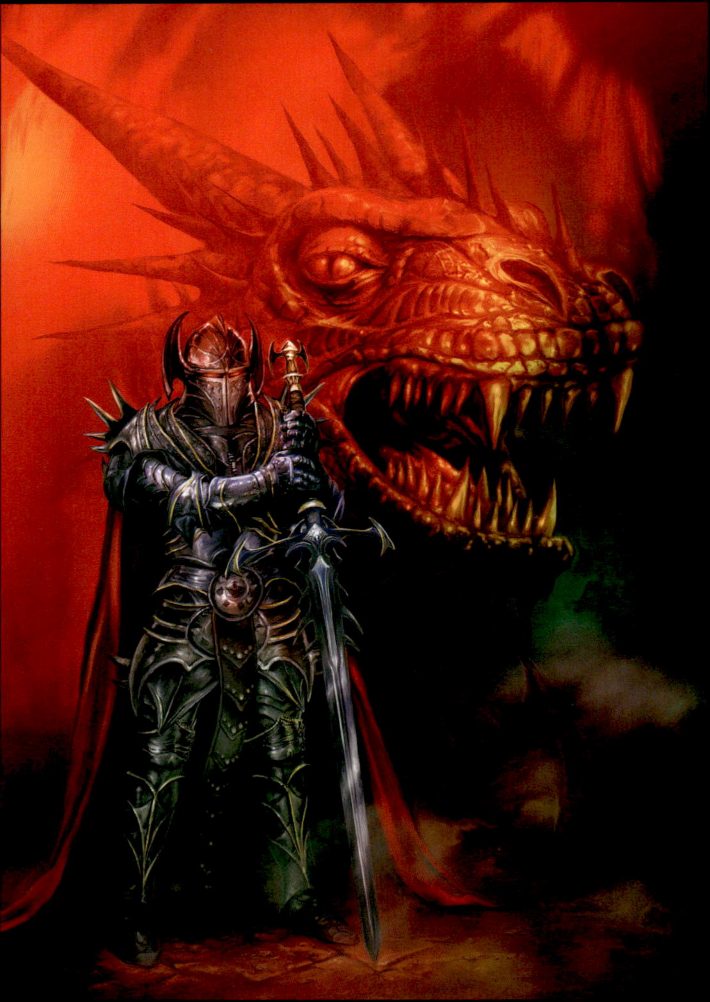

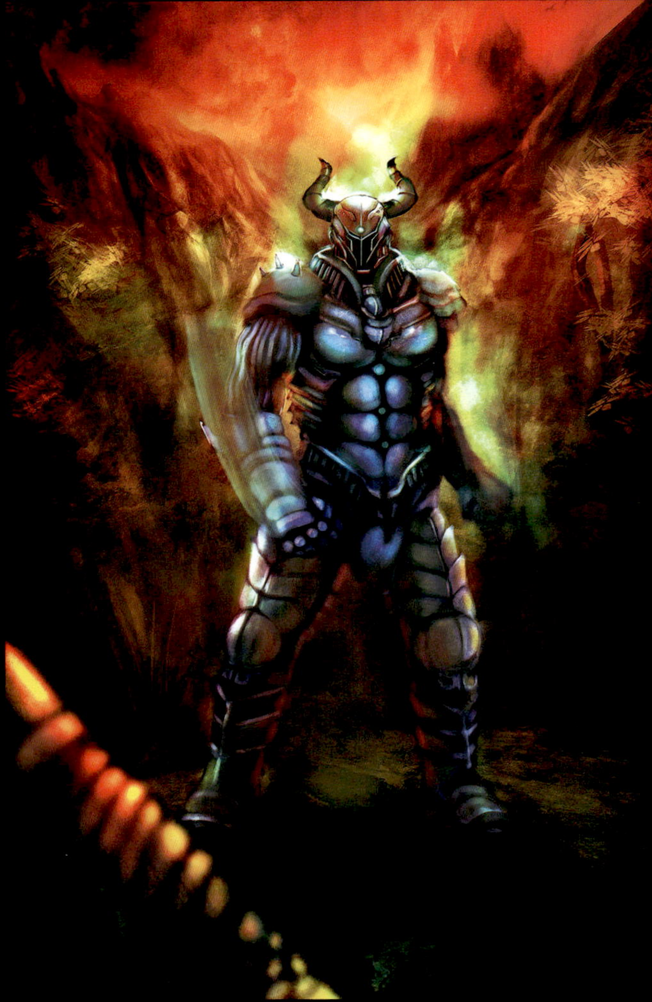

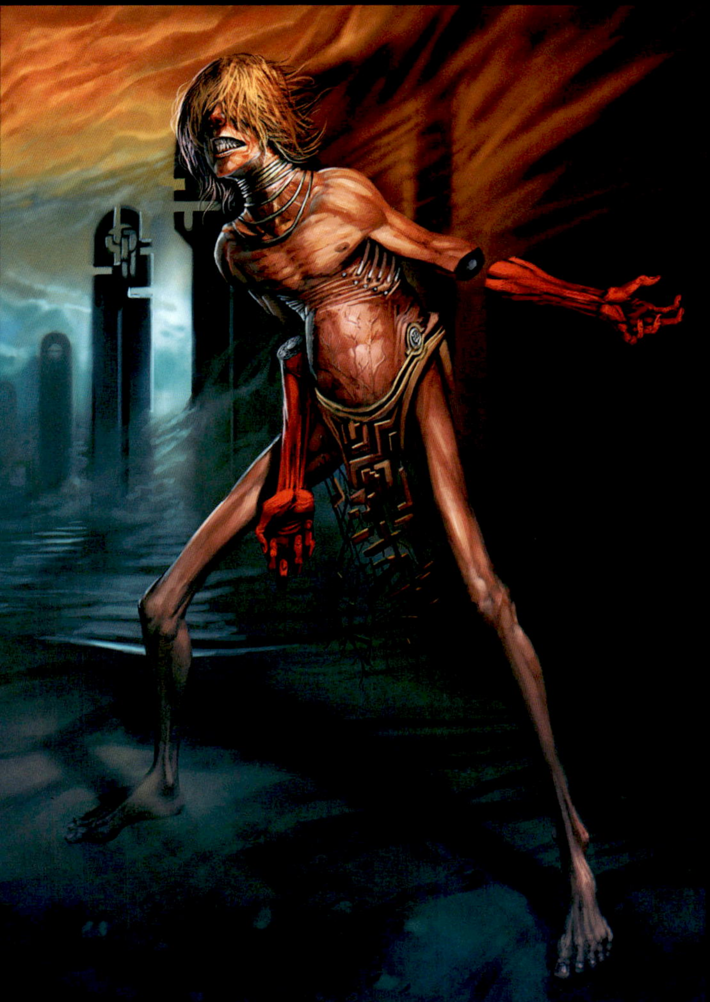

Dragon Knight
Photoshop
Client: Fantom Print
Jan Patrik Krasny, CZECH REPUBLIC
[top left]

The Warlord
Photoshop
Darius Cheong, SINGAPORE
[above]

Af
Photoshop
Peter Mohrbacher, USA
[left]

Red Blaze
Photoshop
Jiansong Chen, LusioSoft Entertainment Co., Ltd, CHINA
[right]

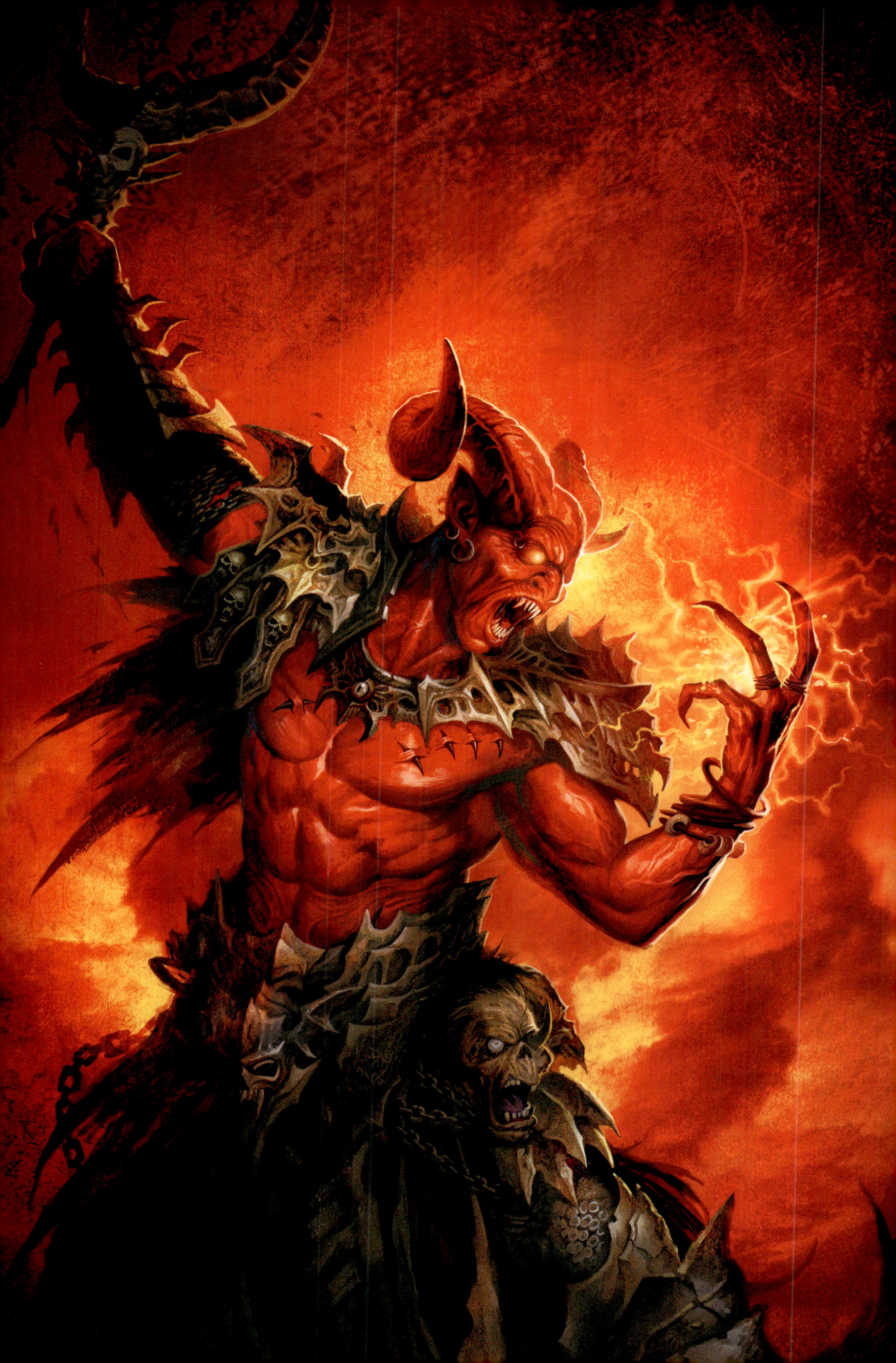

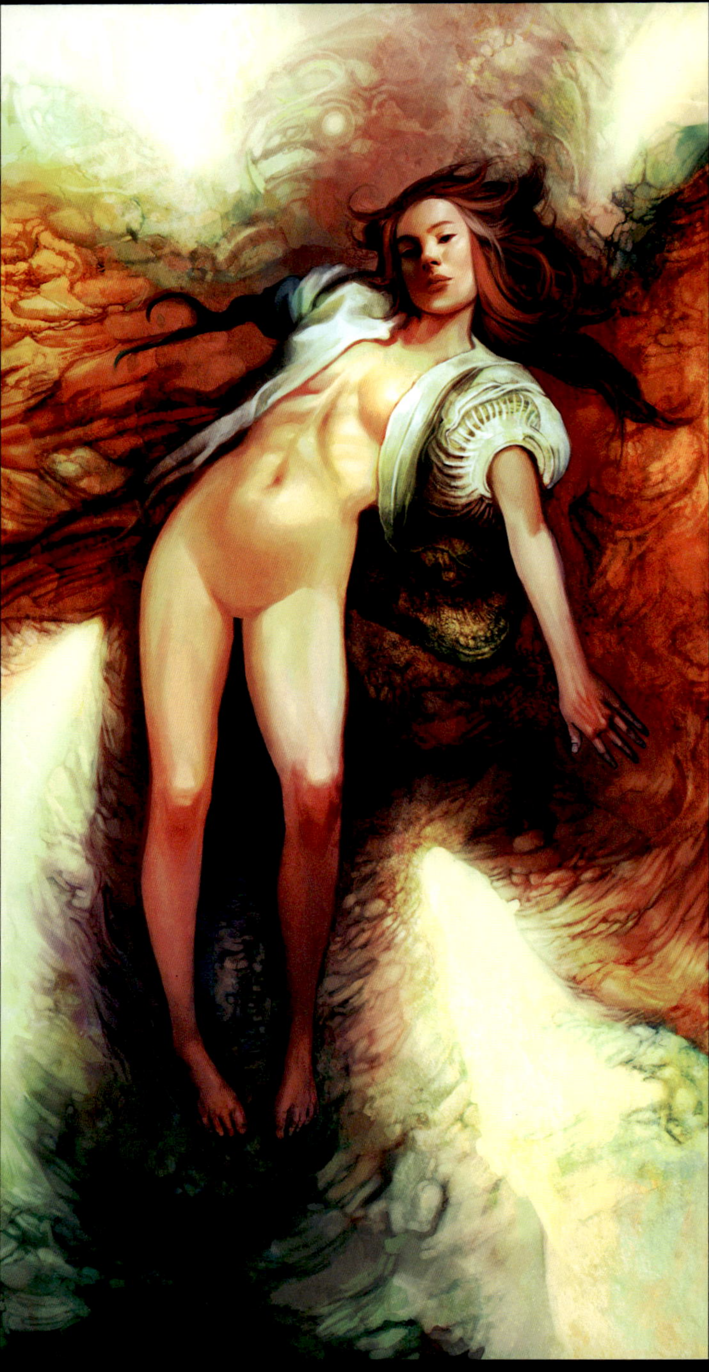

zrk
Photoshop
Falk, GERMANY
[above]

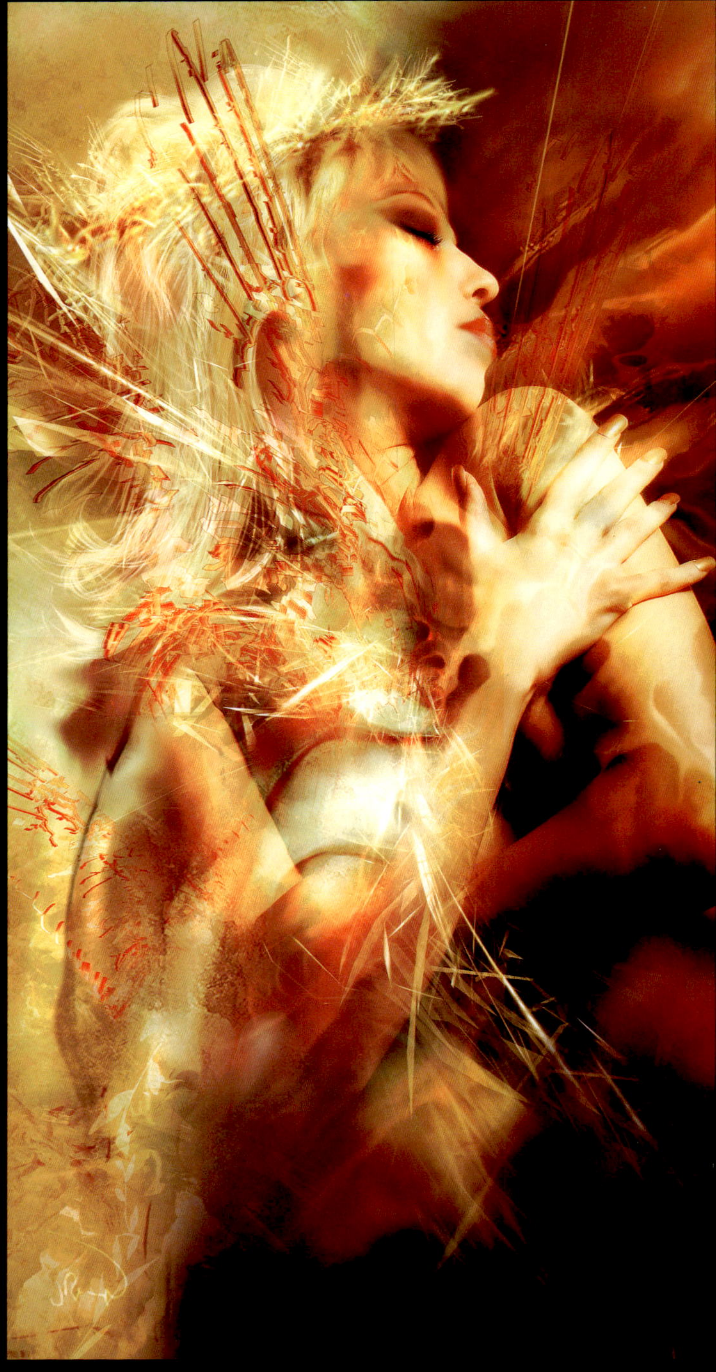

Sin or Salvation
Photoshop, Illustrator, 3ds Max
Jennifer Reagles, saiaii, USA
[above]

Kill the winter
Photoshop
Xiao-chen Fu, CHINA
[right]

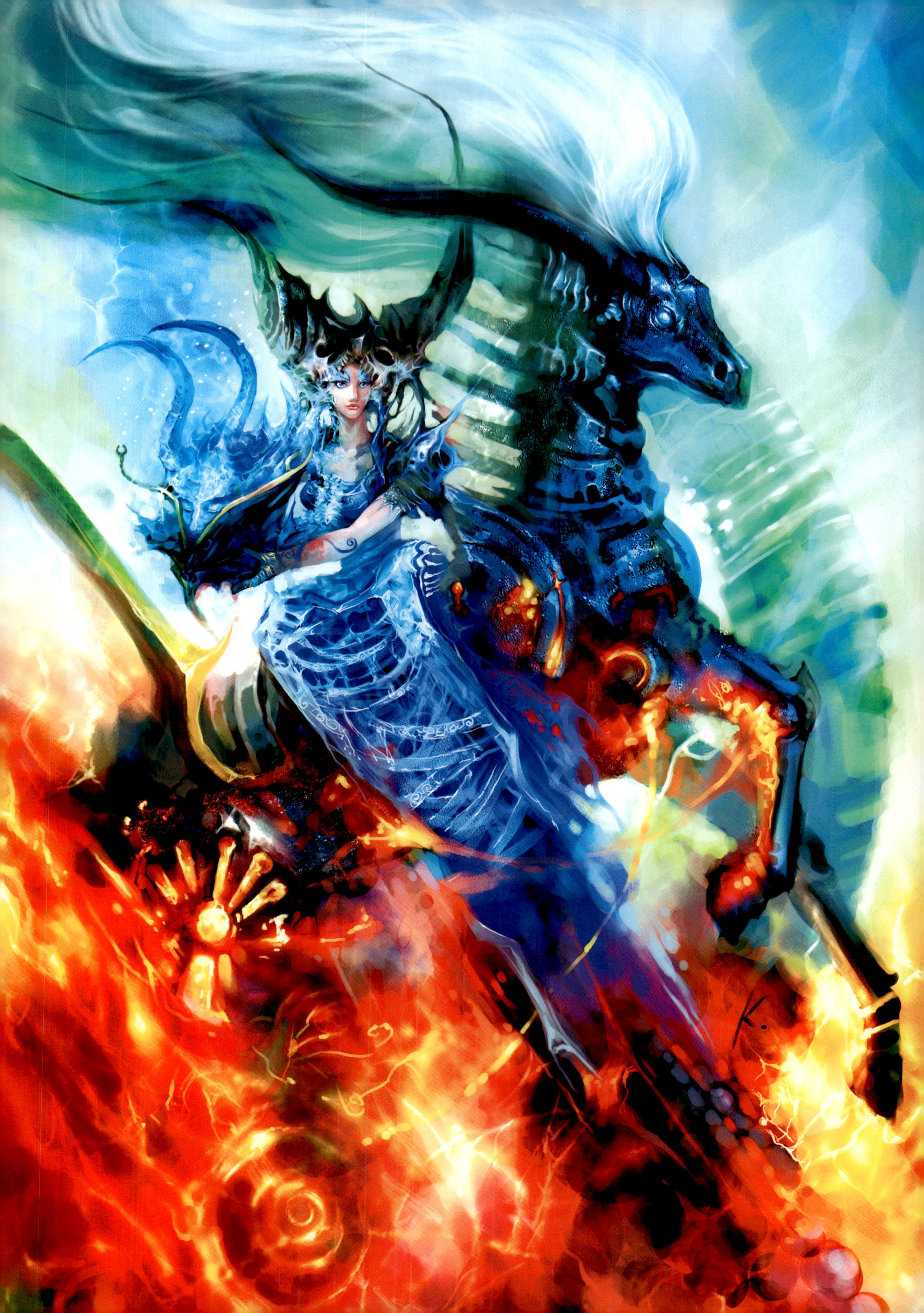

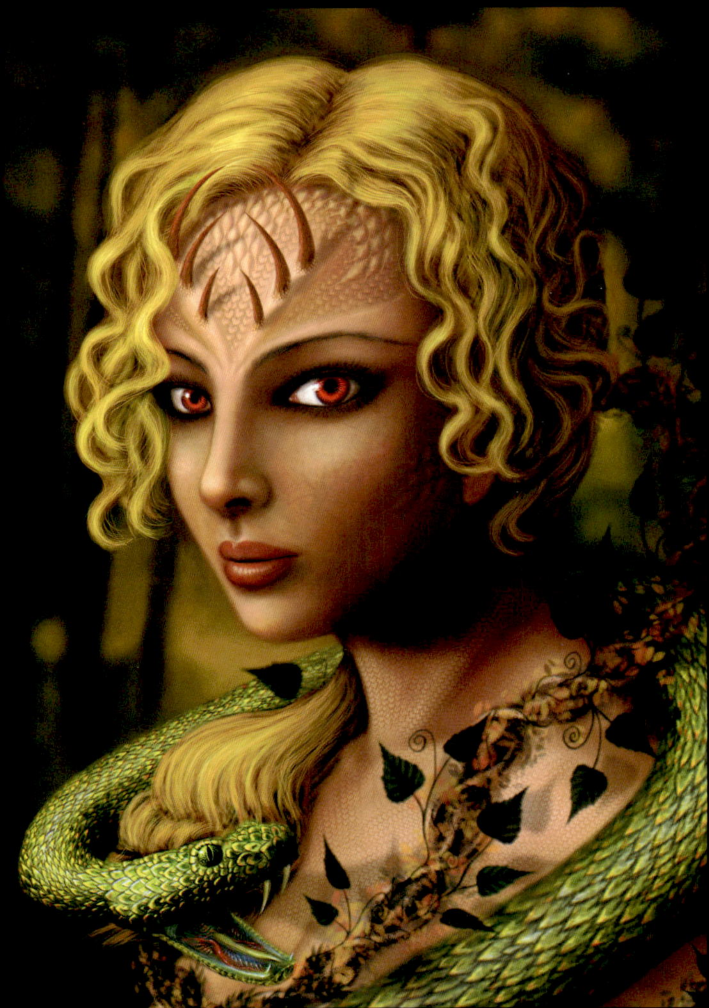

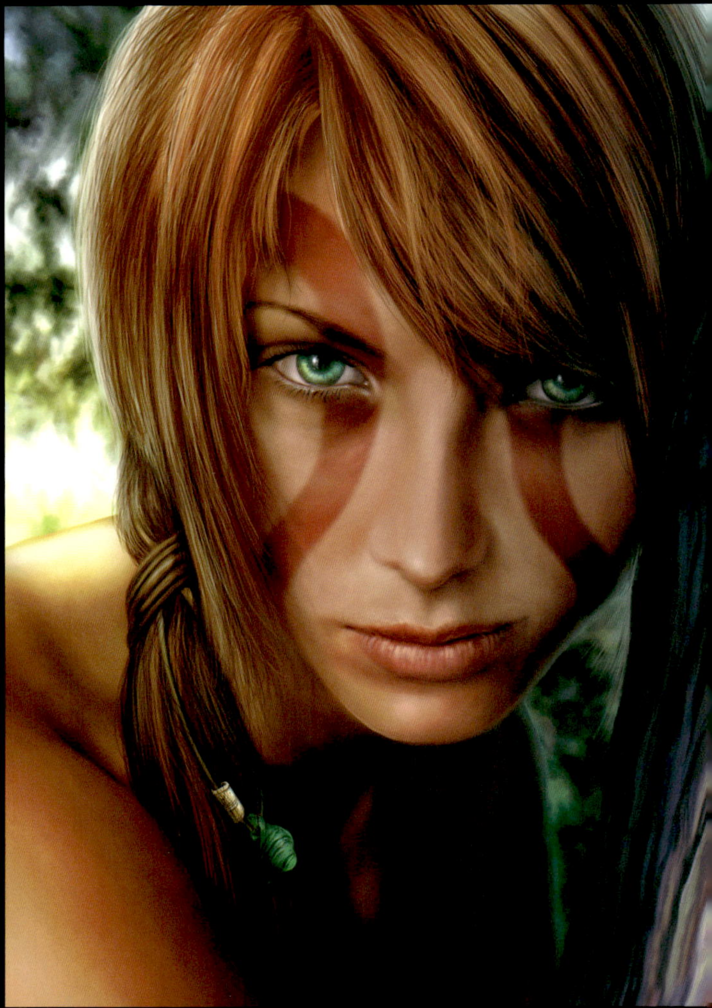

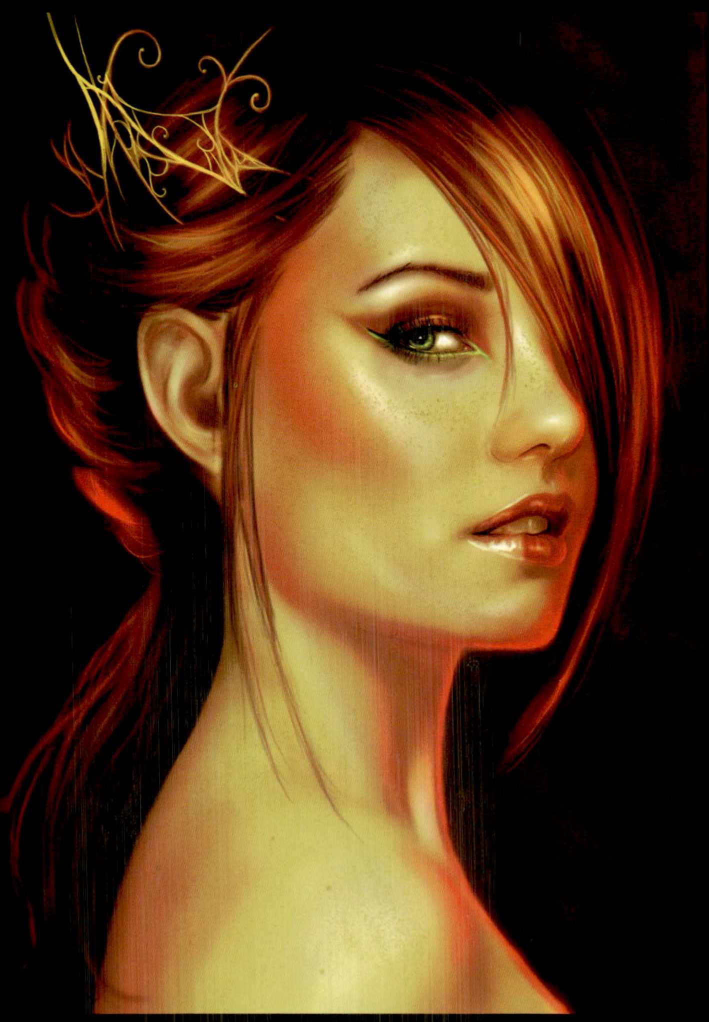

Queen Nothing
Photoshop
Jeffrey M. de Guzman, PHILIPPINES
[top left]

Dangerous women 2: Elven Scout
Painter, Photoshop
Tiziano Baracchi, ITALY
[above]

Yburiath
Photoshop
Suzanne van Pelt, NETHERLANDS
[left]

Kira
Paint Shop Pro, Painter
Client: erthchonicles.com
Jennifer Reagles, saiaii, USA
[right]

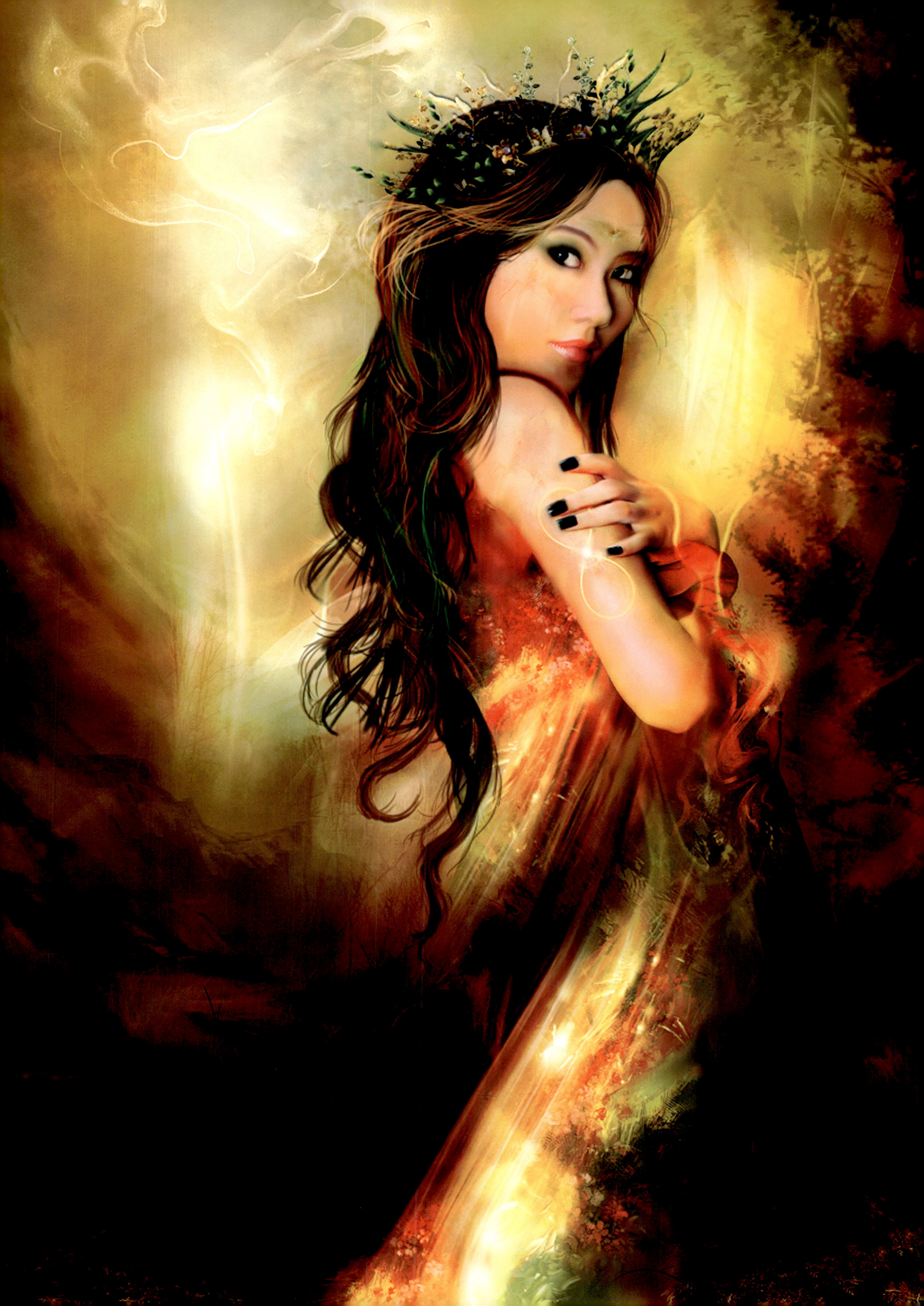

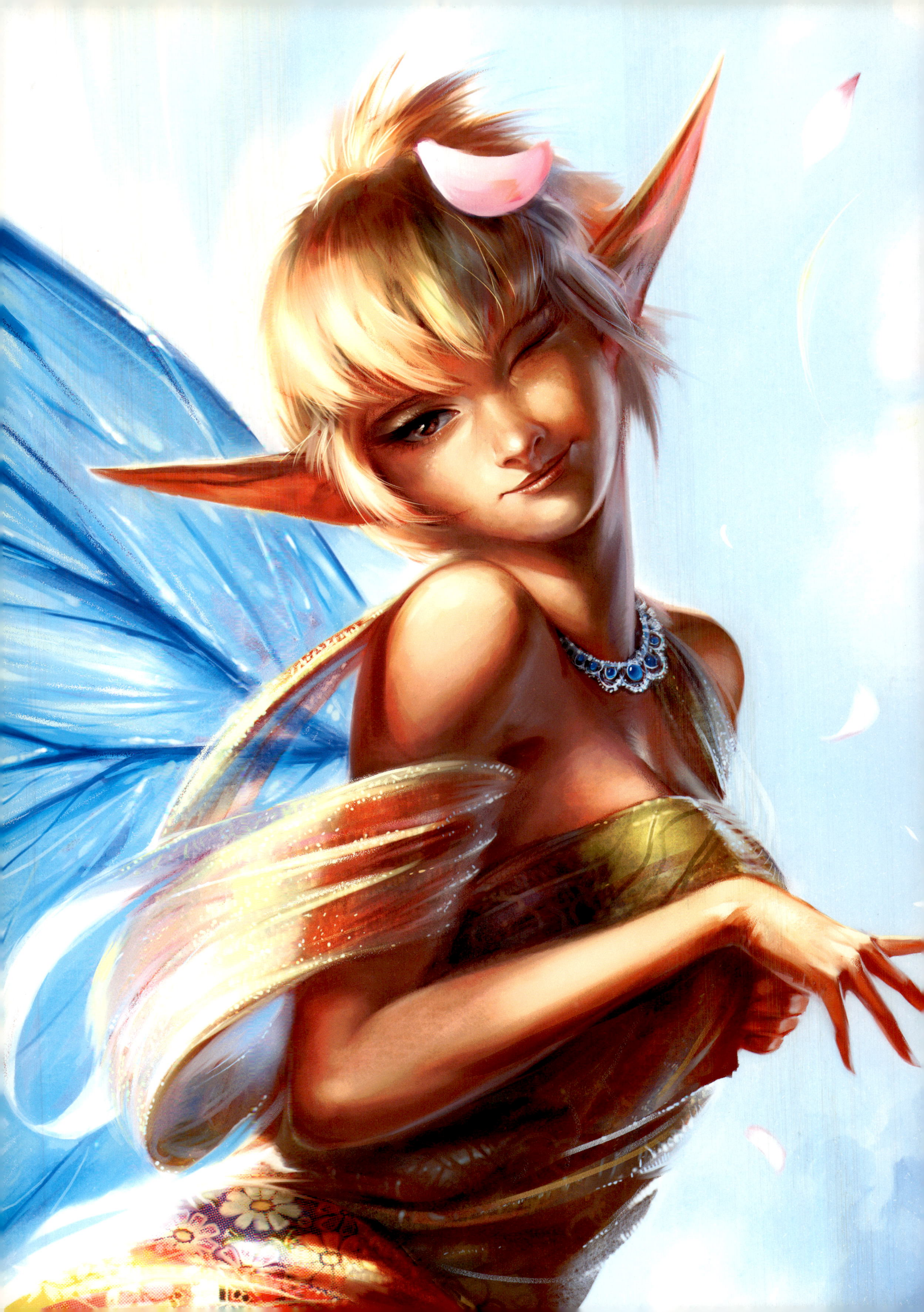

Legend Fairy
Painter, Photoshop
Leonid Kozienko, RUSSIA
[left]

Calypso
Photoshop
Michelle Hoefener, USA
[right]

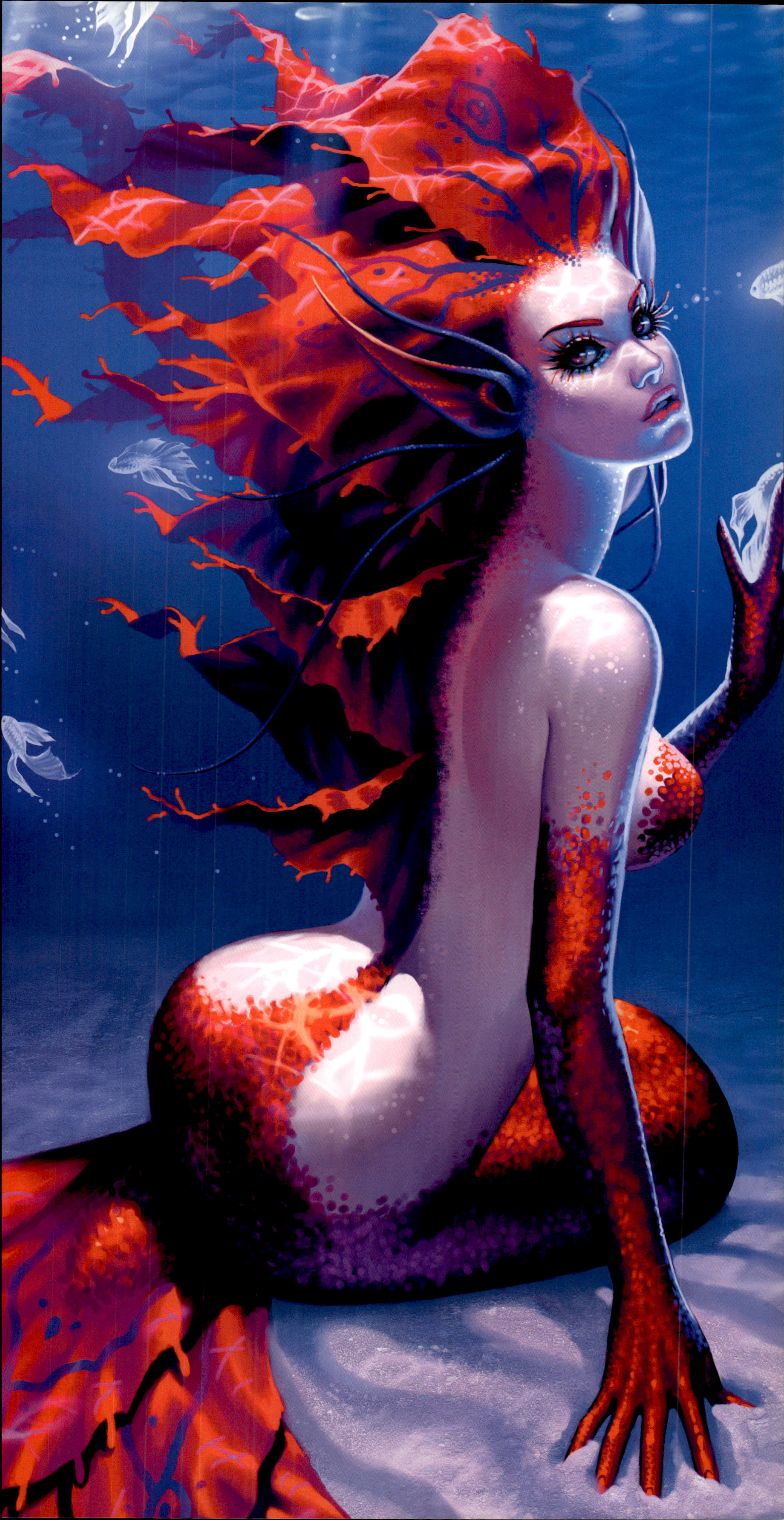

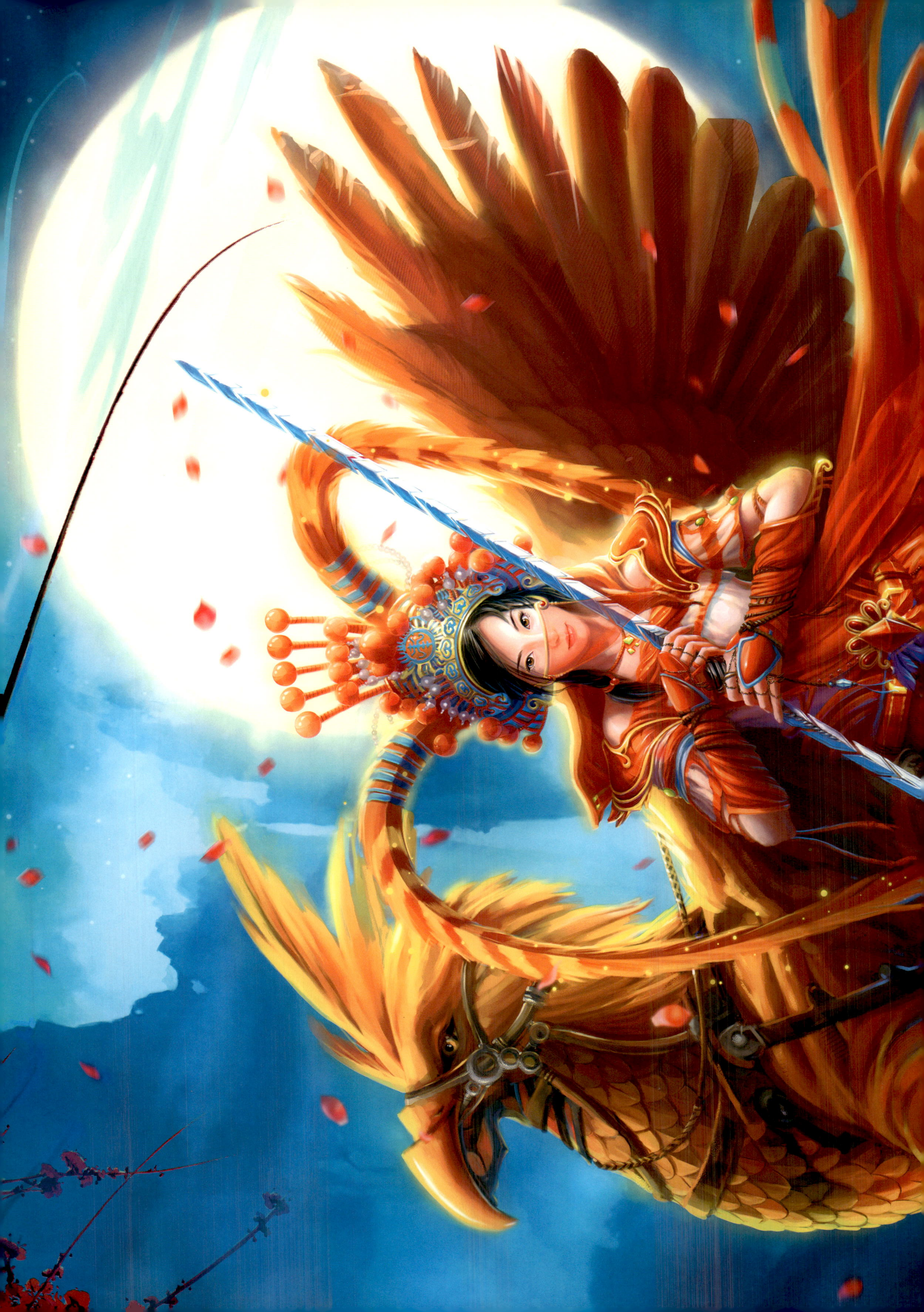

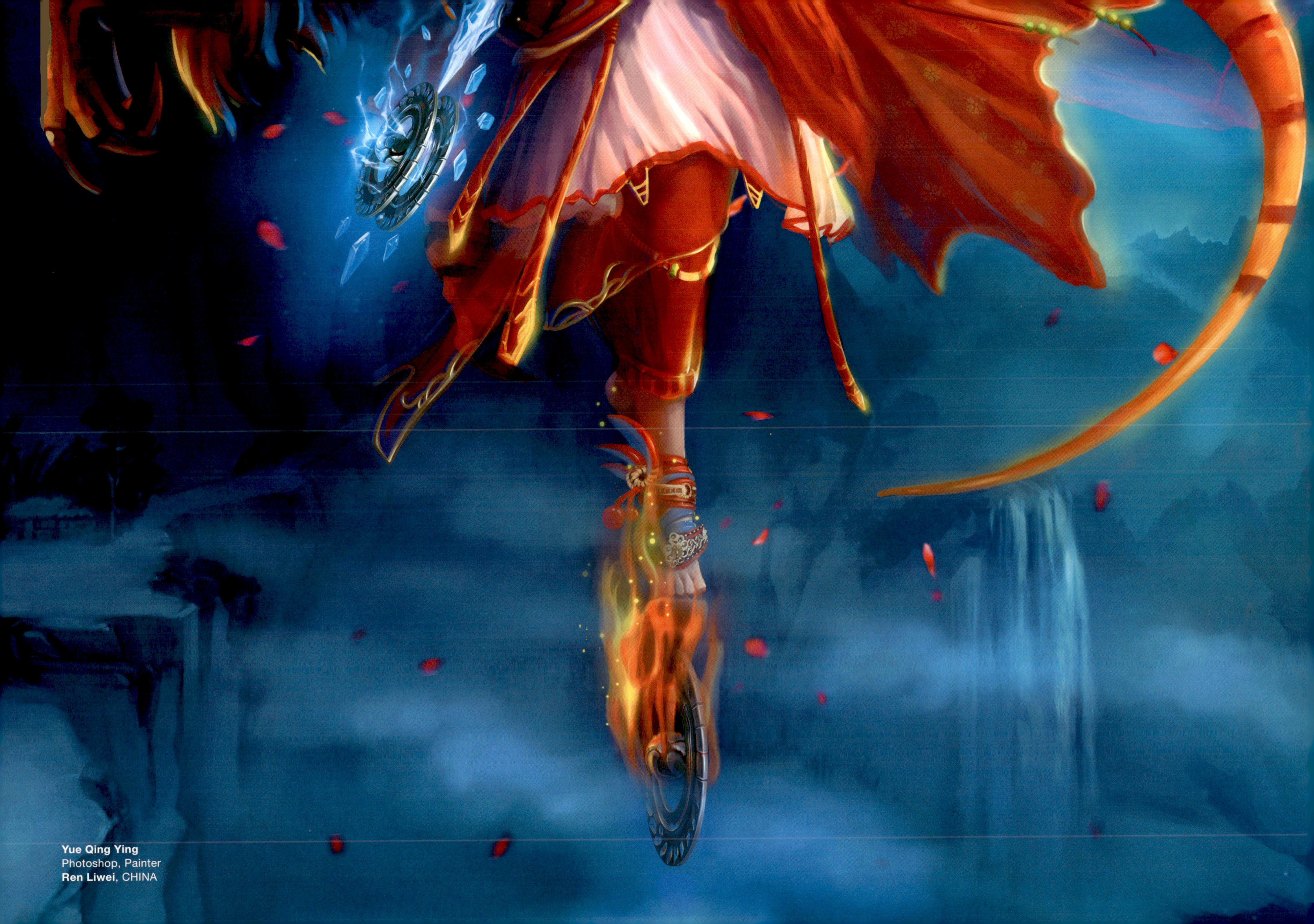

Yue Qing Ying
Photoshop, Painter
Ren Liwei, CHINA

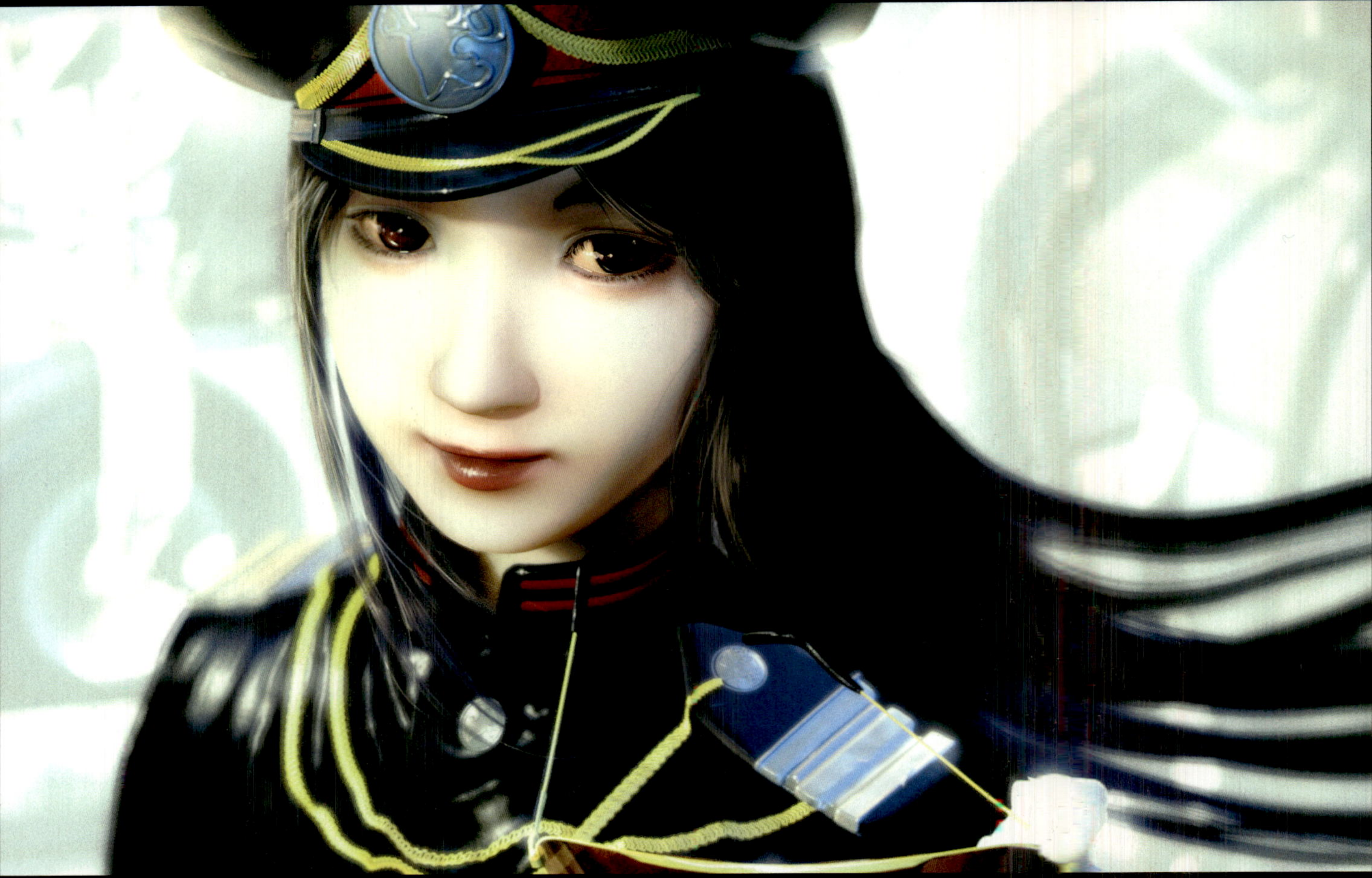

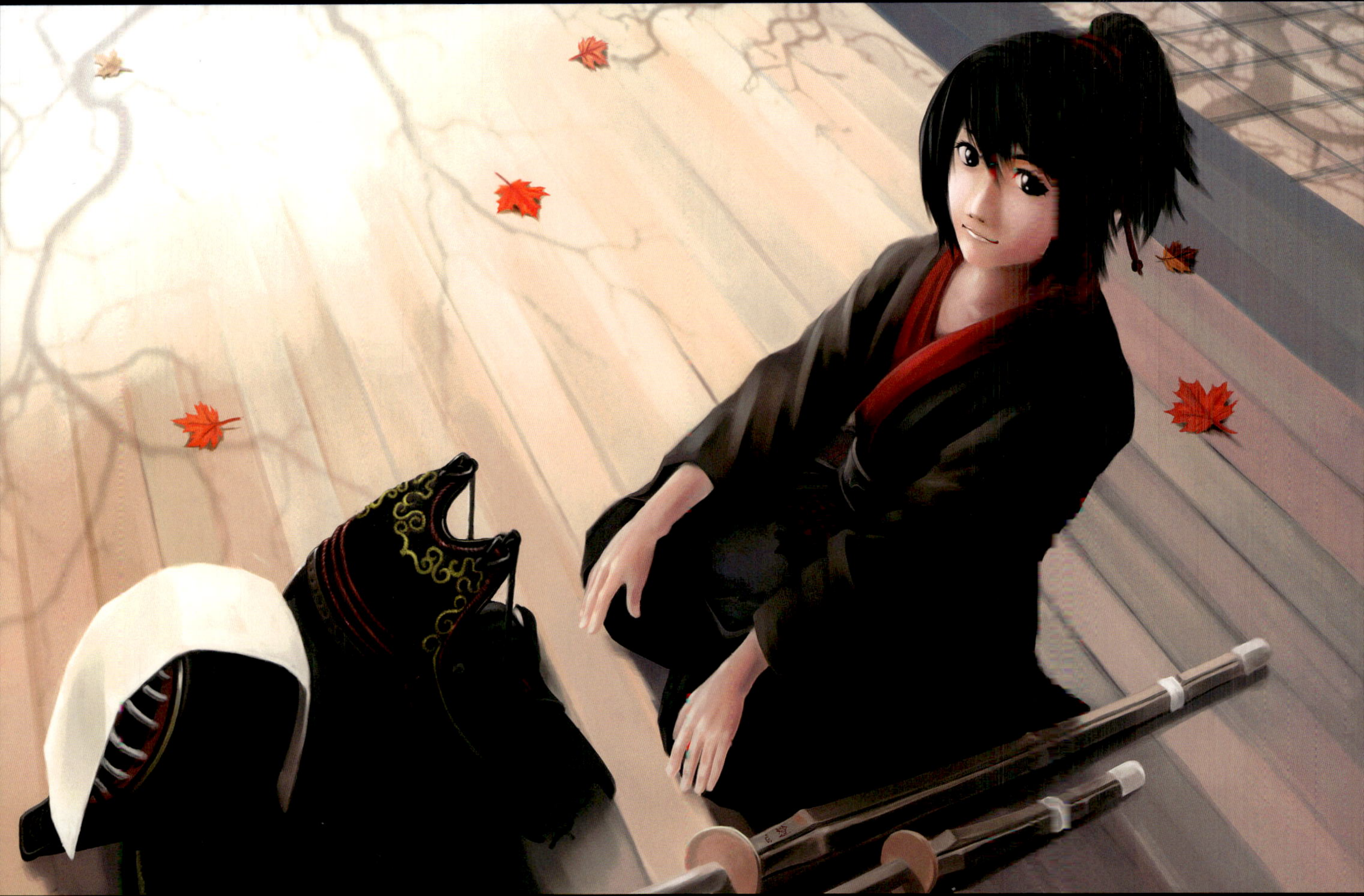

Girl in uniform
3ds Max, mental ray, Photoshop
Dzung Phungdinh, VIETNAM
[top]

Yoko's Autumn
Painter, Photoshop
Leos Ng, SINGAPORE
[above]

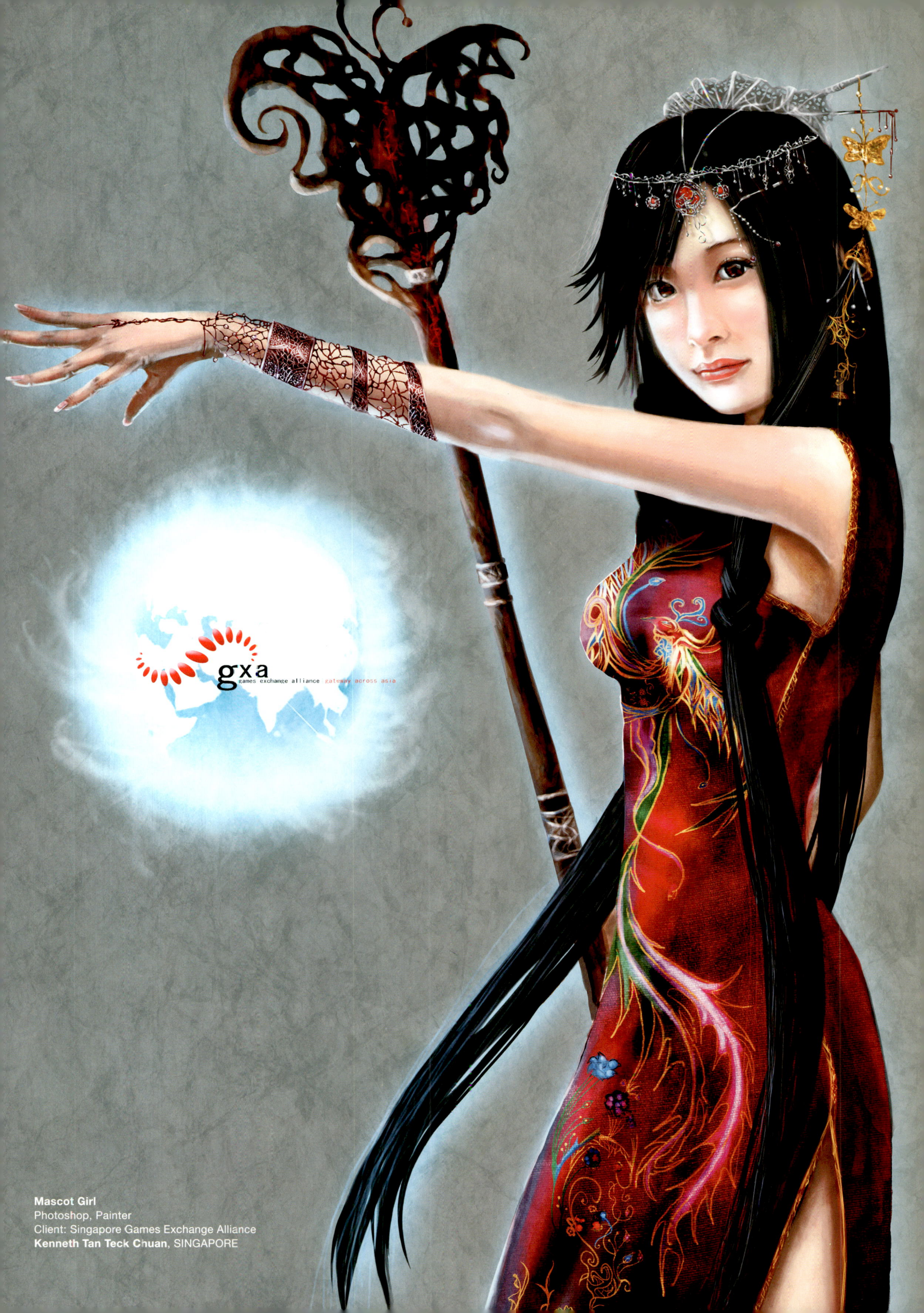

Mascot Girl
Photoshop, Painter
Client: Singapore Games Exchange Alliance
Kenneth Tan Teck Chuan, SINGAPORE

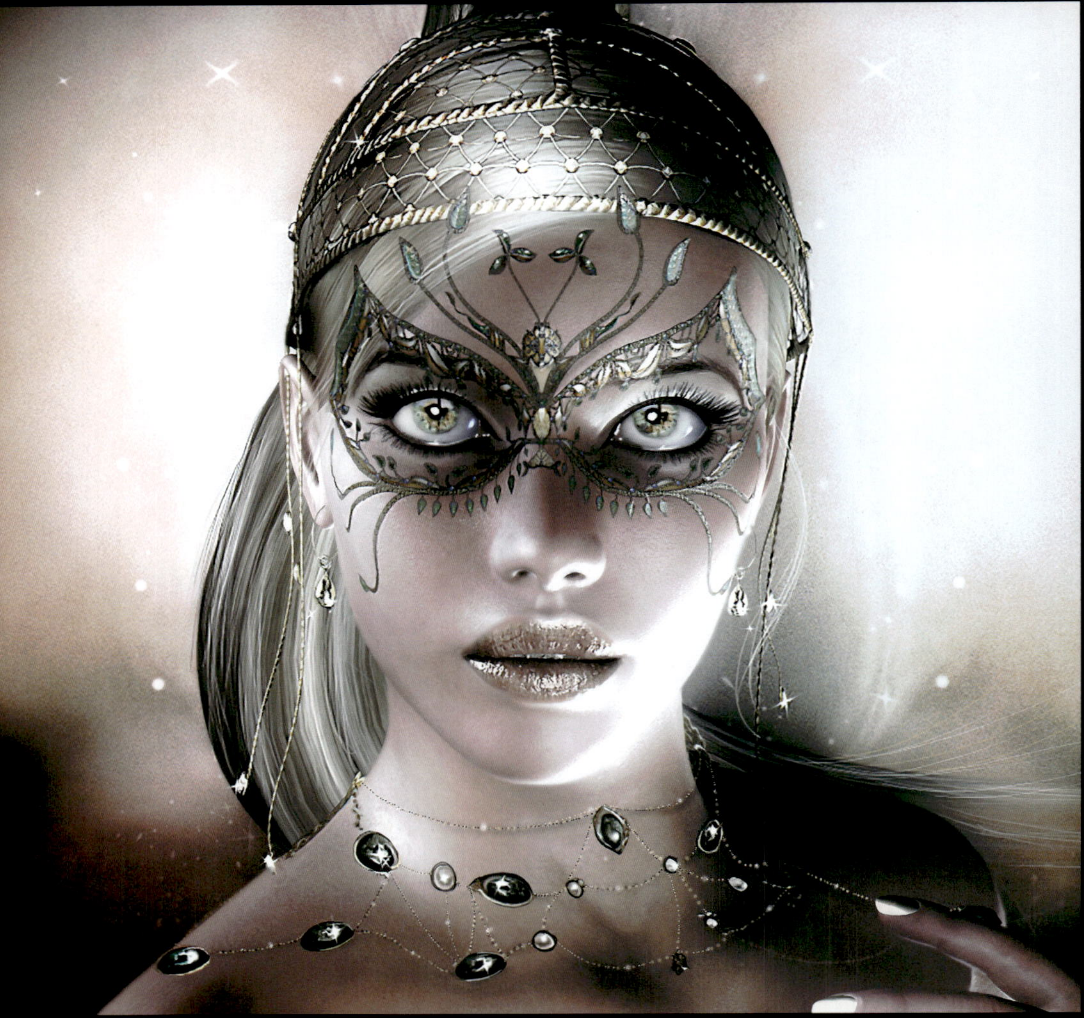

Temptress
Poser, Photoshop, Painter
Lyndsey Hayes, GREAT BRITAIN
[left]

Cameron
3ds Max, Poser, VRay
Adam Potter, AUSTRALIA
[right]

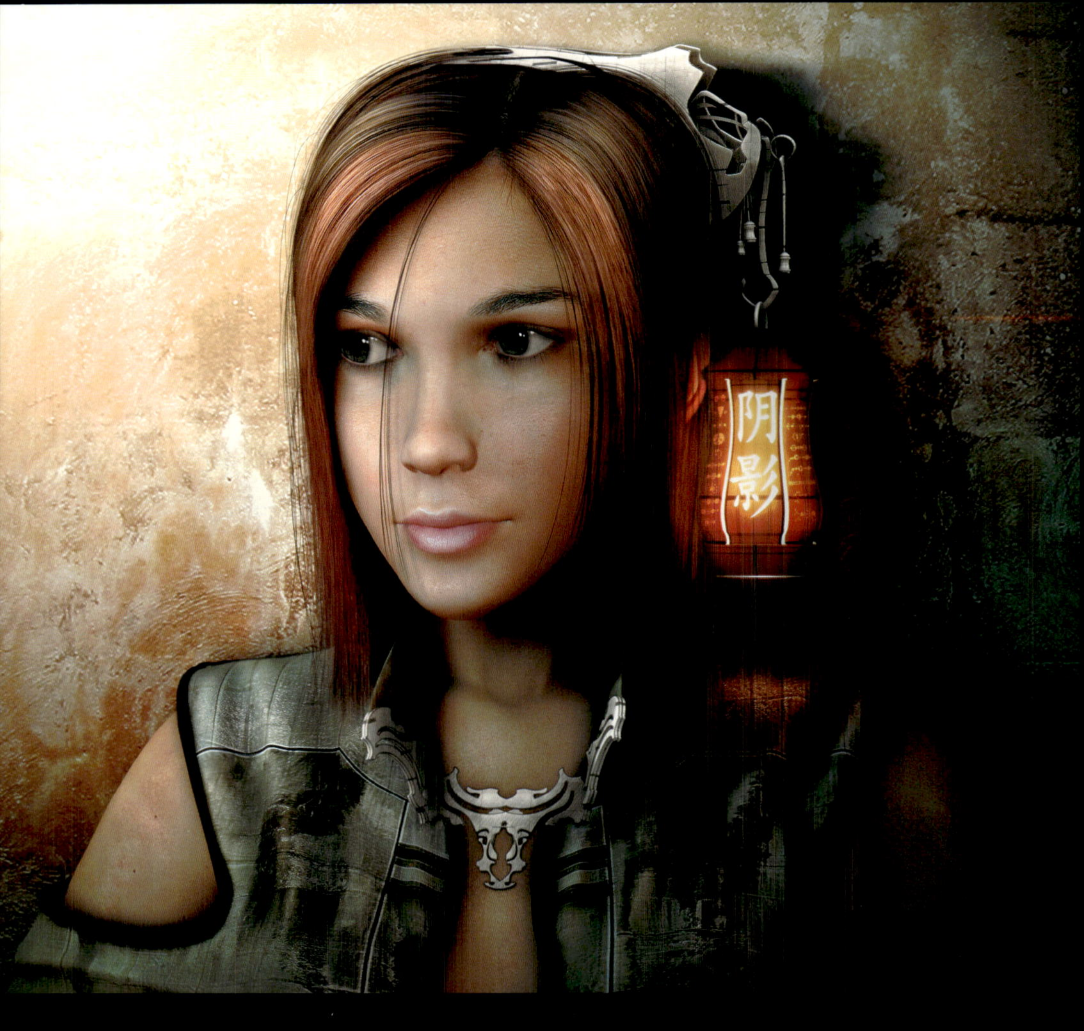

Defying Silence
Maya, Photoshop, mental ray
Marcin Balcerzak, CANADA
[left]

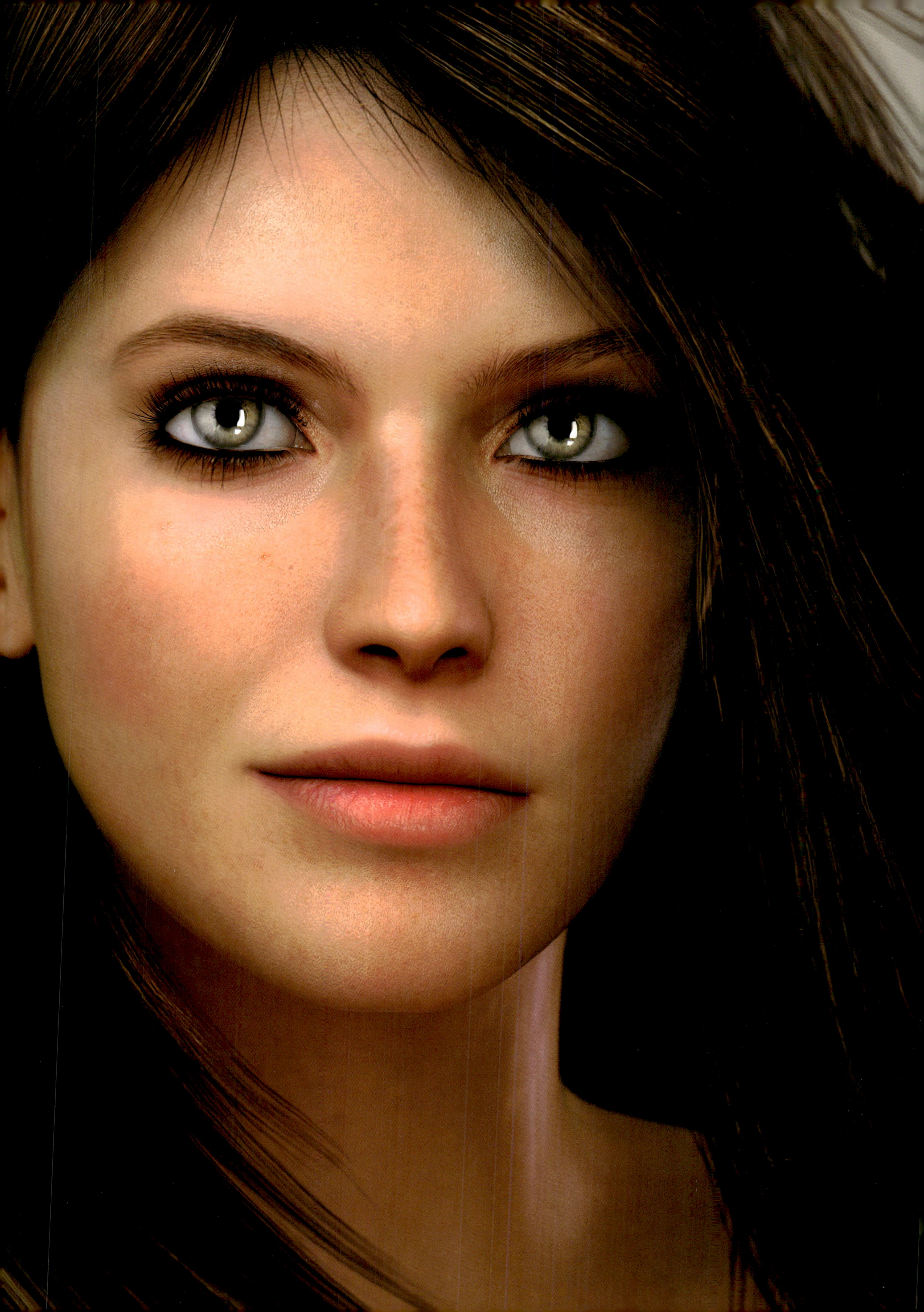

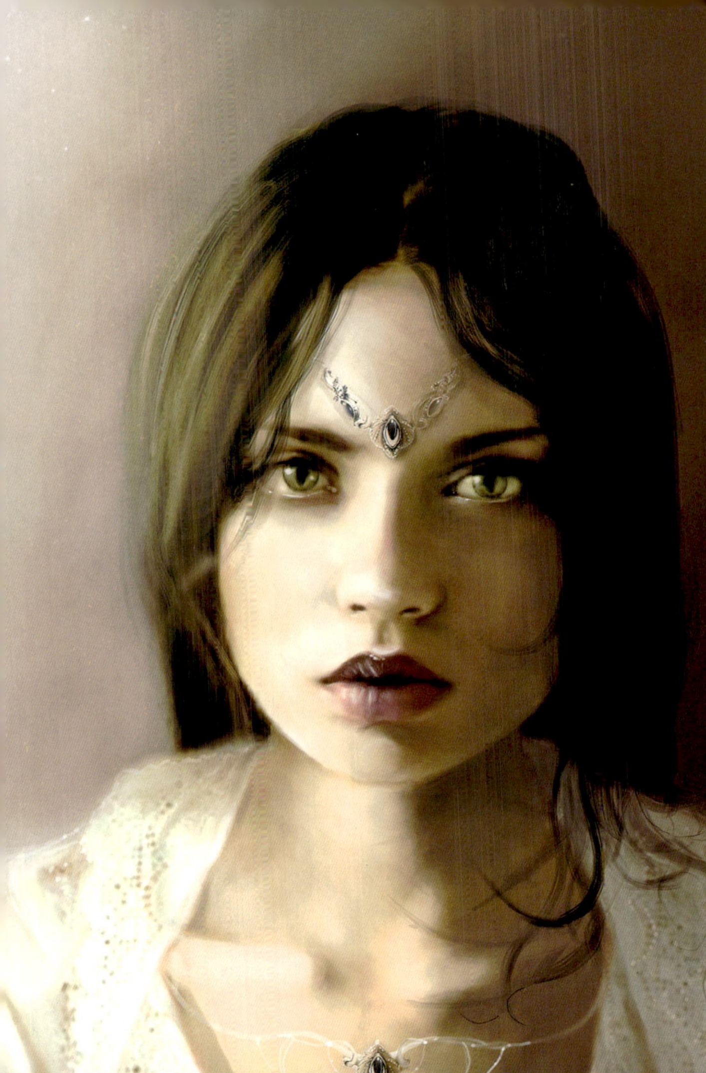

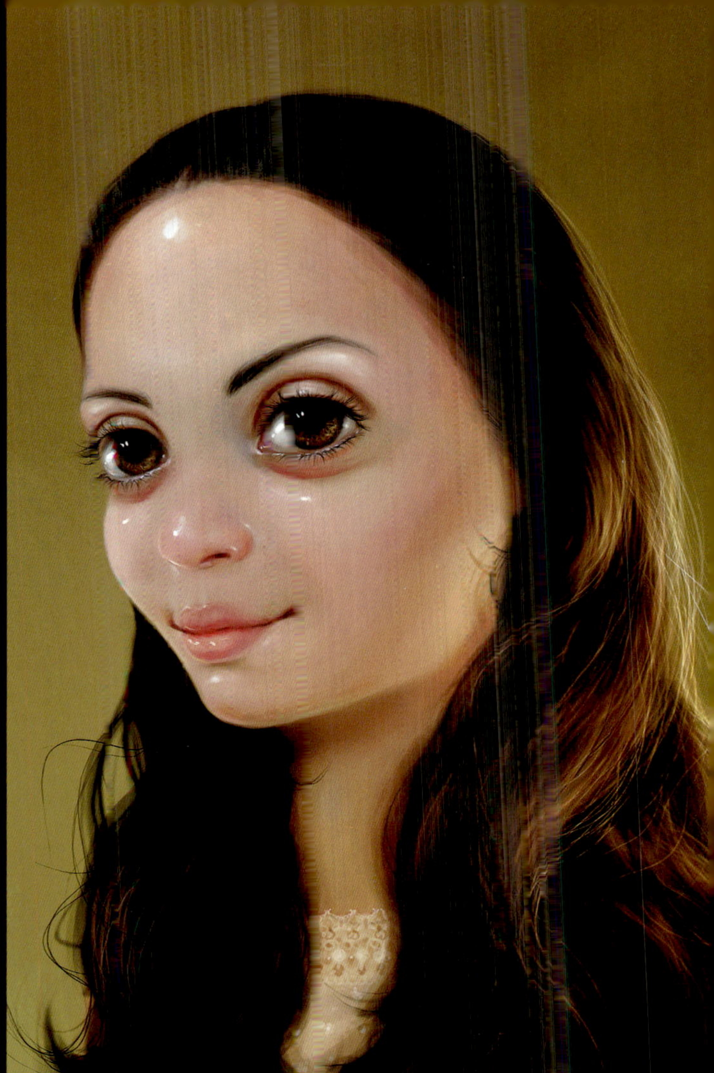

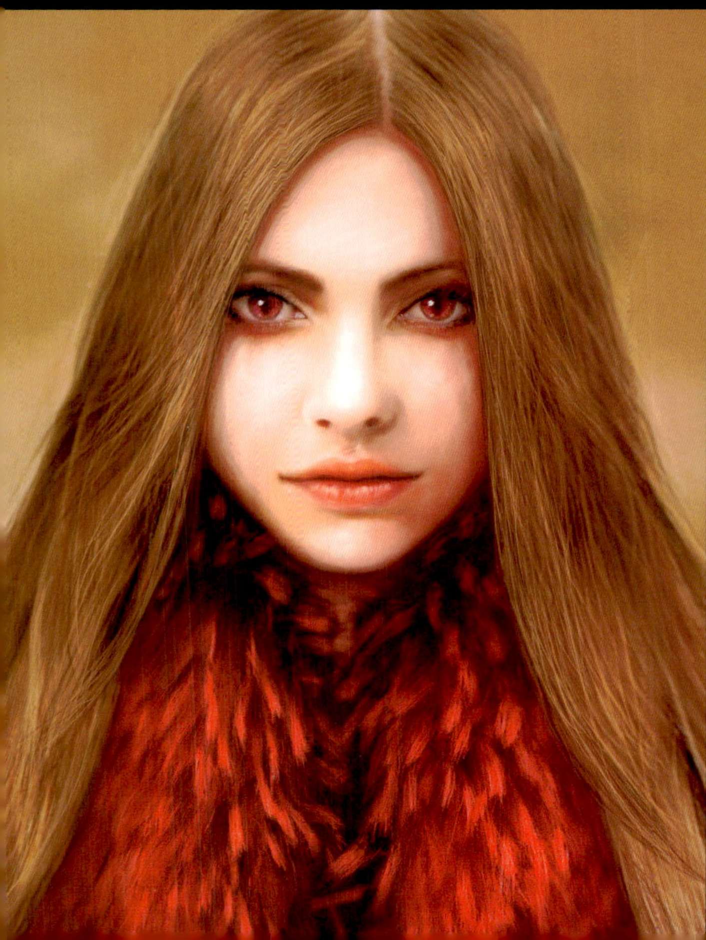

Dusk
Photoshop, Paint Shop Pro
Bente Schlick, GERMANY
[top left]

Cho
Photoshop
Shreya Shetty, INDIA
[above]

Furry
Photoshop
Ann-Christin Pogoda, GERMANY
[left]

Lady of Blood
Painter
Katarina Sokolova, UKRAINE
[right]

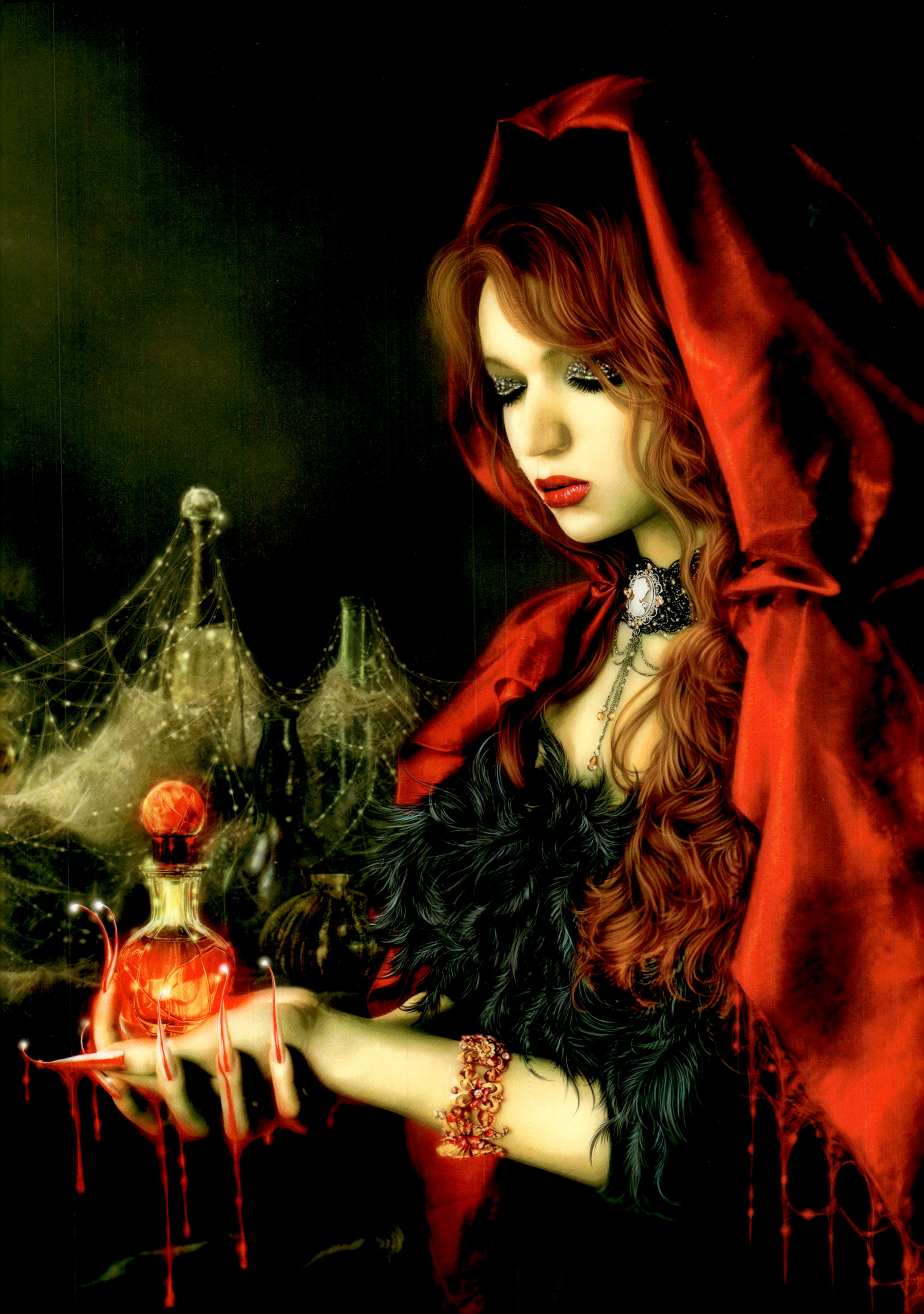

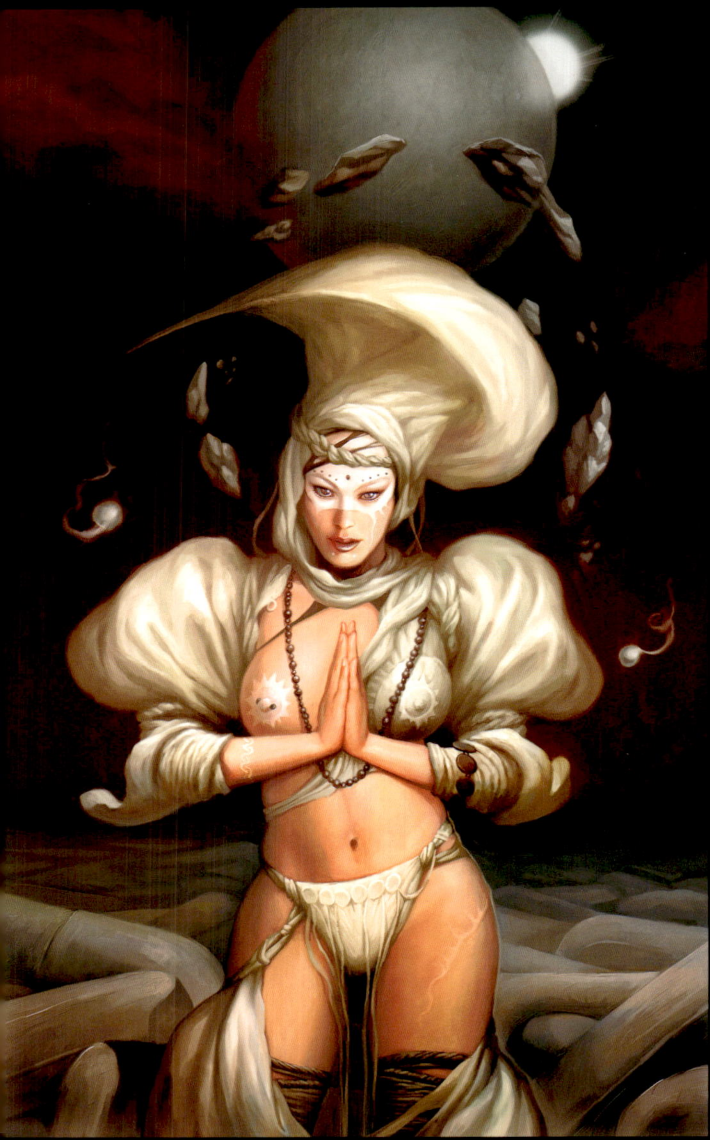

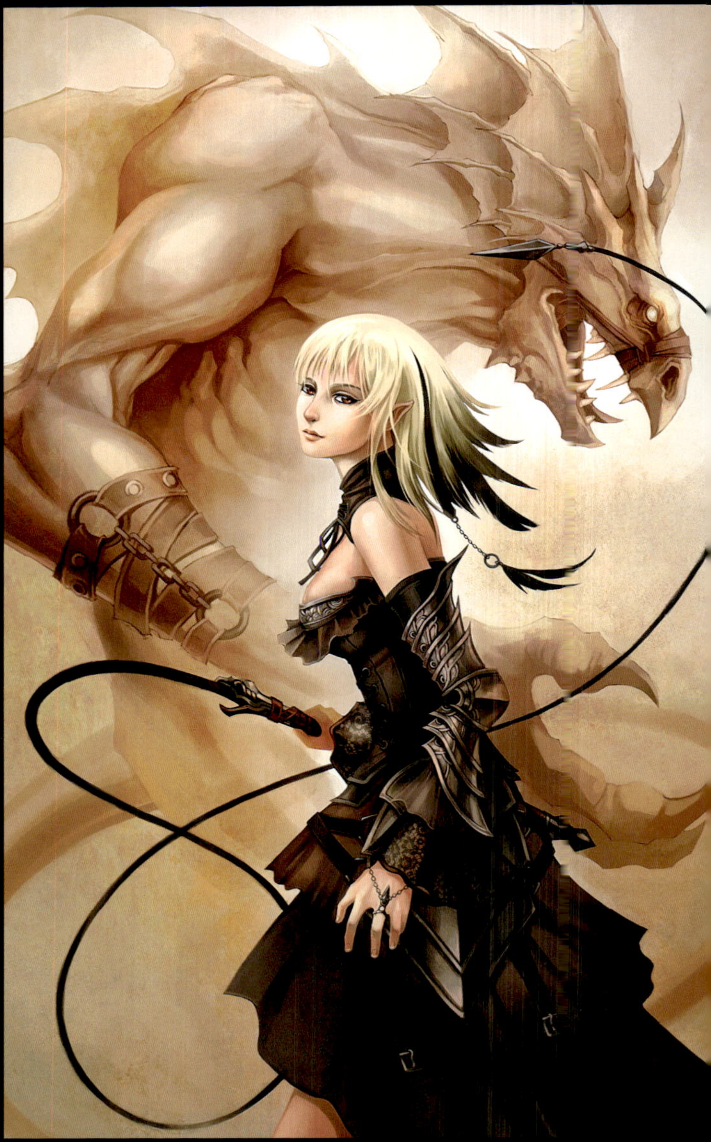

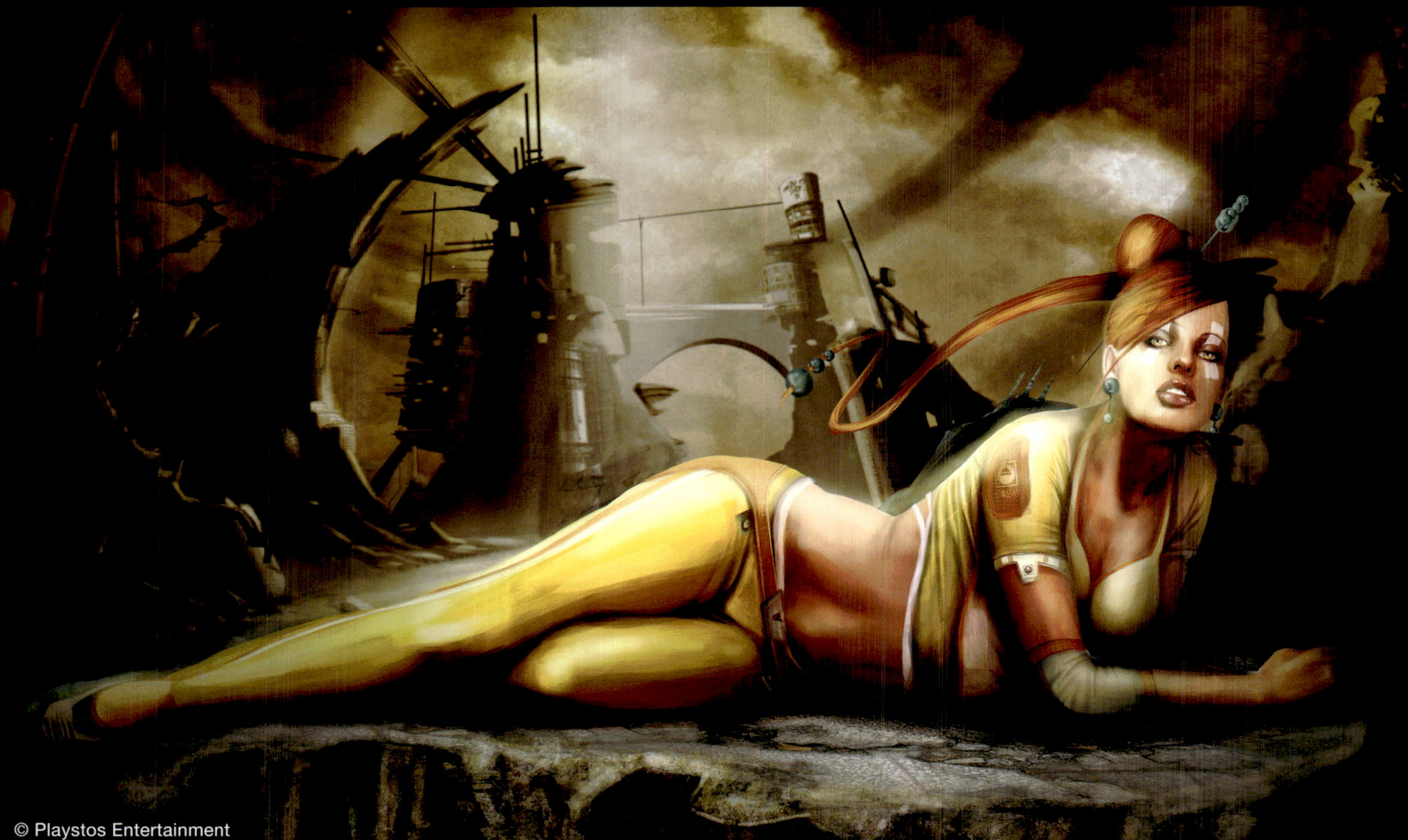

Augur
Photoshop
Jiansong Chen, LusioSoft Entertainment Co., Ltd, CHINA
[far left]

Beast Tamer
Photoshop
Sandara Tang, SINGAPORE
[left]

Valkyr
Painter, Photoshop
Wei Chen, CHINA
[right]

Thelia
Photoshop
Client: Playstos Entertainment
Margherita Premuroso, ITALY
[left]

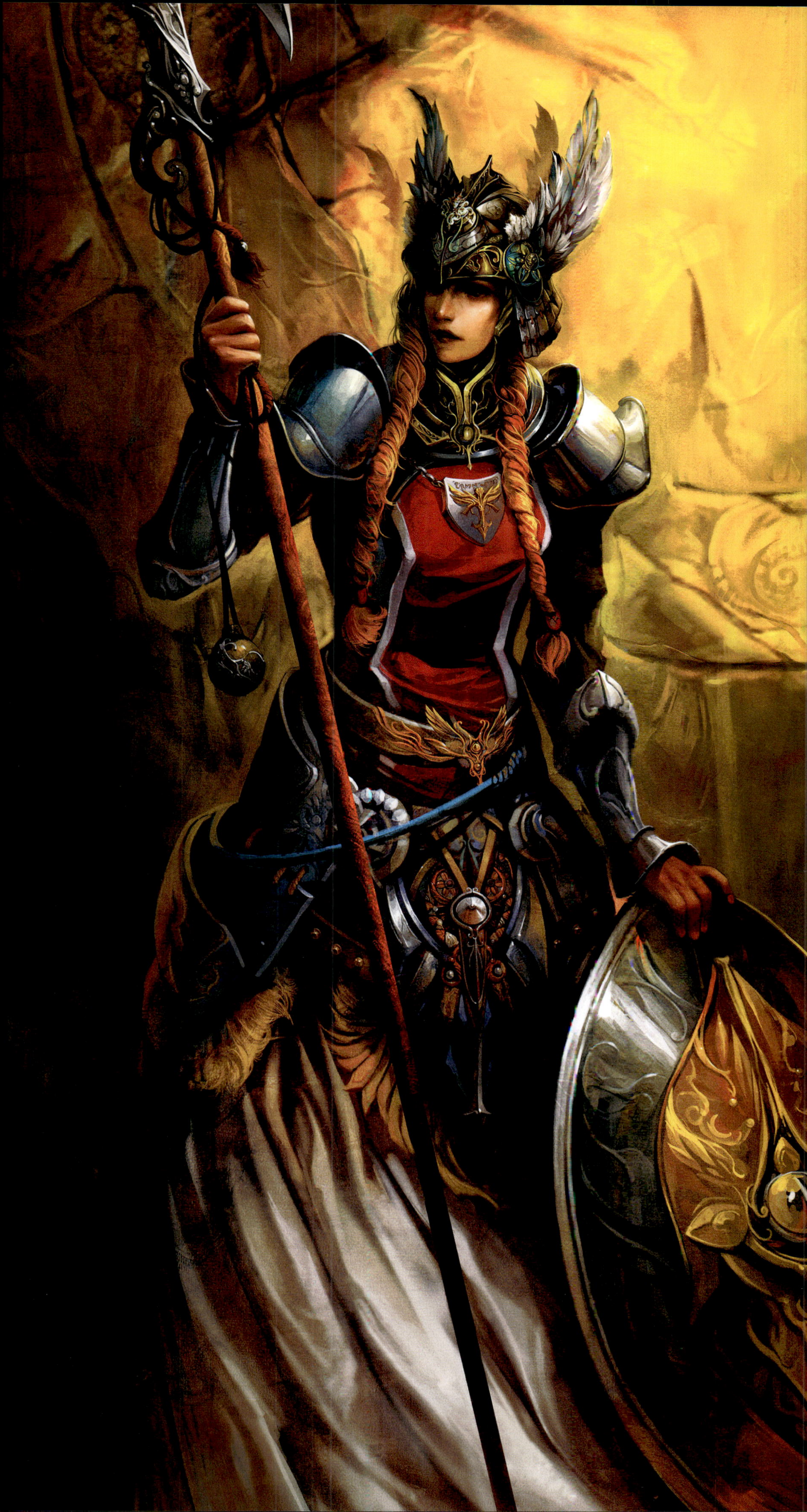

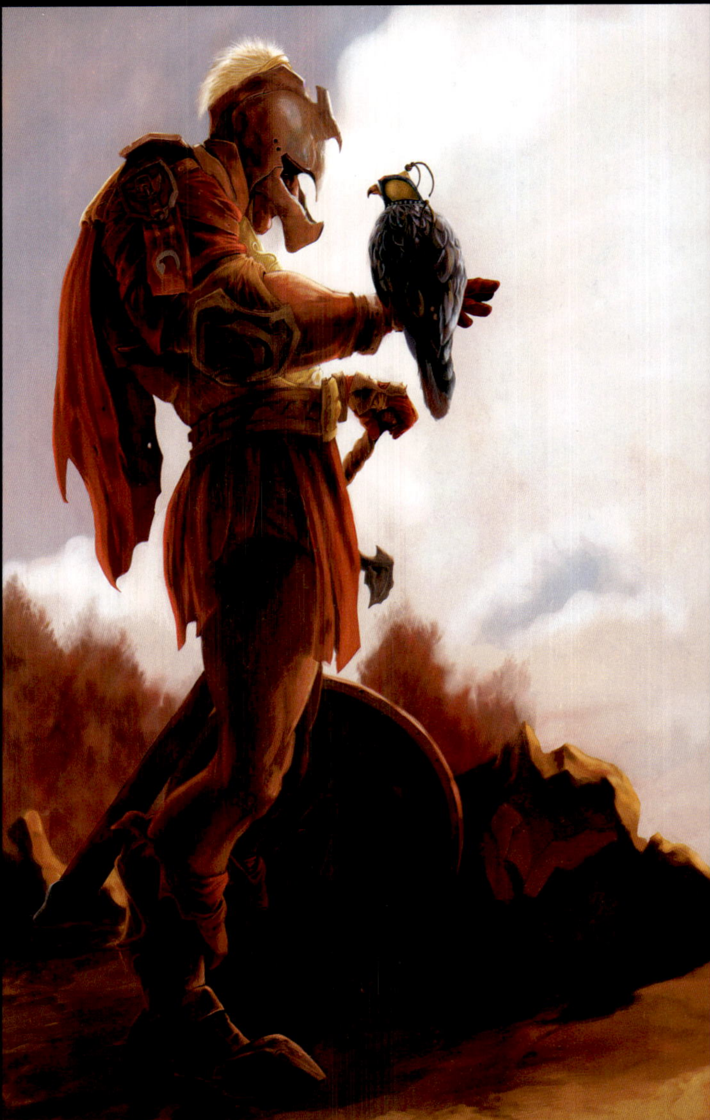

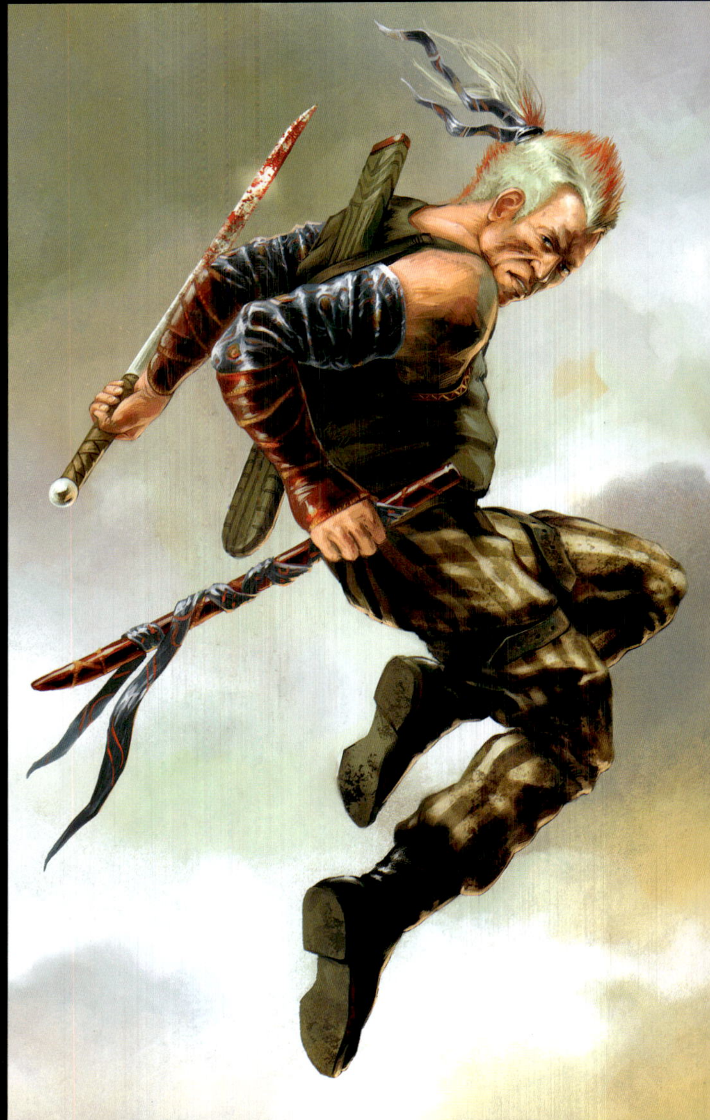

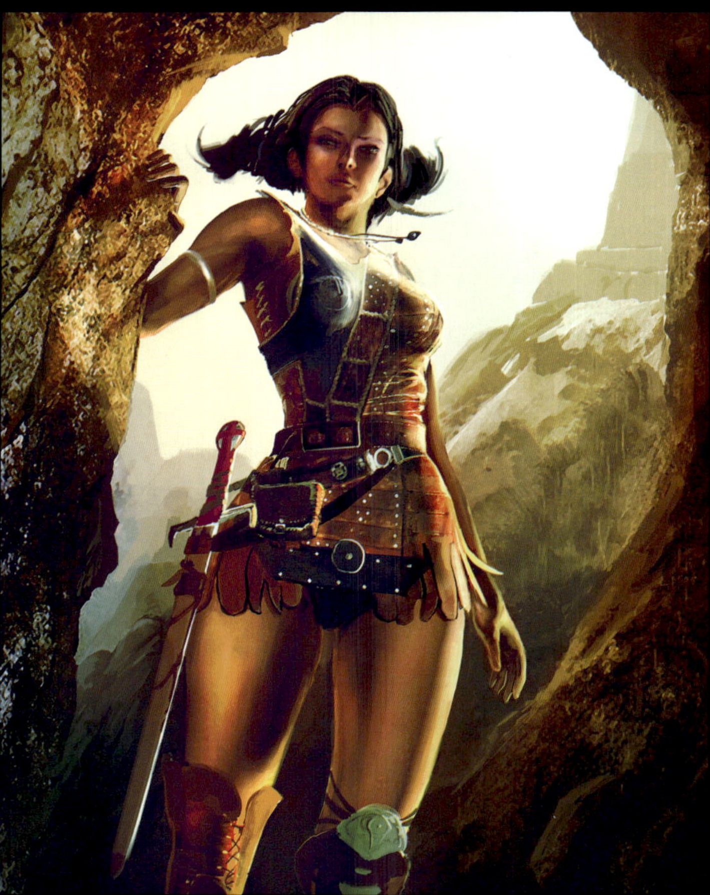

The falcon troop
Painter, Photoshop
Ilker Serdar Yildiz, TURKEY
[top left]

Warrior
Painter, Photoshop
Mateja Petkovic, SERBIA
[above]

Mountain watch
Painter, Photoshop
Bruno Werneck, USA
[left]

Railla Karnokailen
Photoshop
Tomasz Jedruszek, POLAND
[right]

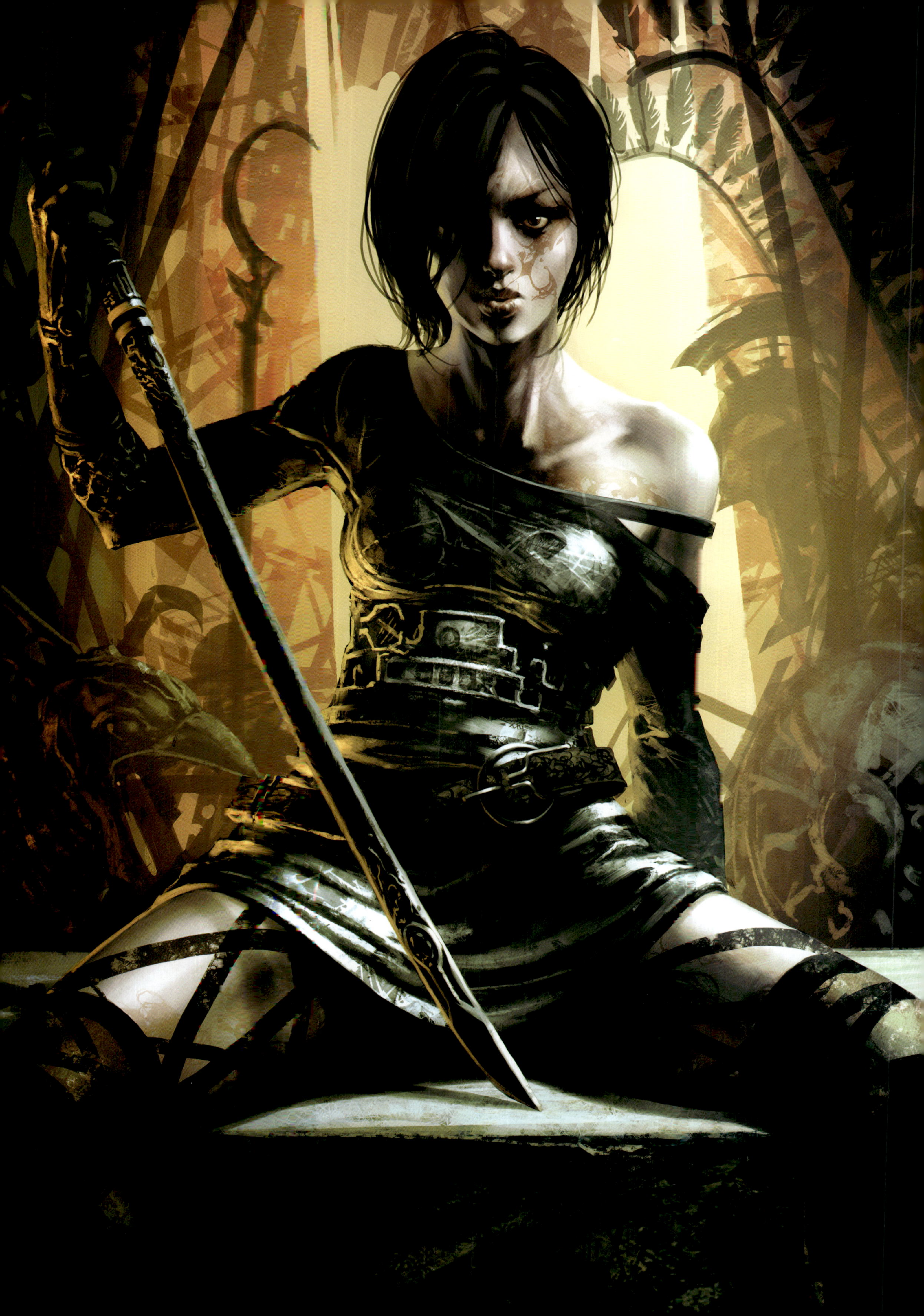

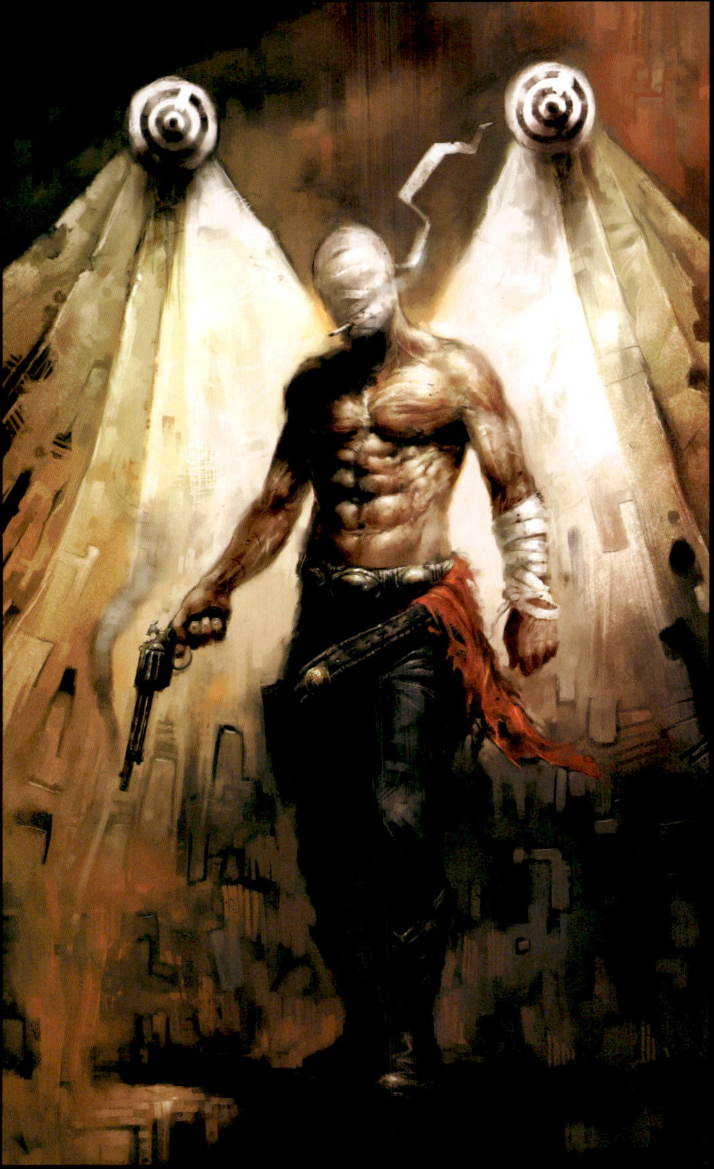

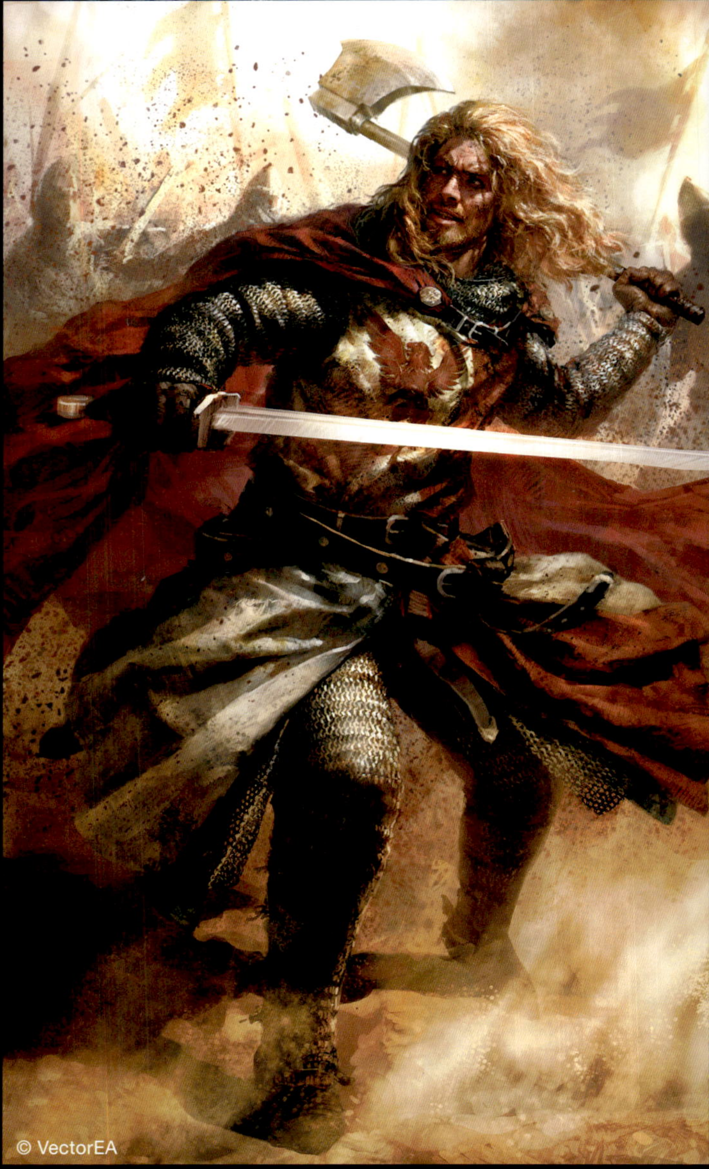

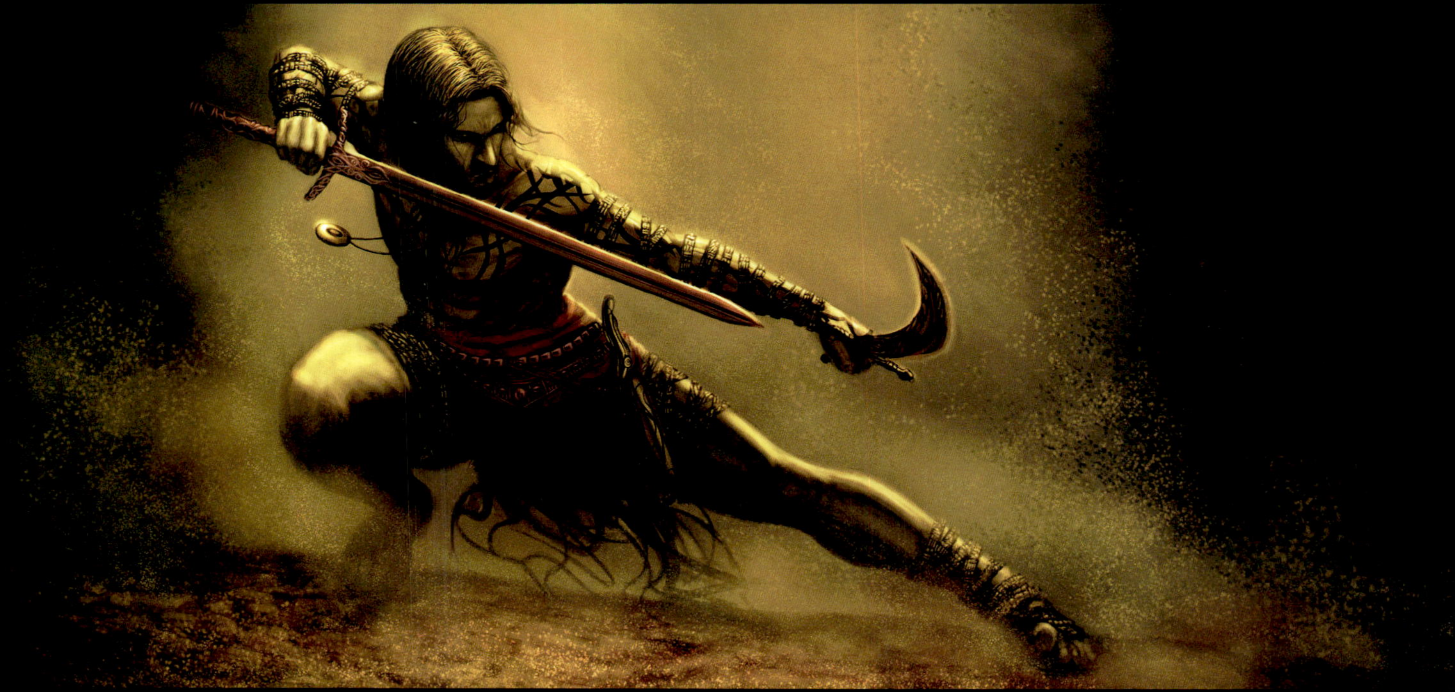

Three bullets
Photoshop
Client: Fabryka Slow
Grzegorz Krysinski, POLAND
[top]

Rise of the prince
Photoshop
John Barry Ballaran,
PHILIPPINES
[above]

Fearless
Photoshop
Client: VectorEA
Alon Chou, TAIWAN
[top]

Kratos vs. Barbarian King
Photoshop, Maya
Andy Park, SCEA,
USA
[right]

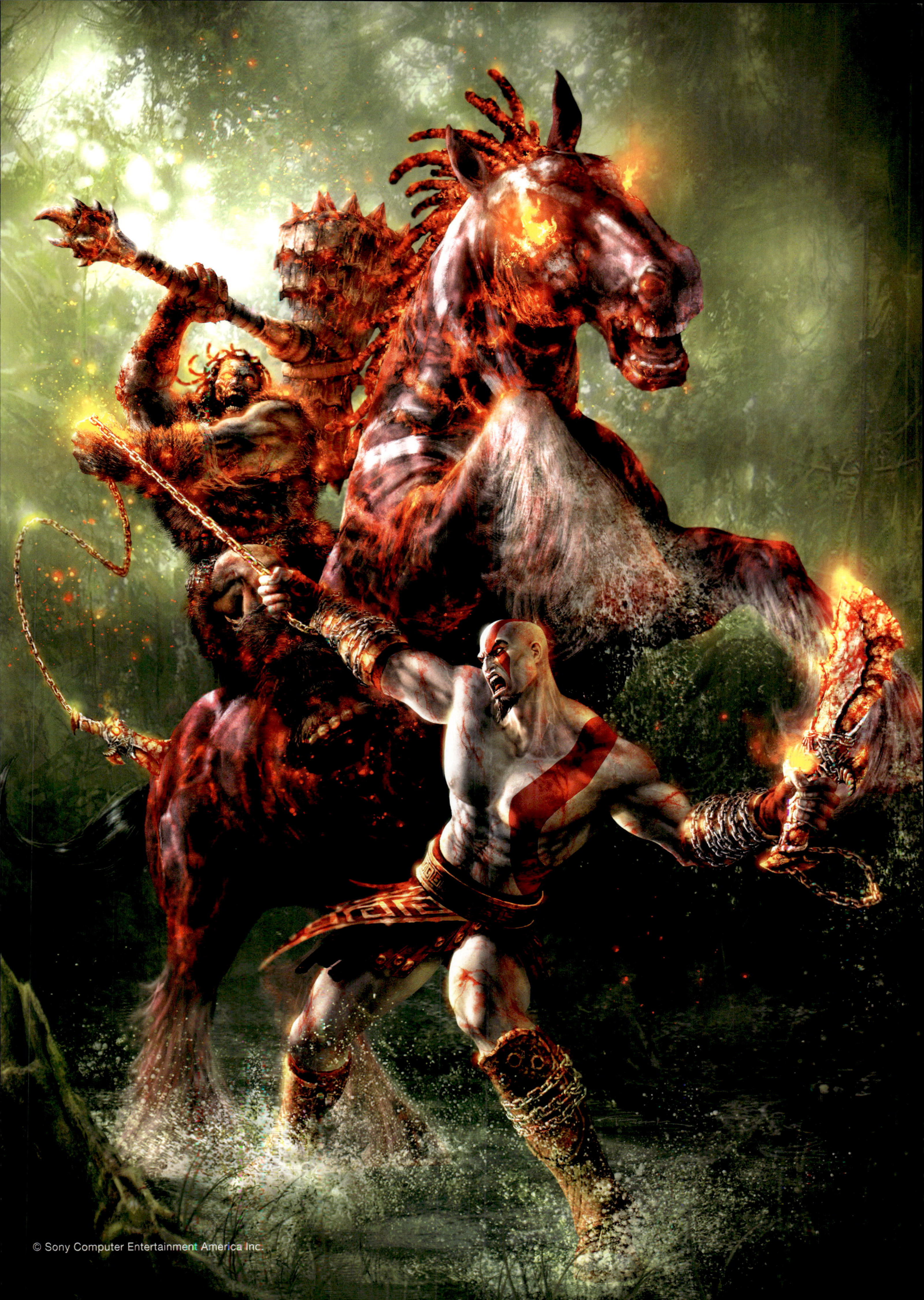

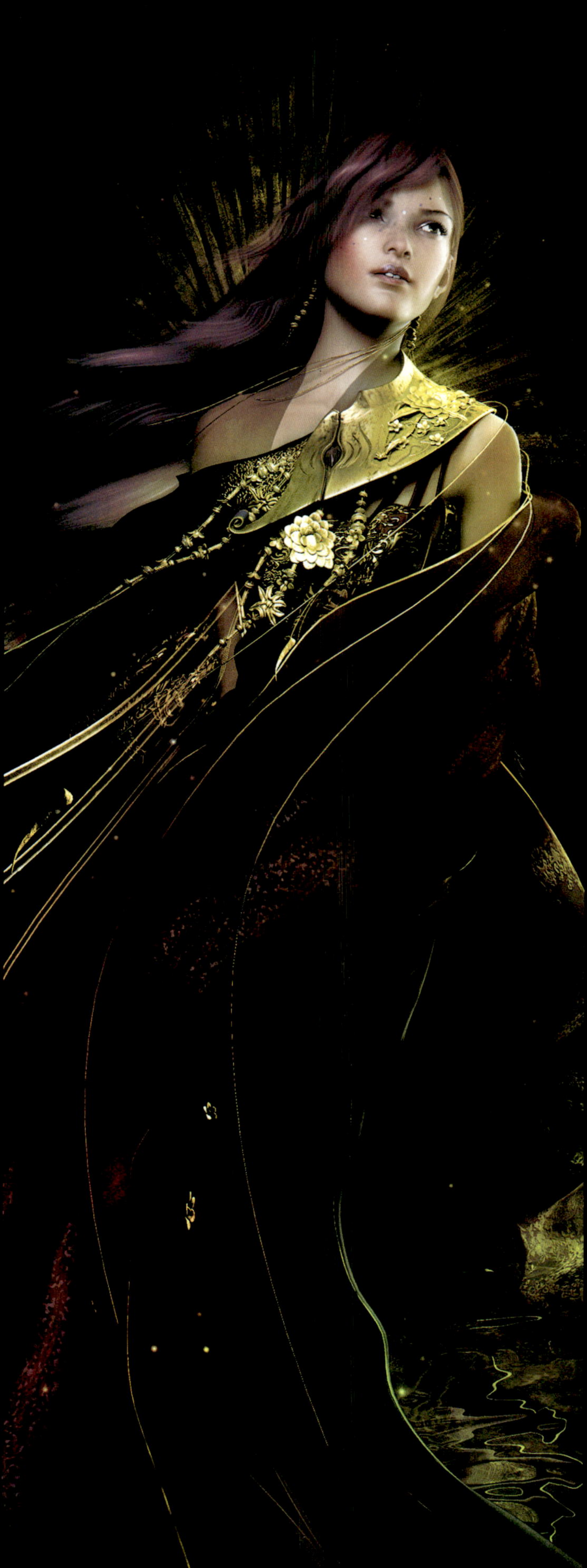

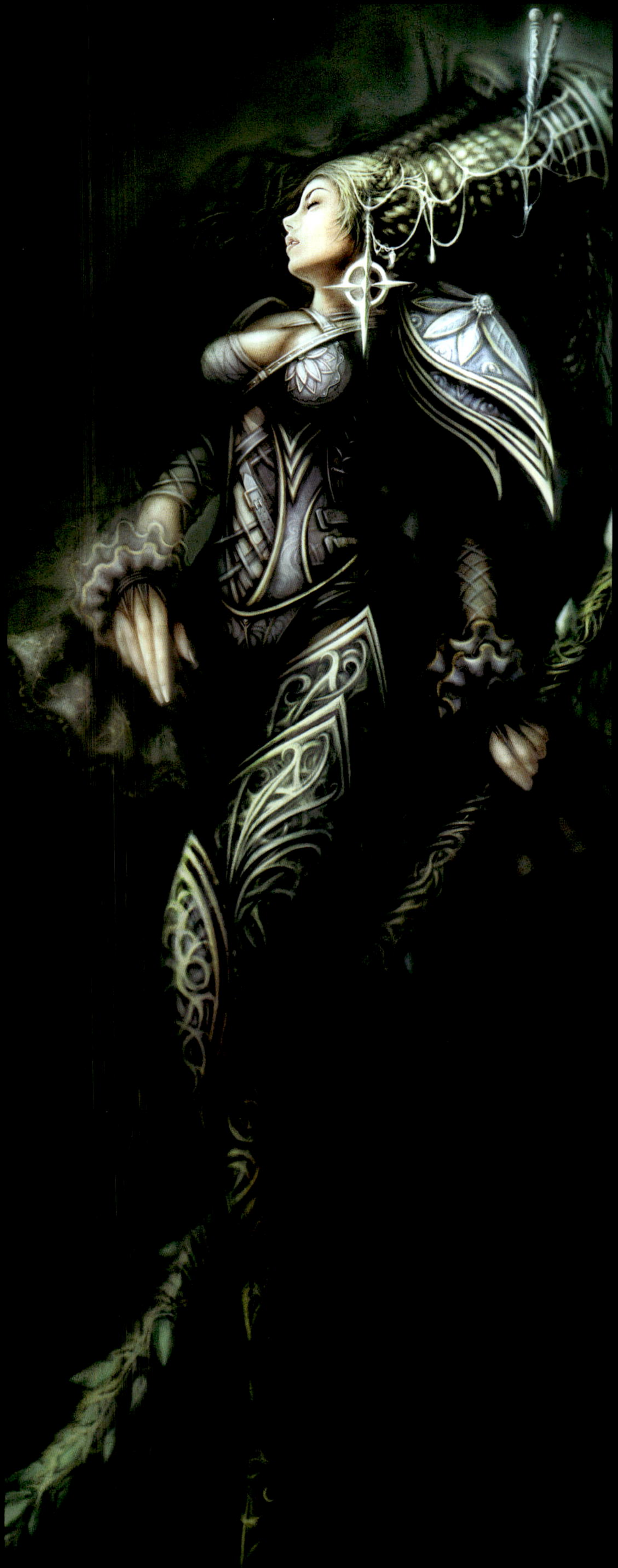

Golden Flow
3ds Max
Olivier Ponsonnet, FRANCE
[above]

Wind Warrior
Photoshop, Painter
Kyung Up Hyun, KOREA
[above]

Queen of Blades
ZBrush, Photoshop
Marek Okon, POLAND
[right]

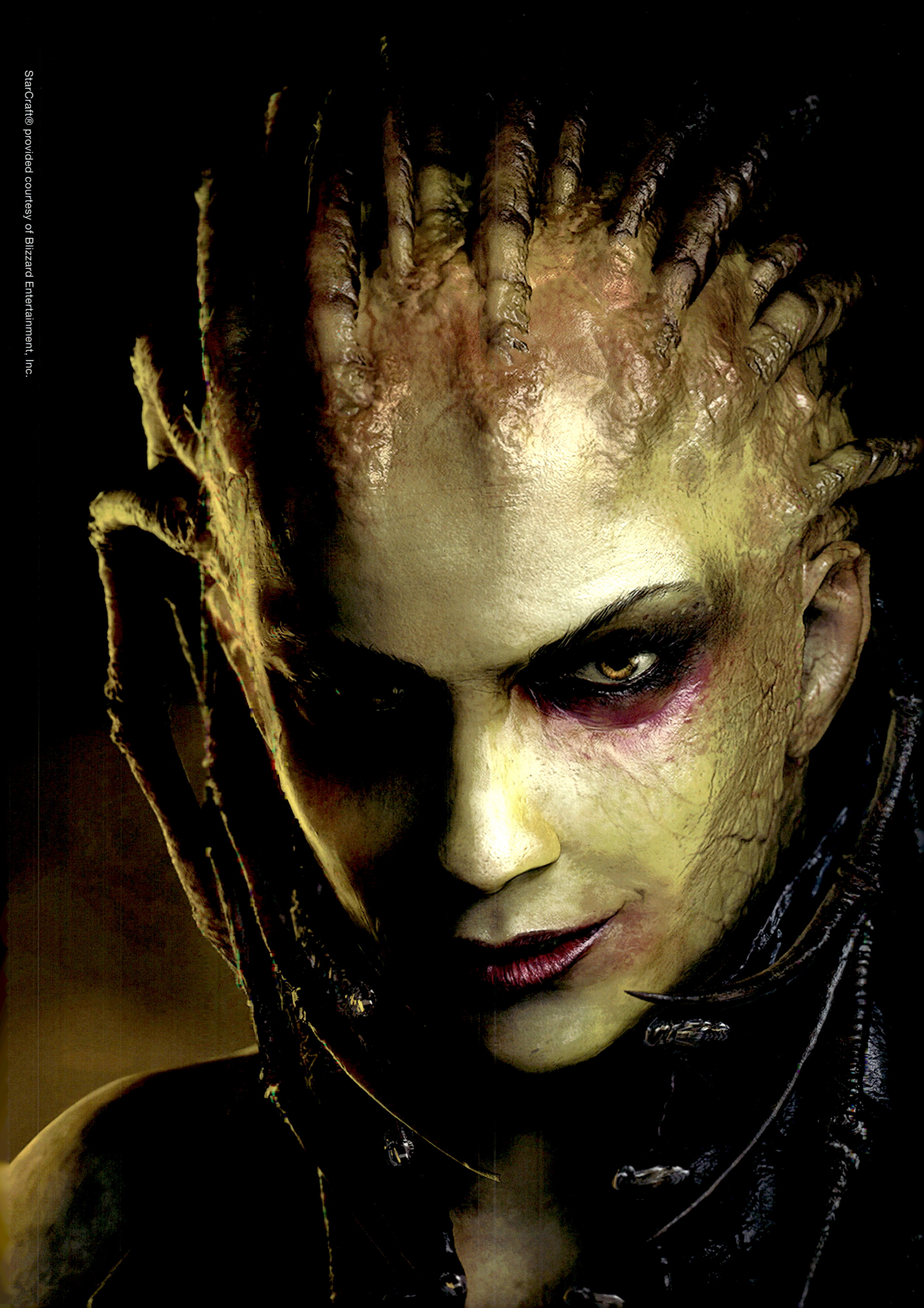

StarCraft® provided courtesy of Blizzard Entertainment, Inc.

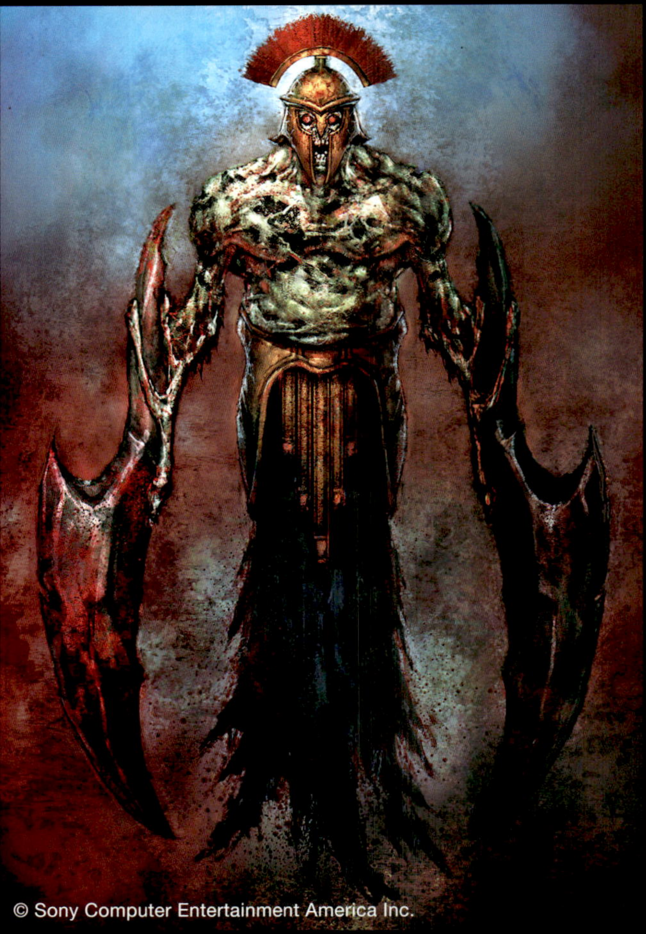

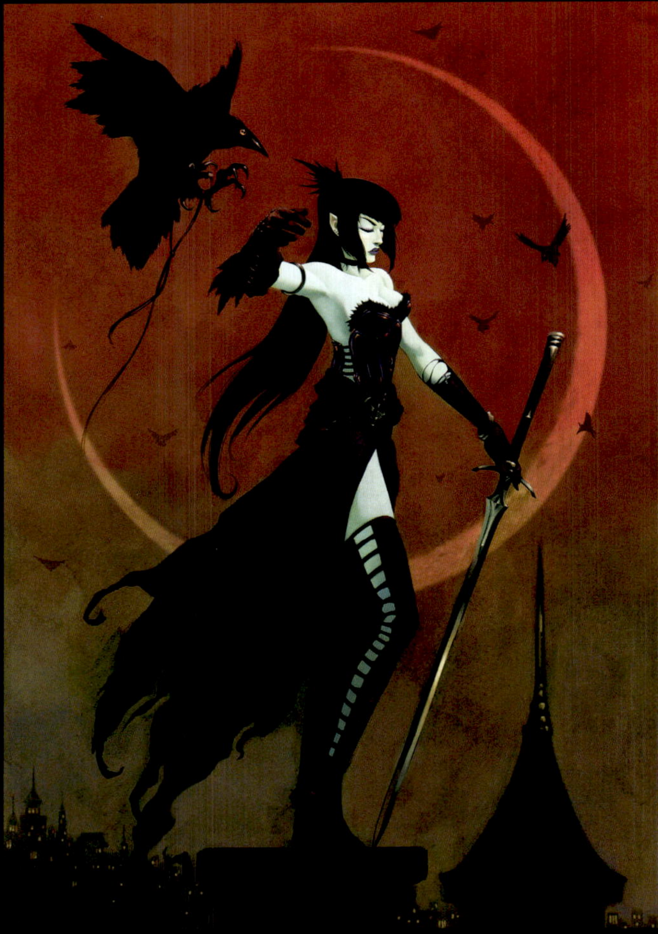

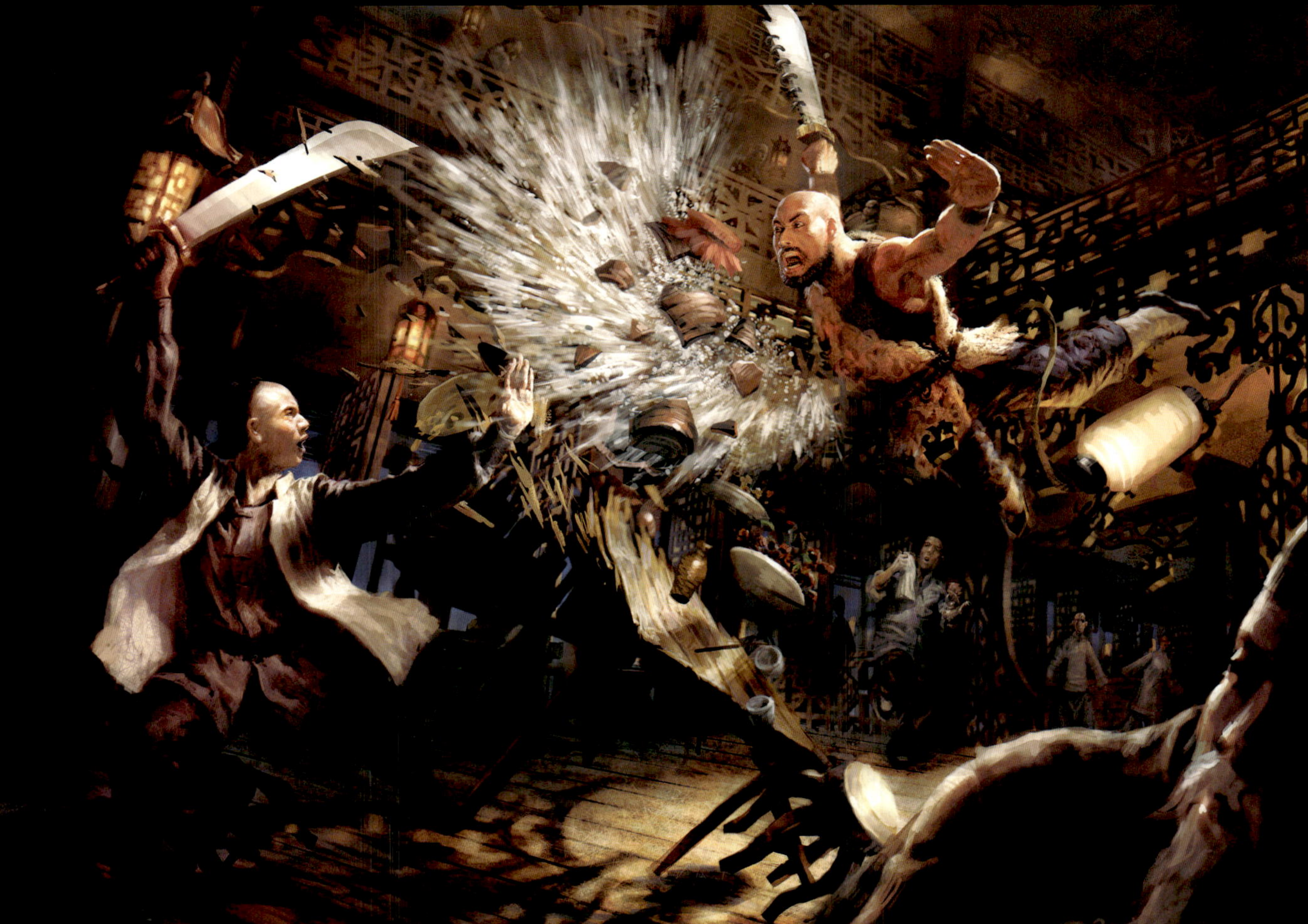

Dive Skele 2
Photoshop
Andy Park, SCEA, USA
[top]

Fight
Photoshop
Alon Chou, TAIWAN
[above]

Crow Tamer
Painter, Photoshop
Paulo Toledo, CHILE
[top]

Exodus
Photoshop
Peter Mohrbacher, USA
[right]

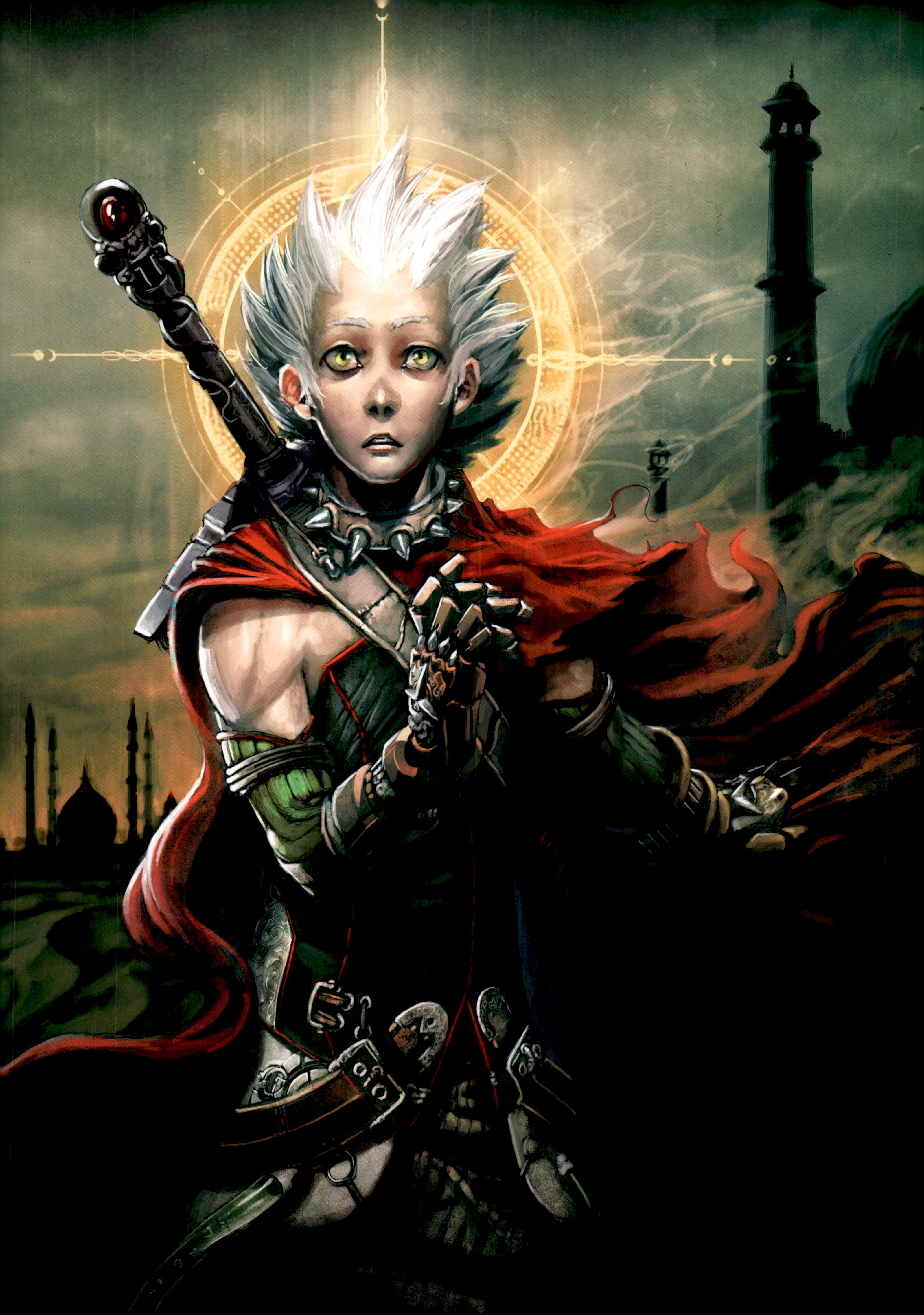

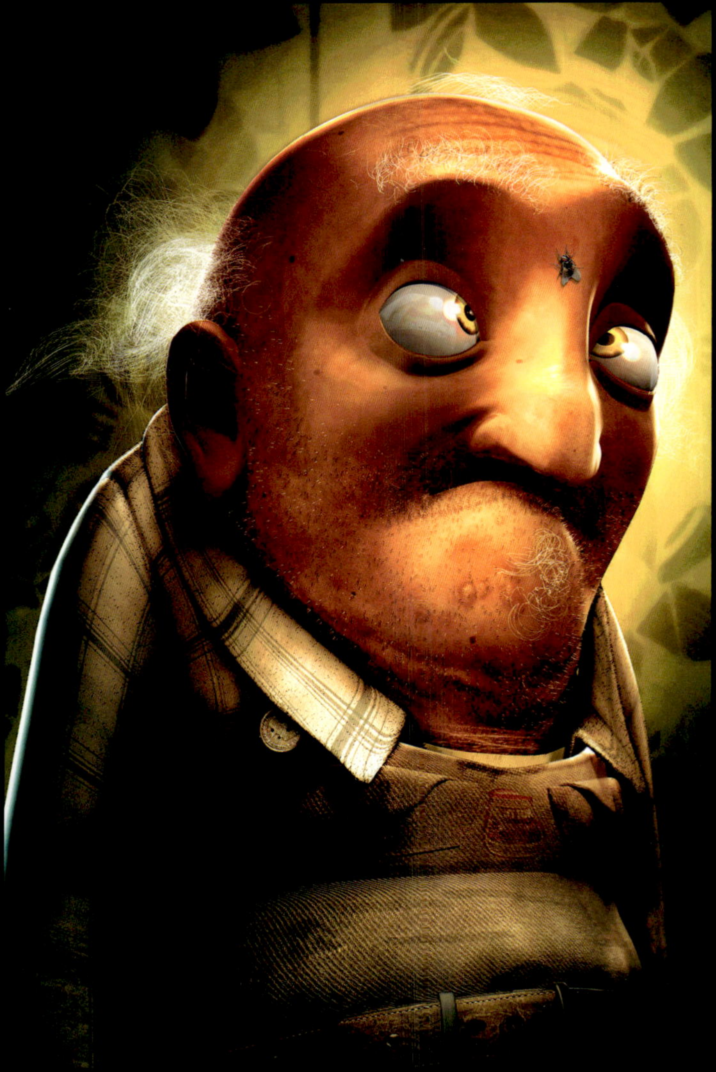

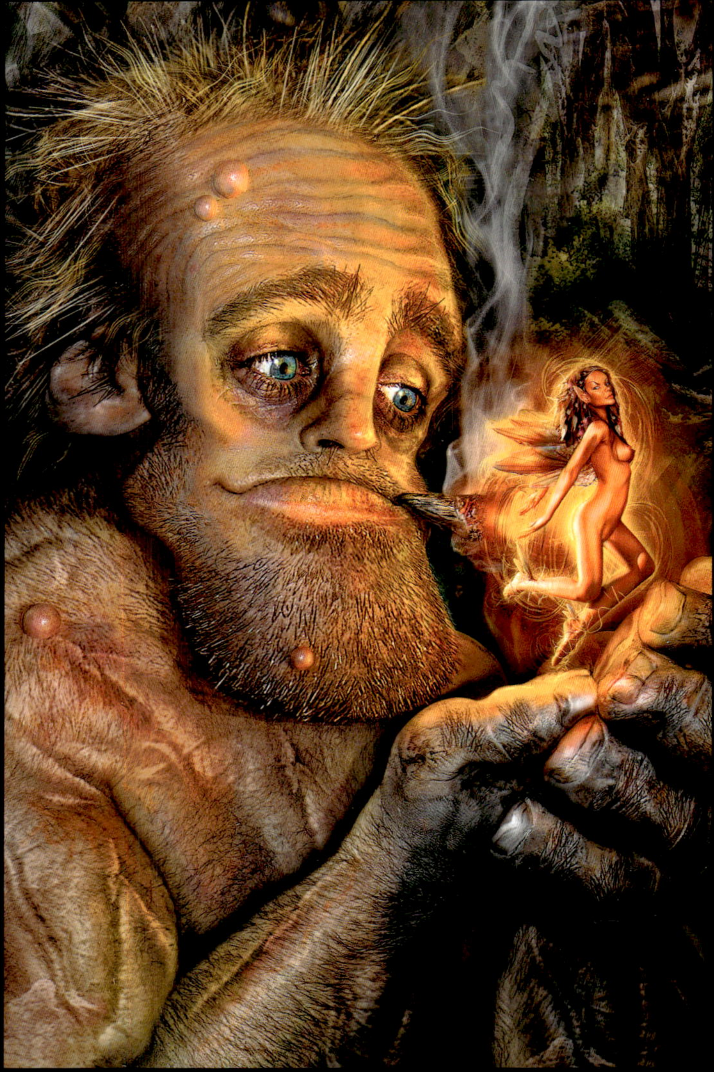

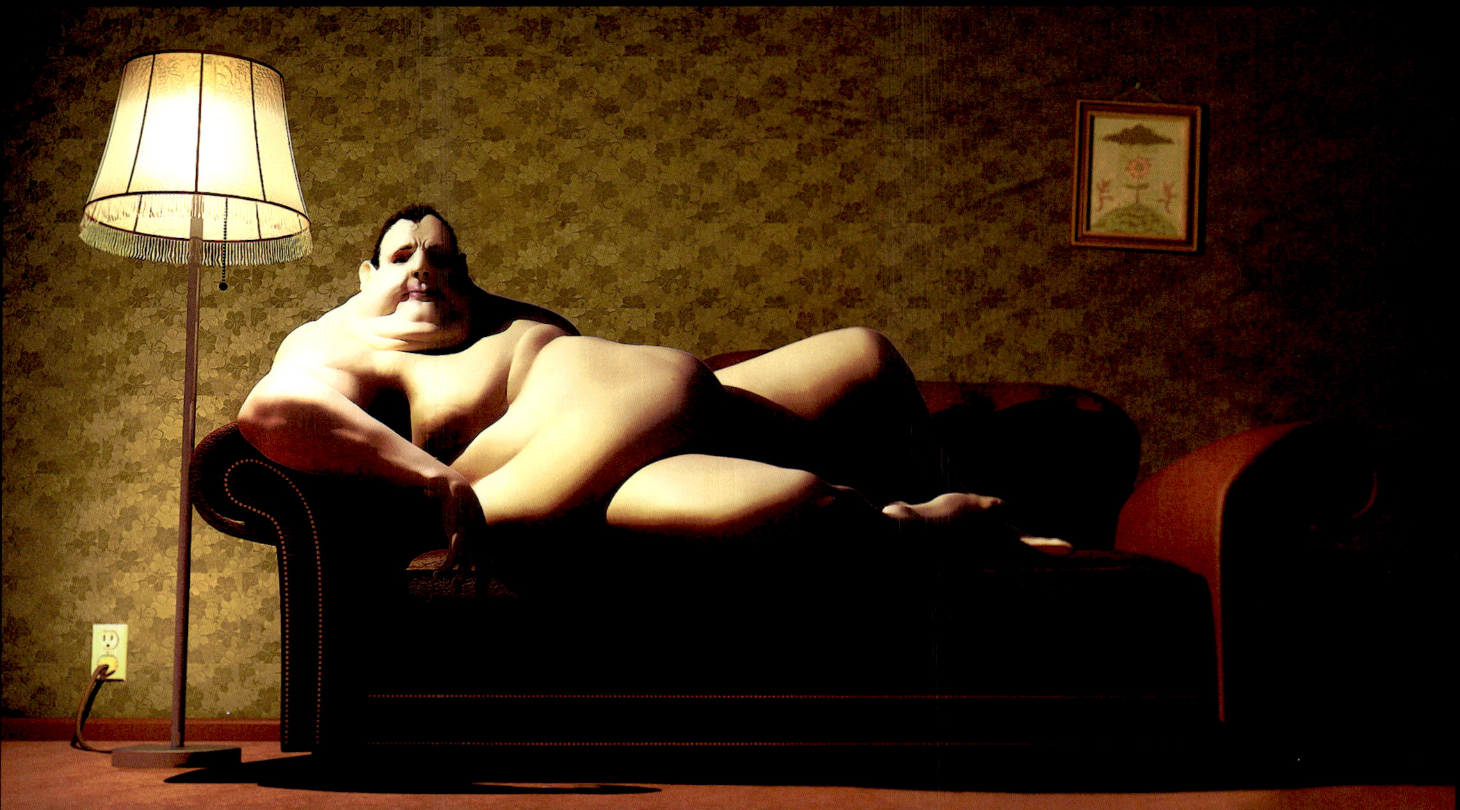

Fern 1903-1996
3ds Max, VRay
Patrick Beaulieu, CANADA
[top]

Seduction
3ds Max
Alex Nice, USA
[above]

Keep'n da faeries warm
Photoshop
Paul Roget, AUSTRALIA
[top]

Railway
Photoshop
Corey Loving, USA
[right]

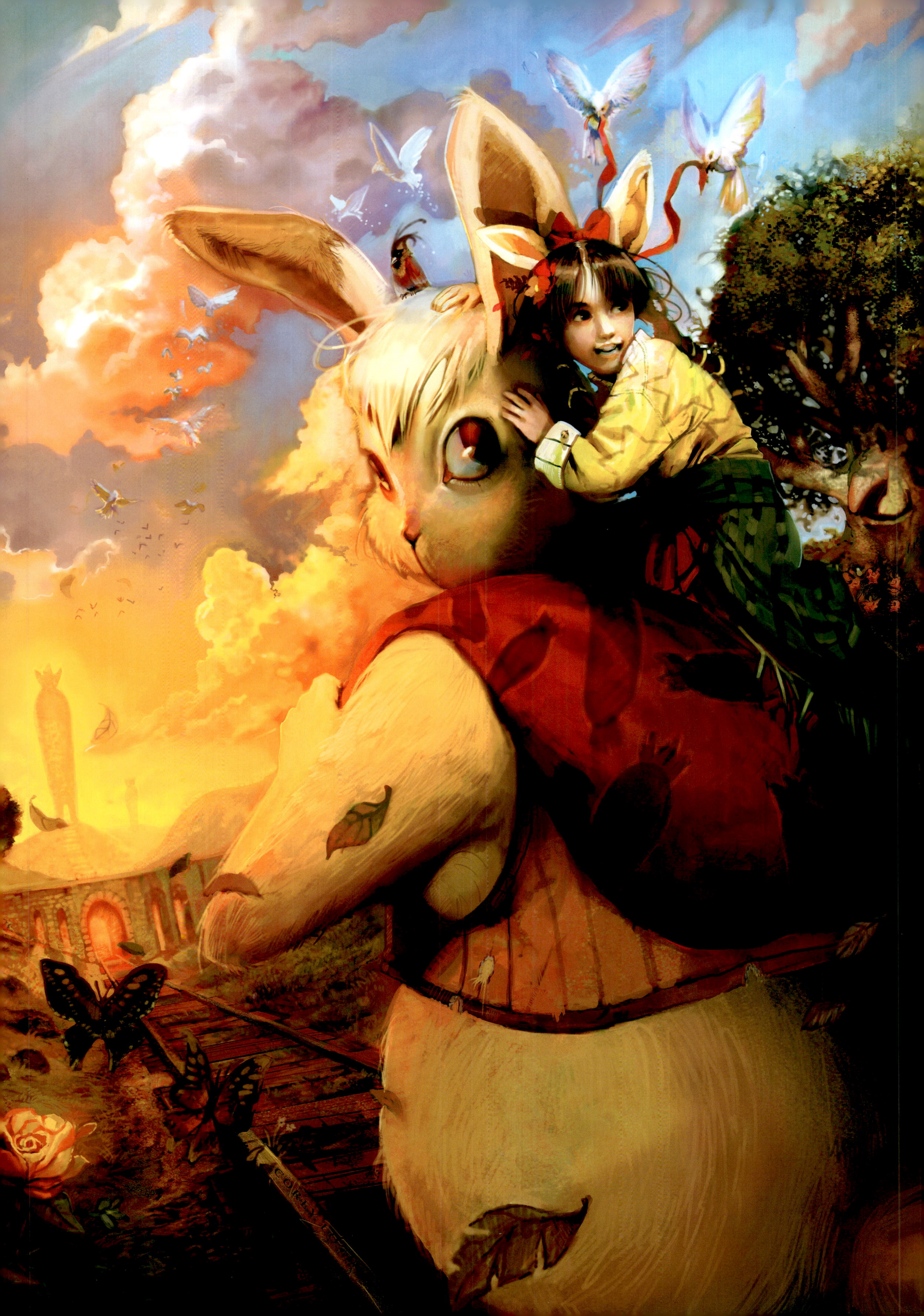

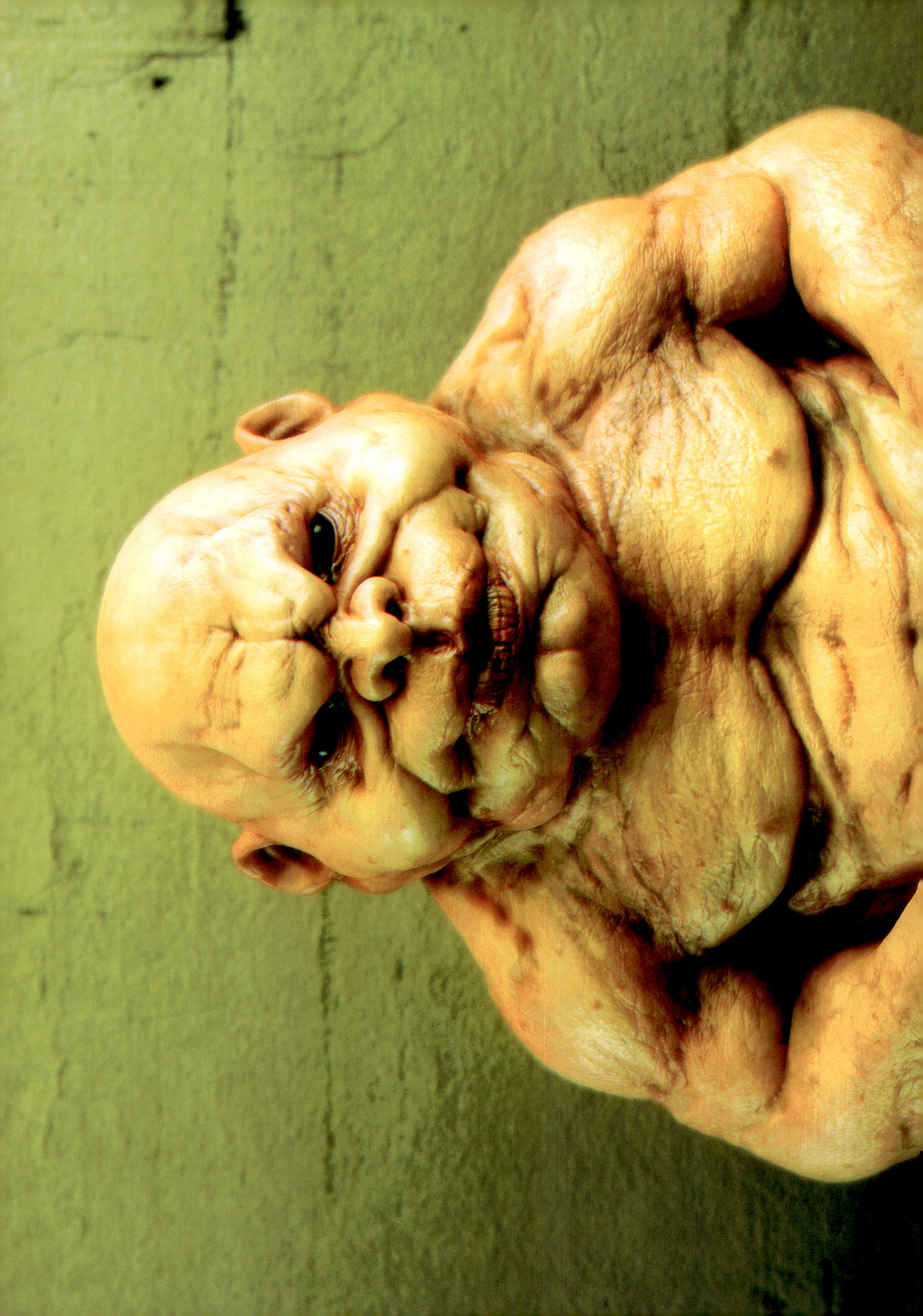

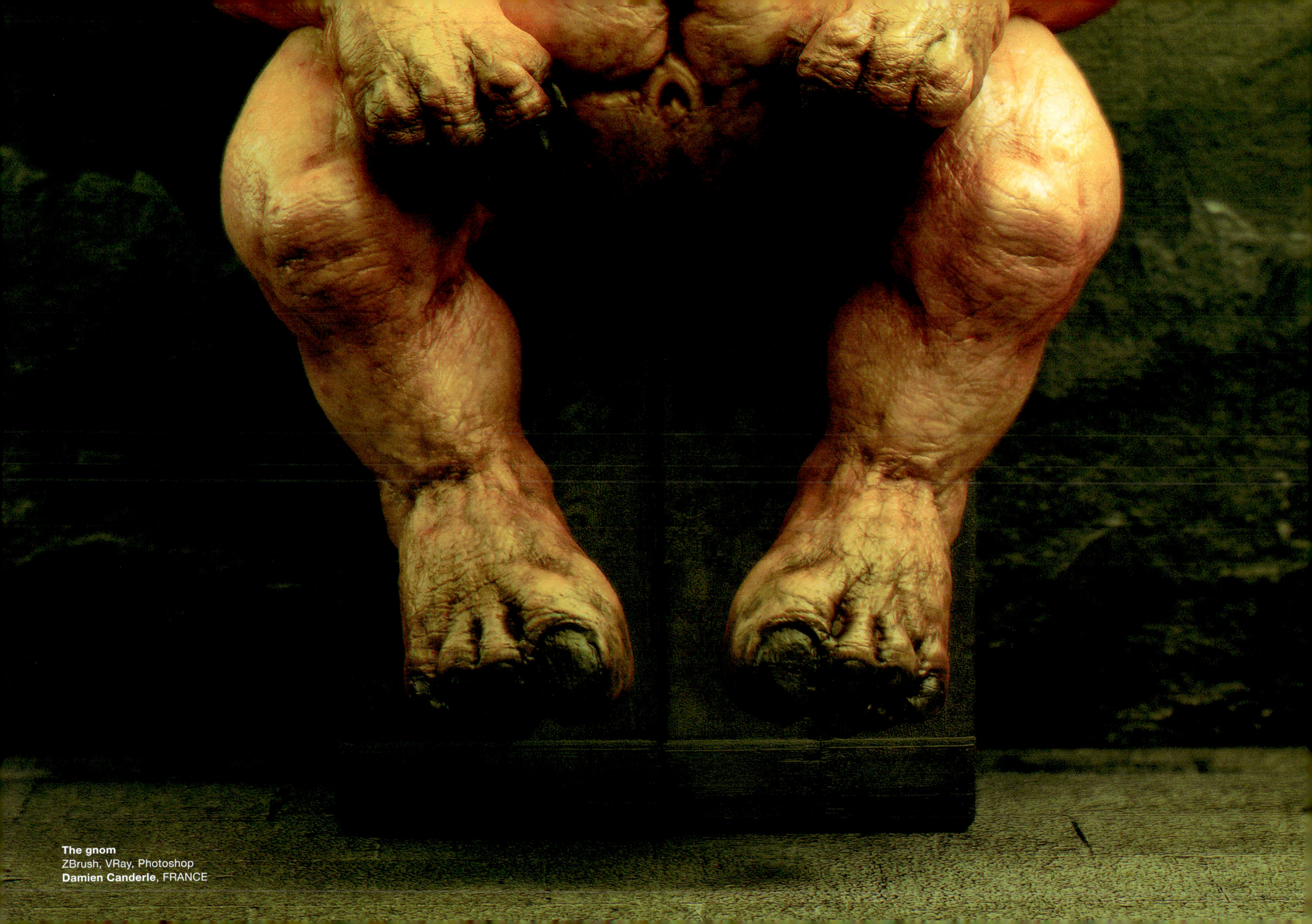

The gnom
ZBrush, VRay, Photoshop
Damien Canderle, FRANCE

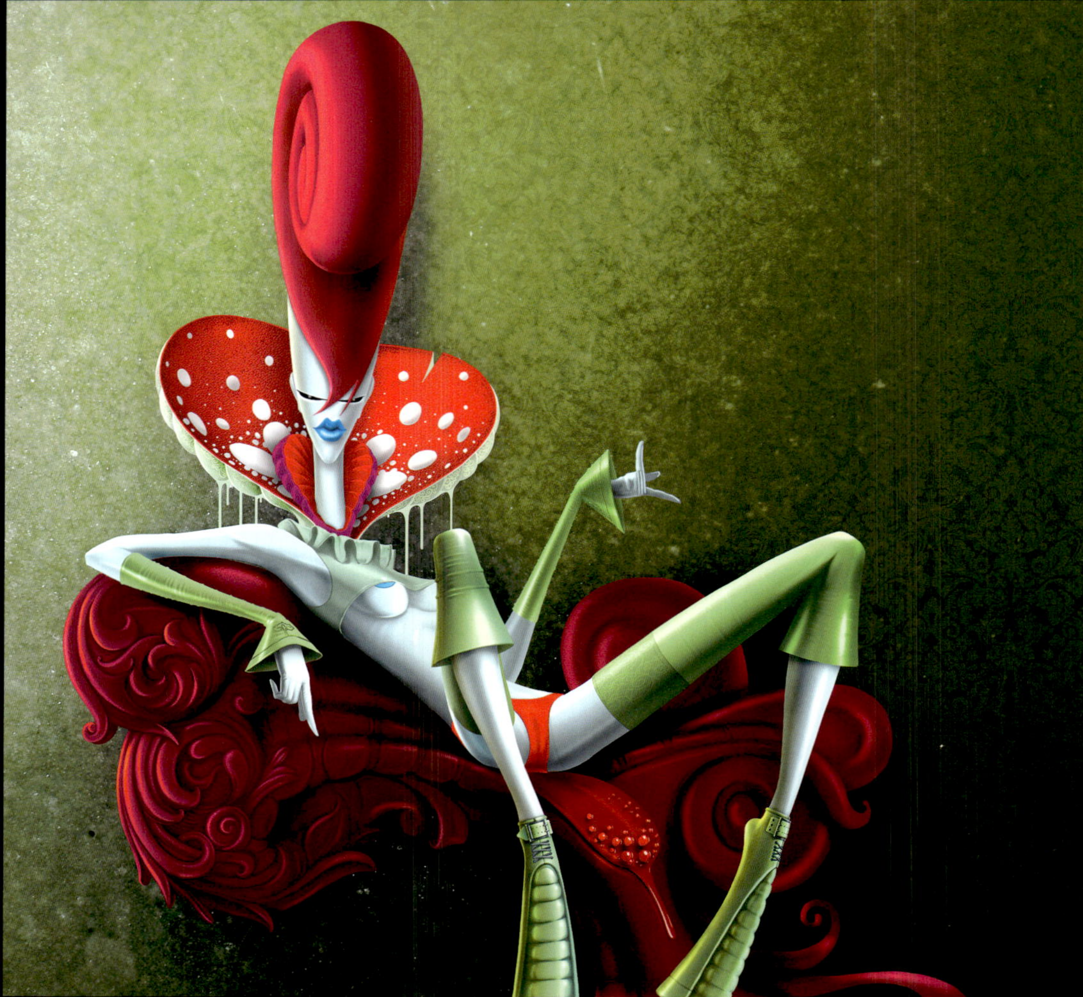

Umpyachka
Photoshop
Vladimir Tikhonov, E-SH, RUSSIA
[left]

Le Neunoeil
ZBrush, BodyPaint 3D, Photoshop
Concept: Jean-Baptiste Reynaud
Damien Canderle, FRANCE
[right]

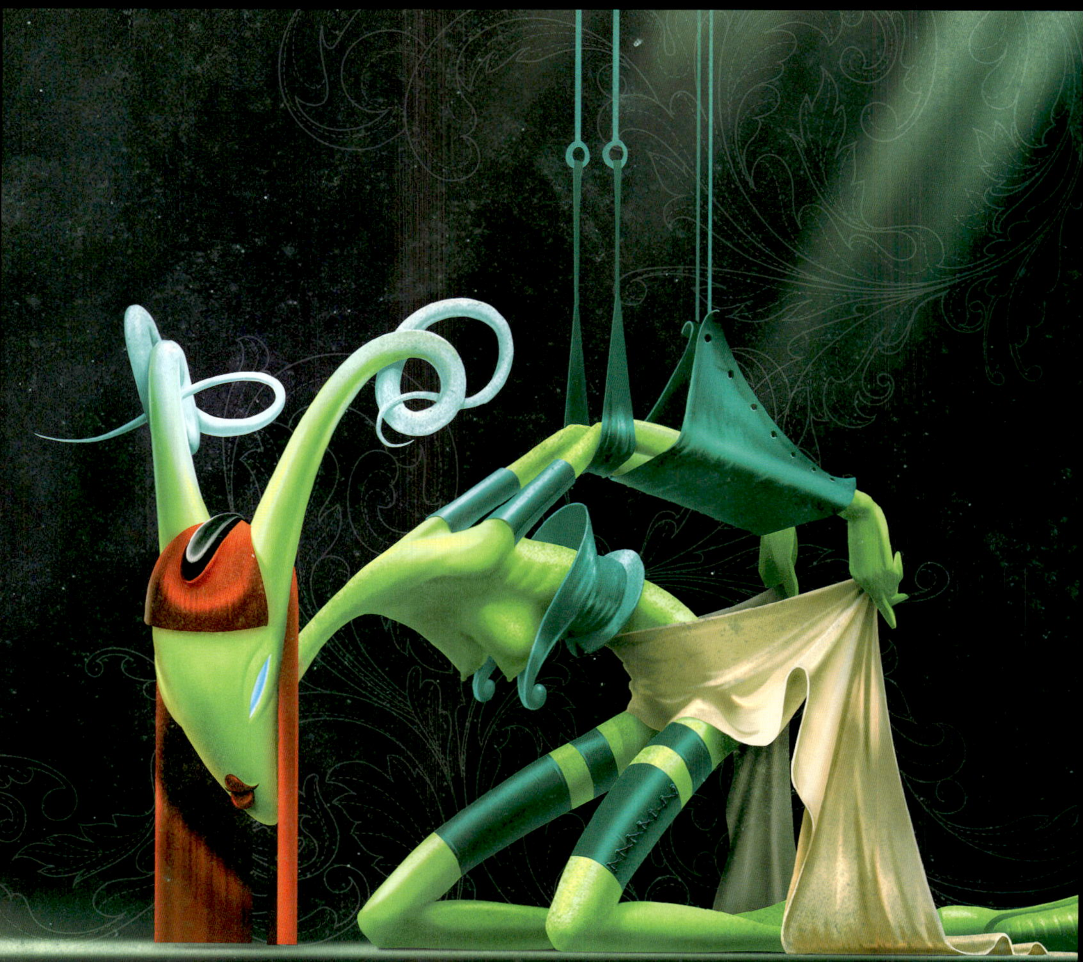

Vachka
Photoshop
Vladimir Tikhonov, E-SH, RUSSIA
[left]

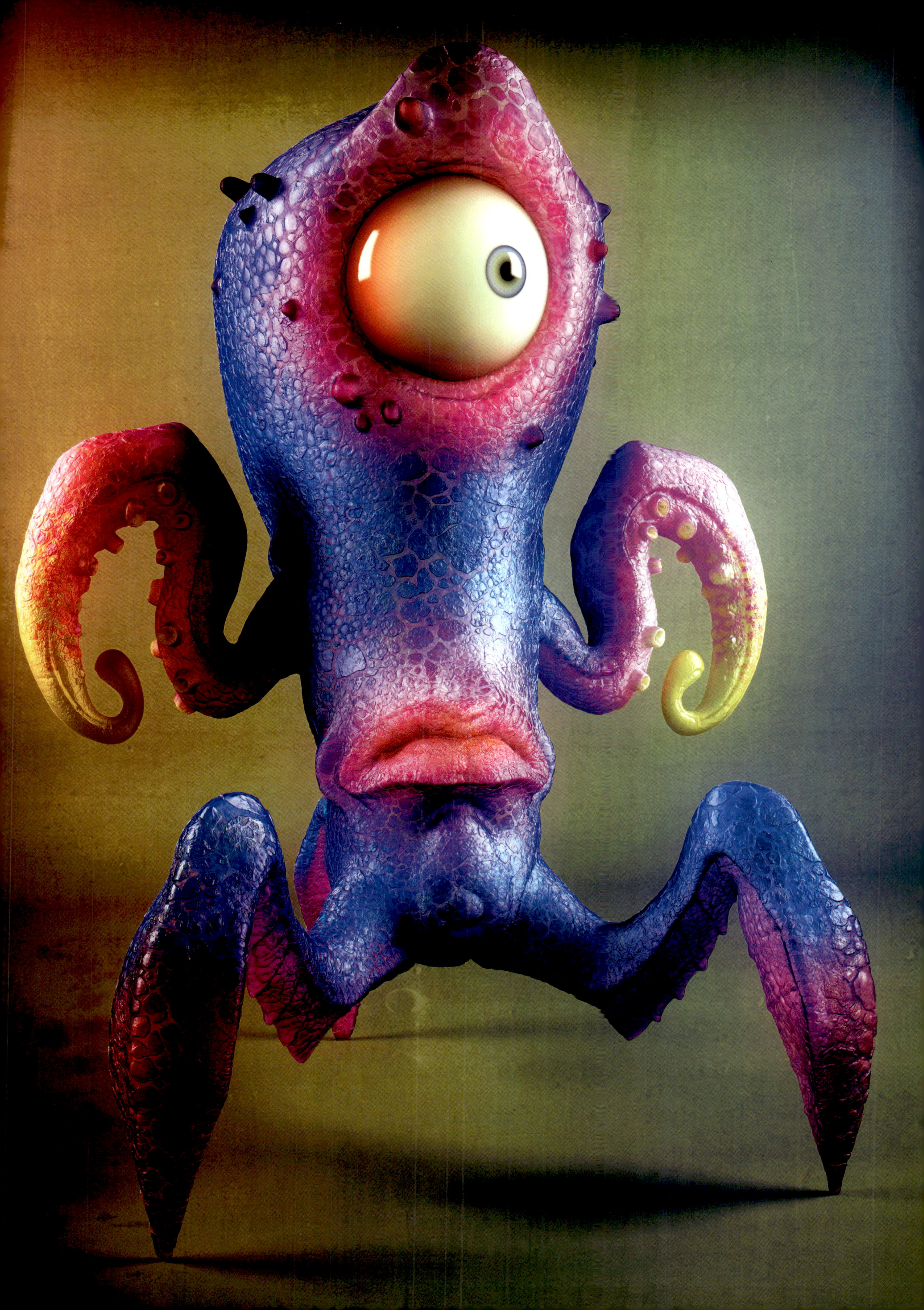

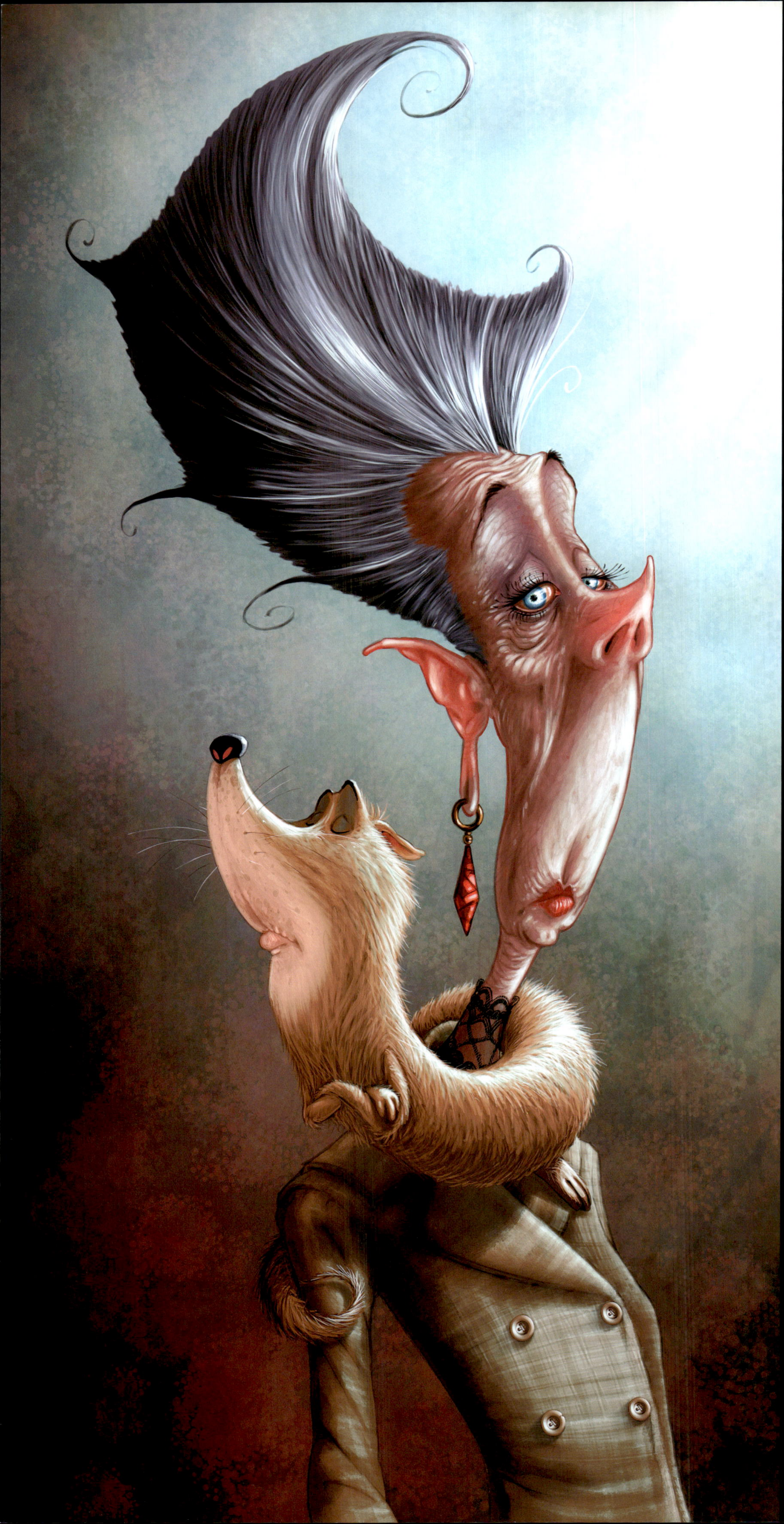

Mis 'Air'
Photoshop
Client: Advanced Photoshop Magazine
Michael van den Bosch, NETHERLANDS
[left]

The Card Player 'Mamoulian'
ZBrush, Photoshop
Inspired by Clive Barker's 'The Damnation Game.'
Leigh Bamforth, GREAT BRITAIN
[right]

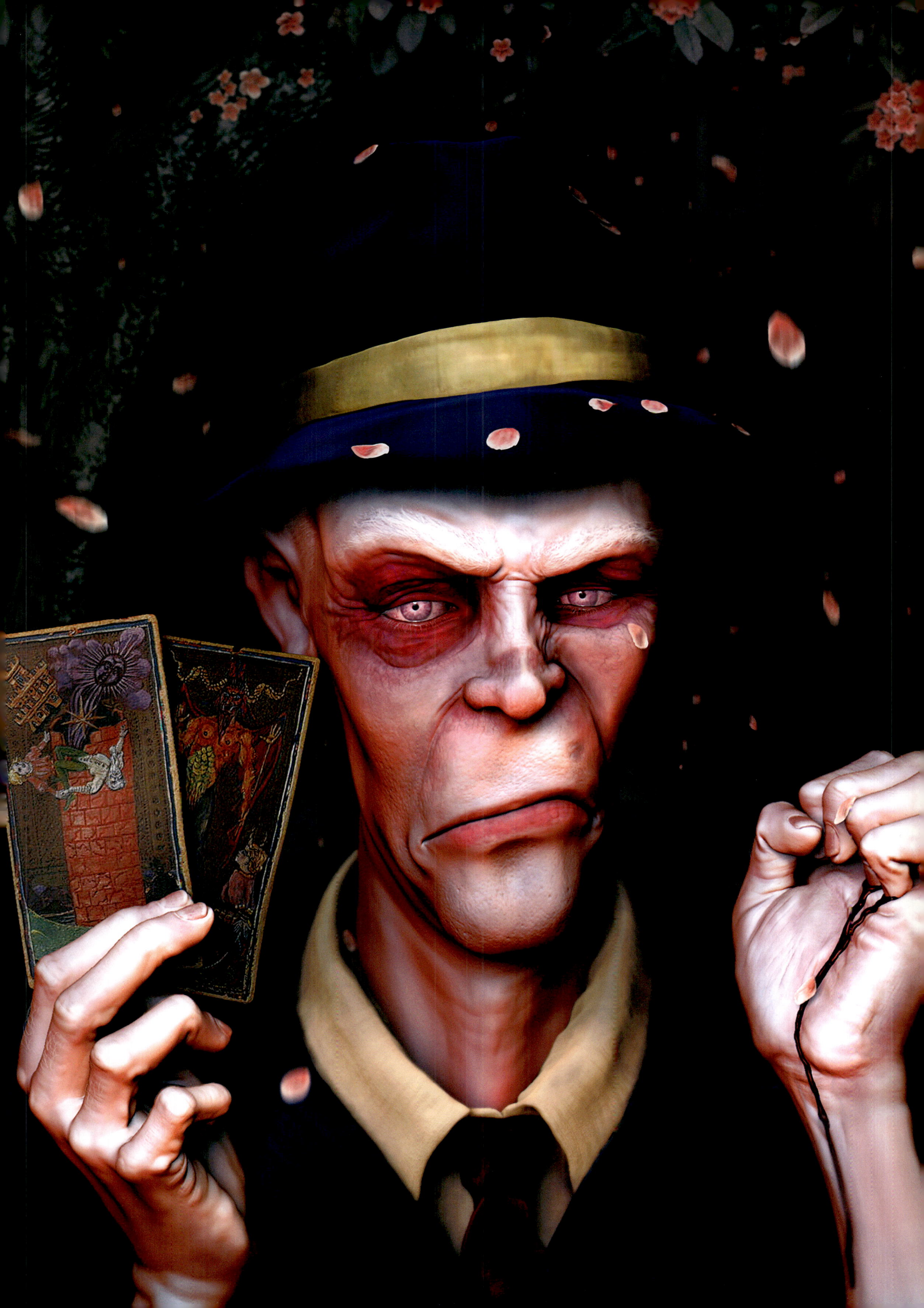

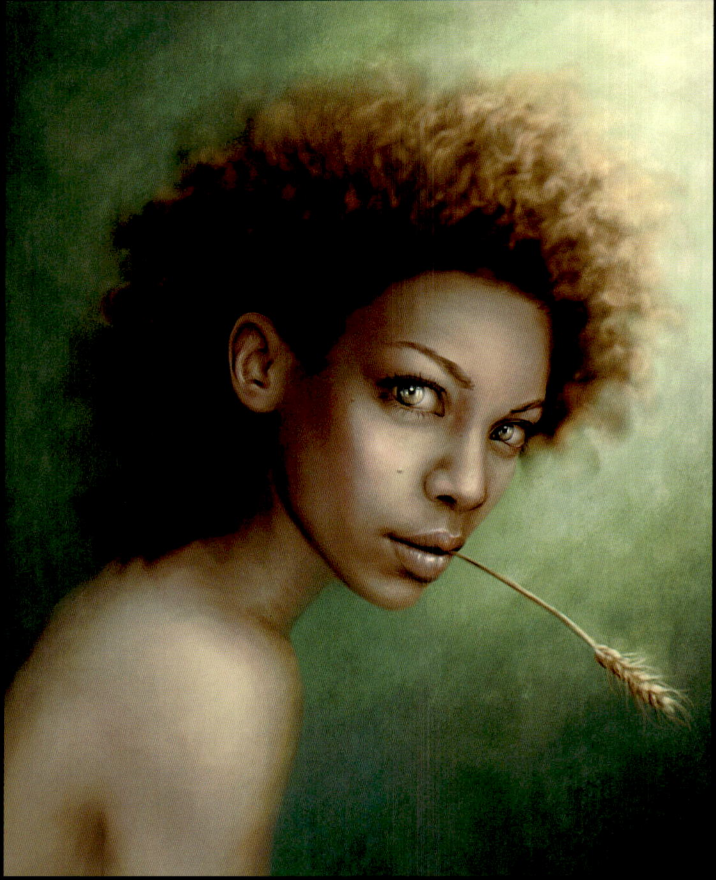

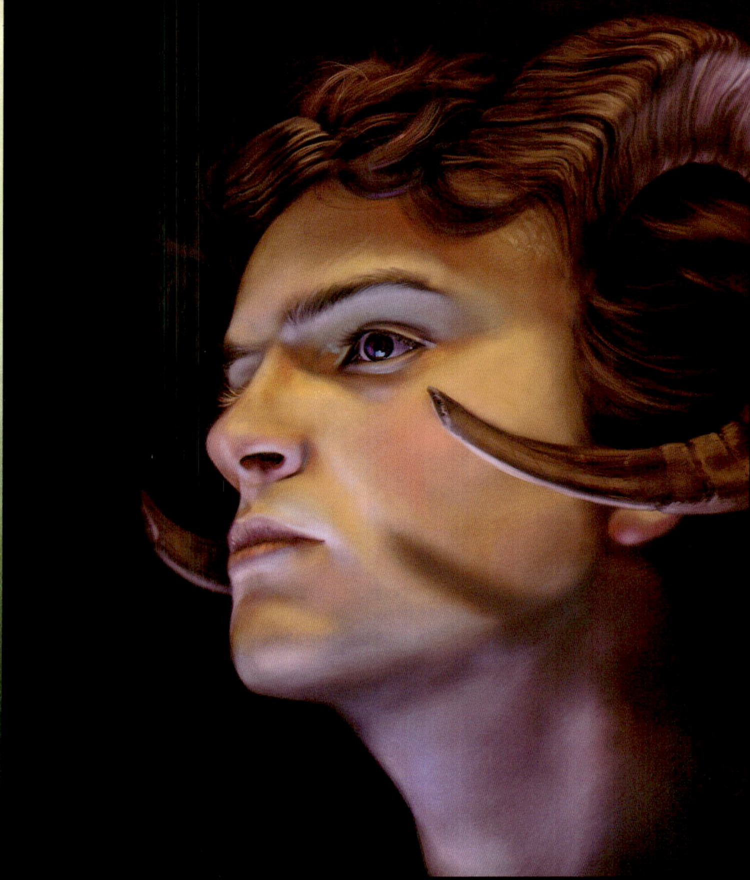

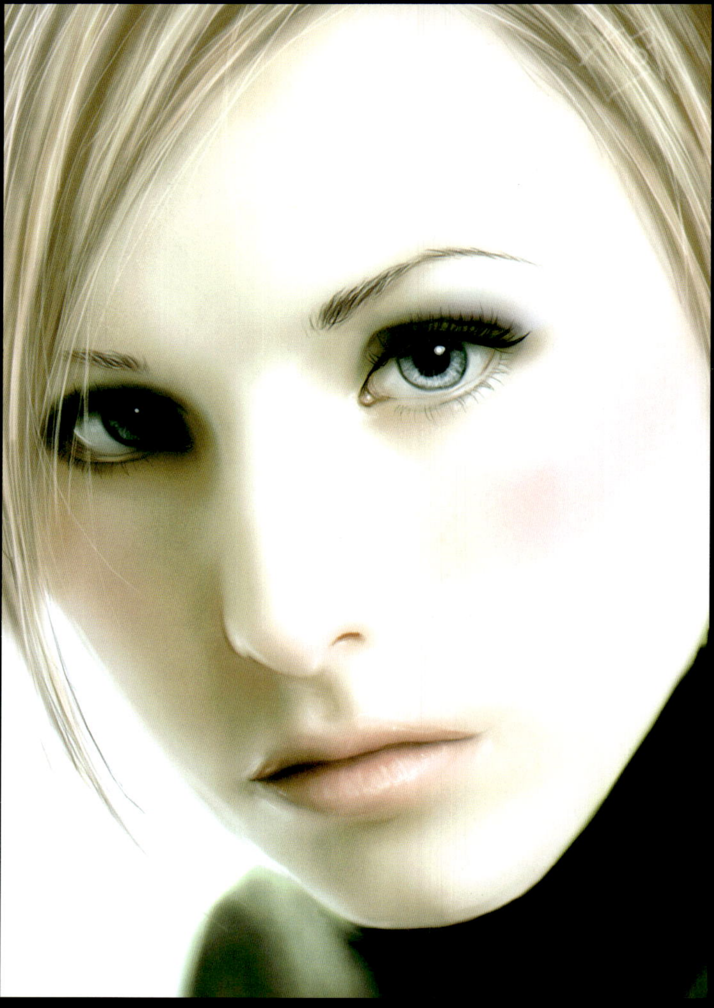

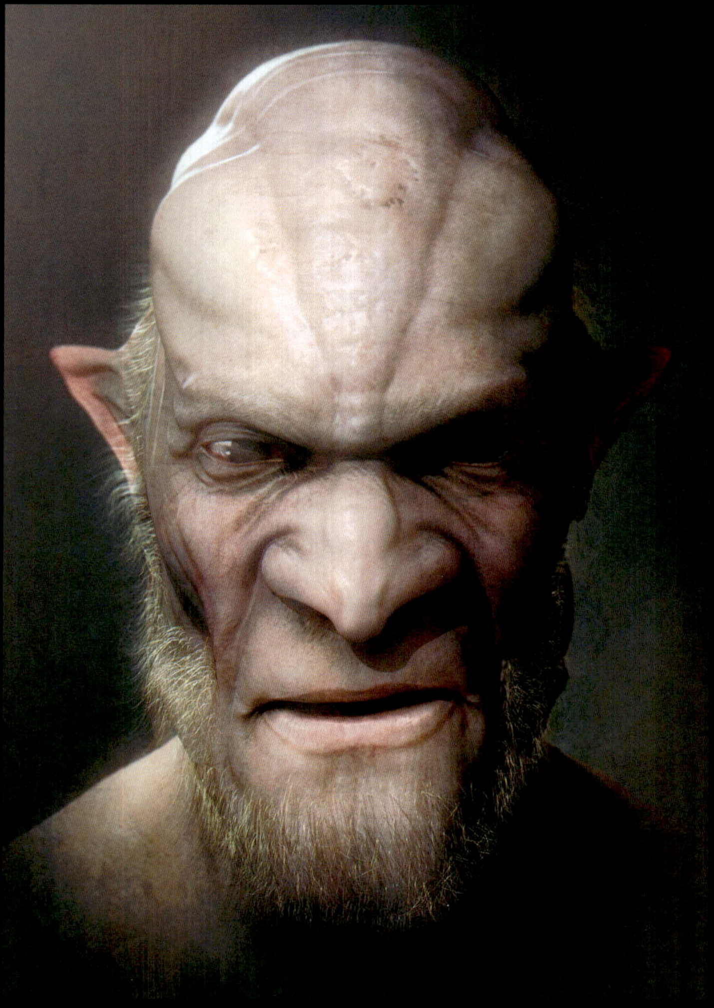

Aubadien
Painter, Photoshop
Doris Mantair, NETHERLANDS
[top]

Up close
Photoshop
Suzanne van Pelt, NETHERLANDS
[above]

The last fauna
Photoshop, Painter
Krystal Camprubi, FRANCE
[top]

The mirror
3ds Max, ZBrush, Photoshop
Sergio Santos, SPAIN
[above]

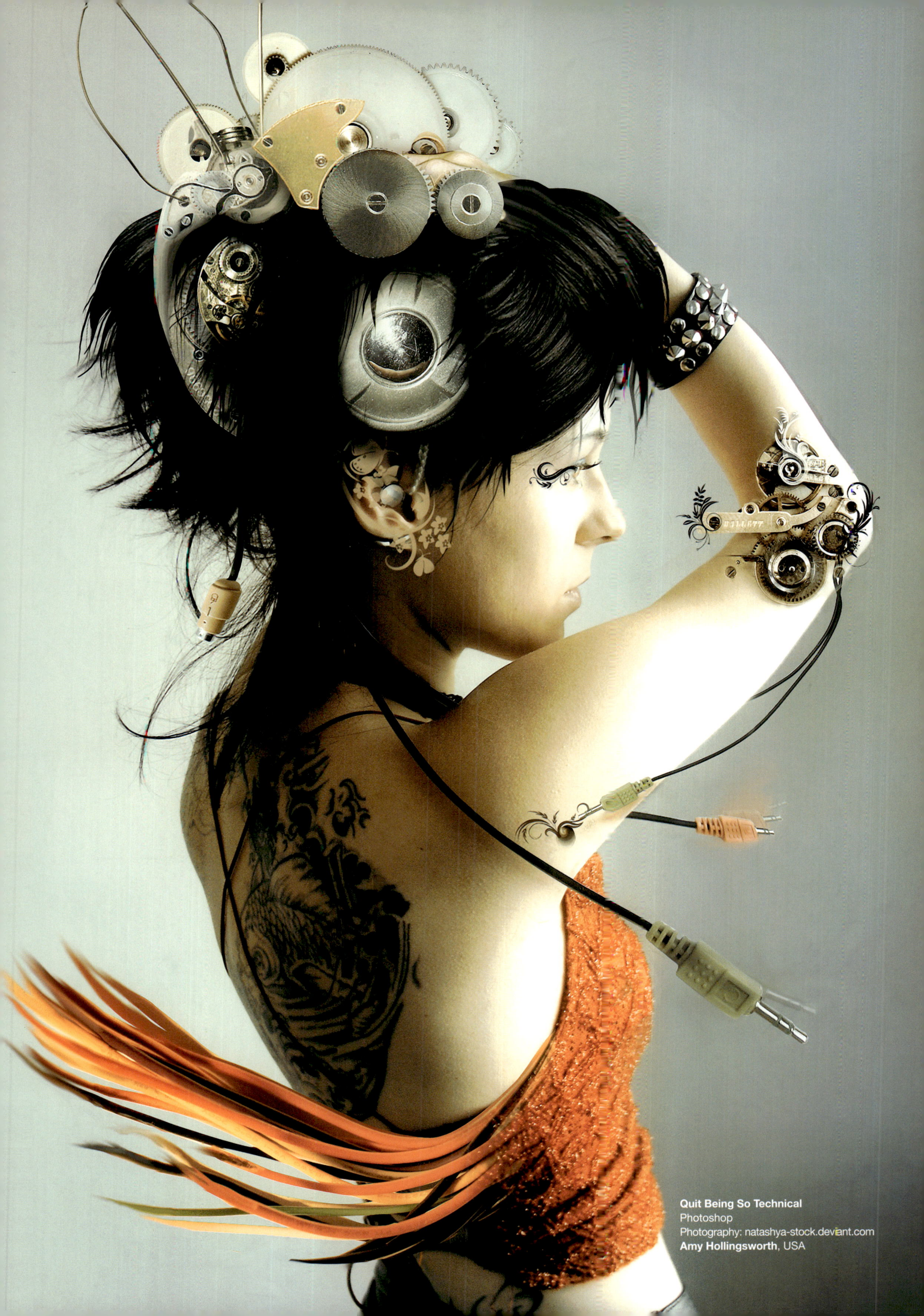

Quit Being So Technical
Photoshop
Photography: natashya-stock.deviant.com
Amy Hollingsworth, USA

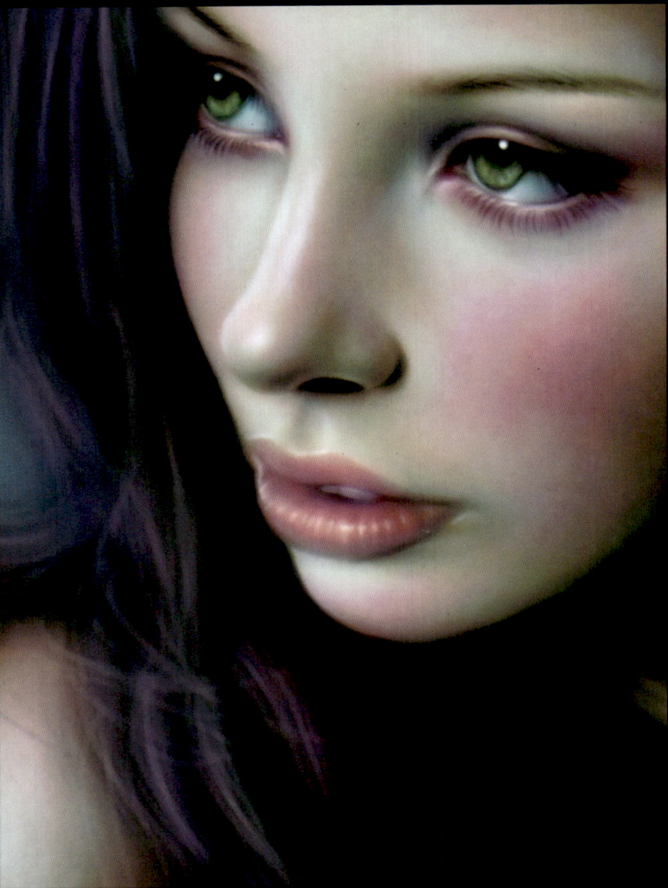

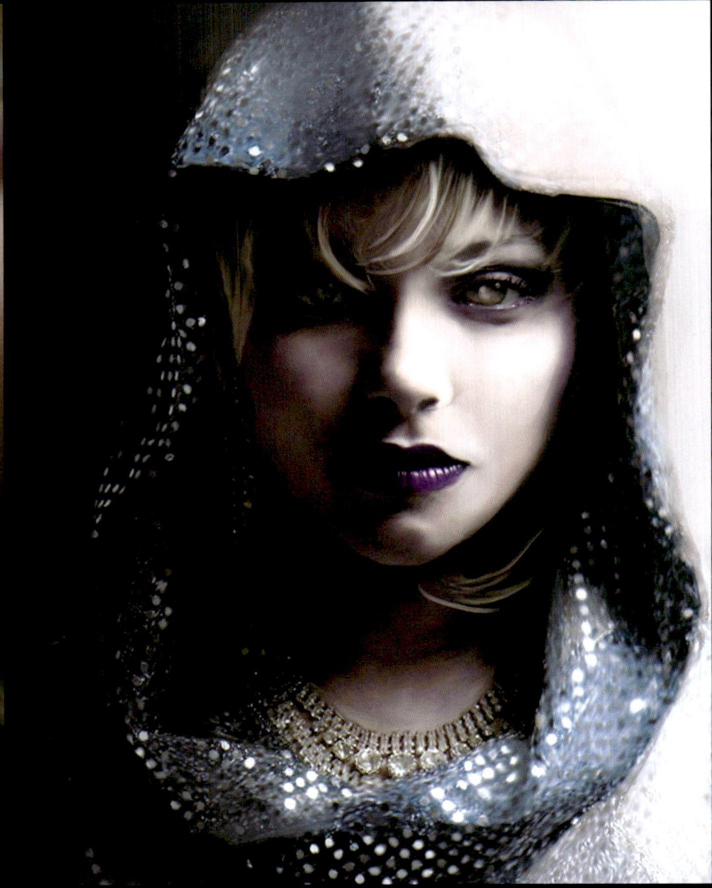

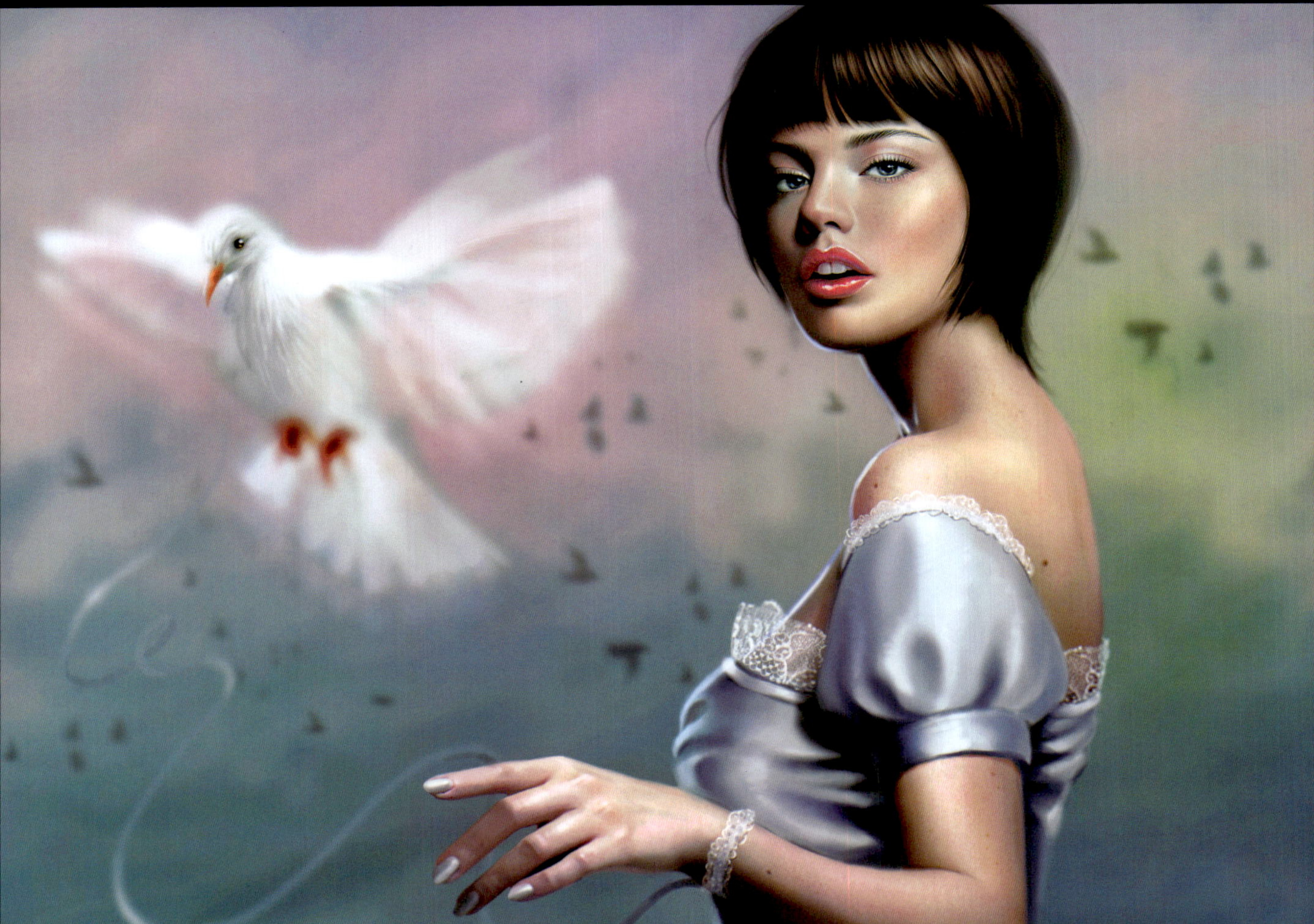

Regard
Painter, Photoshop, ArtWeaver
Michael Hideux,
FRANCE
[top]

Freedom
Photoshop
Hoang Le,
VIETNAM
[above]

Dawn
Photoshop, Paint Shop Pro
Photographer: Thomas Brucher
Bente Schlick, GERMANY
[top]

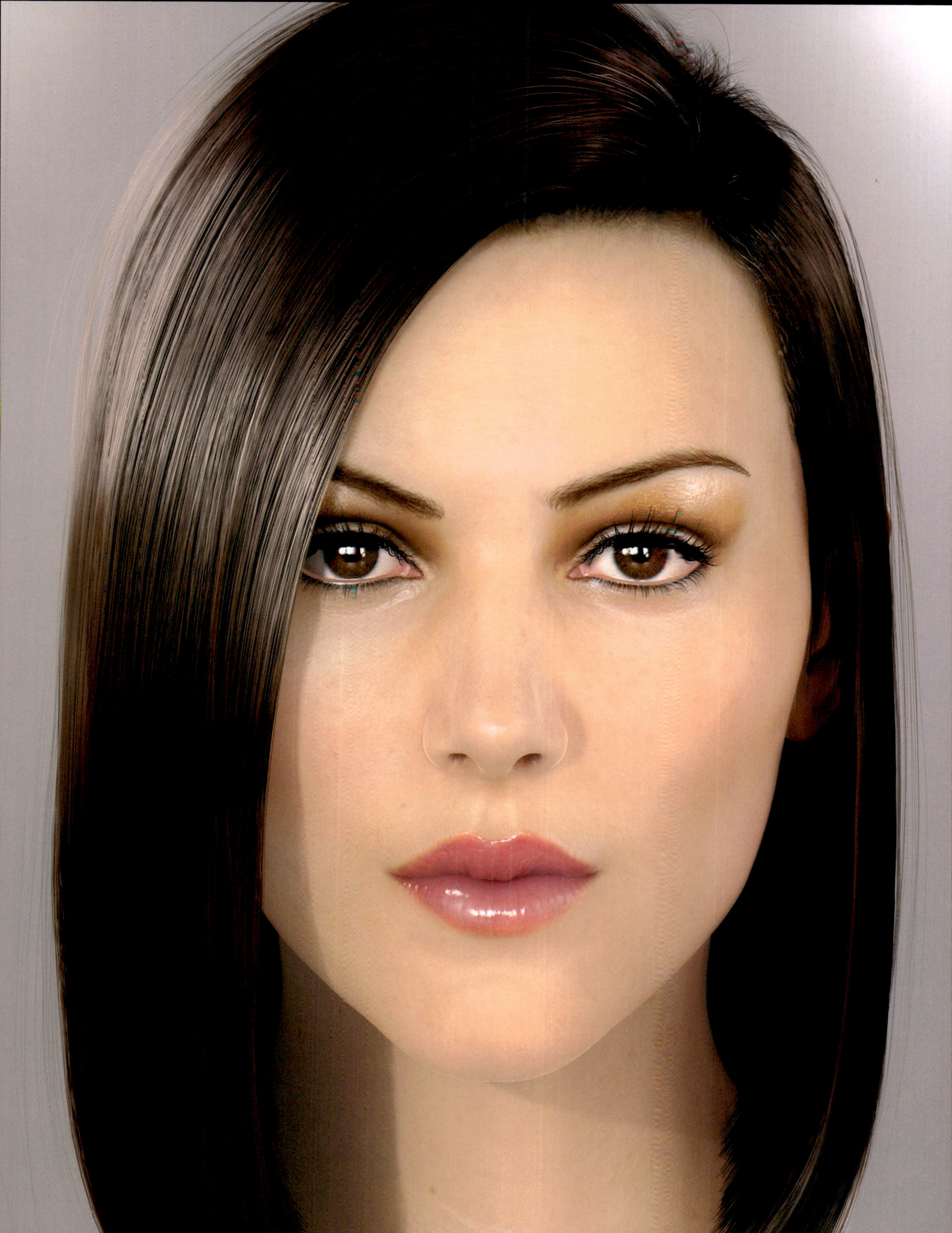

Cortina Digital Woman #1
Maya, ZBrush, BodyPaint 3D, mental ray
Francisco A. Cortina, USA

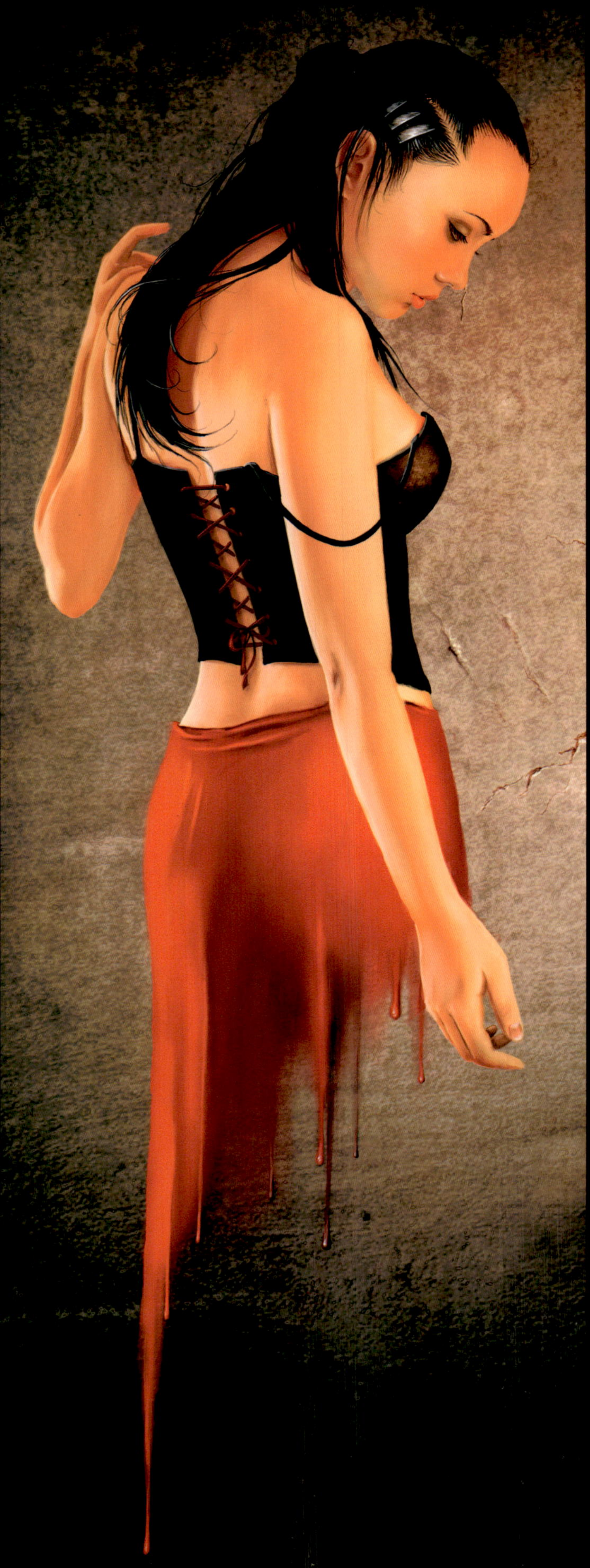

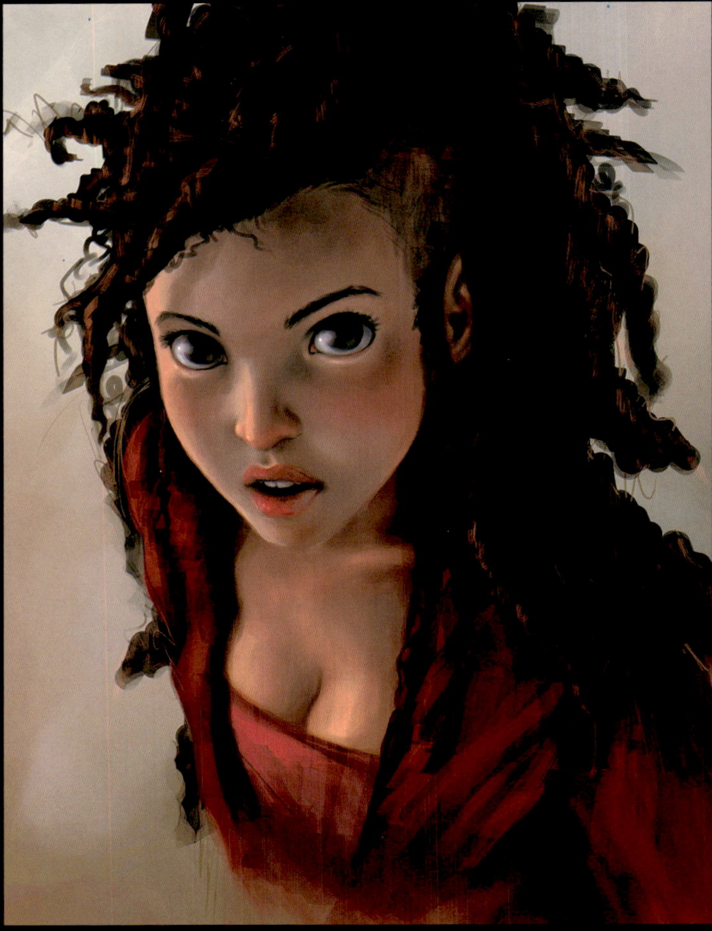

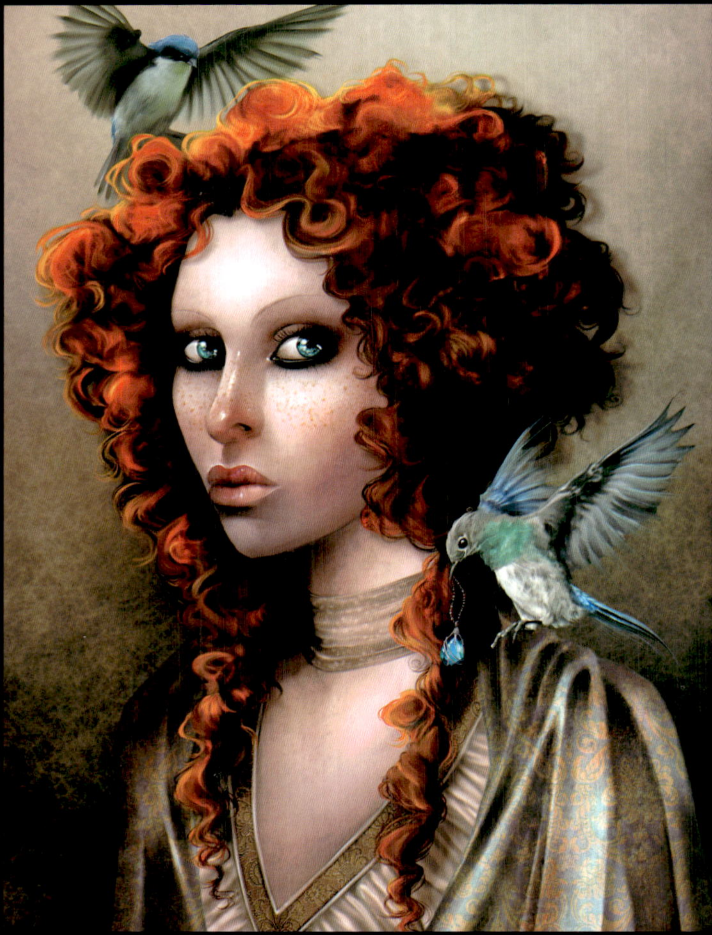

Lady
Photoshop
Benjamin Friess,
FRANCE
[above]

Lolita
Photoshop
Daniela Uhlig,
GERMANY
[top]

Unspoken
Photoshop
Client: .PSD magazine
Gracjana Zielinska, POLAND
[above]

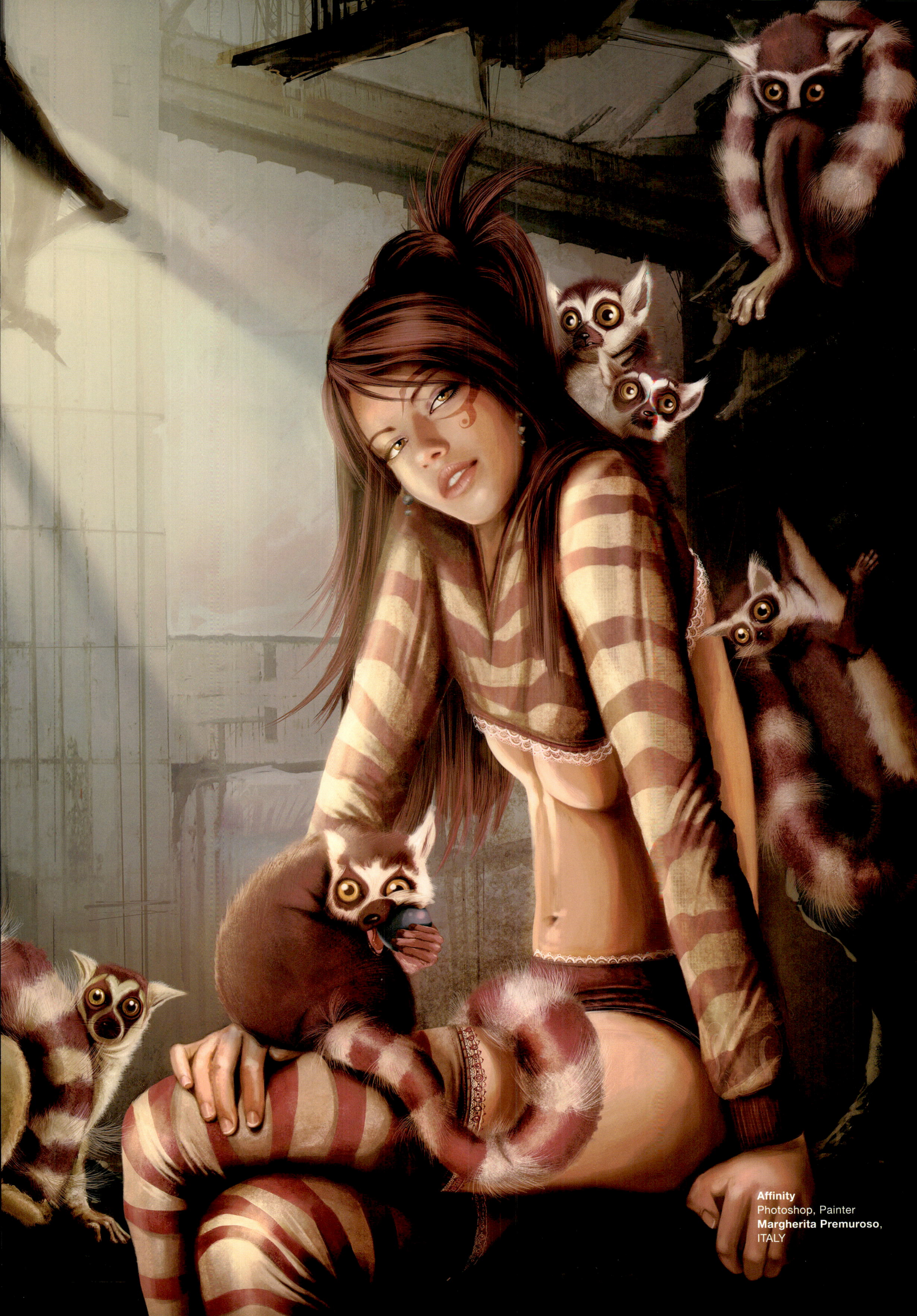

Affinity
Photoshop, Painter
Margherita Premuroso, ITALY

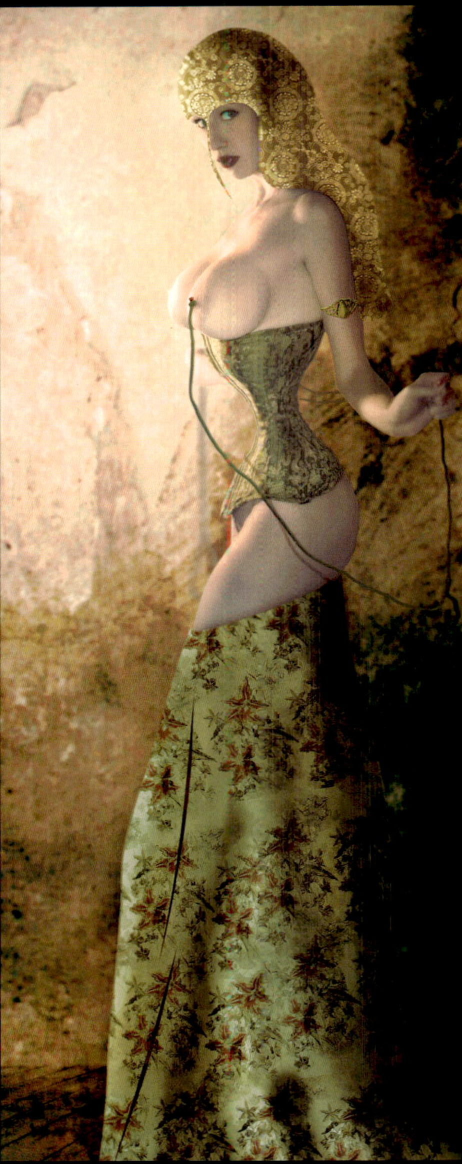

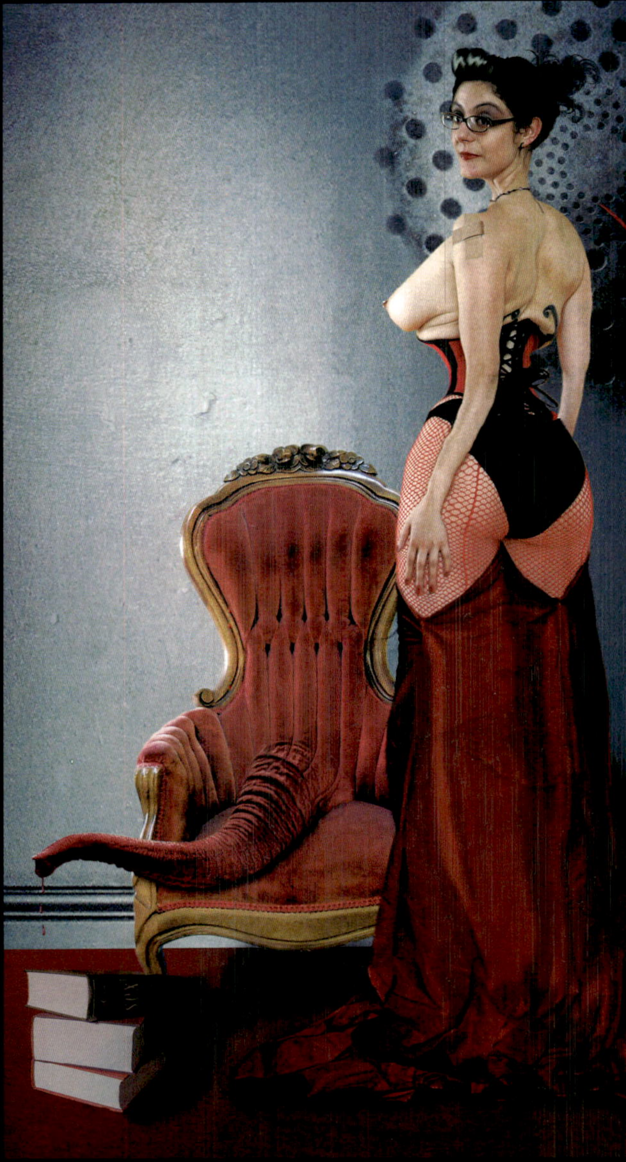

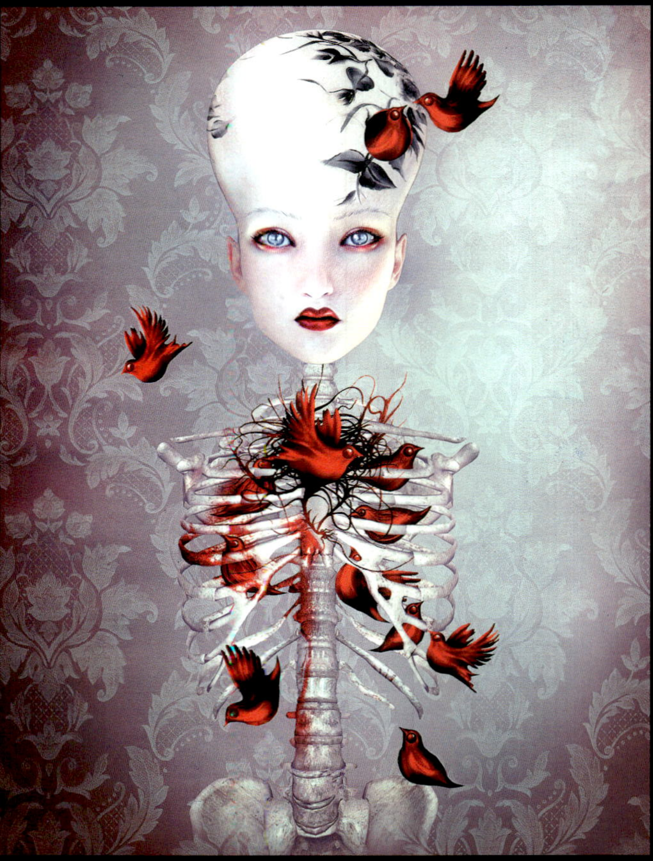

Natalie portrait
Photoshop
Japi Honoo, ITALY
[top left]

Audacia Ray portrait
Photoshop
Japi Honoo, ITALY
[above]

Lady of Broken Hearts
Photoshop, Poser
Client: Master Creating Game Studio
Natalie Shau, LITHUANIA
[left]

Magnolia
Photoshop
Dorache Liliana, ROMANIA
[right]

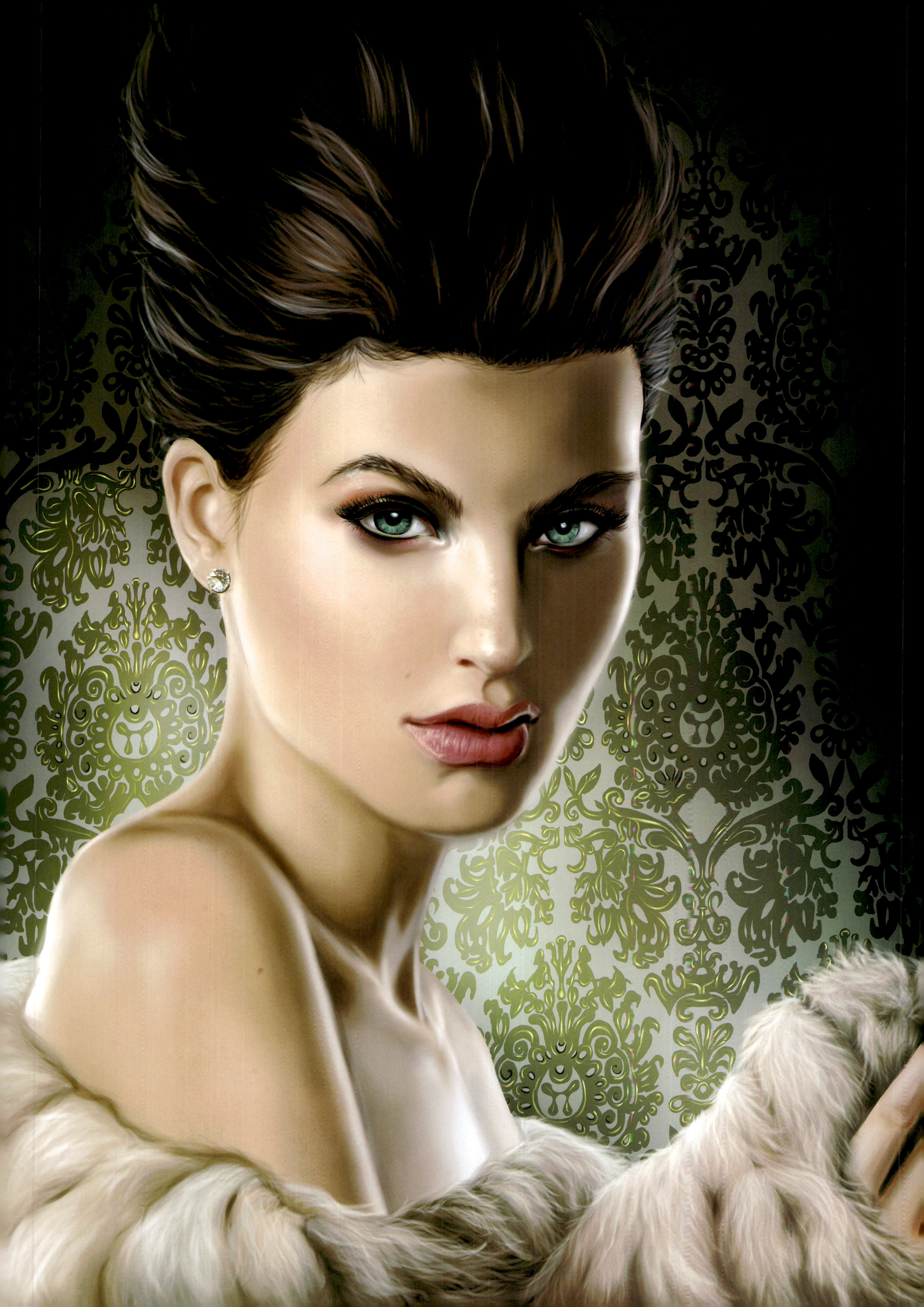

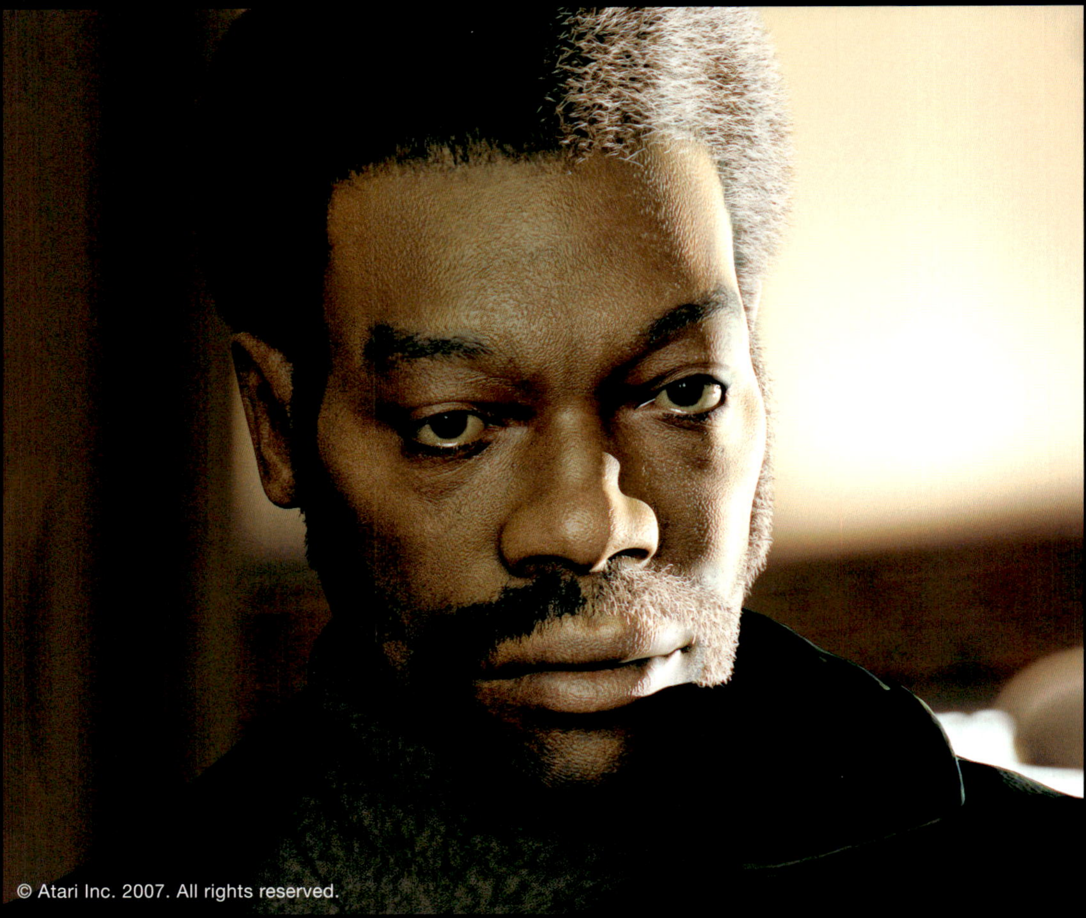

Bishop
LightWave 3D, Fusion
Client: Reflections/Atari Inc.
Richard Wright, GREAT BRITAIN
[left]

The artist himself
Maya, ZBrush, Photoshop, mental ray
Piotr Fox Wysocki, POLAND
[right]

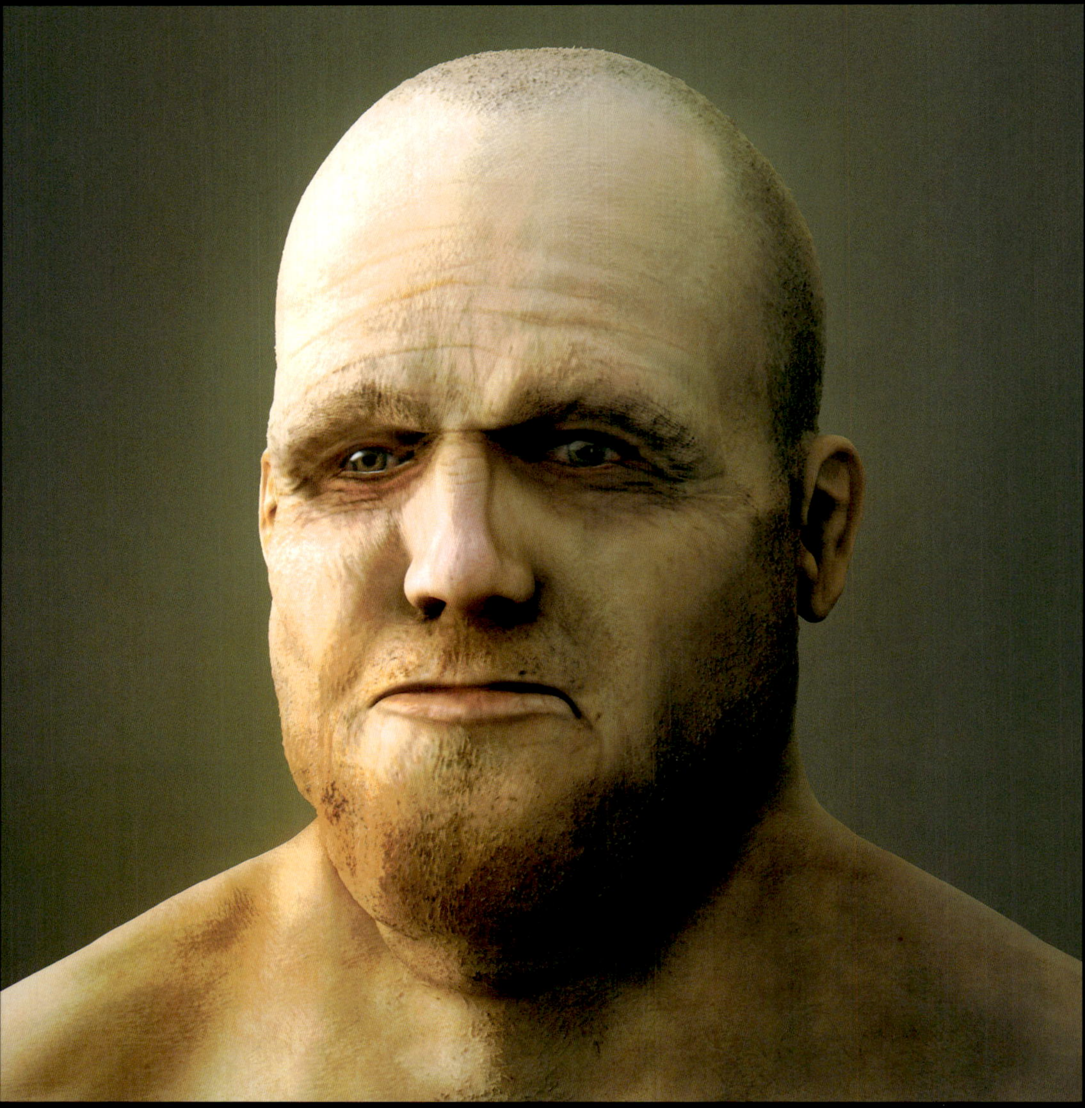

Colosus
modo, Mudbox, Photoshop
Jean Christophe Largillier, FRANCE
[left]

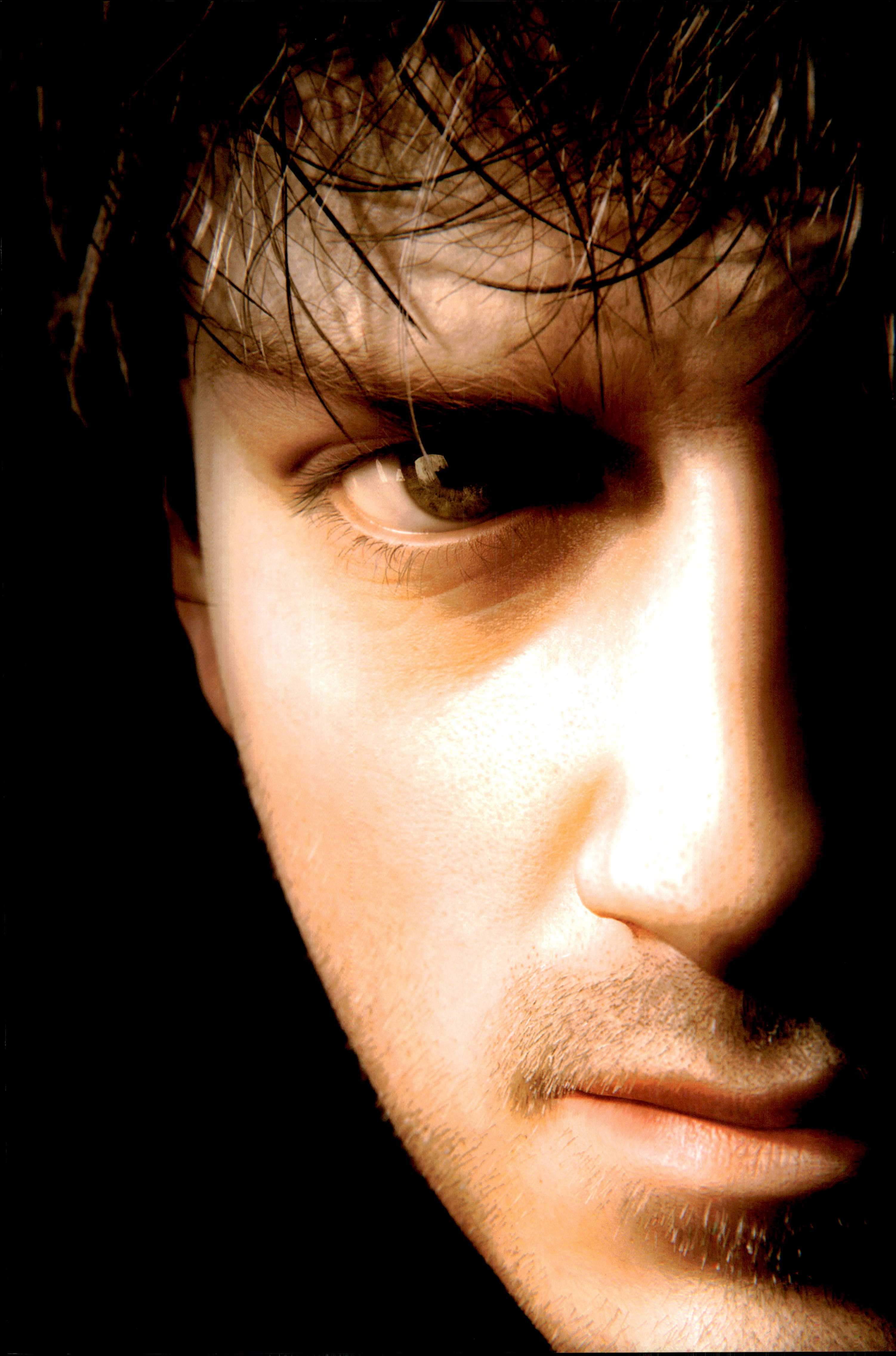

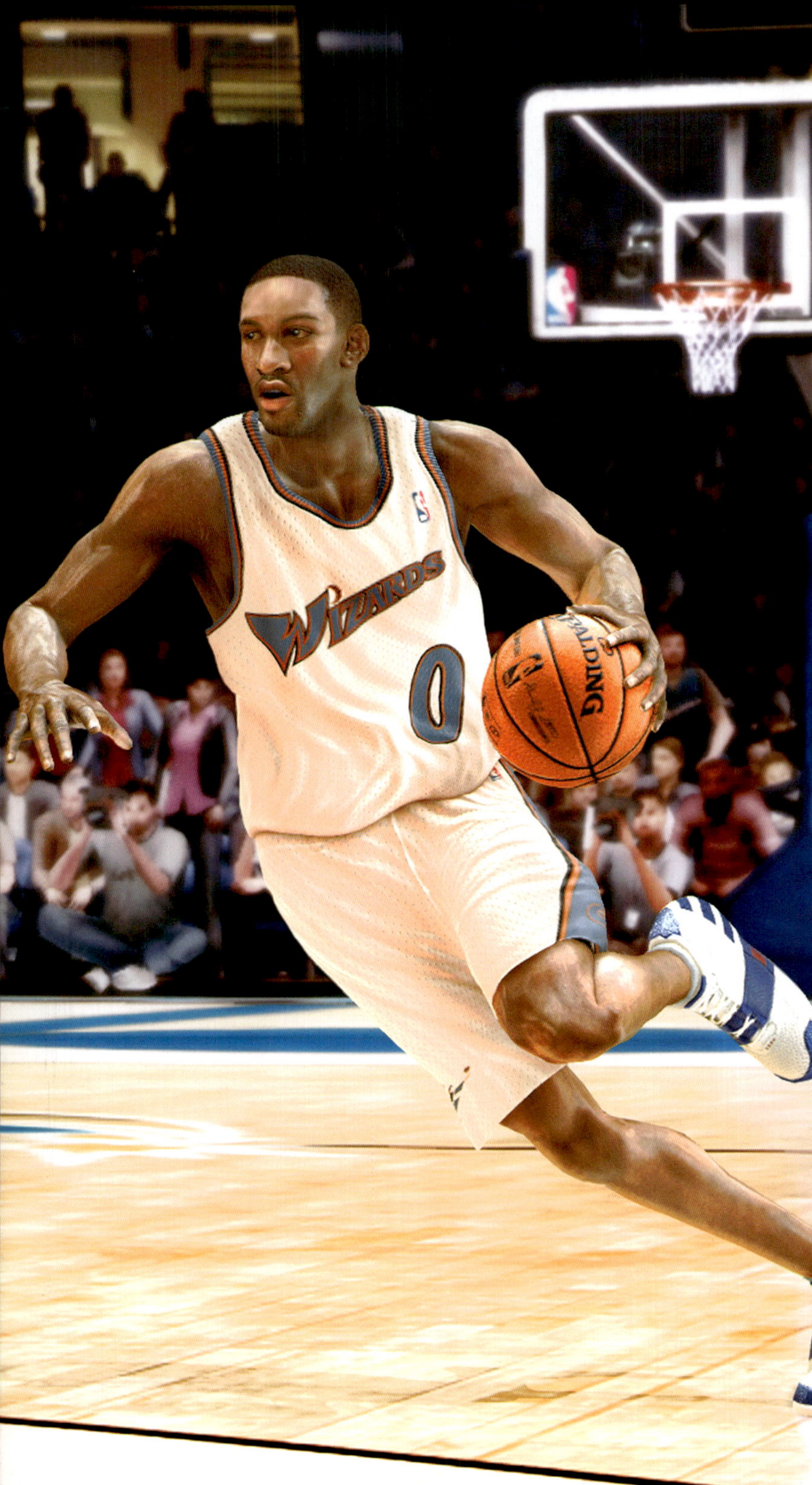

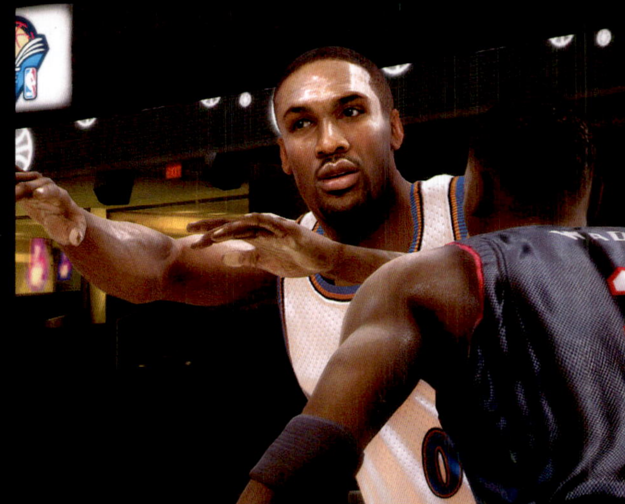

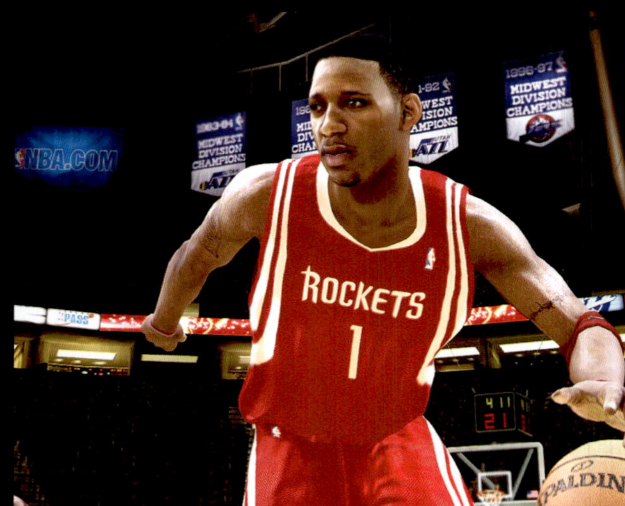

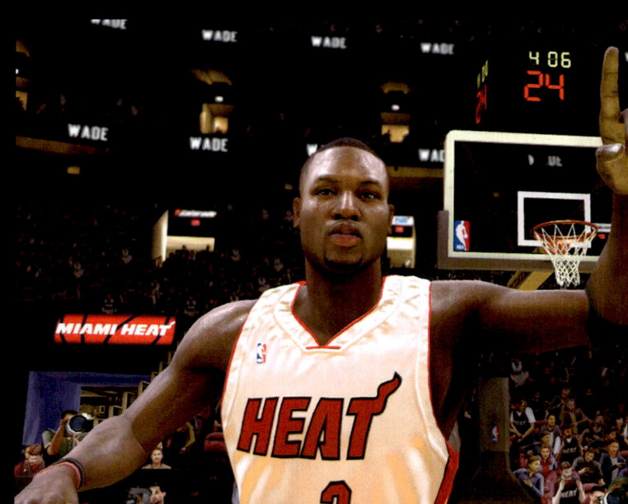

Gilbert poster [above], Gilbert [top right], TMac [center right], Wade [above right], Kobe [opposite]

NBA LIVE 08
Maya, MotionBuilder, Photoshop, Renderware
Modeling: Steve Wing Yin Chan, David Lam
Textures: Steve Wing Yin Chan, Andy Yi Shen
Lighting: Andy Yi Shen, Yuka Chi, Kay Darby
Environments: Rob Tchir, Morgan Hall

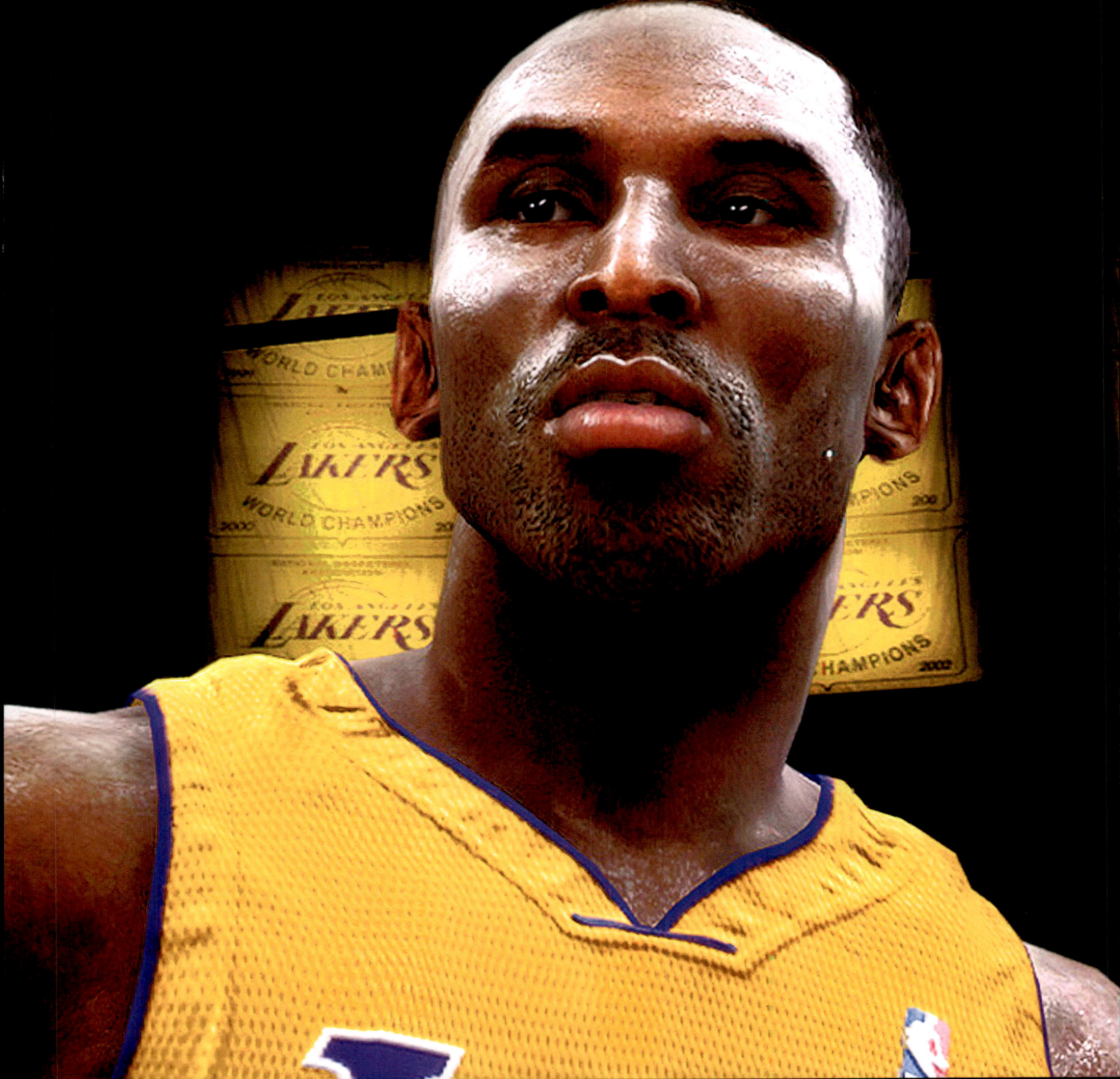
LAKERS
WORLD CHAMPIONS
2000
LAKERS
WORLD CHAMPIONS
2002

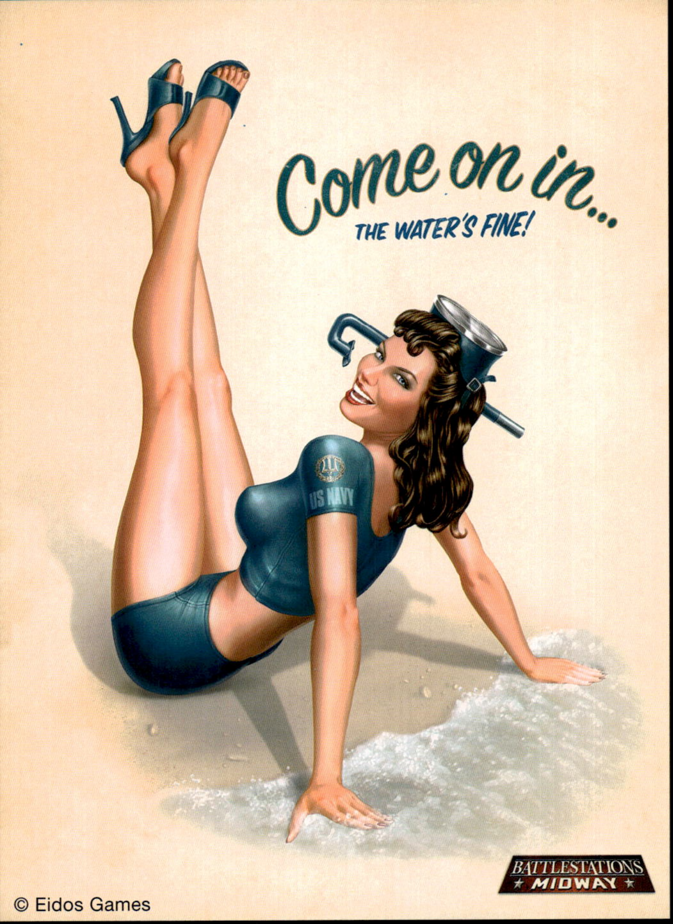

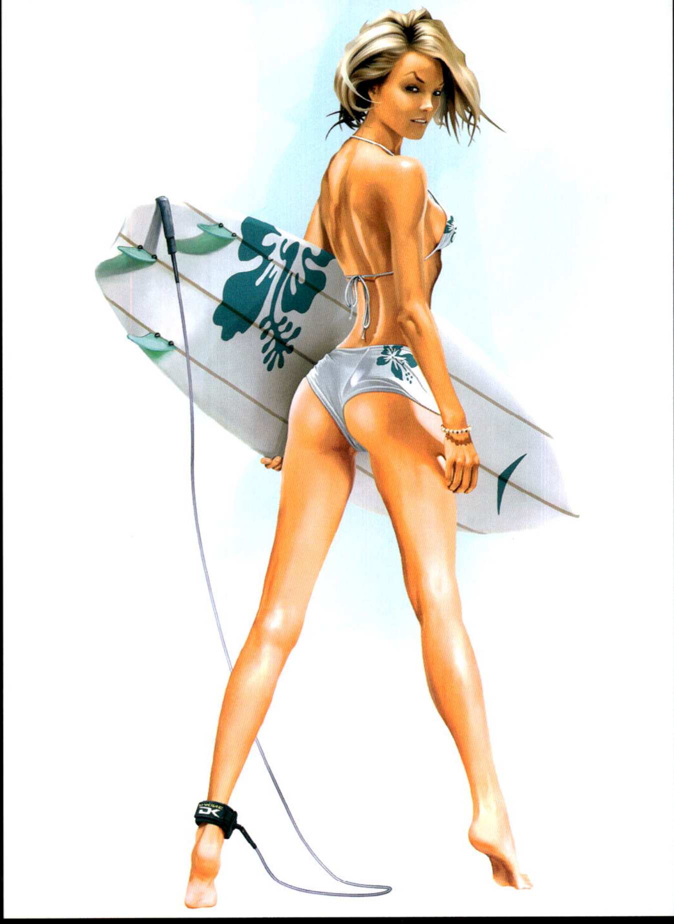

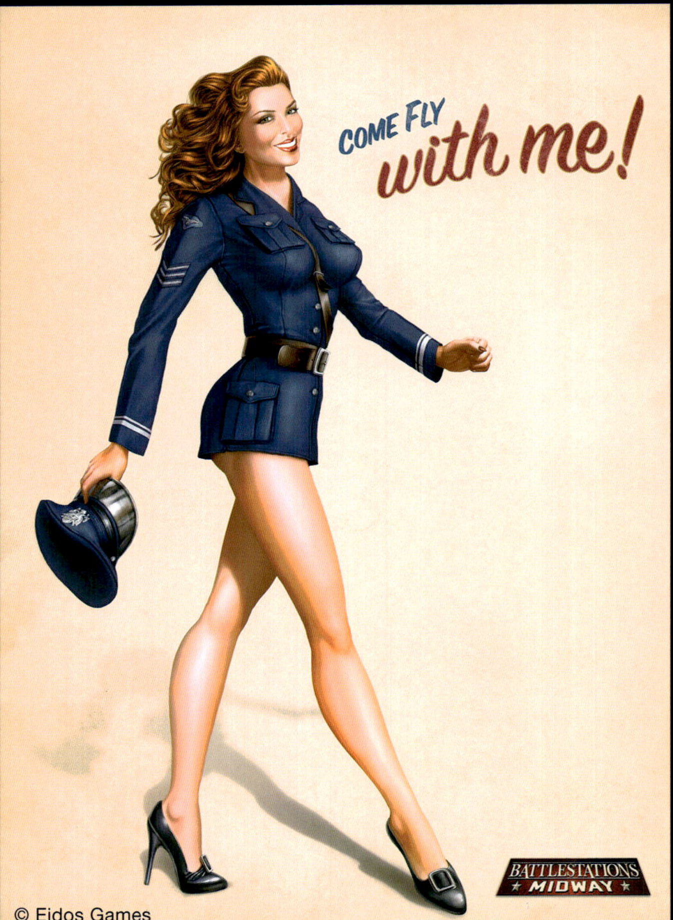

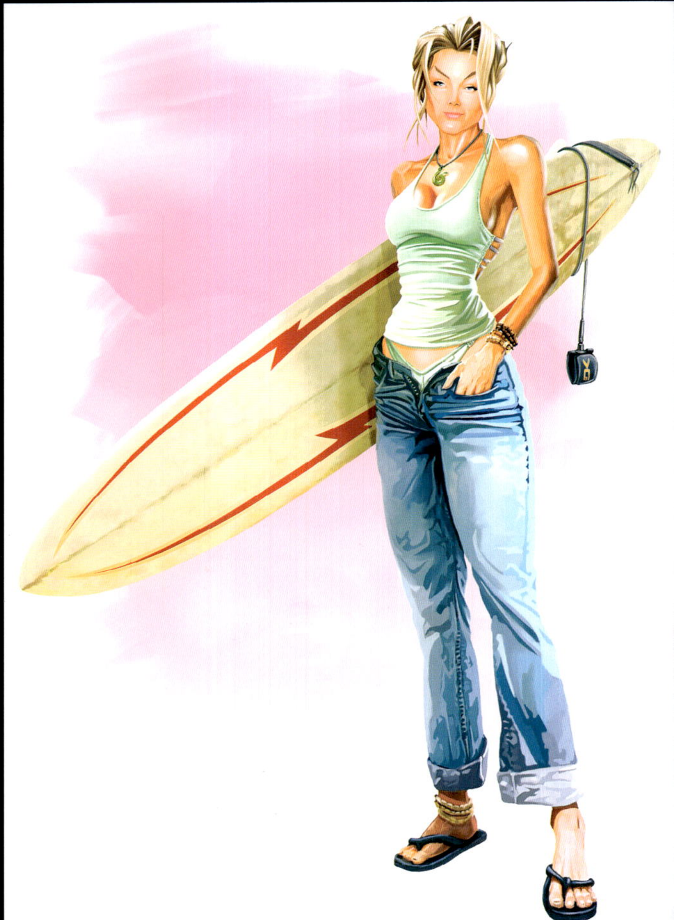

Battlestations Midway: submarine girl
Photoshop
Client: Eidos Games
Henning Ludvigsen, NORWAY
[top]

Battlestations Midway: air girl
Photoshop
Client: Eidos Games
Henning Ludvigsen, NORWAY
[above]

White Hibiscus
Photoshop, Painter
Joerg Warda,
GERMANY
[top]

Red special
Photoshop, Painter
Joerg Warda,
GERMANY
[above]

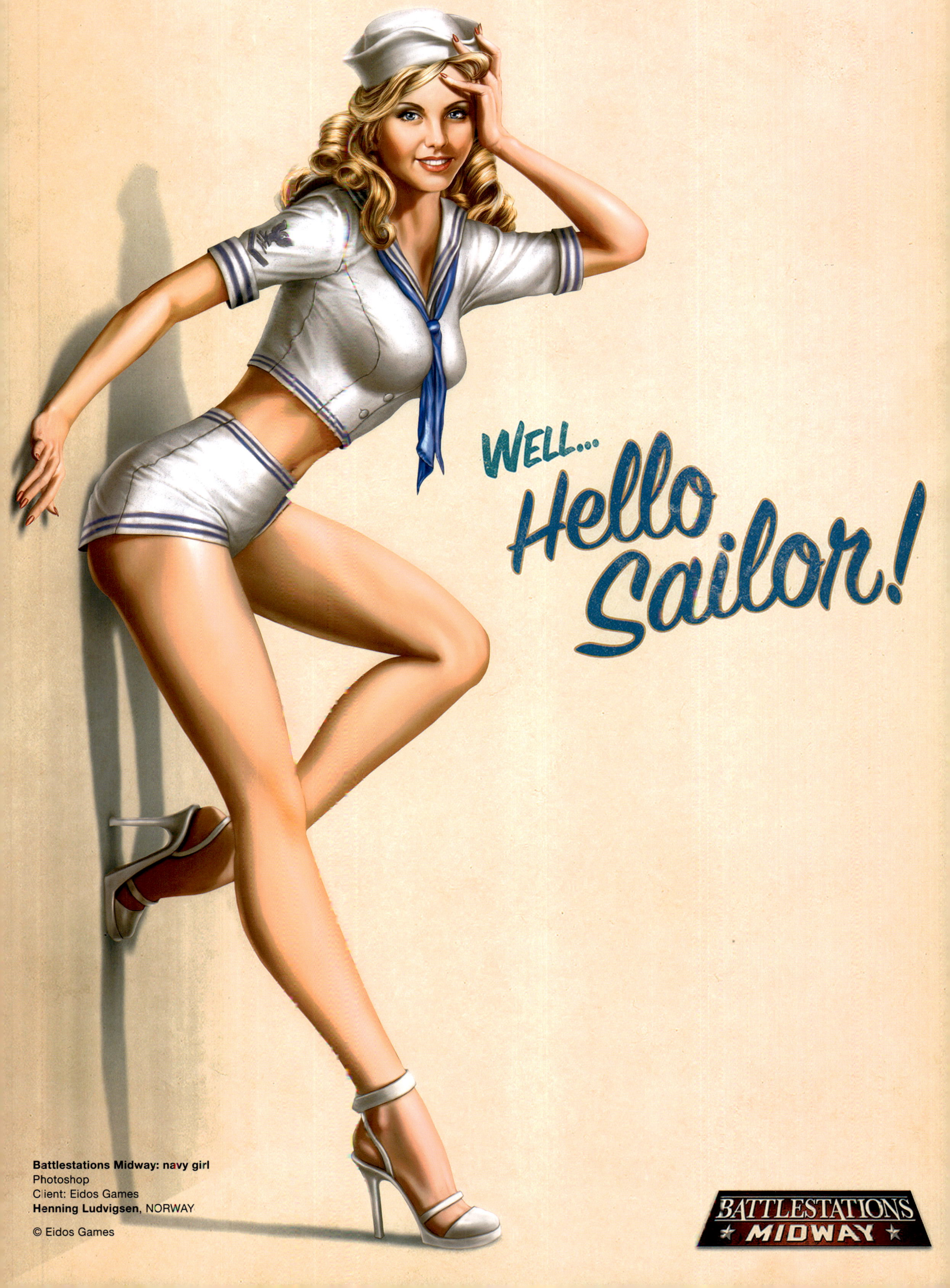

Battlestations Midway: navy girl
Photoshop
Client: Eidos Games
Henning Ludvigsen, NORWAY

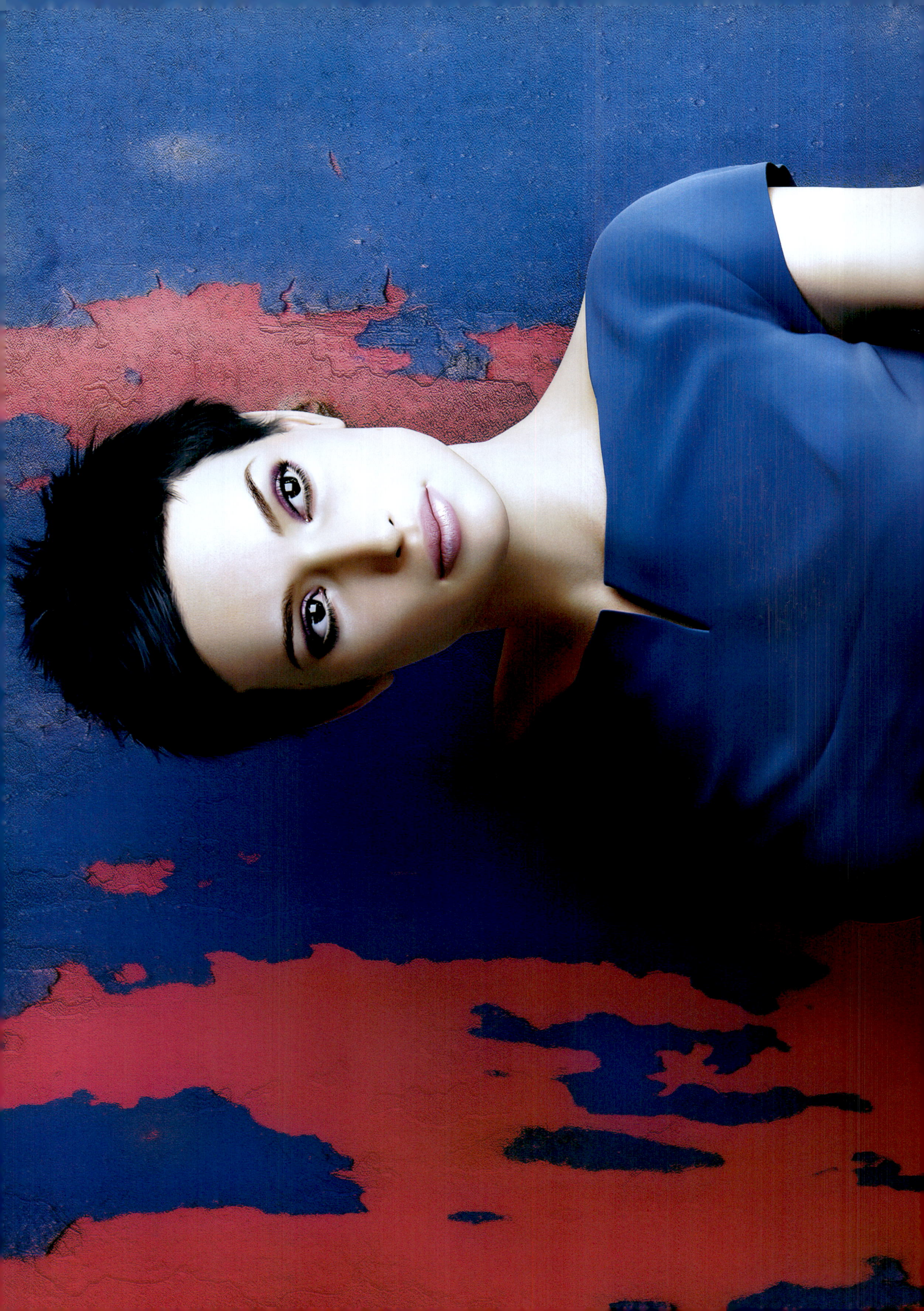

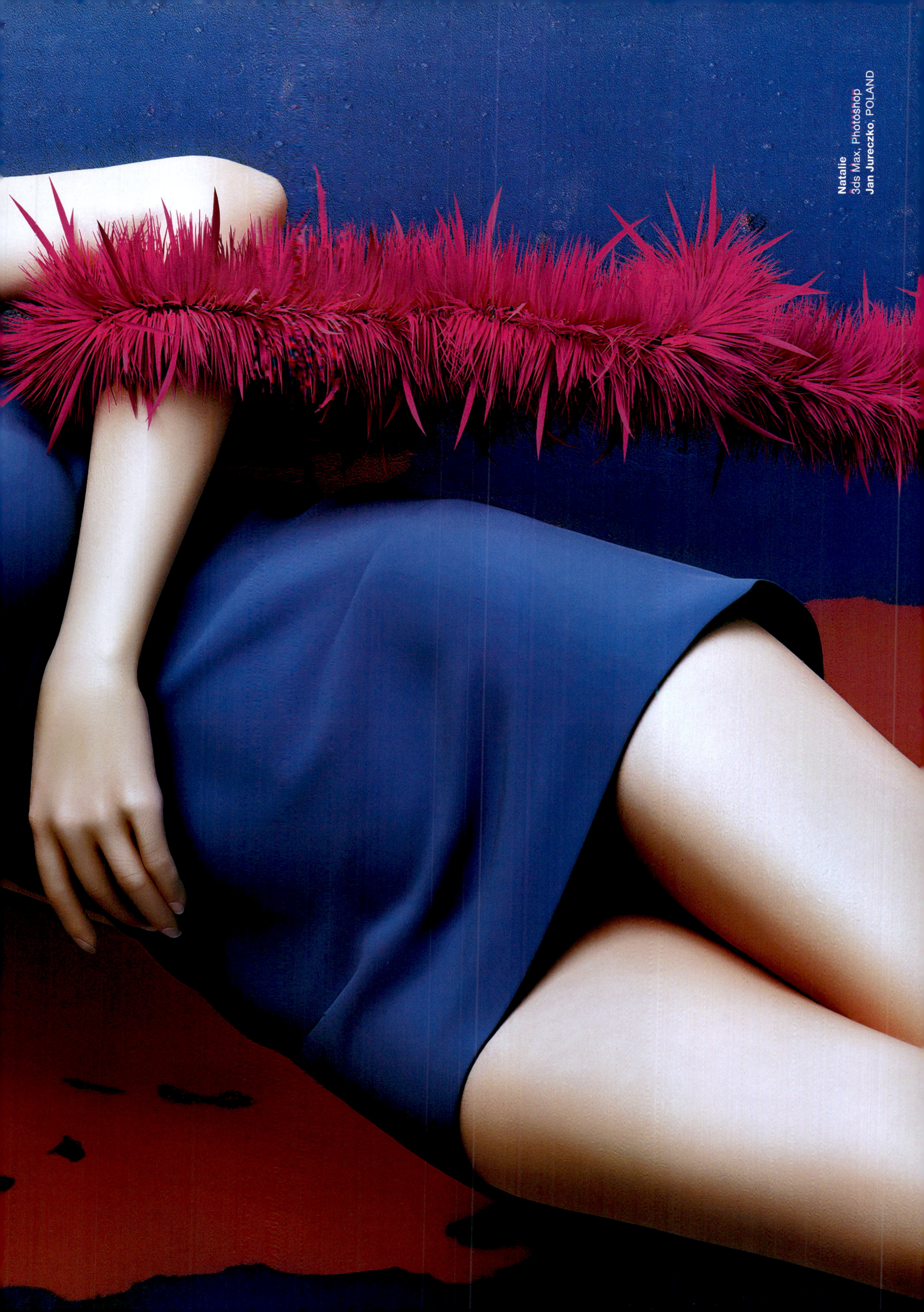

Natalie
3ds Max, Photoshop
Jan Jureczko, POLAND

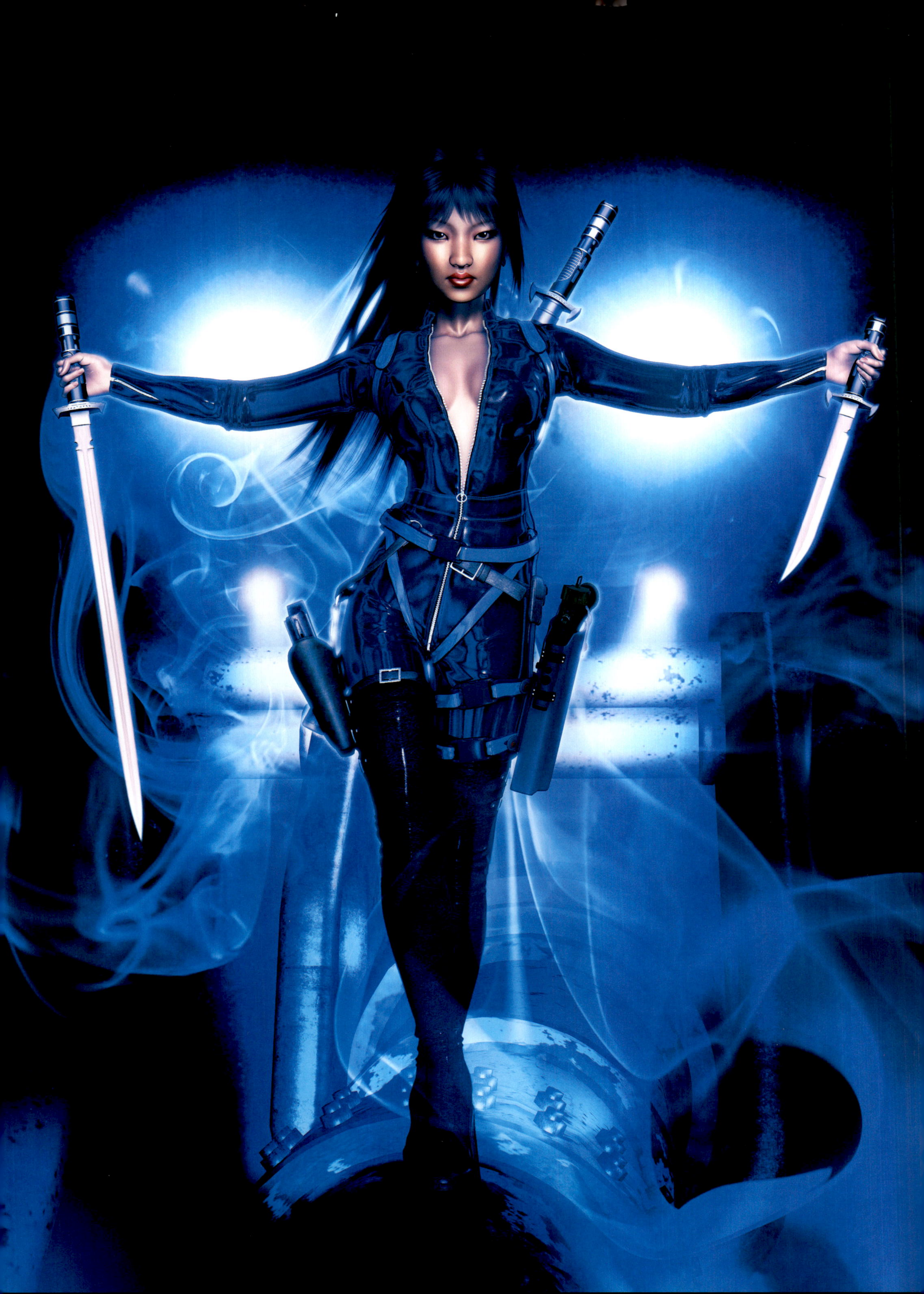

Shadow Dancer
DAZ Studio, Poser, Photoshop
Matt 'Shimuzu' Smith, GREAT BRITAIN
[above]

Red rider: second generation
Maya, mental ray, Photoshop
Hyun-hee Lee, KOREA
[right]

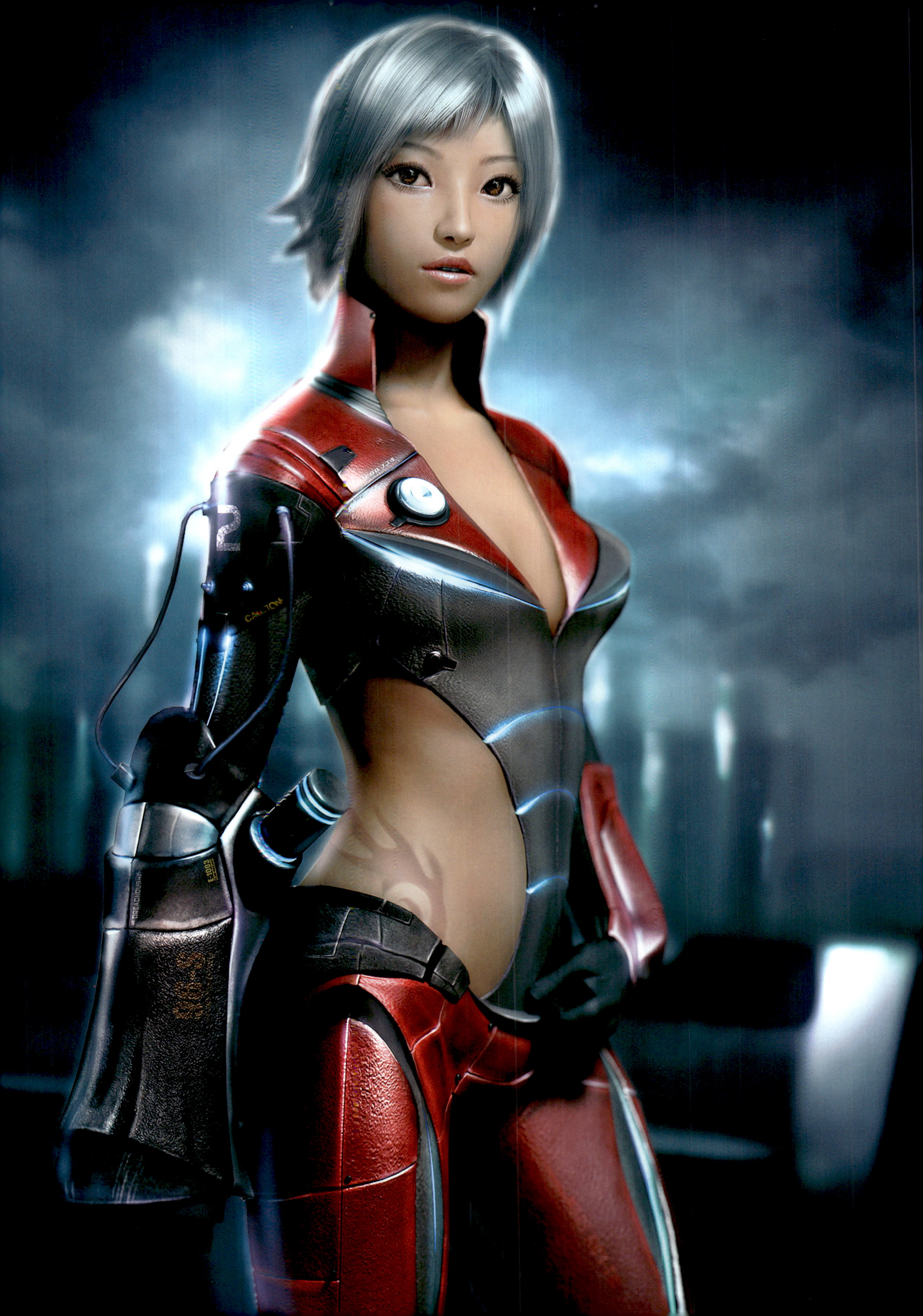

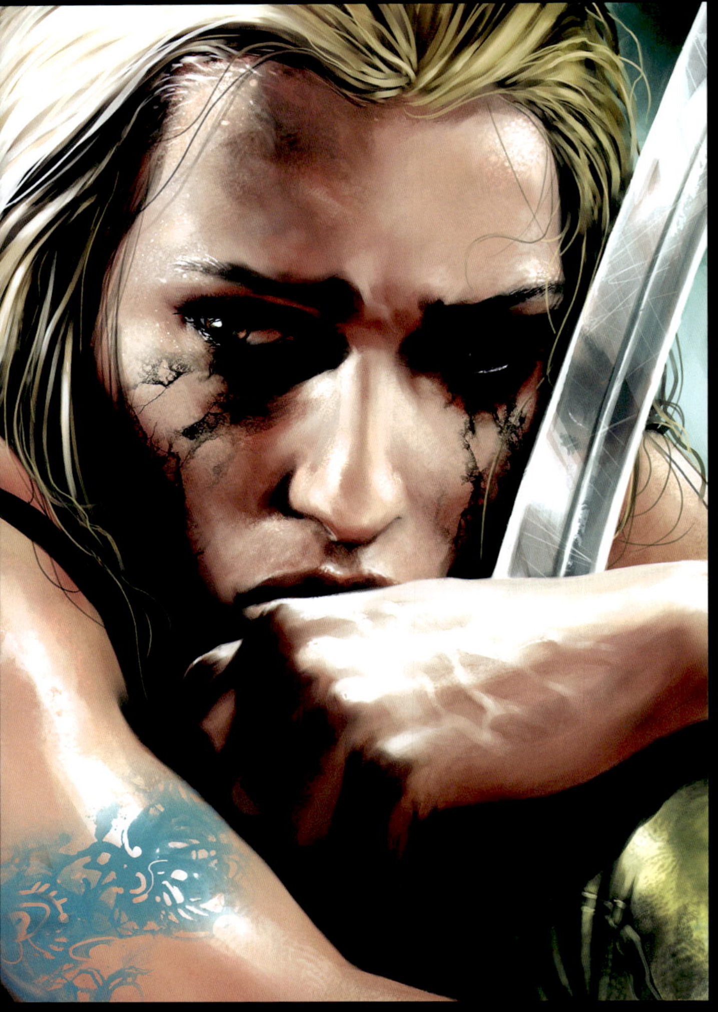

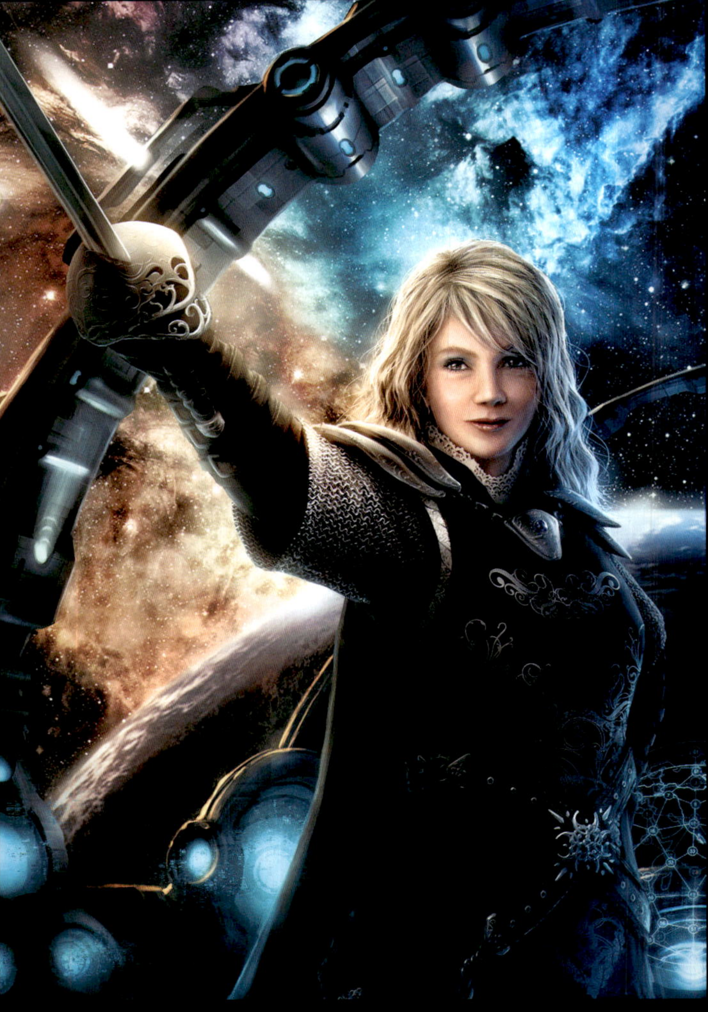

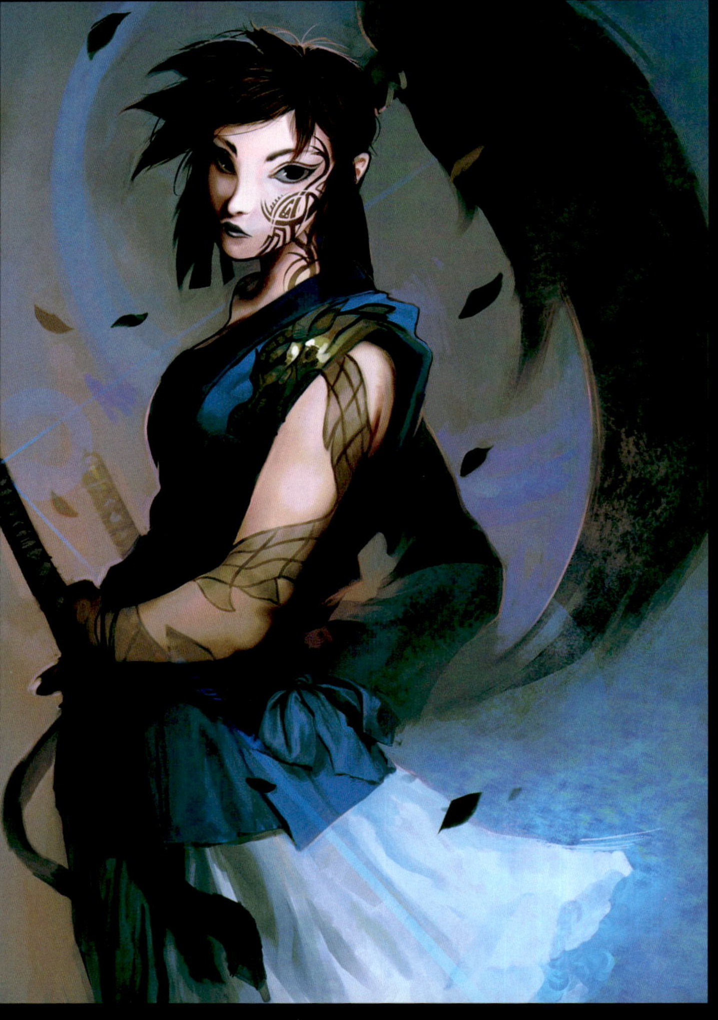

Defeated
Photoshop, Painter
Tomasz Jedruszek, POLAND
[top left]

Star Crusade
Photoshop
Client: Fabryka Slow
Marek Okon, POLAND
[above]

Samurai Girl
Painter, Photoshop
Corey Loving, USA
[left]

Night Elf
Photoshop, Poser
Antje Darling, USA
[right]

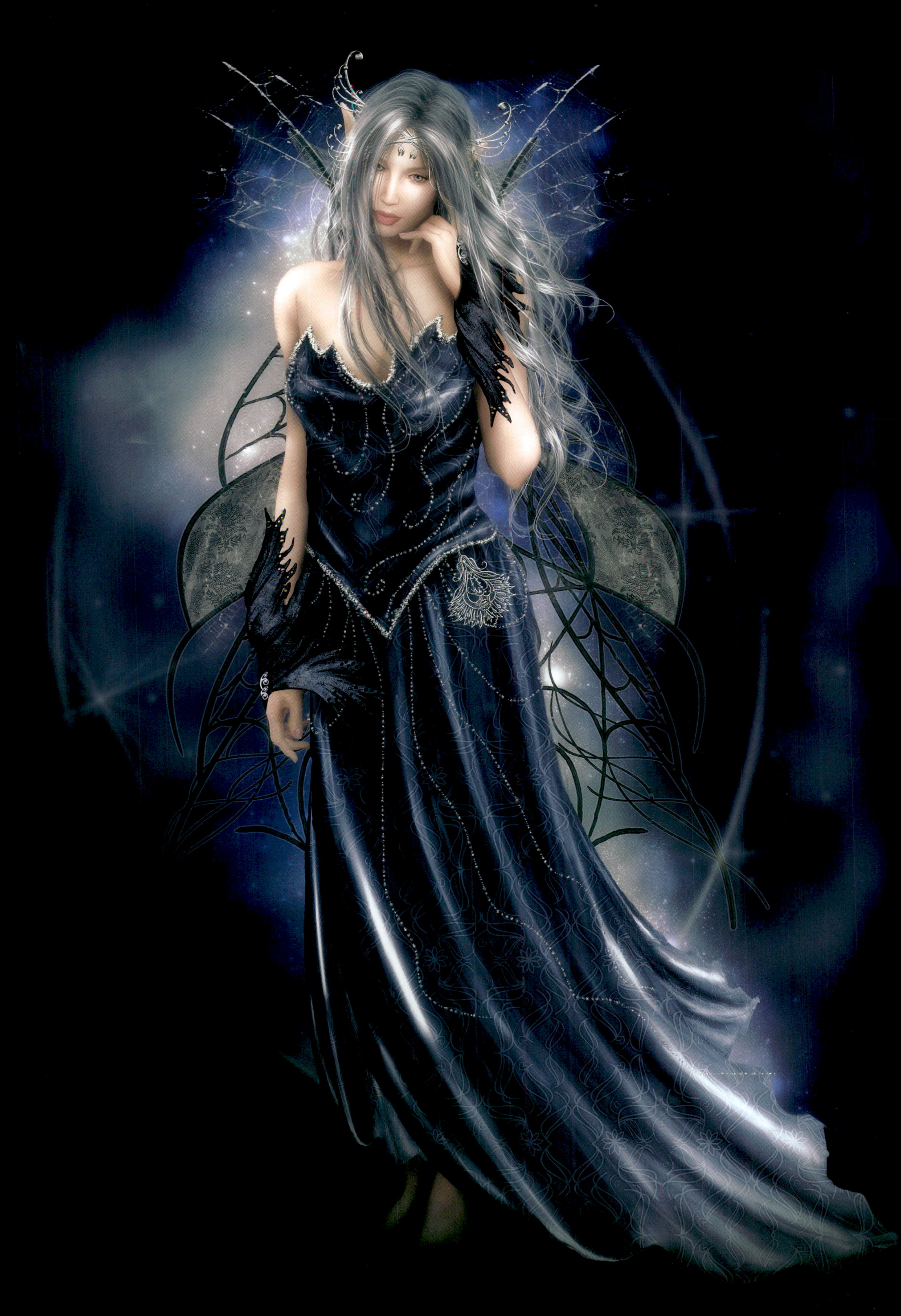

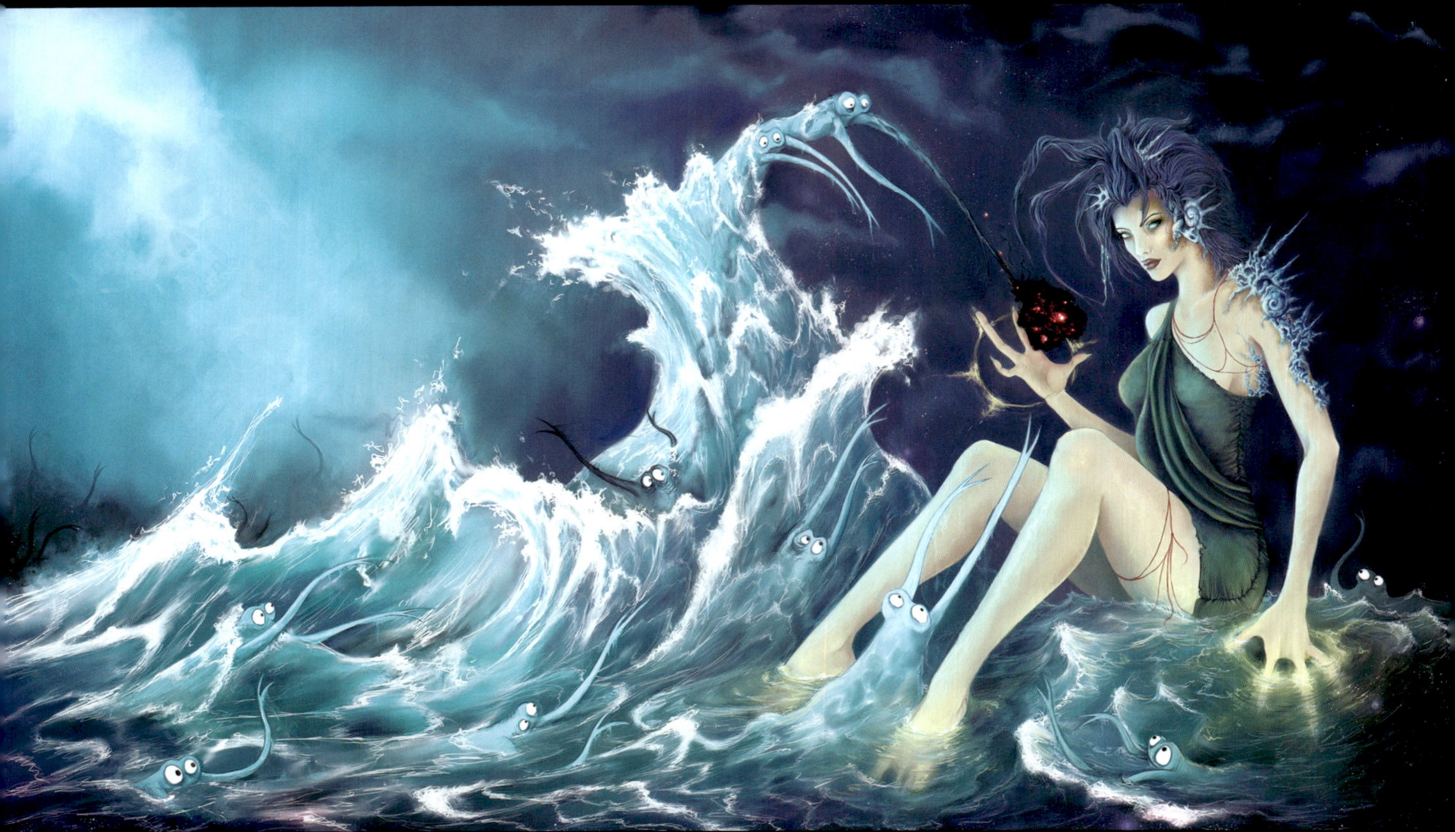

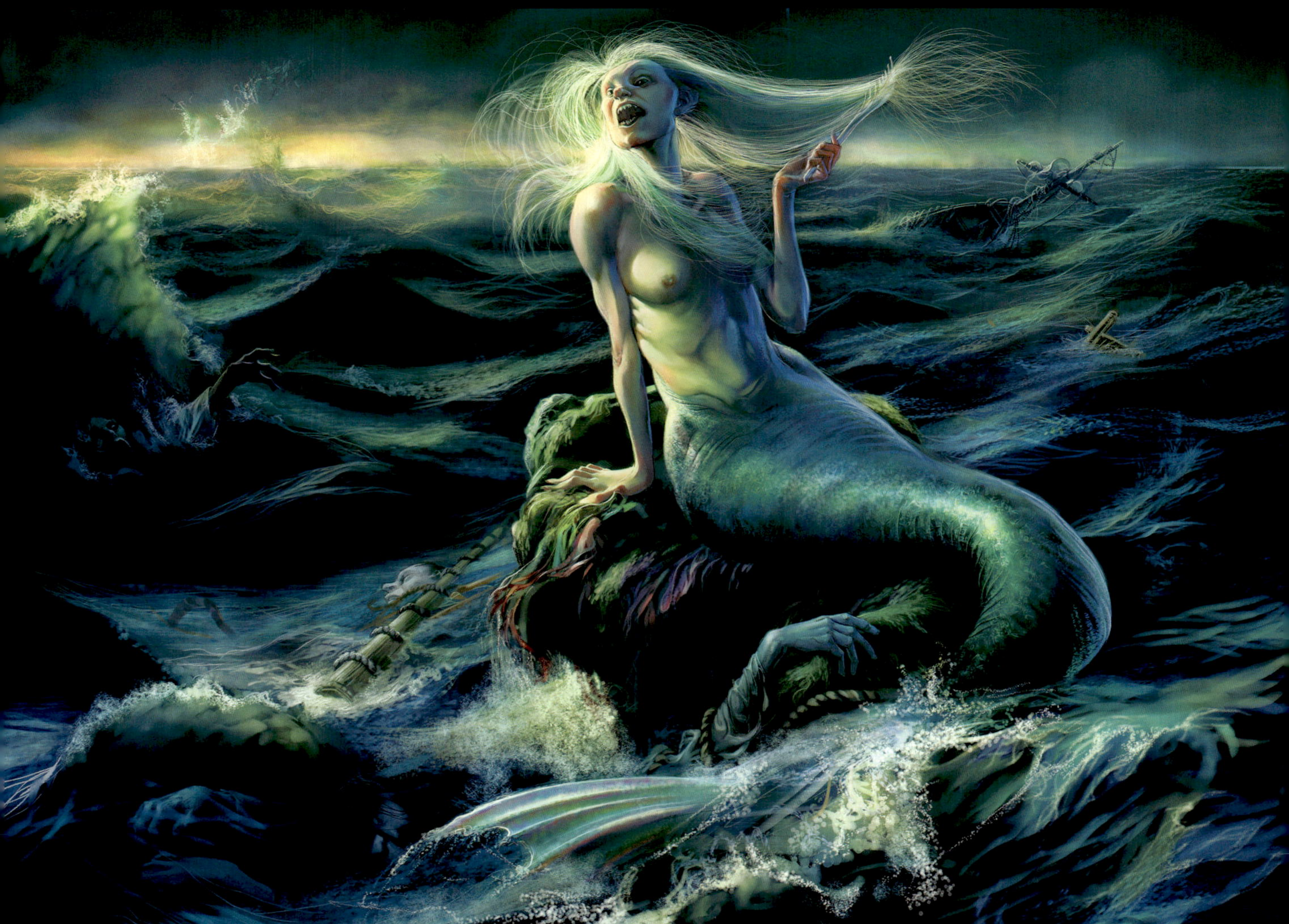

Vater: Story After Oil
Photoshop
Belinda Day, AUSTRALIA
top]

Siren song
Painter, Photoshop
Nick Harris, GREAT BRITAIN
[above]

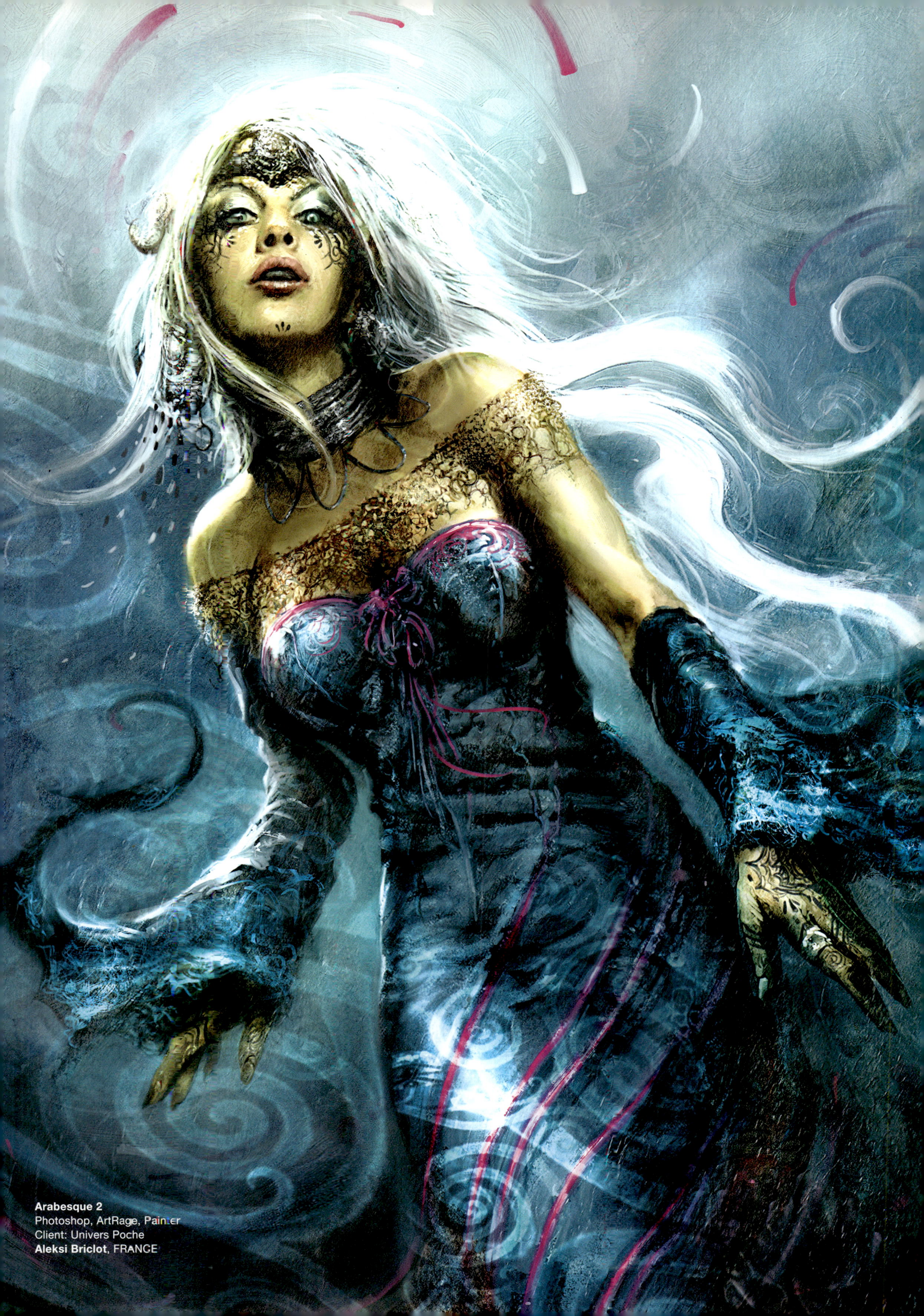

Arabesque 2
Photoshop, ArtRage, Painter
Client: Univers Poche
Aleksi Briclot, FRANCE

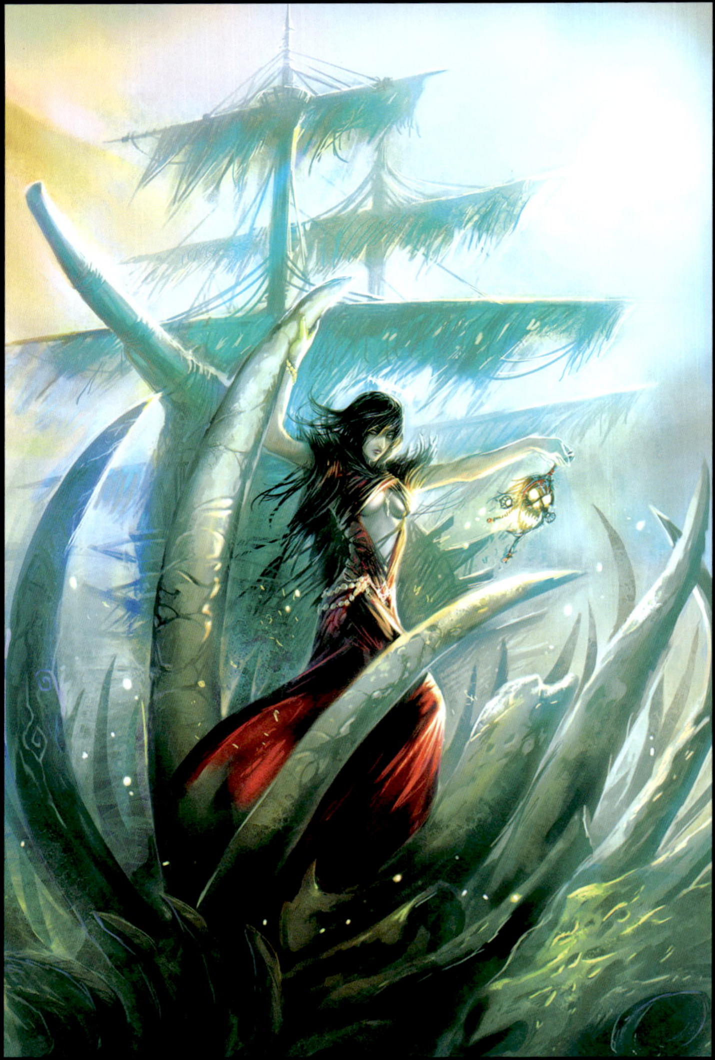

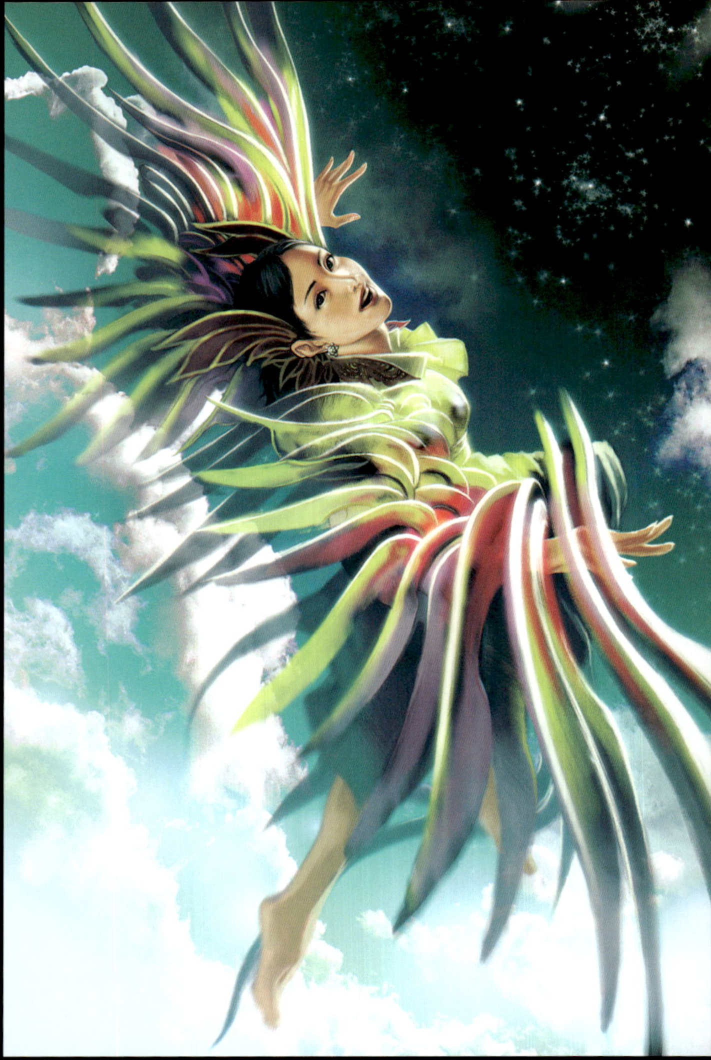

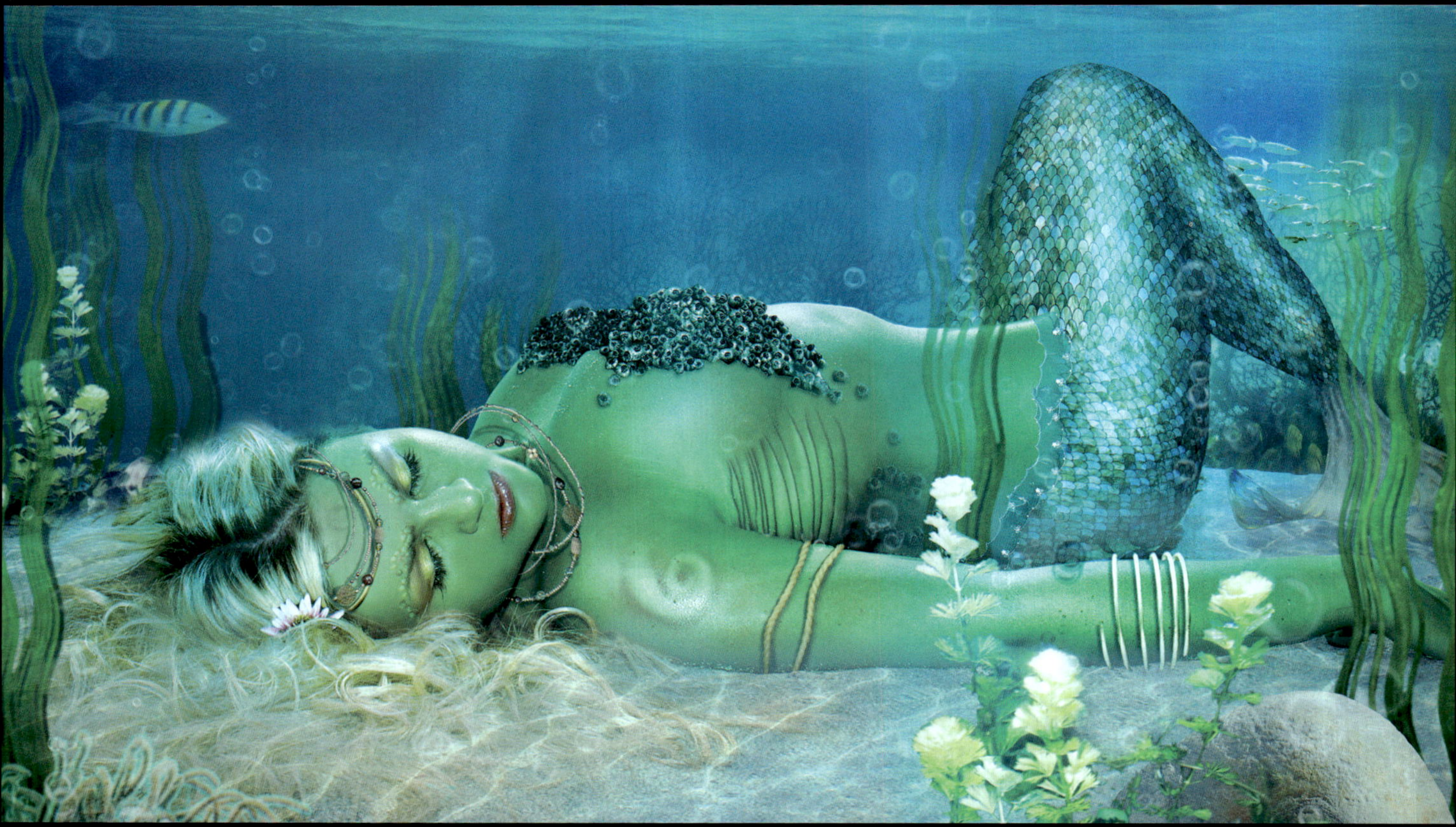

Bone of the ocean
Painter
Jian Guo, CHINA
[top]

Mermaid Queen
Photoshop
Holli Alvarado, USA
[above]

Naramantari
Photoshop
Rafi Adrian Zulkarnain, INDONESIA
[top]

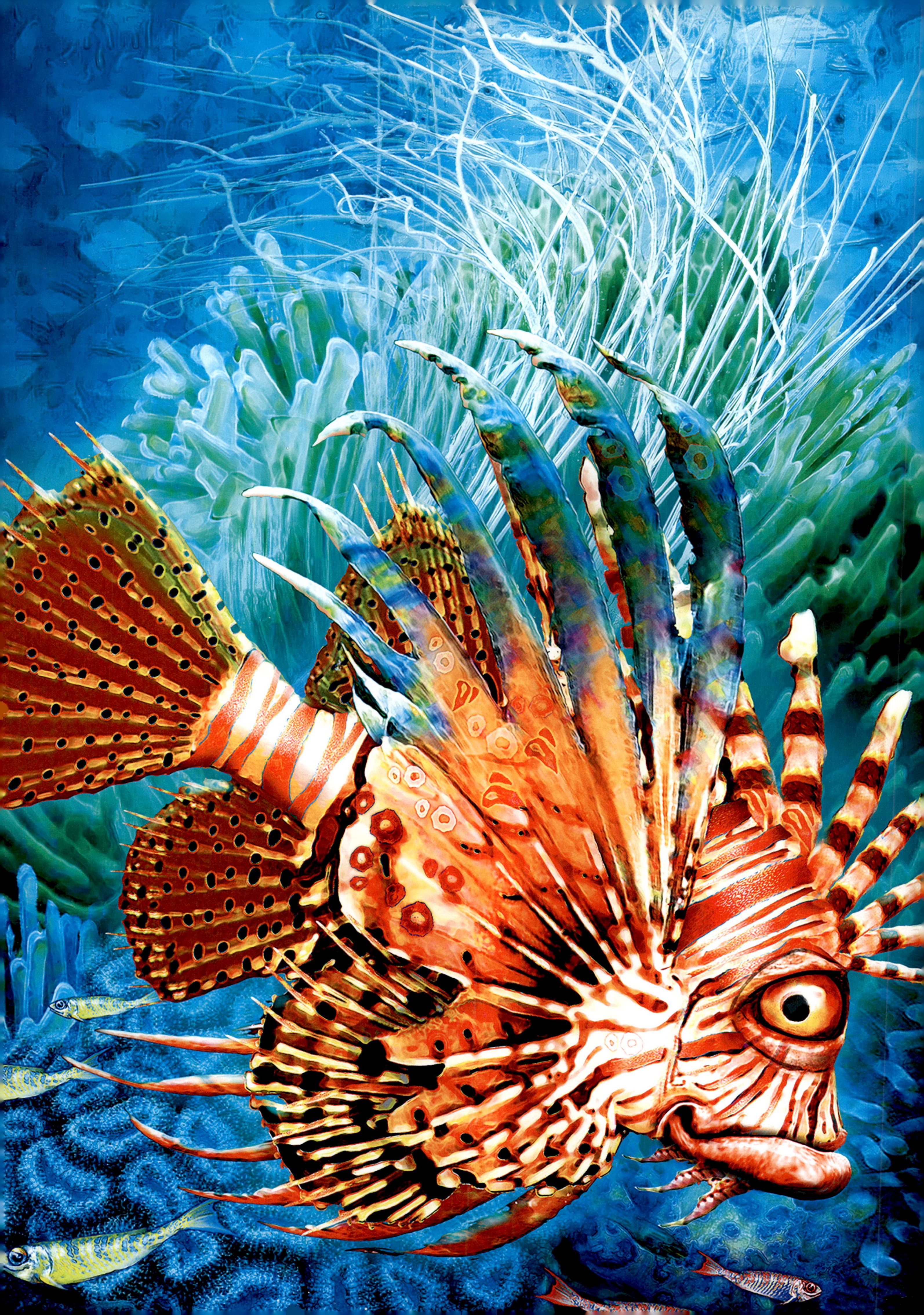

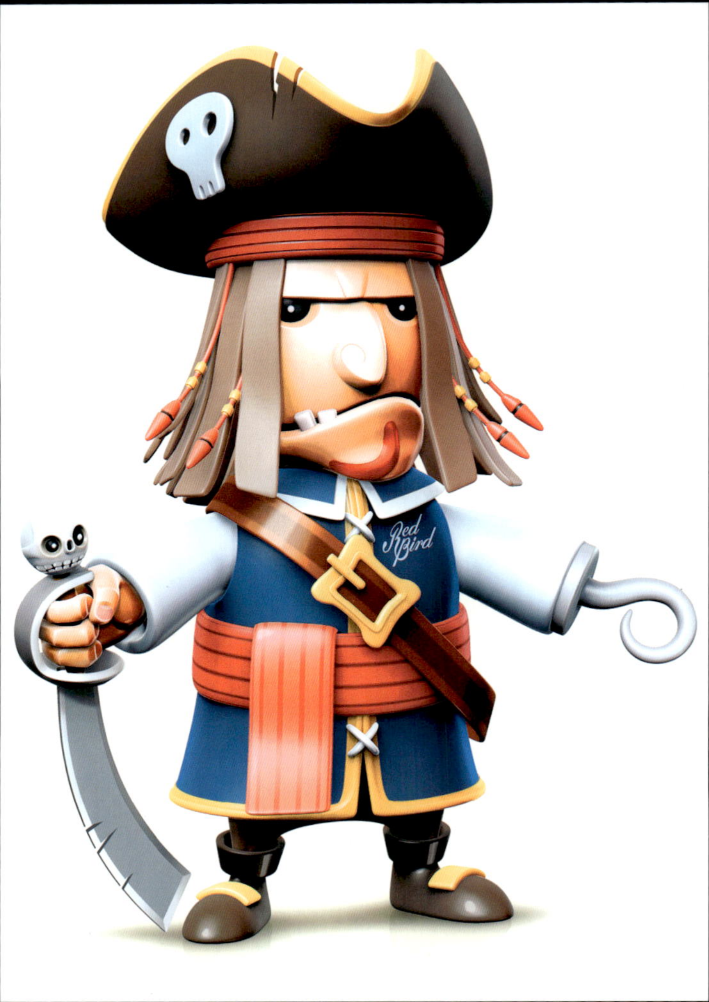

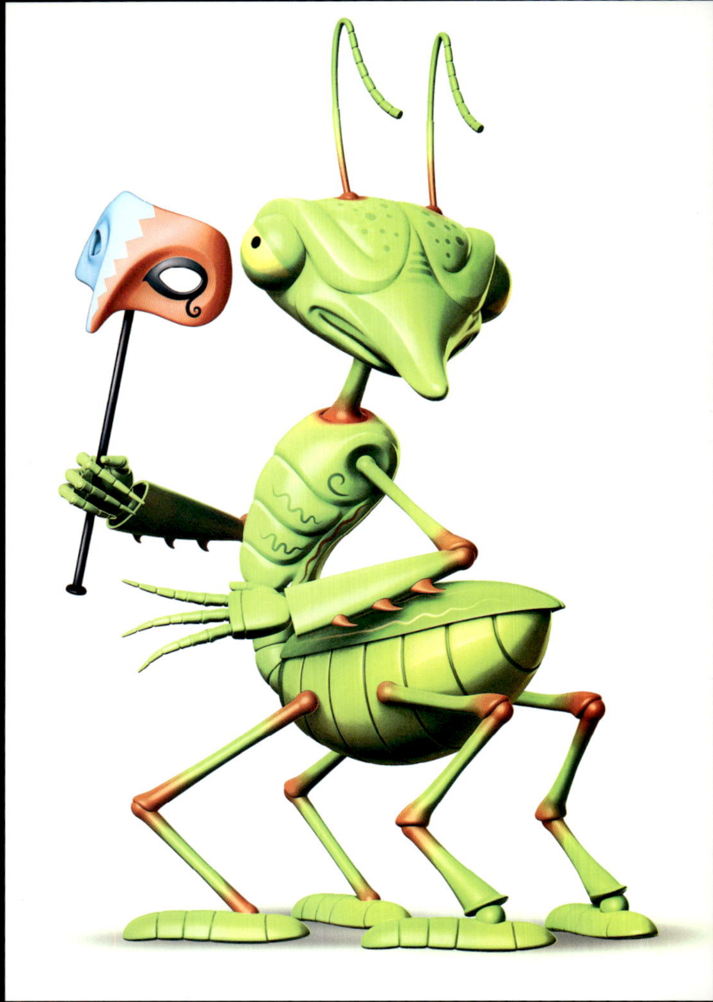

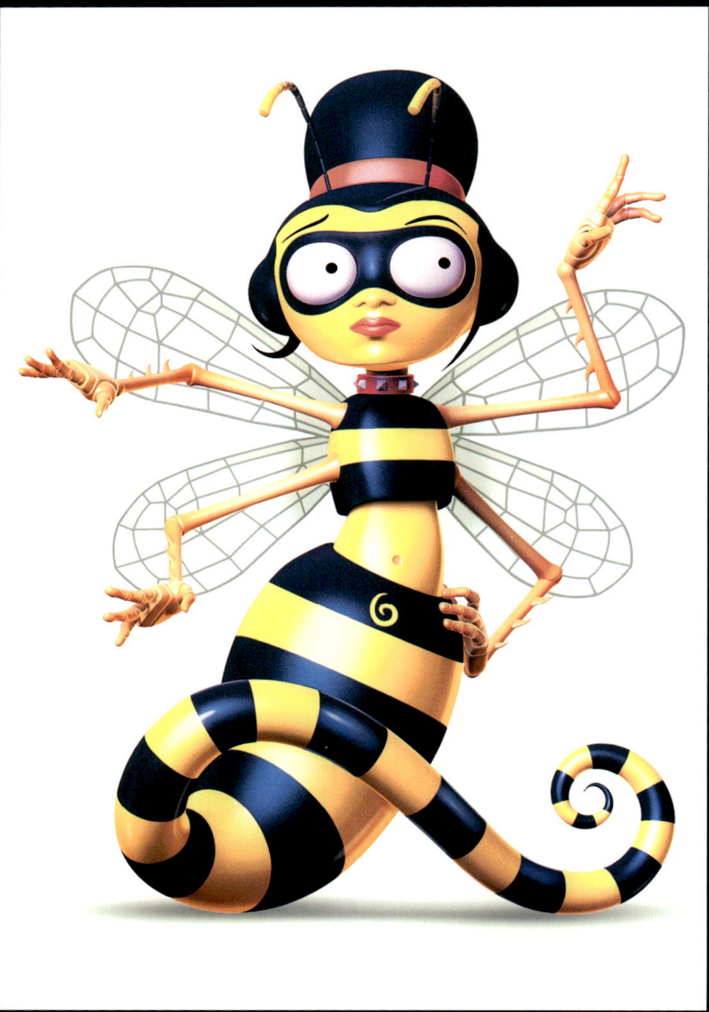

Pirate Redbird
ZBrush, Maya, Photoshop
Ralf Stumpf, GERMANY
[top left]

Venice Mantis
ZBrush, Maya, Photoshop
Ralf Stumpf, GERMANY
[above]

Hornet Girl
ZBrush, Maya, Photoshop
Ralf Stumpf, GERMANY
[left]

Little geisha
Painter, Photoshop
Kei Acedera, CANADA
[right]

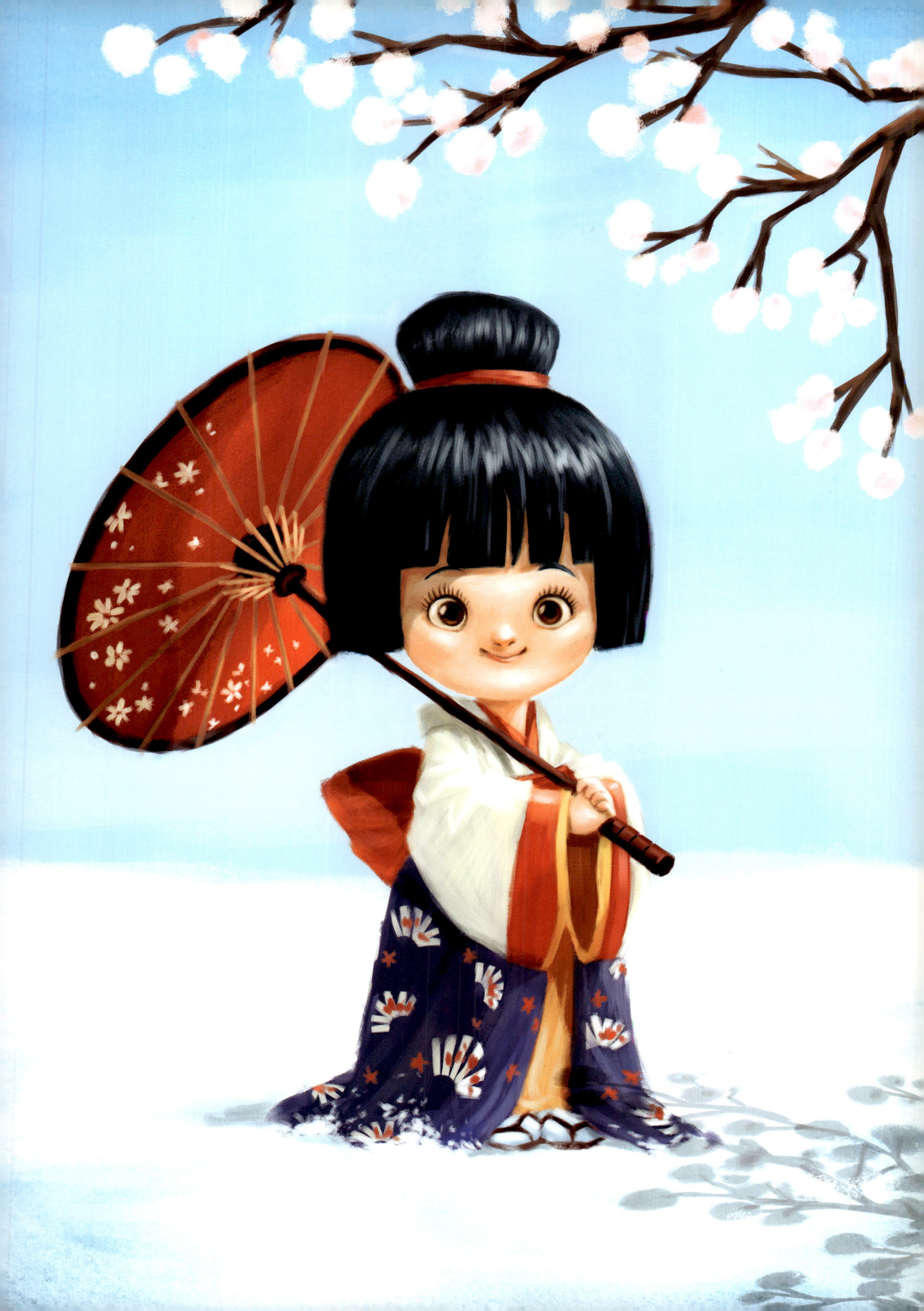

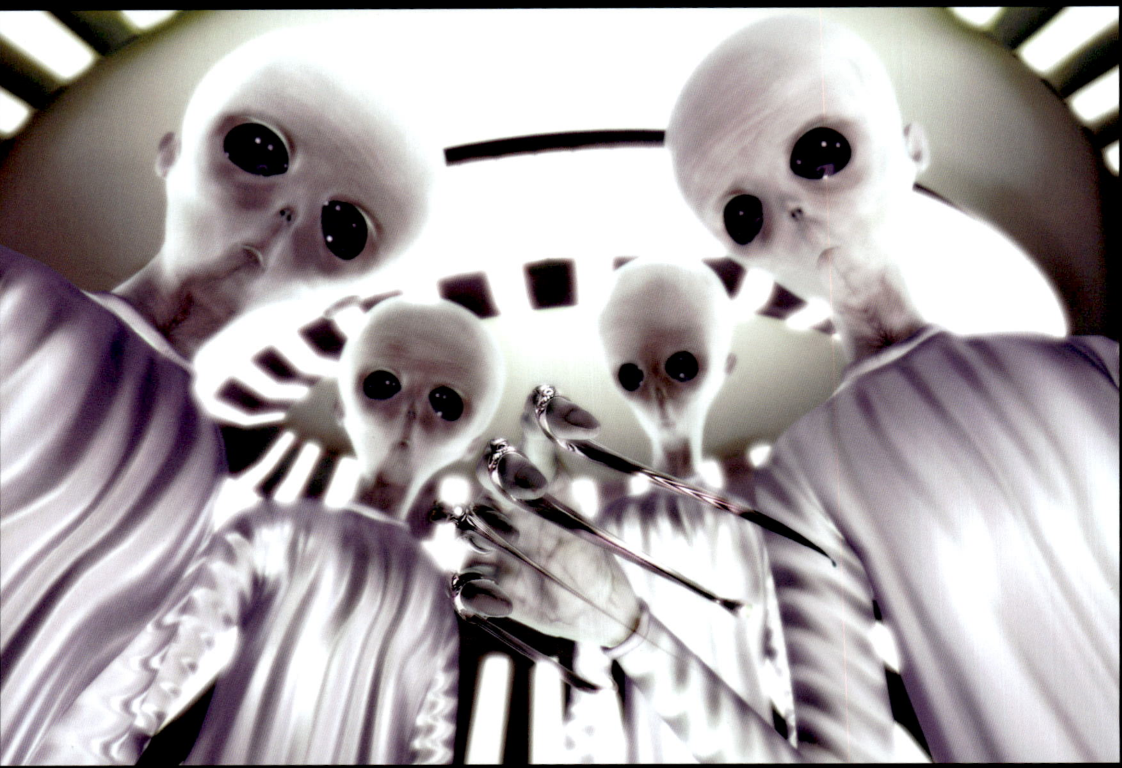

Aliens
LightWave 3D, Photoshop
Paolo Morucci, ITALY
[left]

O_2
Photoshop, Bryce
Antonio Javier Caparó Salgad
CANADA
[right]

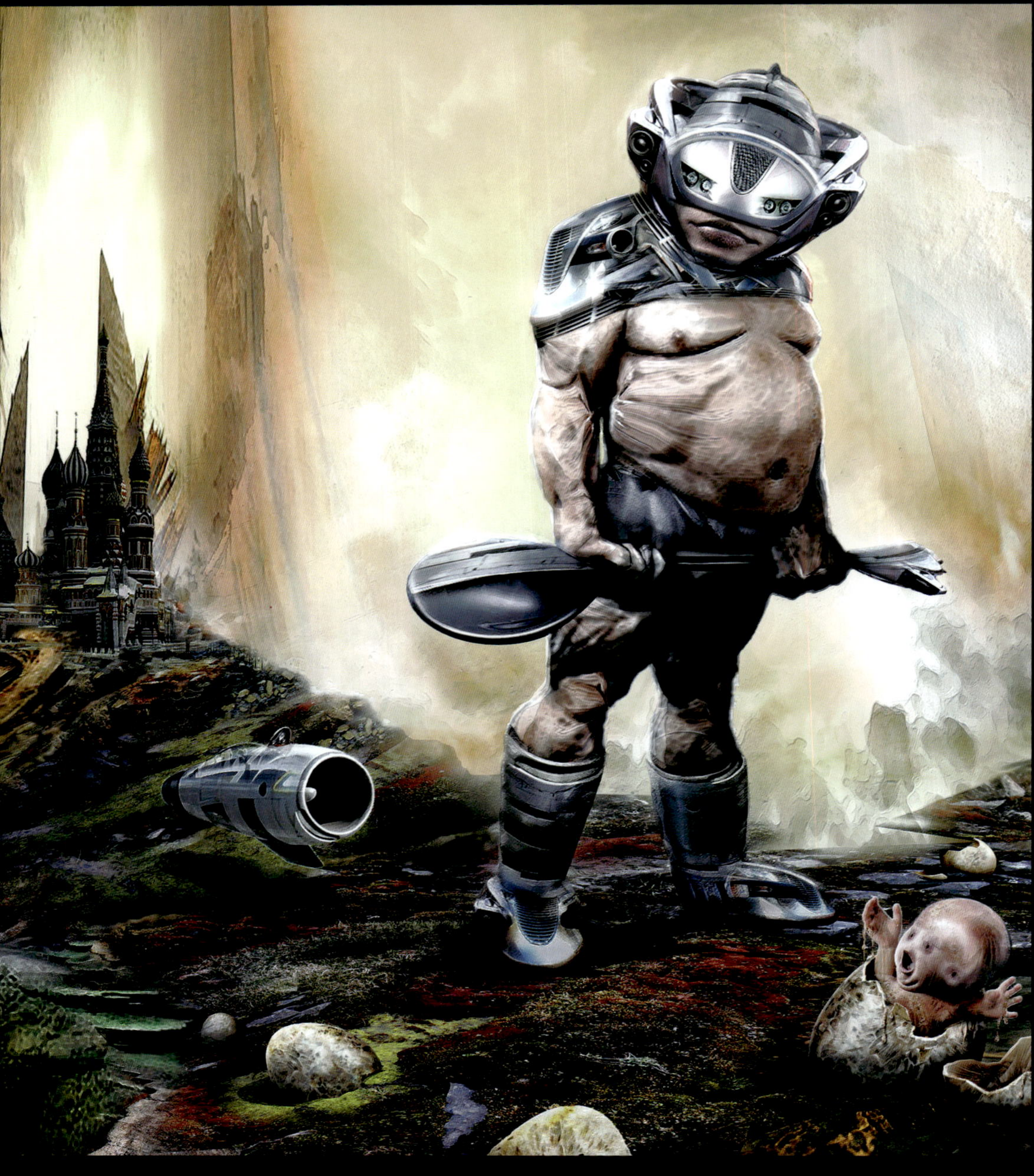

The Birther
Photoshop
Paul Roget, AUSTRALIA
[left]

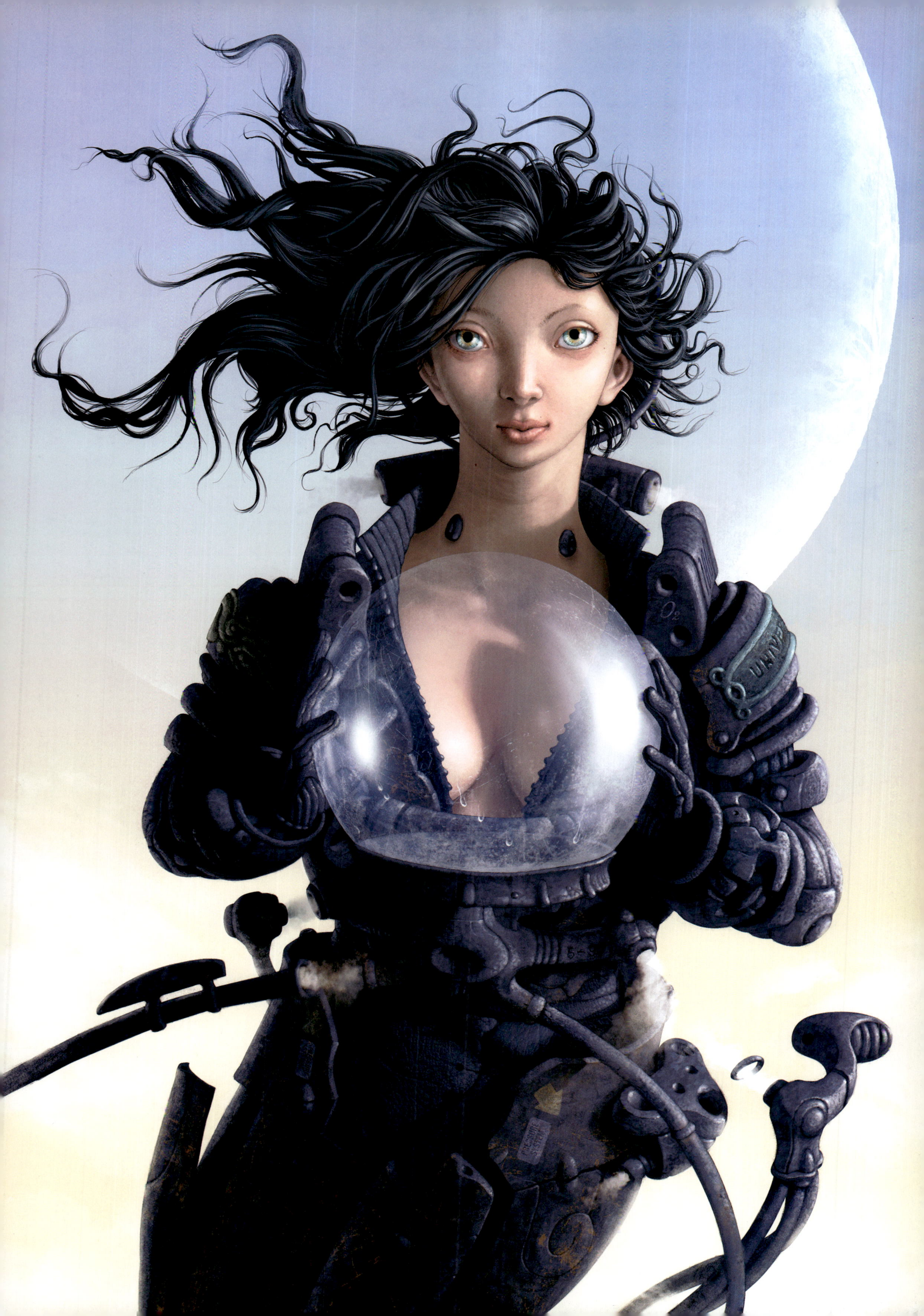

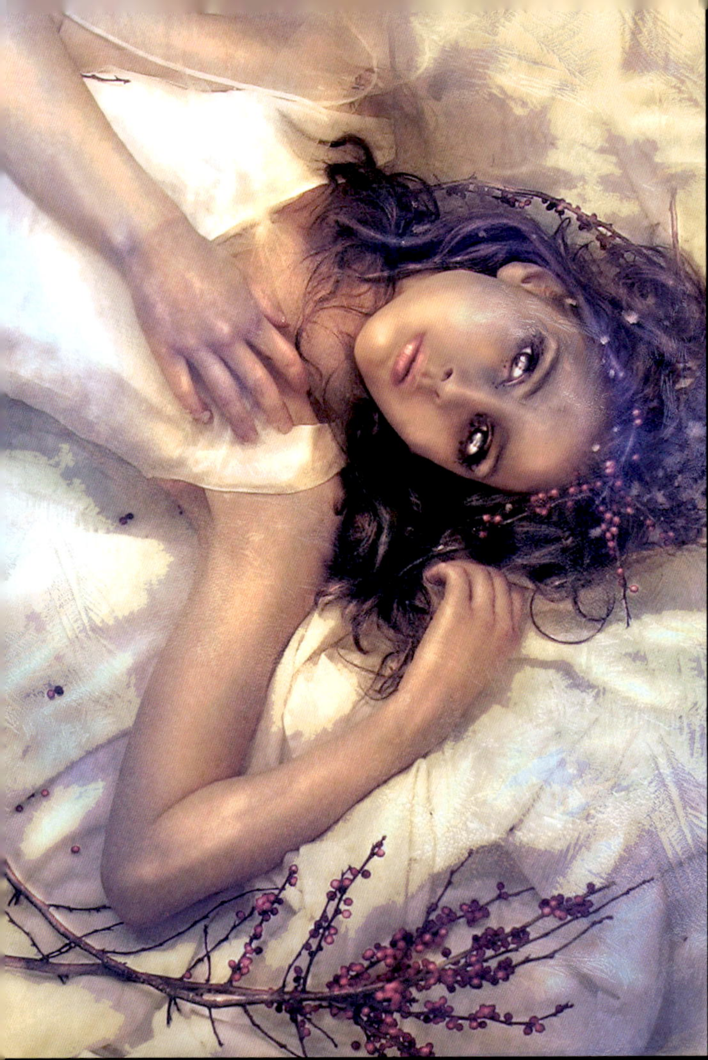

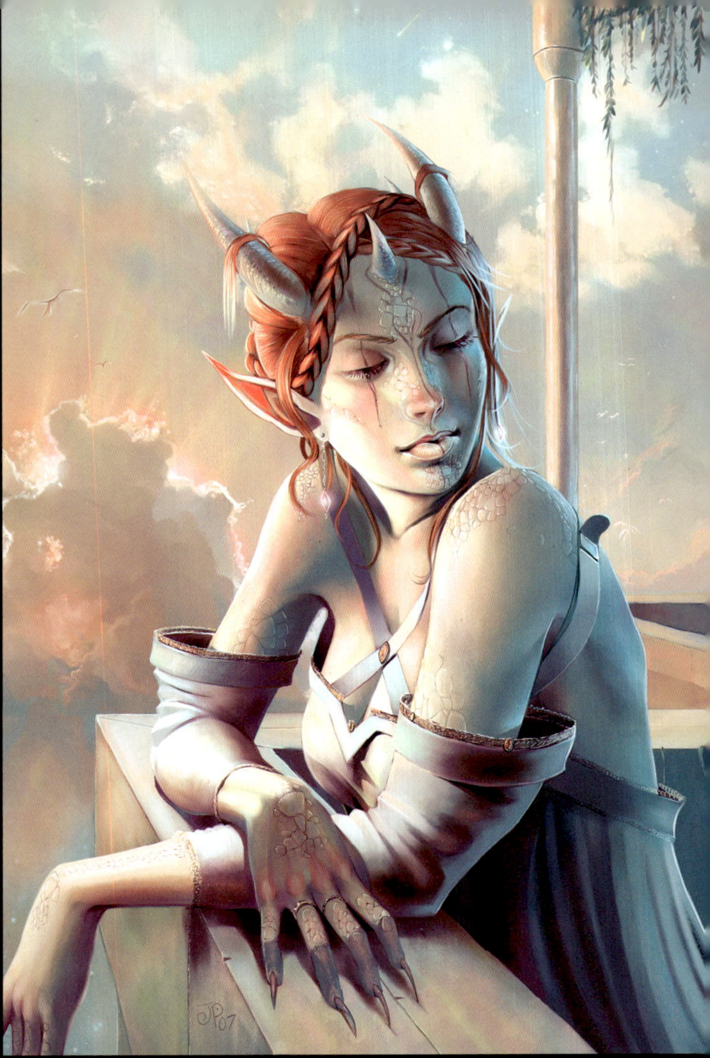

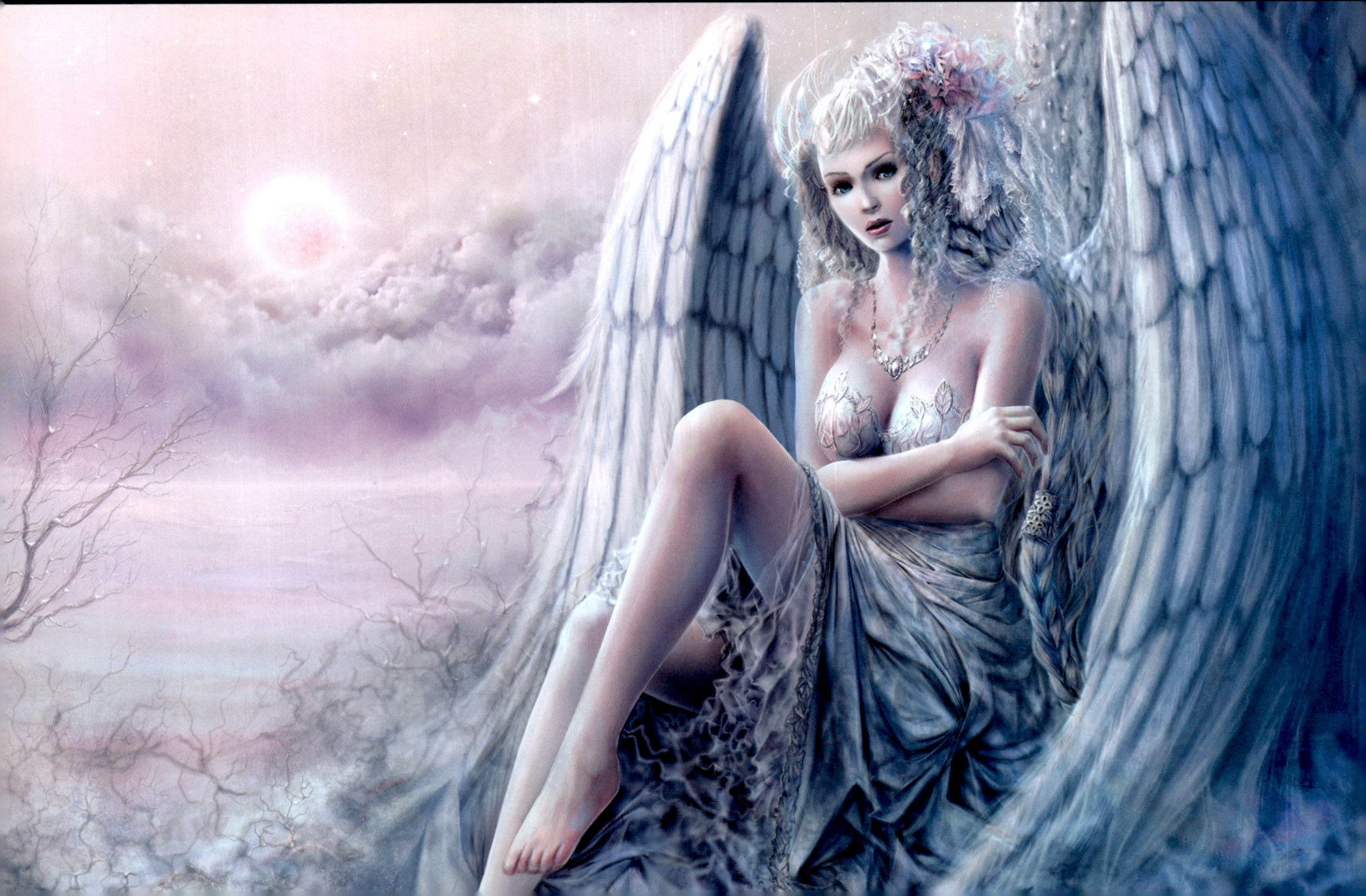

Frost
Photoshop
Model: Odessa Sawyer
Ida Mary Walker Larsen, DENMARK
[far left]

Longnail
Painter
Jacob Probelski, USA
[left]

After the rain
Photoshop, LightWave 3D
Karl Poulson, USA
[right]

Angel of Ice
Photoshop
Agnieszka Mirosław, POLAND
[left]

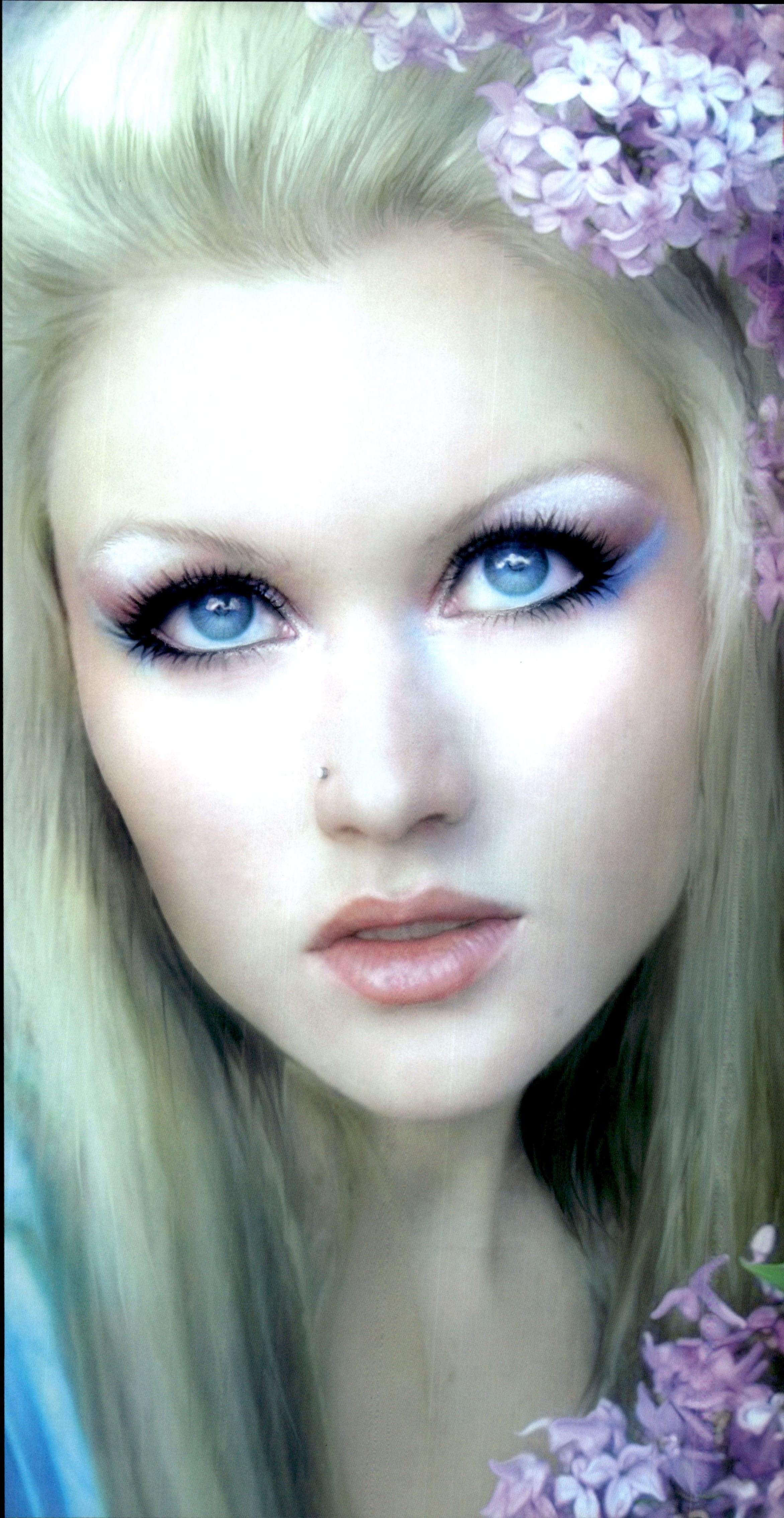

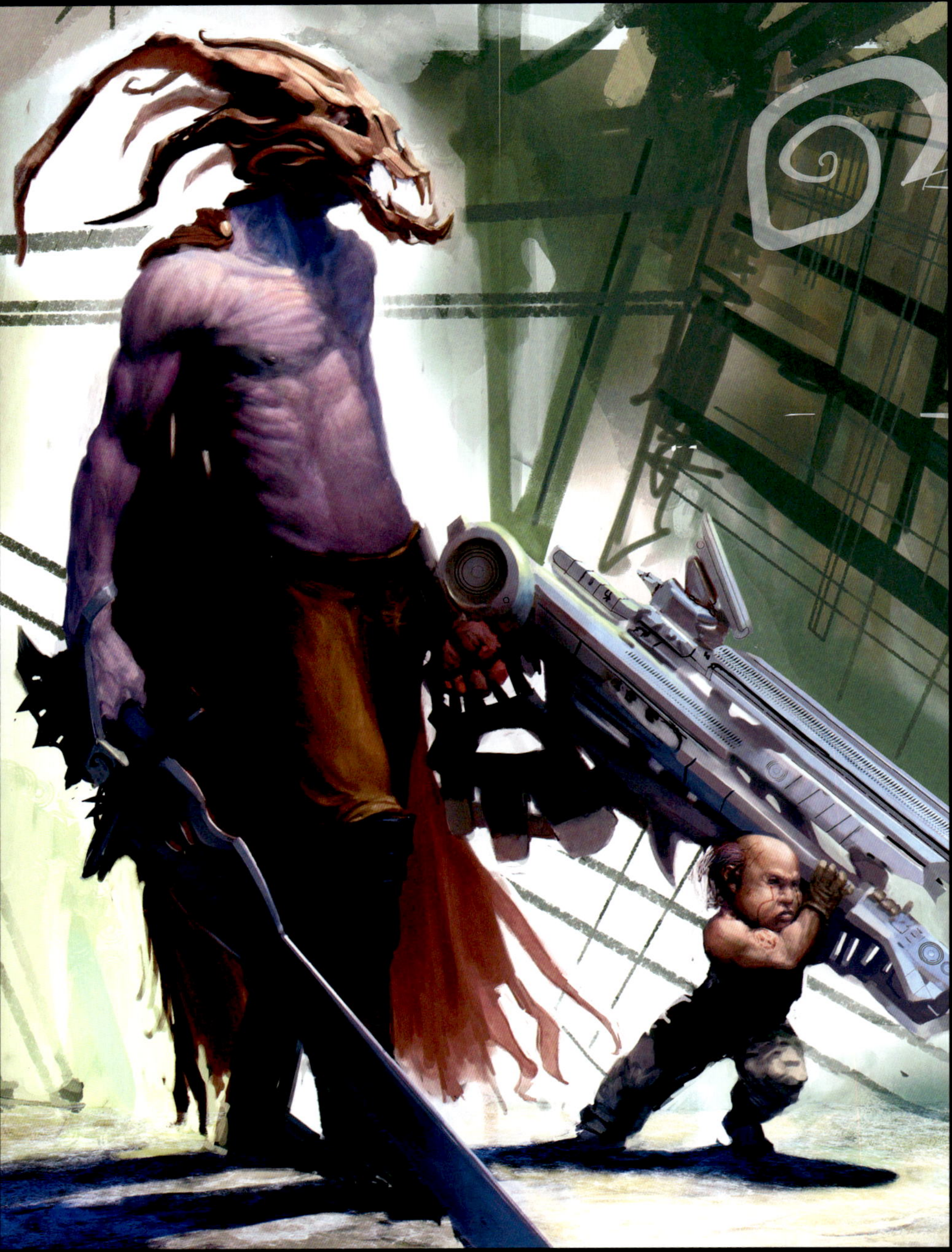

Two man army
Photoshop, Painter
Branko Bistrovic, CANADA
[left]

Beautiful
Photoshop
Photographer: Steven Perry
Samantha Hogg, GREAT BRITAIN
[right]

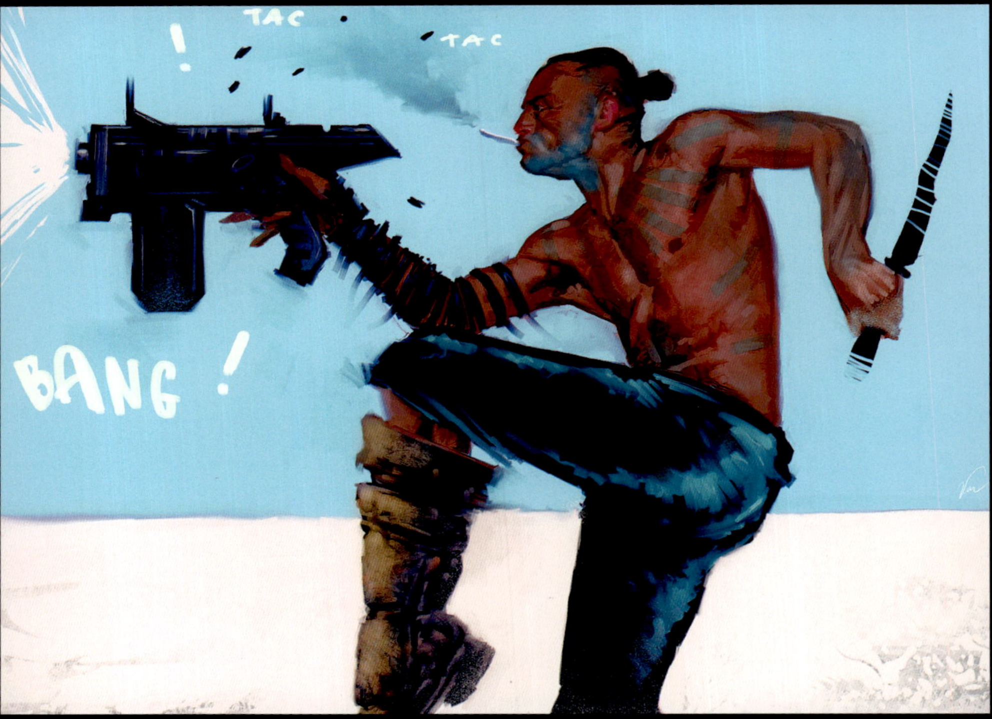

J.W.Hardin (Self portrait)
Painter, Photoshop
Kan Muftic, streamatica,
SWITZERLAND
[left]

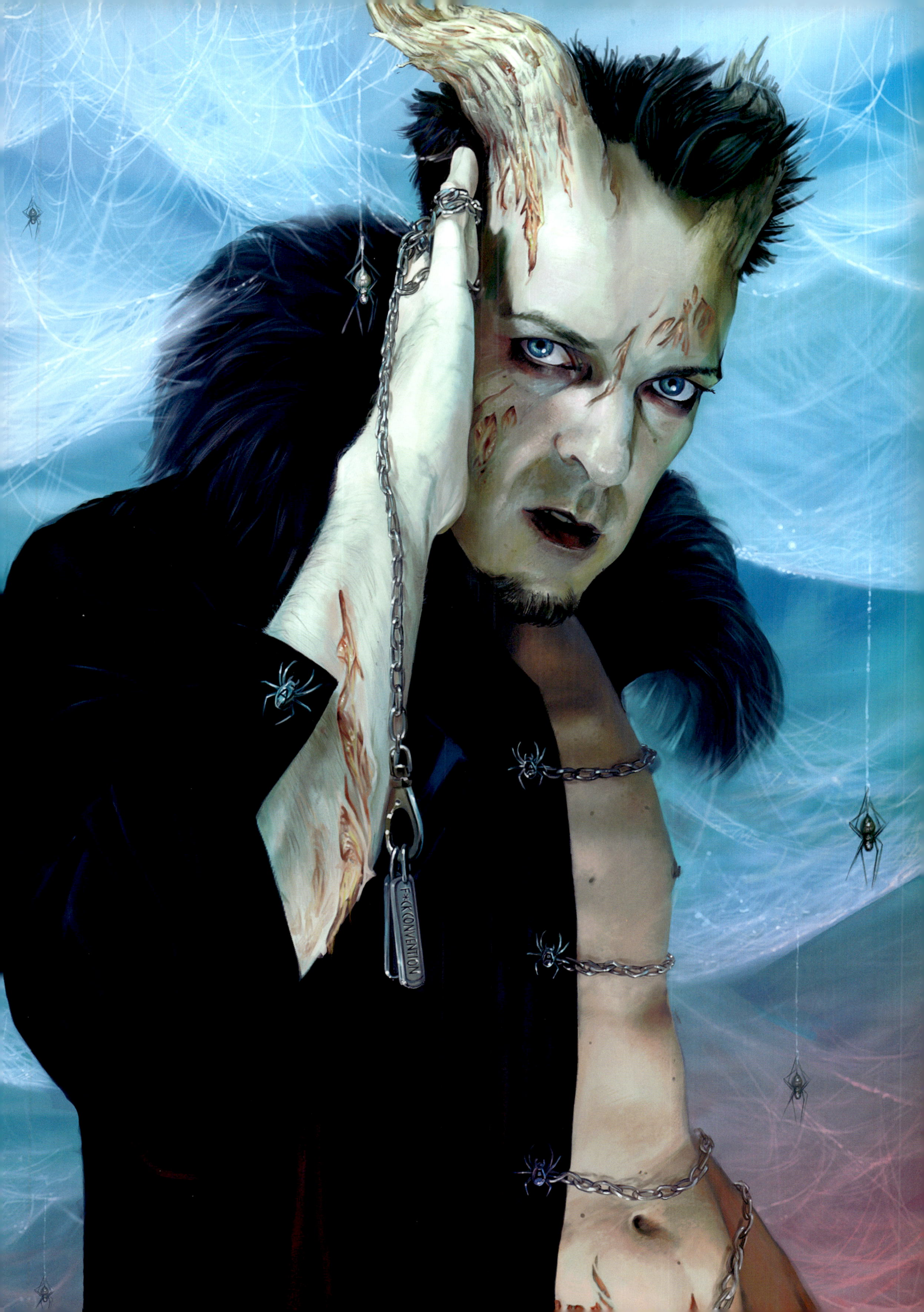
F*CKCONVENTION

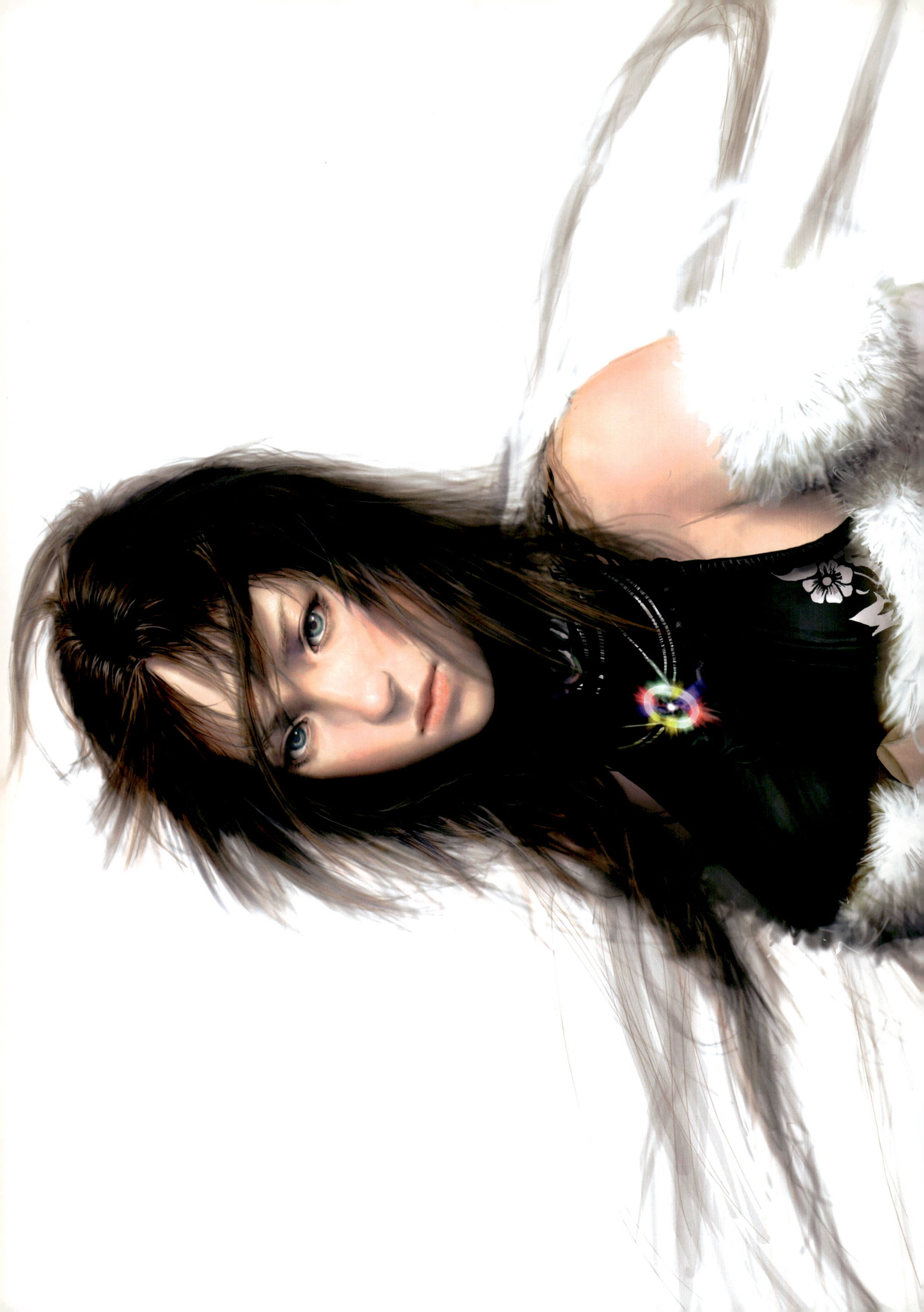

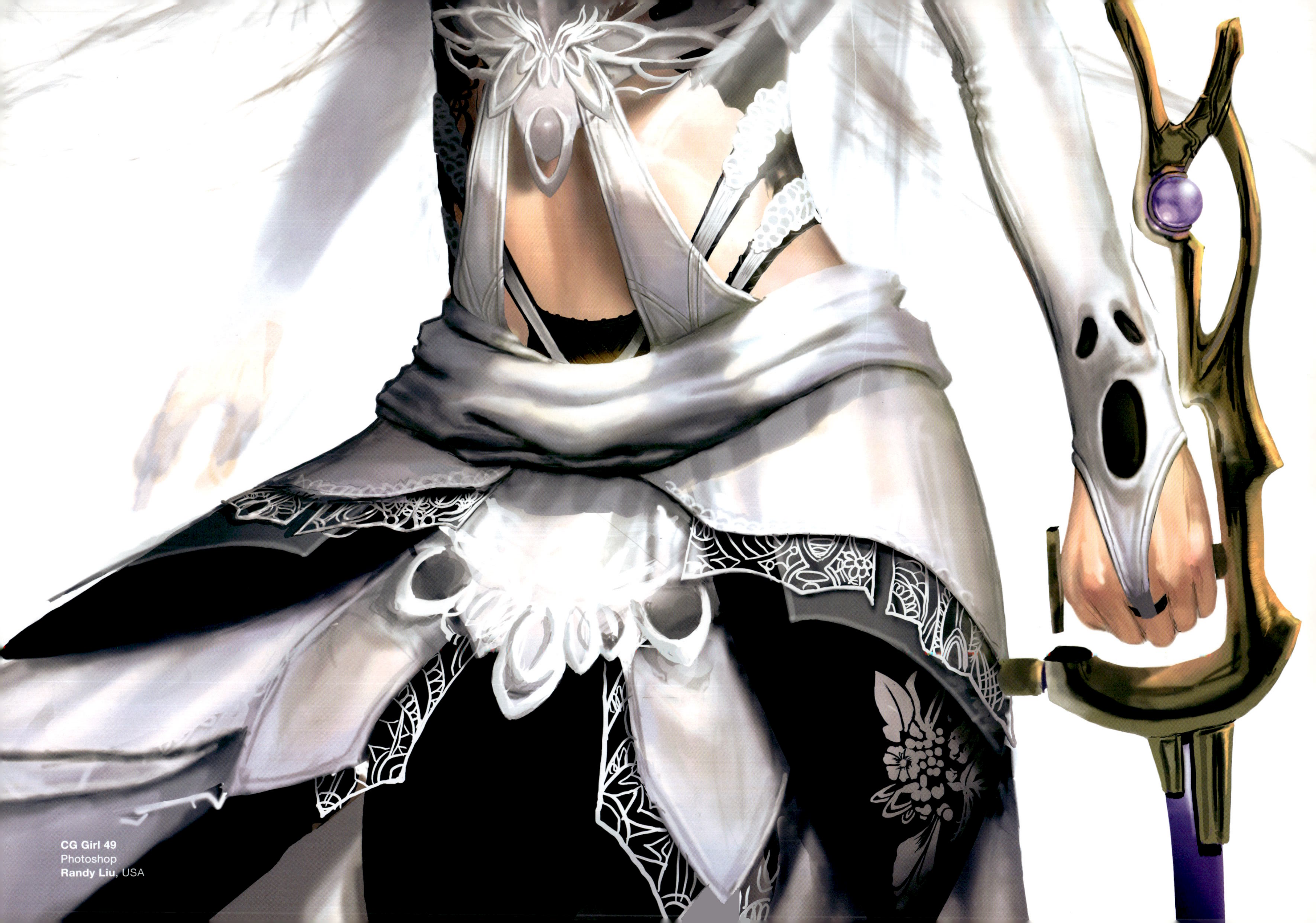

CG Girl 49
Photoshop
Randy Liu, USA

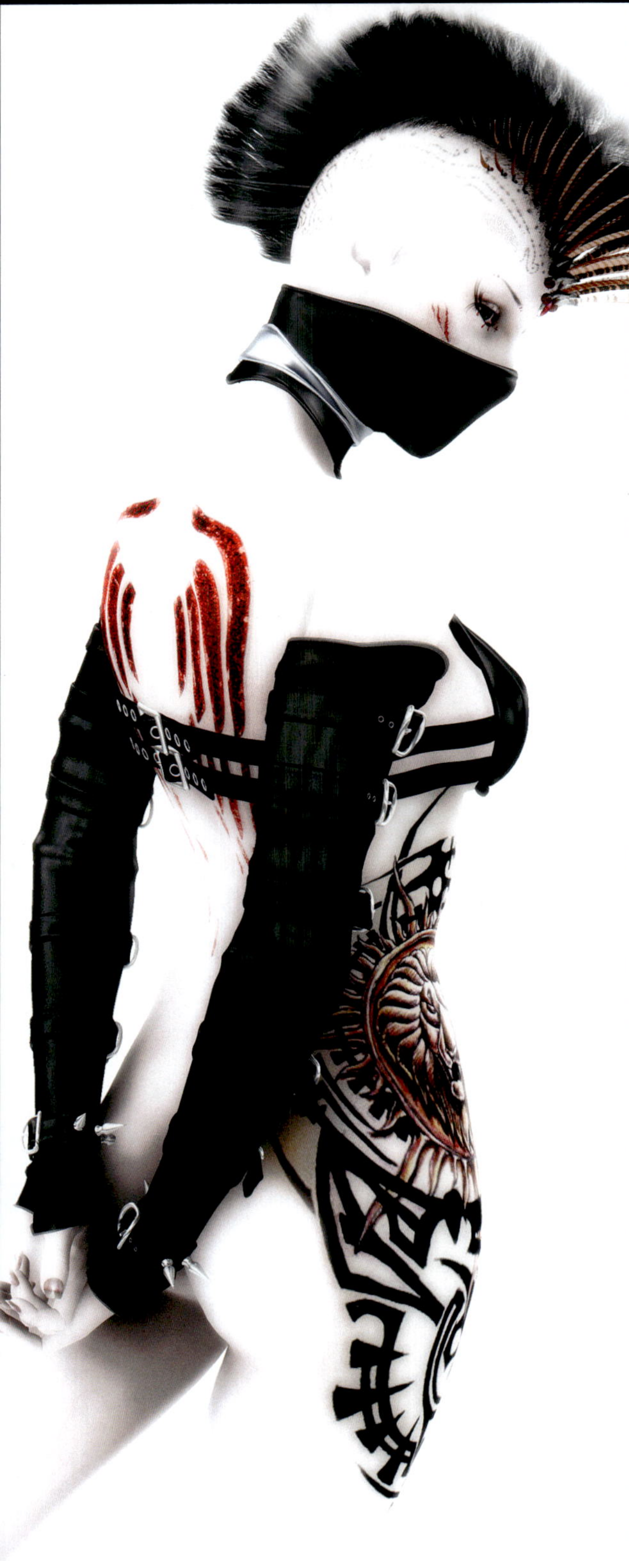

Fetish
Poser, Photoshop

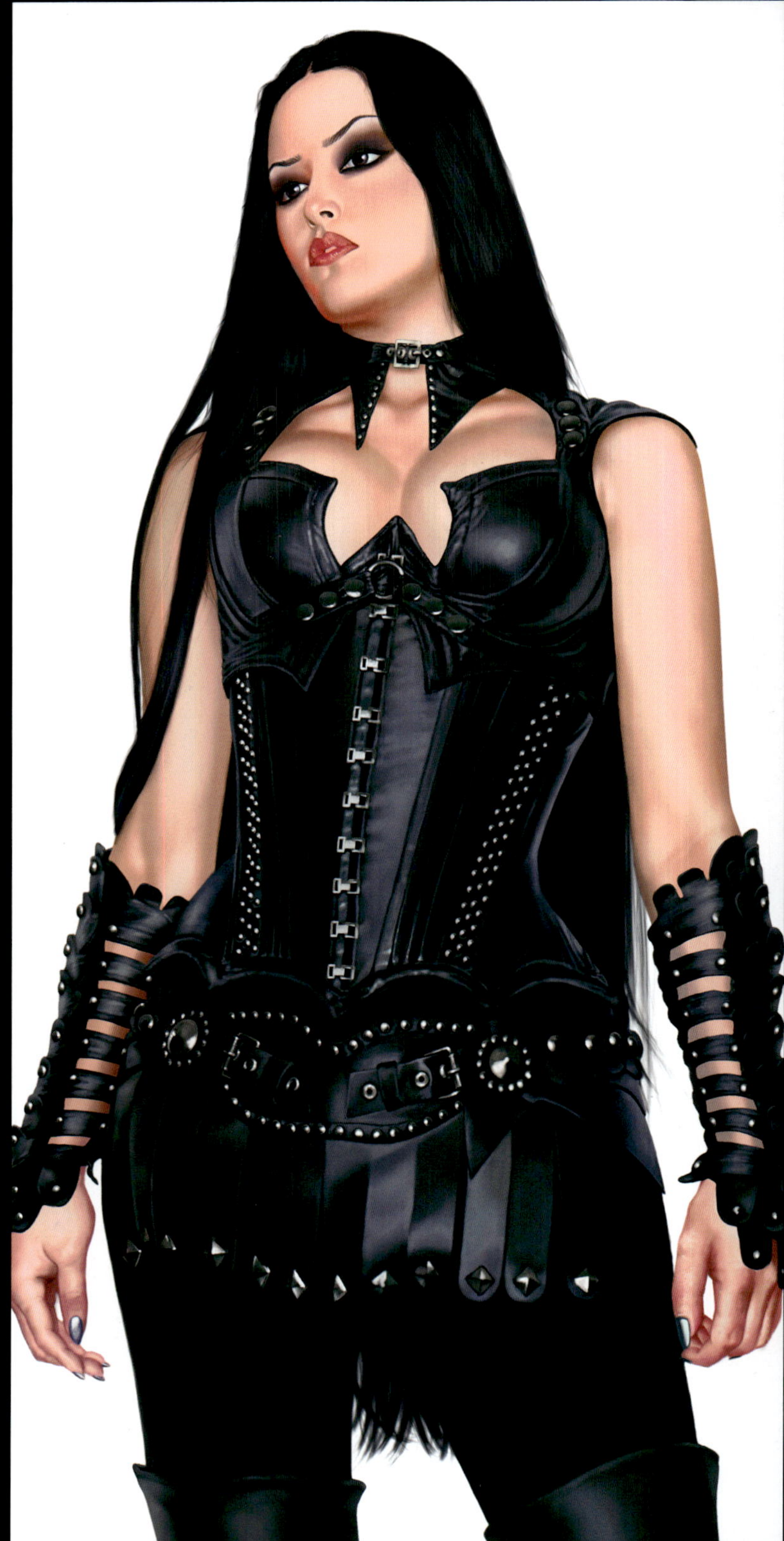

Gothic Girl
Painter

Gold Lion
3ds Max

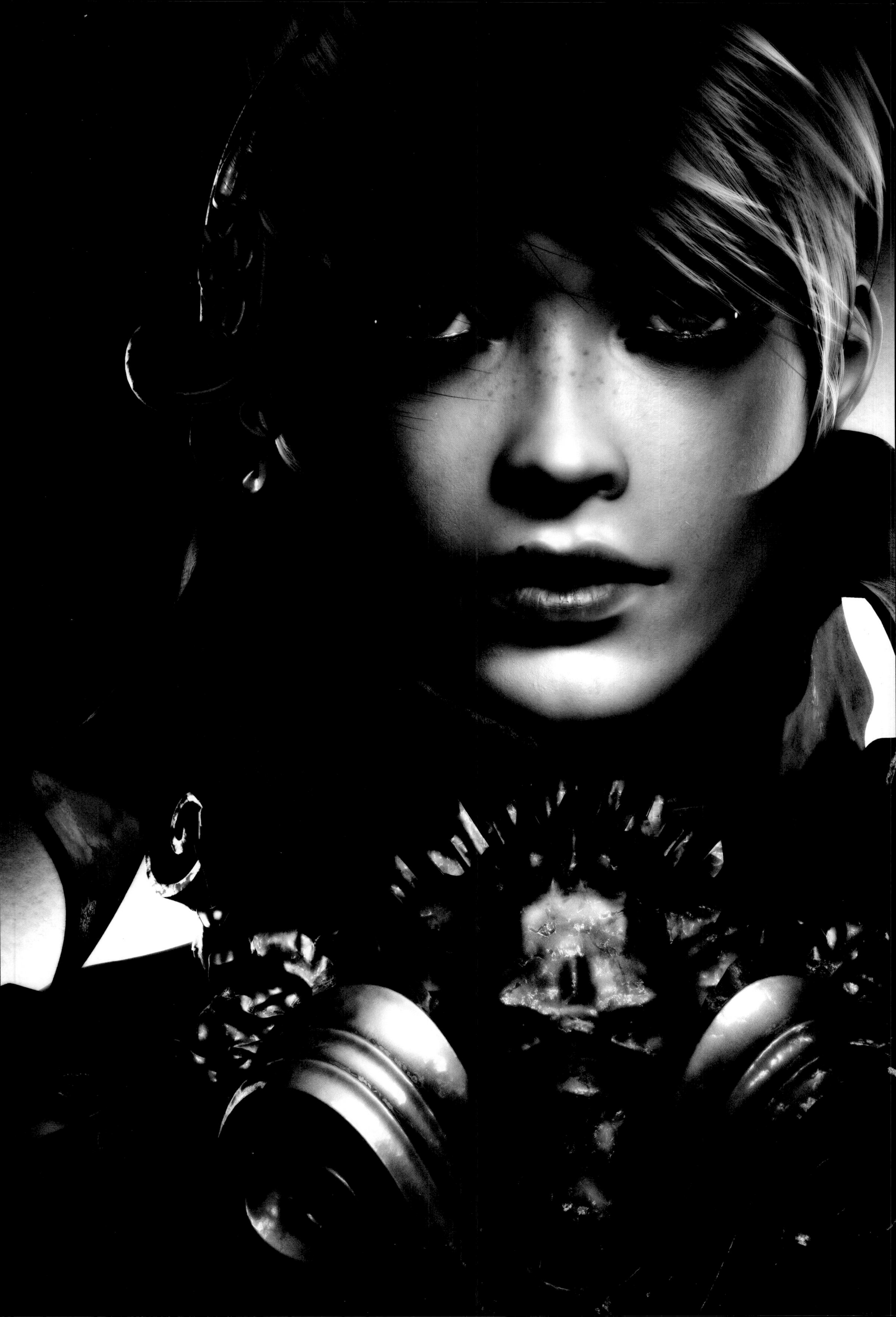

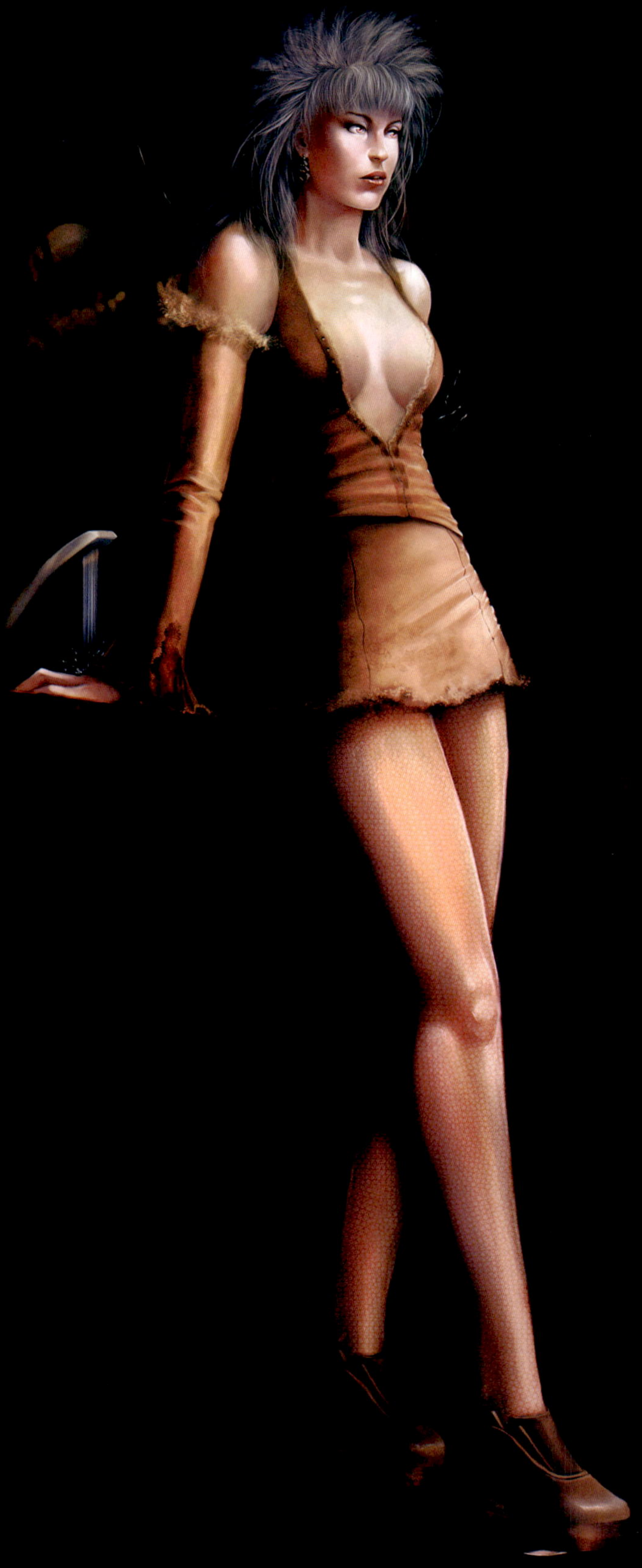

Mea Culpa
Photoshop
Sandra Hirschmann, GERMANY
[above]

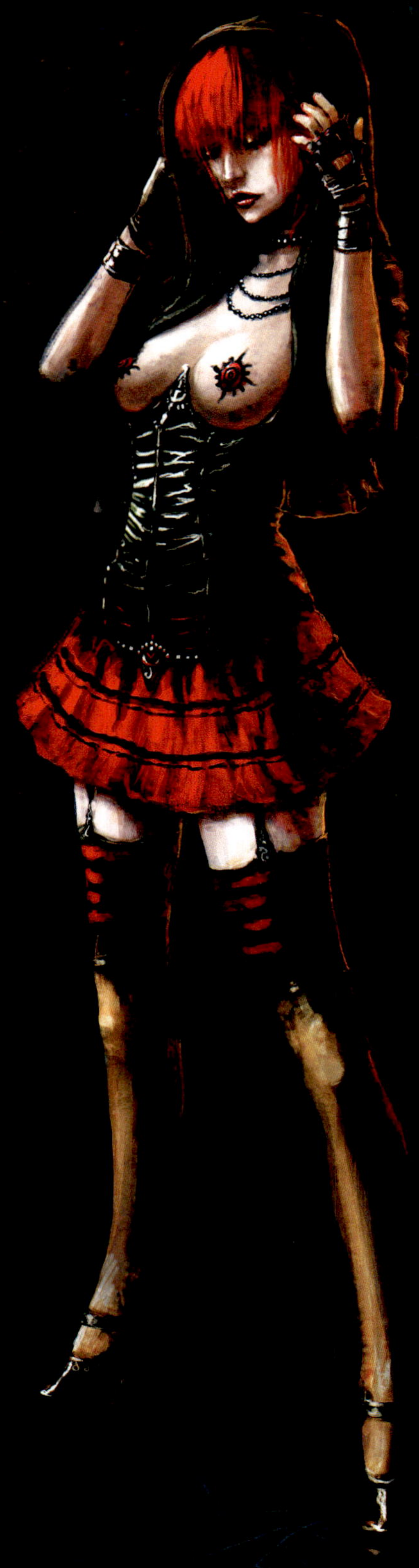

Hooded Girl
Photoshop
Alex Tornberg, NORWAY
[above]

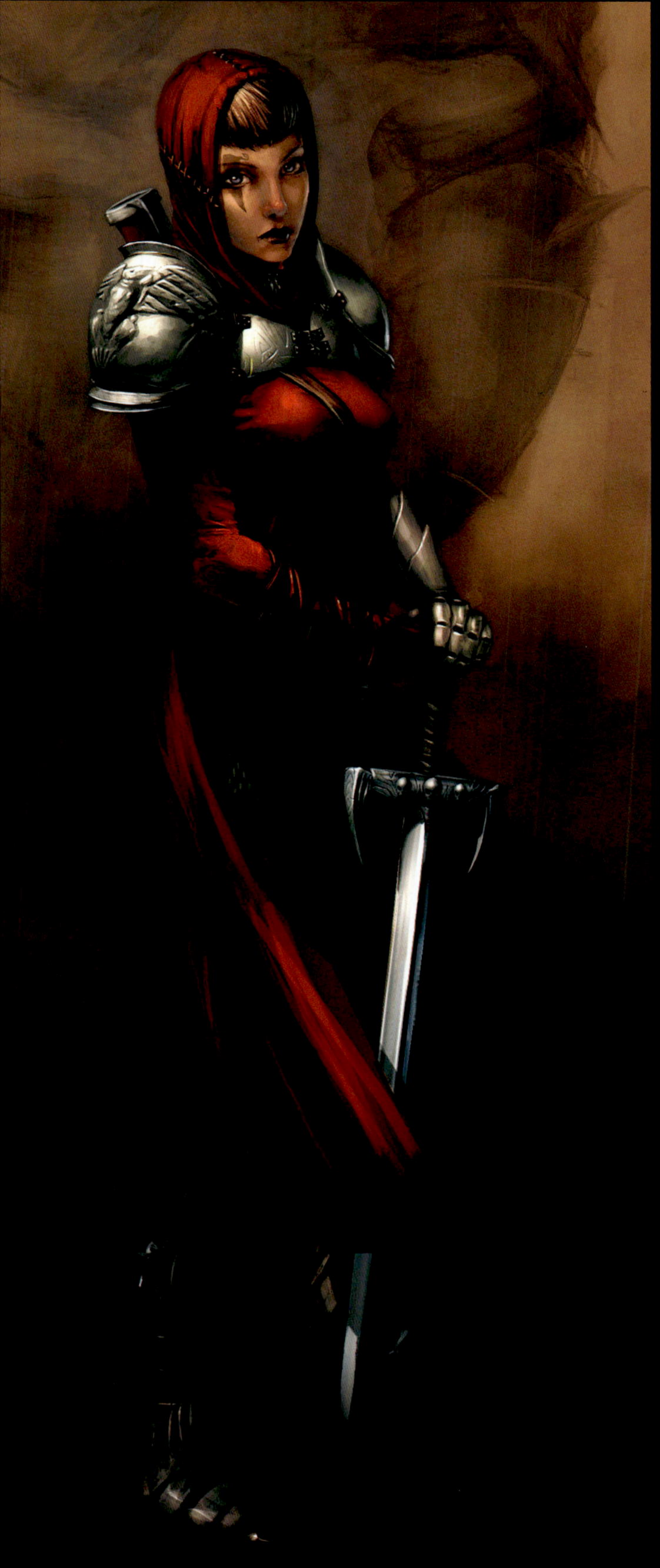

Guardians: Autumn
Photoshop
Kai Spannuth, GERMANY
[above]

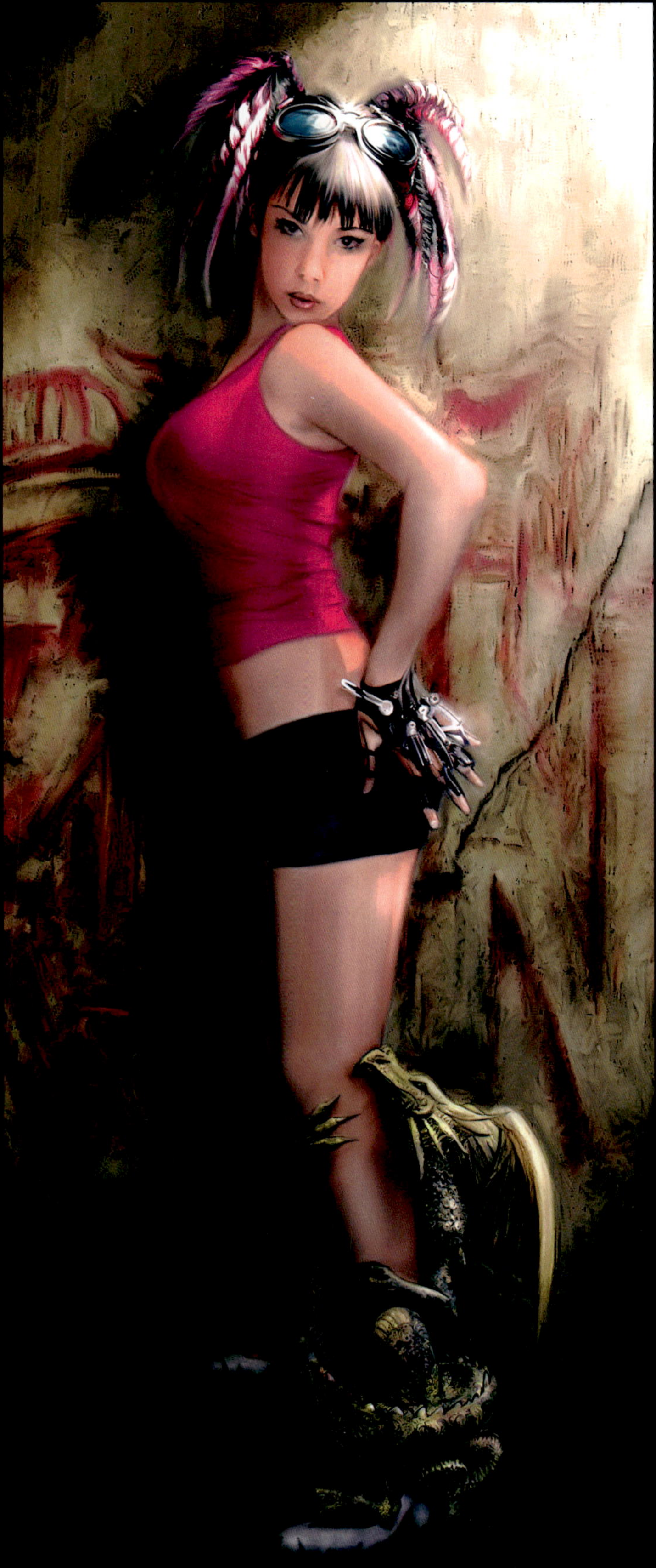

Anita
Photoshop, Paint Shop Pro
Marisa 'Sarima' Lopez Moreno, SPAIN
[above]

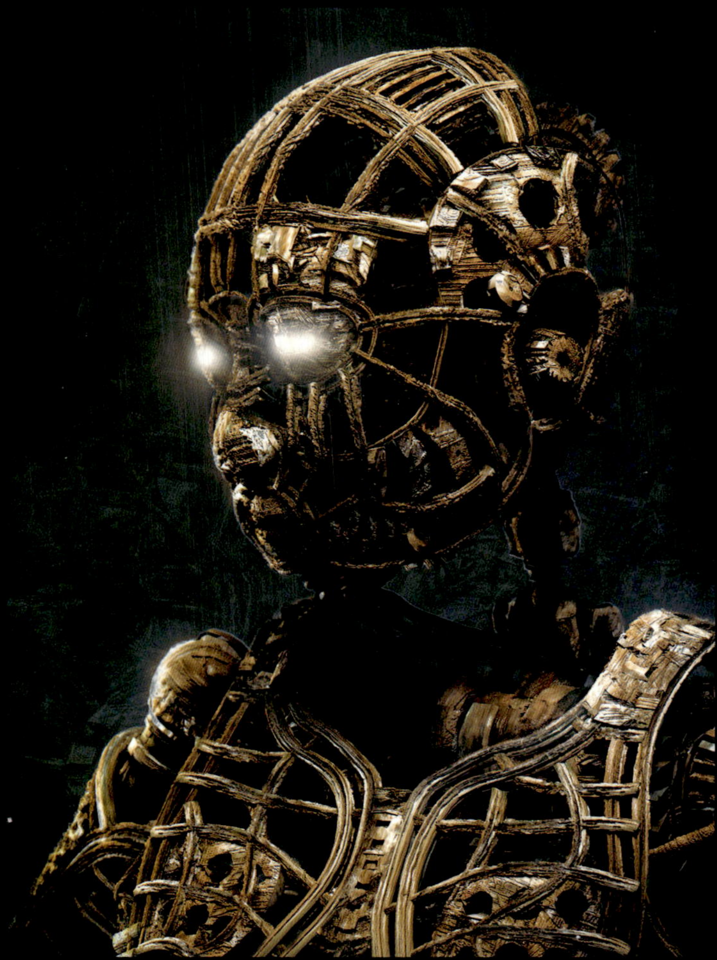

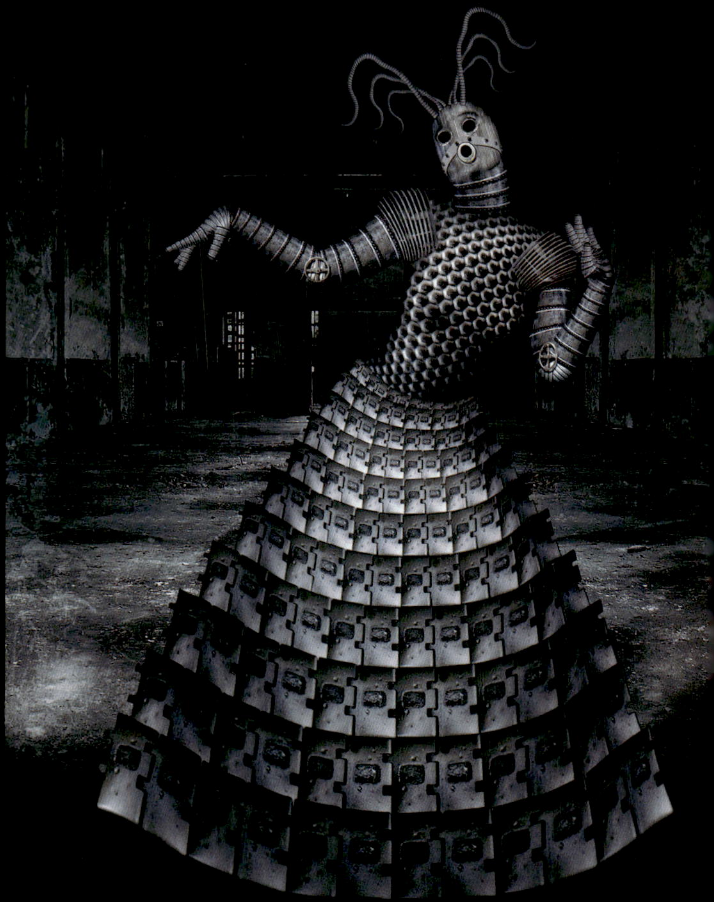

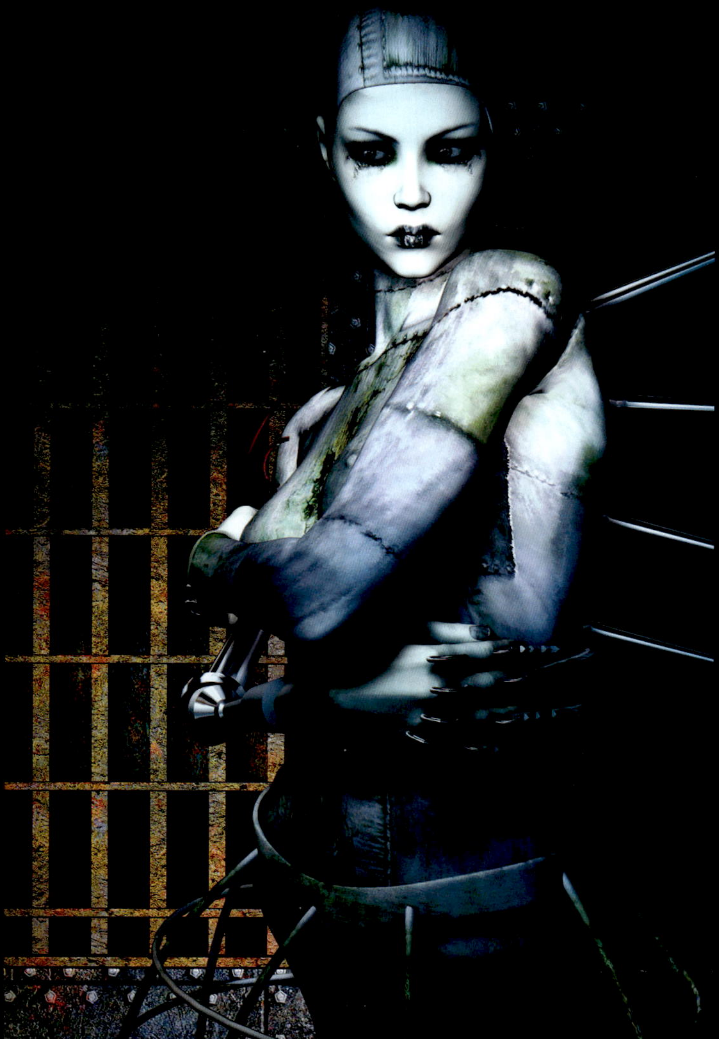

Rust
Maya, Painter
Daniel Arnold-Mist, GREAT BRITAIN
[top left]

The Silent Dancer
Photoshop
Alexei Solha, BRAZIL
[above]

Cheap Replacement
Poser, Photoshop
Jennifer Neveloff, USA
[left]

Black Cat White Cat
Photoshop
Eli Effenberger, ISRAEL
[right]

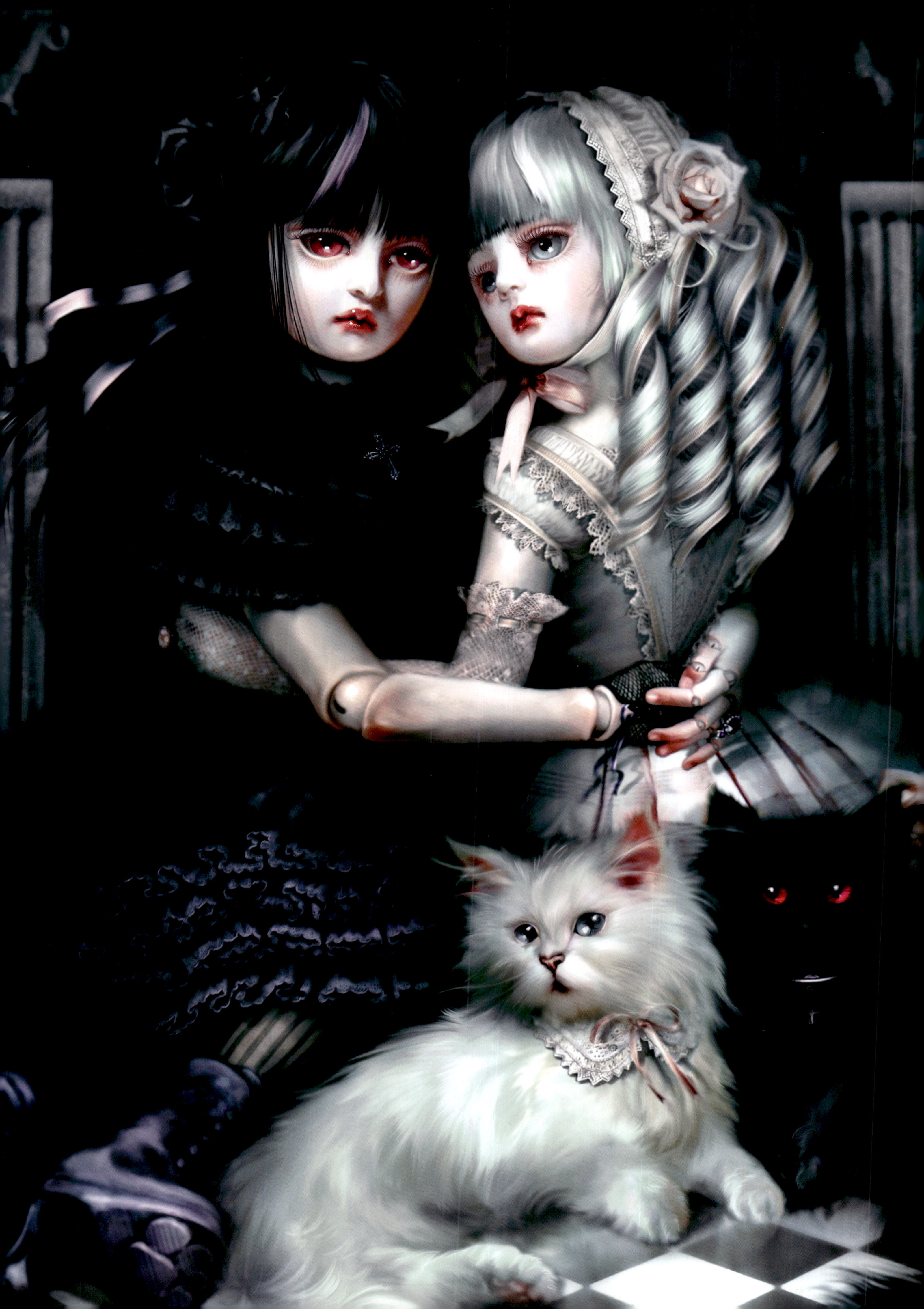

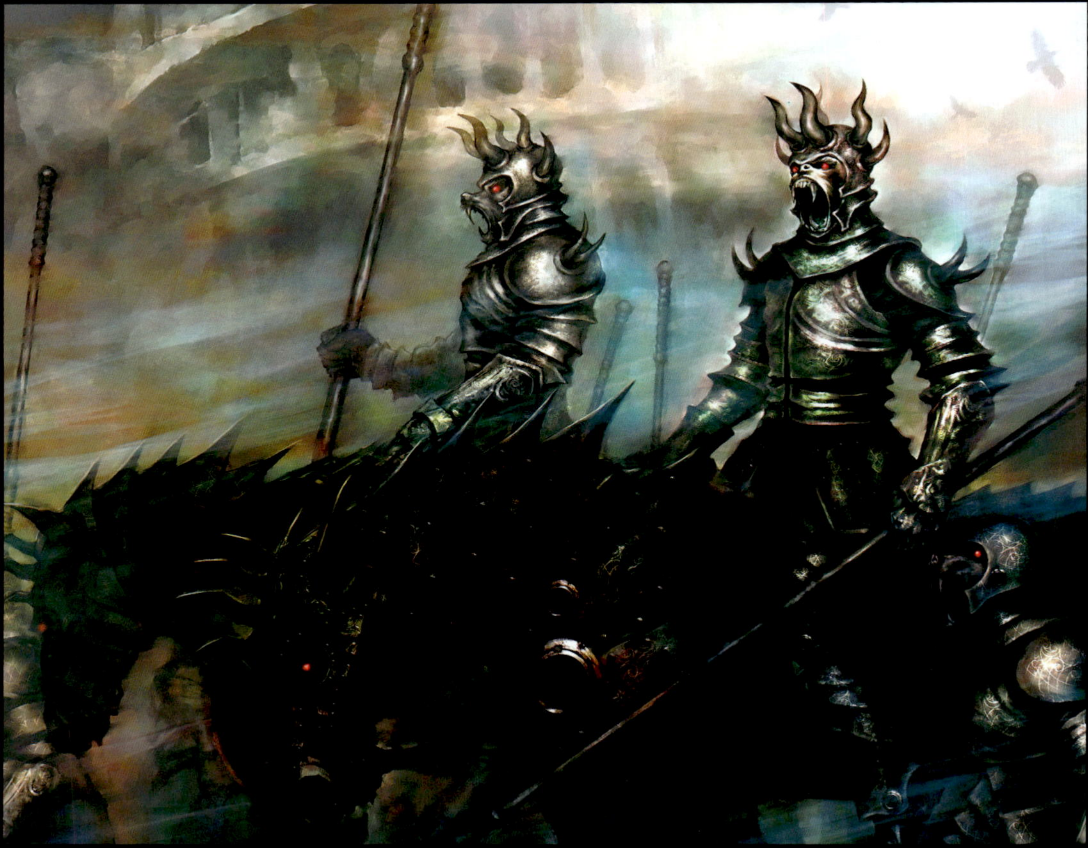

Battle cry
Painter, Photoshop
Kyushik Shin, USA
[left]

Corak the Hunter
3ds Max, ZBrush, Maya, Photoshop
Philip Herman, INDONESIA
[right]

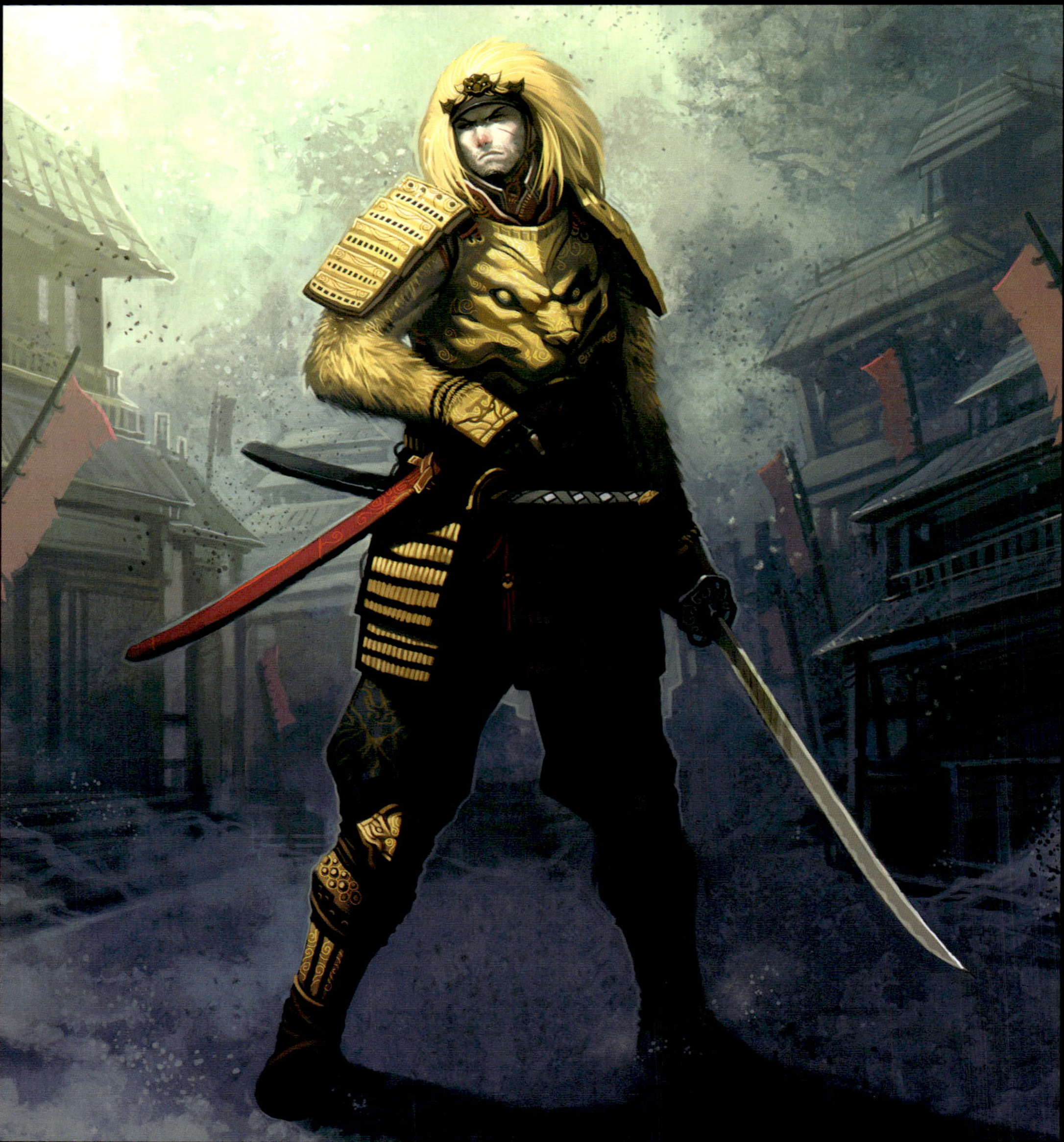

Lionclan Samurai
Photoshop
Andrew Hou, CANADA
[left]

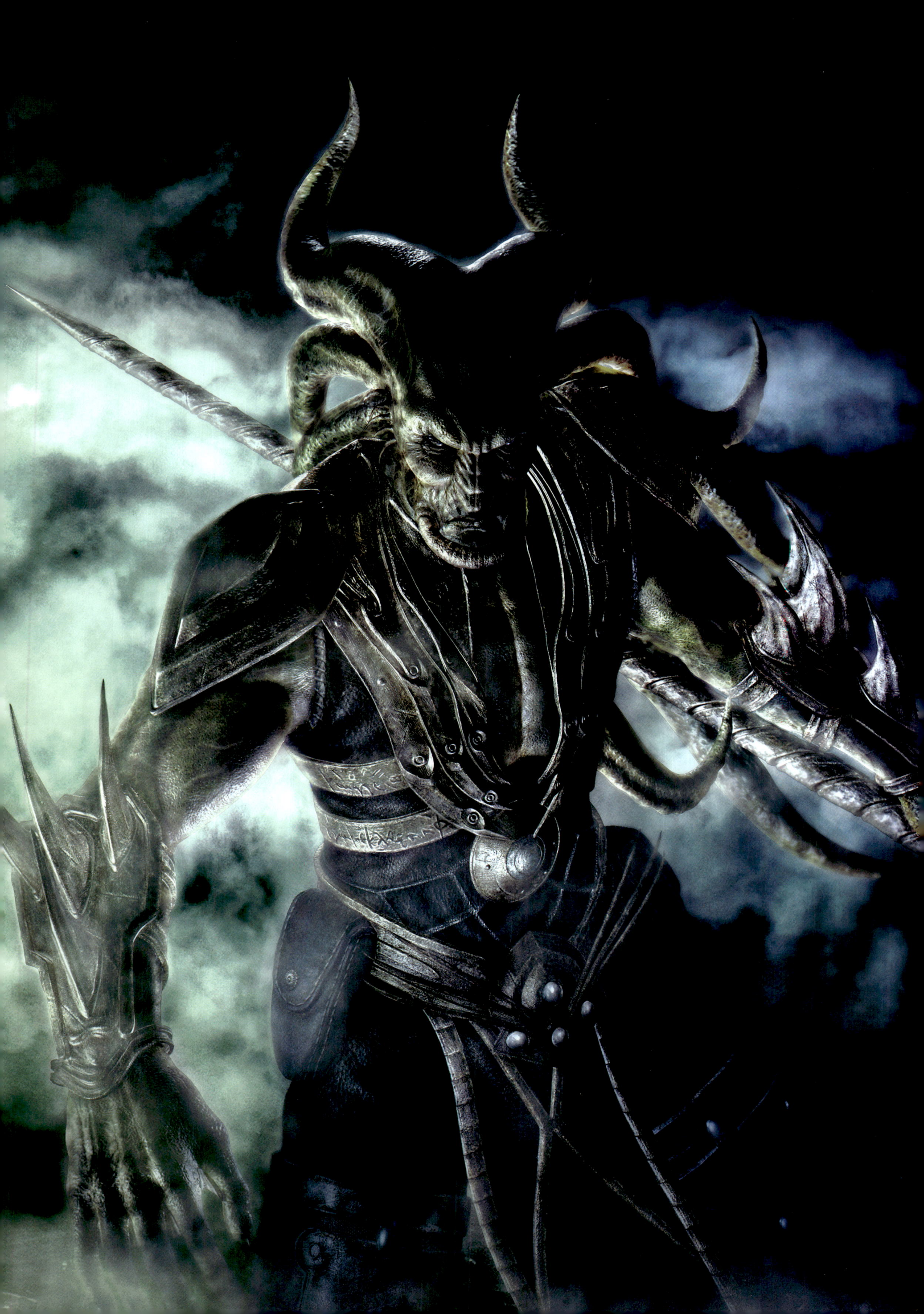

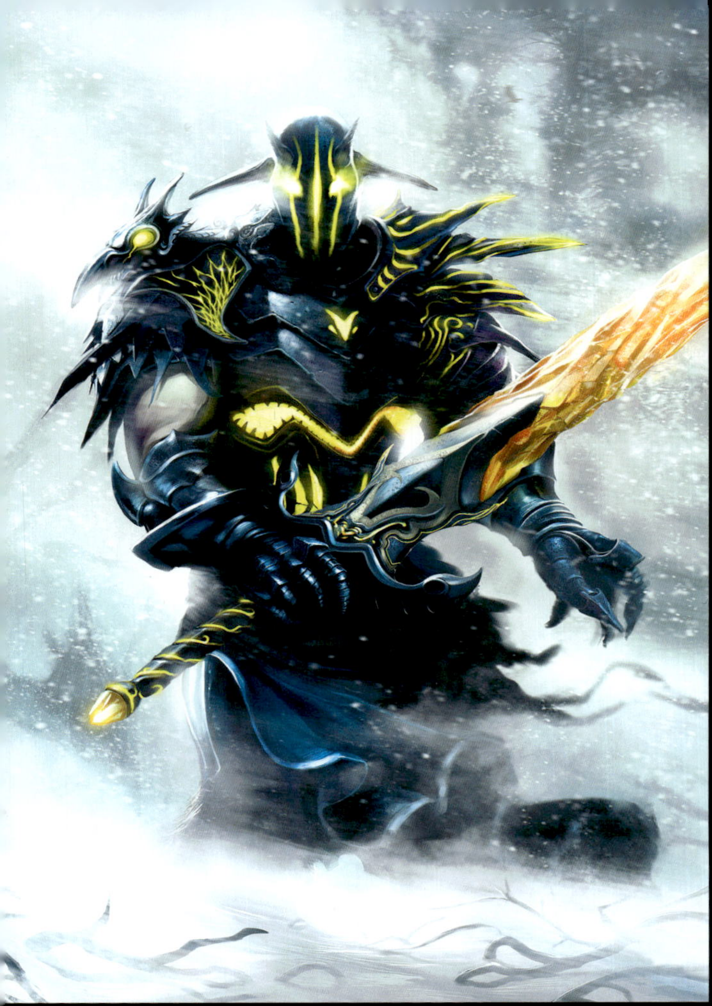

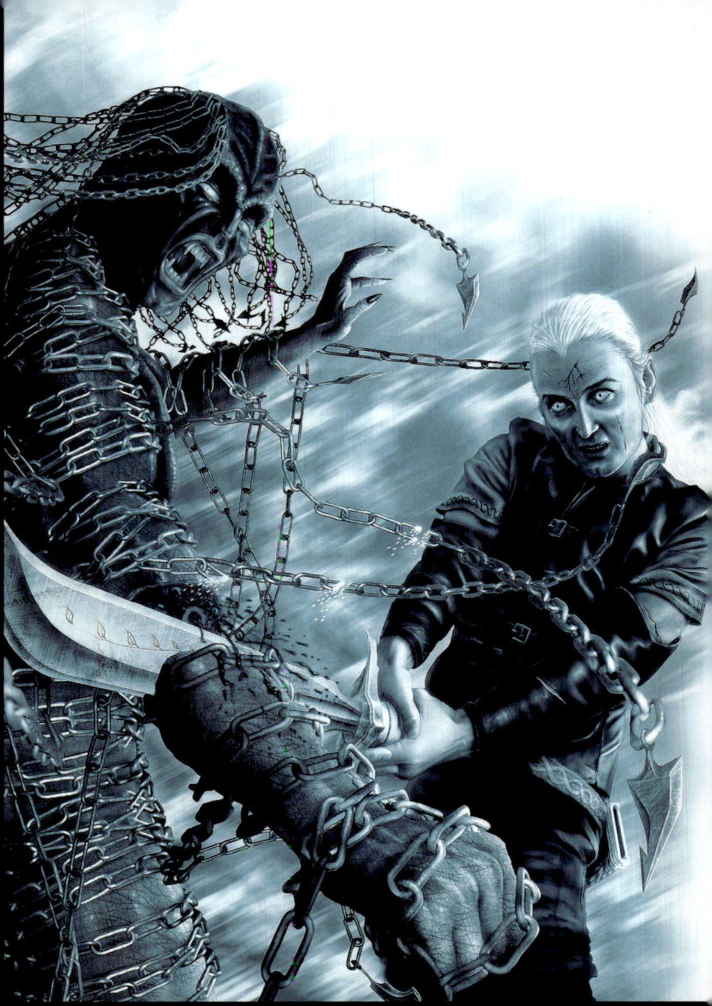

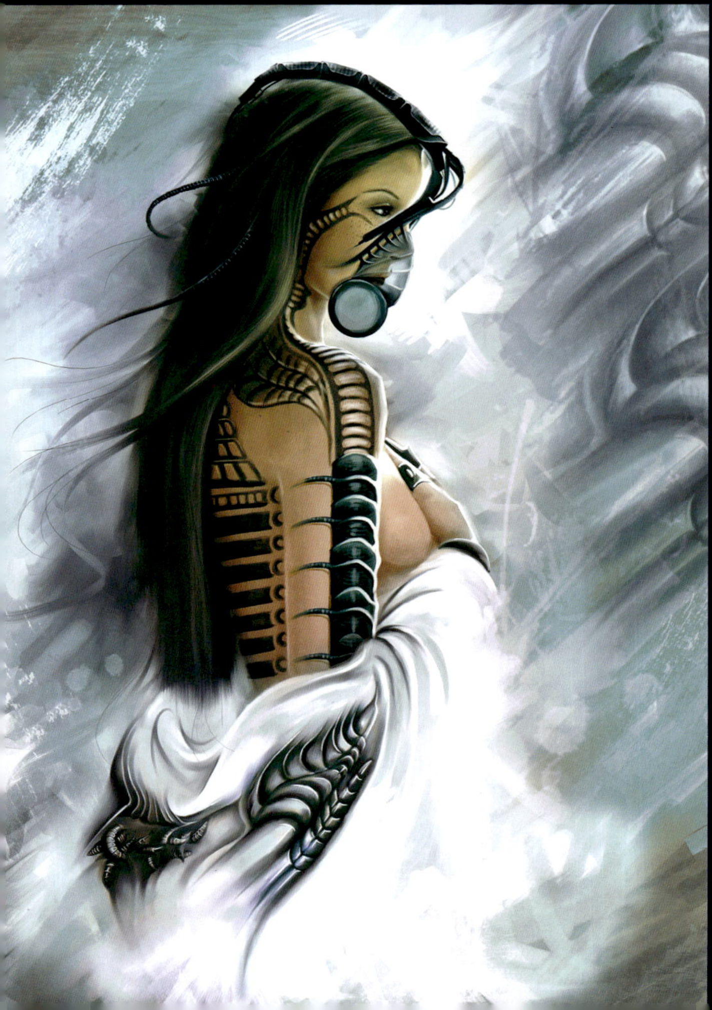

The Visitor
Photoshop
Simon Robert, ROMANIA
[top left]

Combat
Photoshop
Client: Bastion Press
Phillip James, GREAT BRITAIN
[above]

Transmogrify
Painter, Photoshop
Michael Krenzin, GERMANY
[left]

Dragon hunter
Painter
Erik Holmen, ROBRADY Design,
USA
[right]

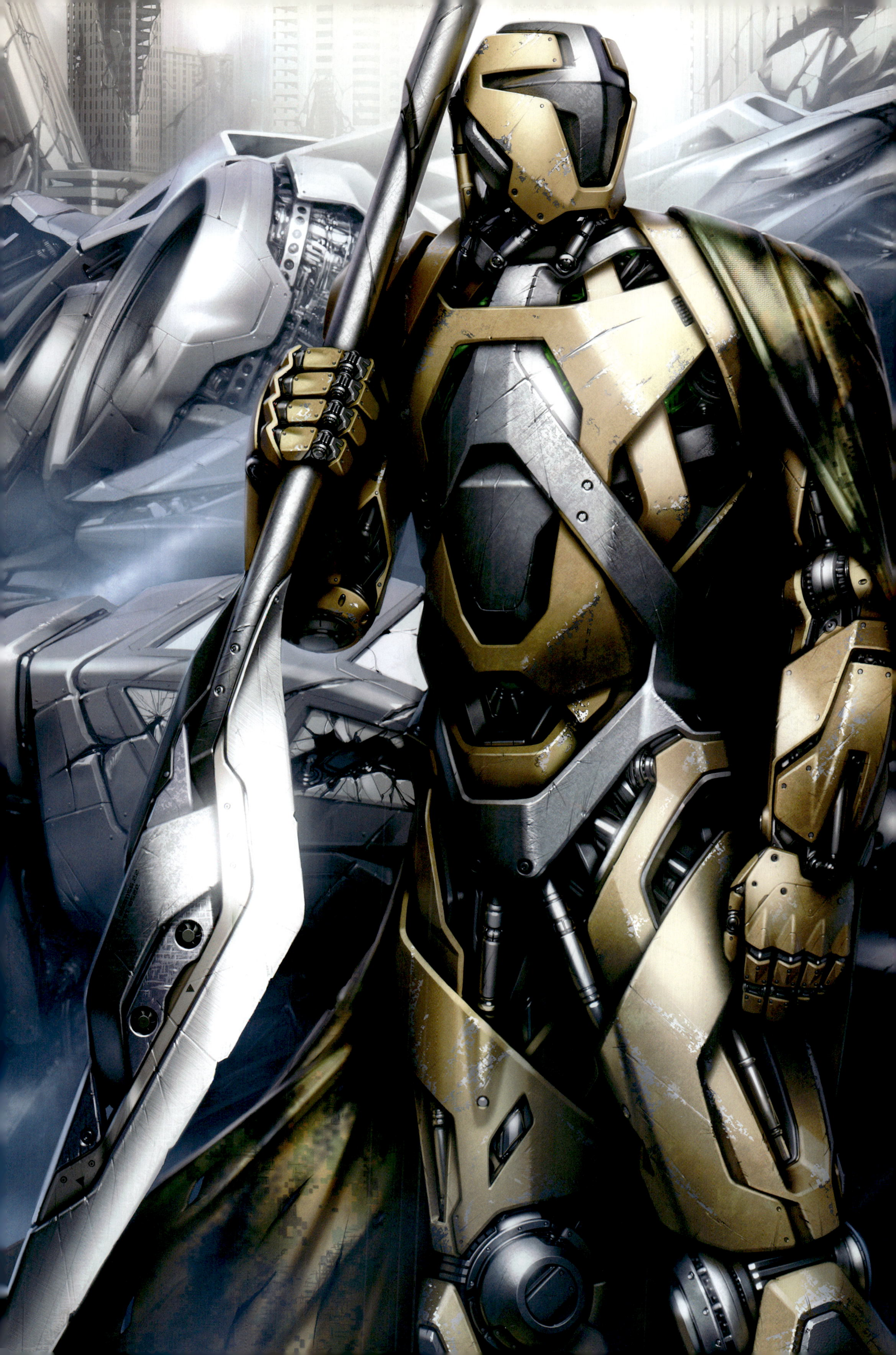

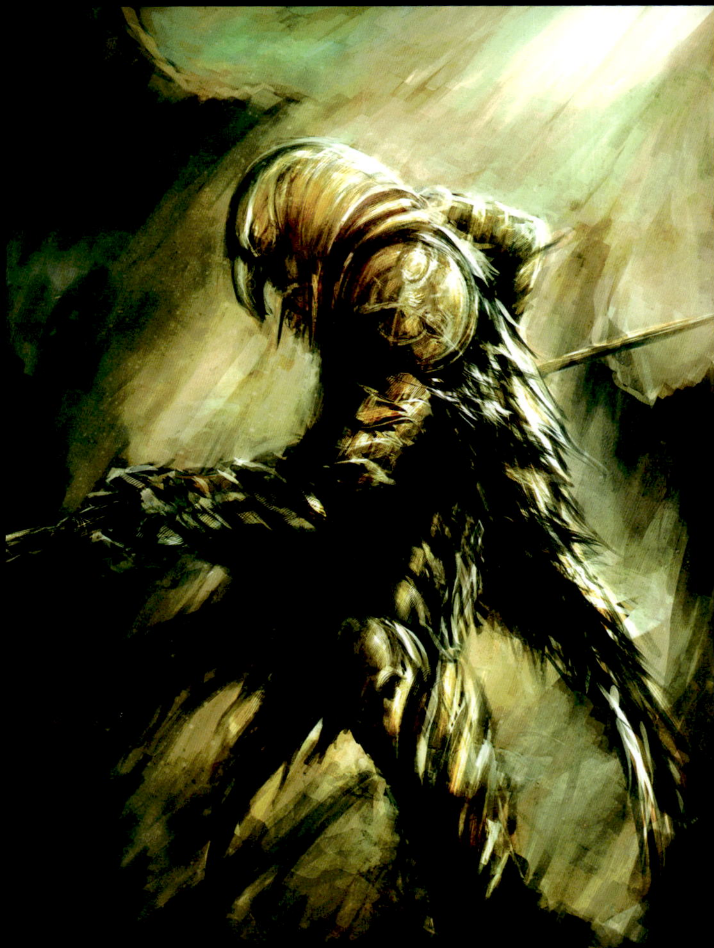

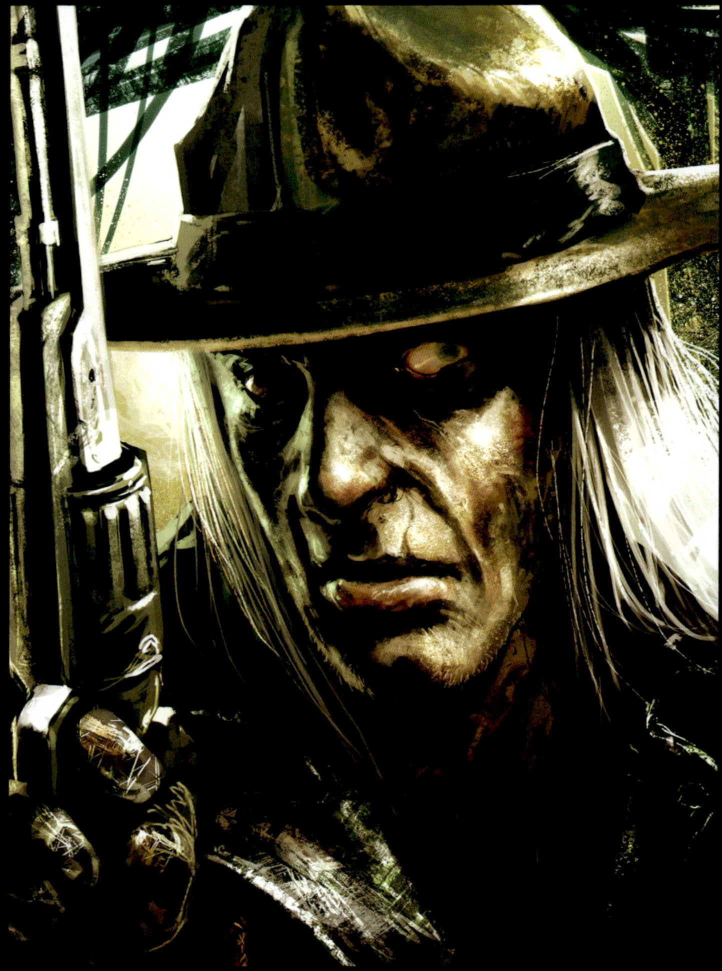

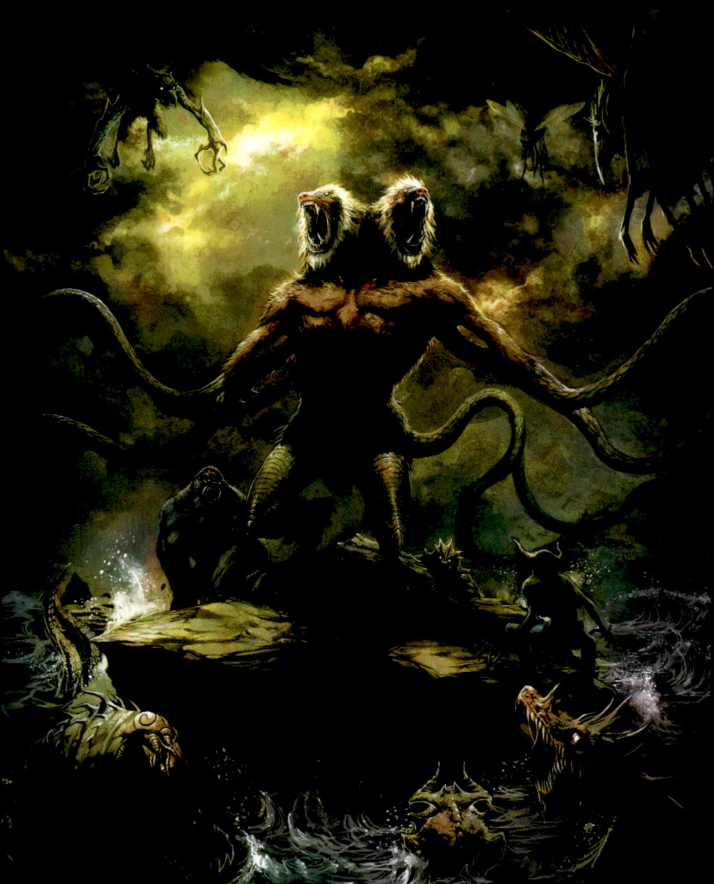

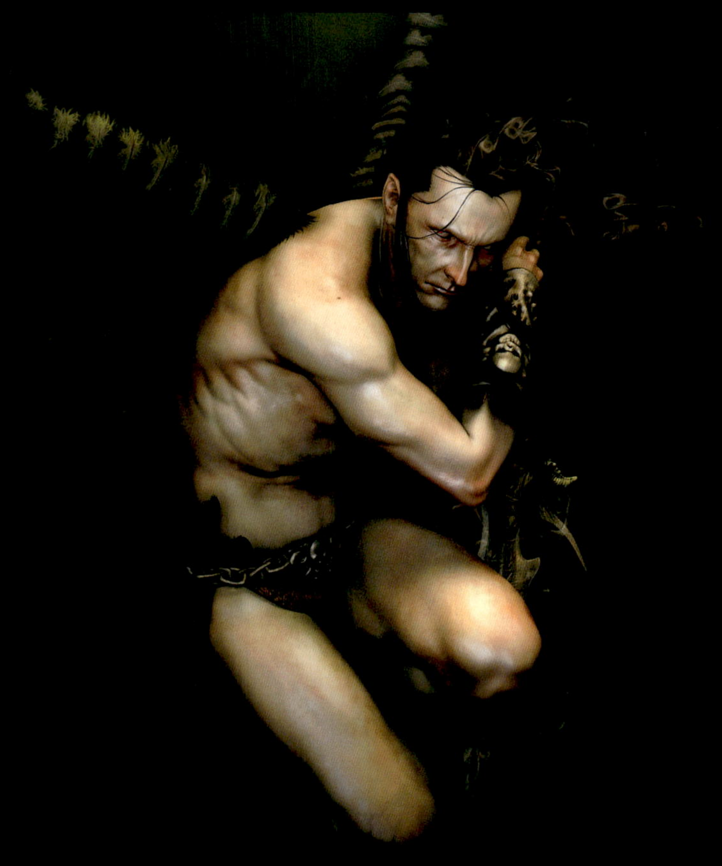

Arcanian
Photoshop
Riyahd Cassiem, SOUTH AFRICA
[top]

Demogorgon
Photoshop
Client: Paizo Publishing
Andrew Hou, CANADA
[above]

One eyed judge
Photoshop
Tomasz Jedruszek, POLAND
[top]

Lucifer: The fallen Angel
Softimage|XSI, Mudbox, ZBrush, Photoshop
Diego Maia, BRAZIL
[above]

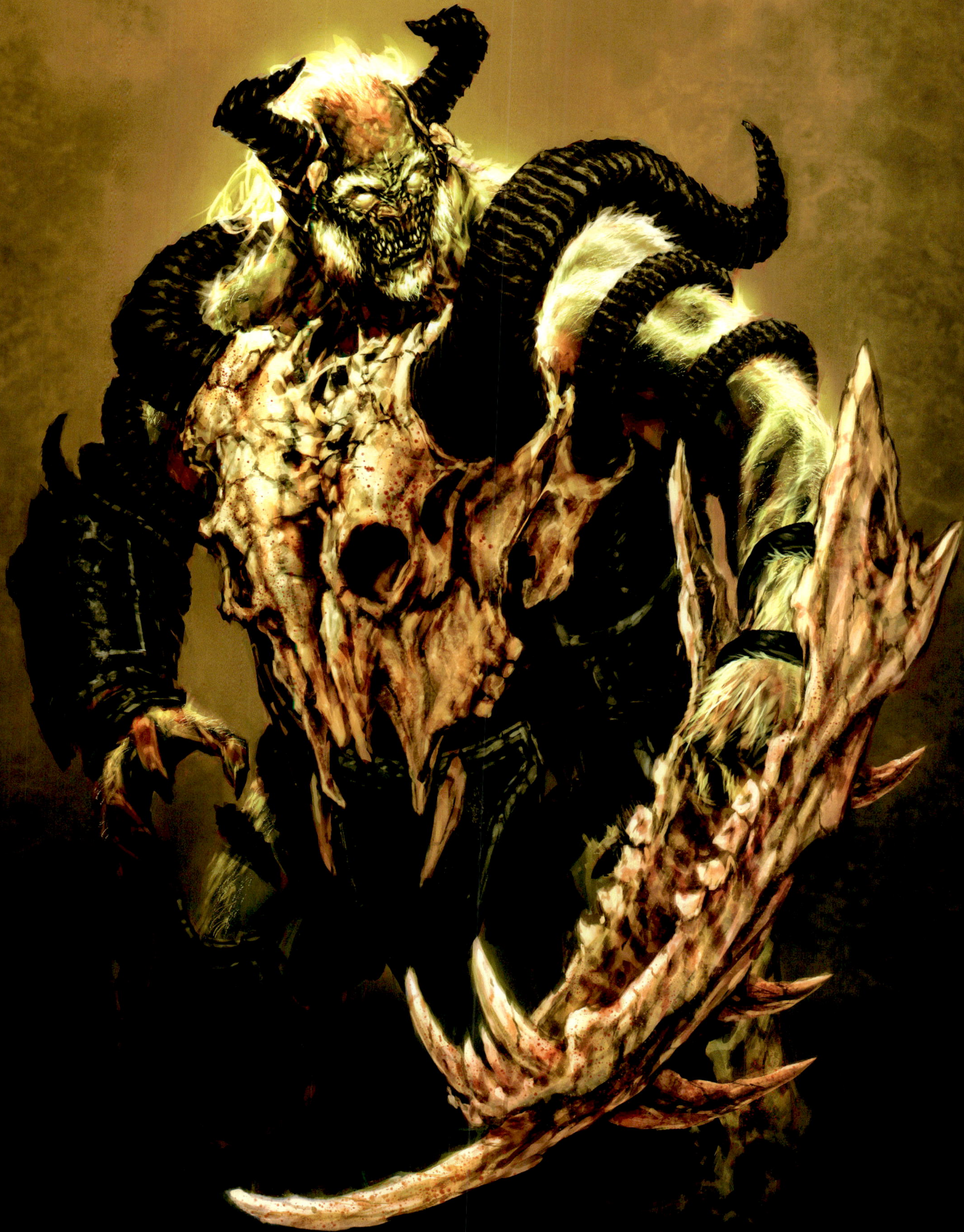

Hades Juggernaut
Photoshop
Andy Park, SCEA, USA

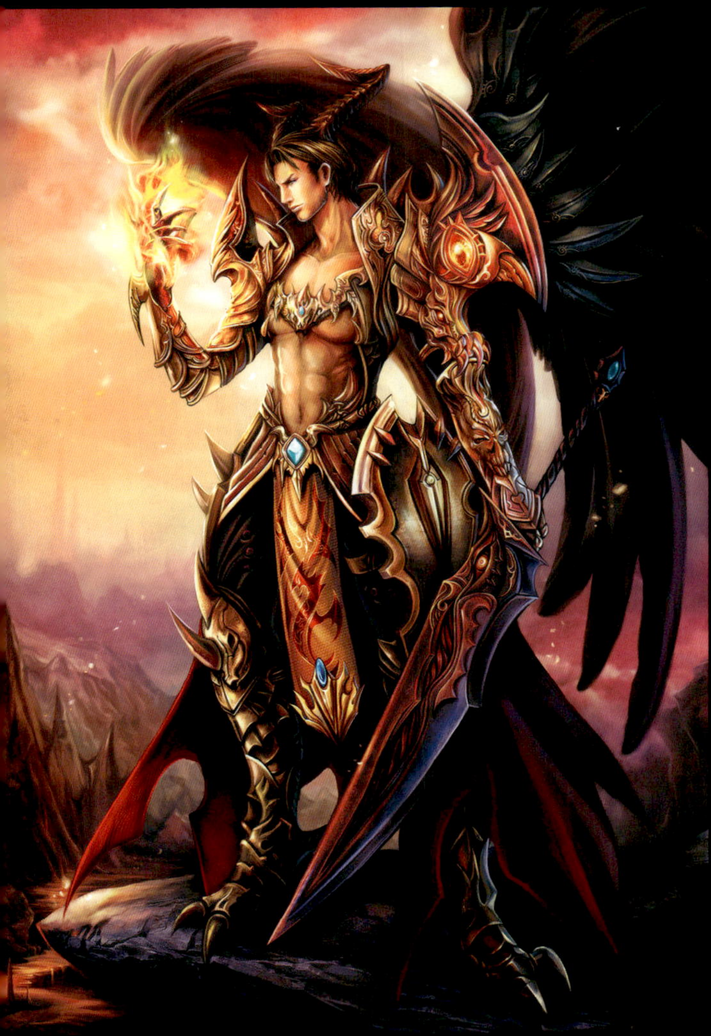

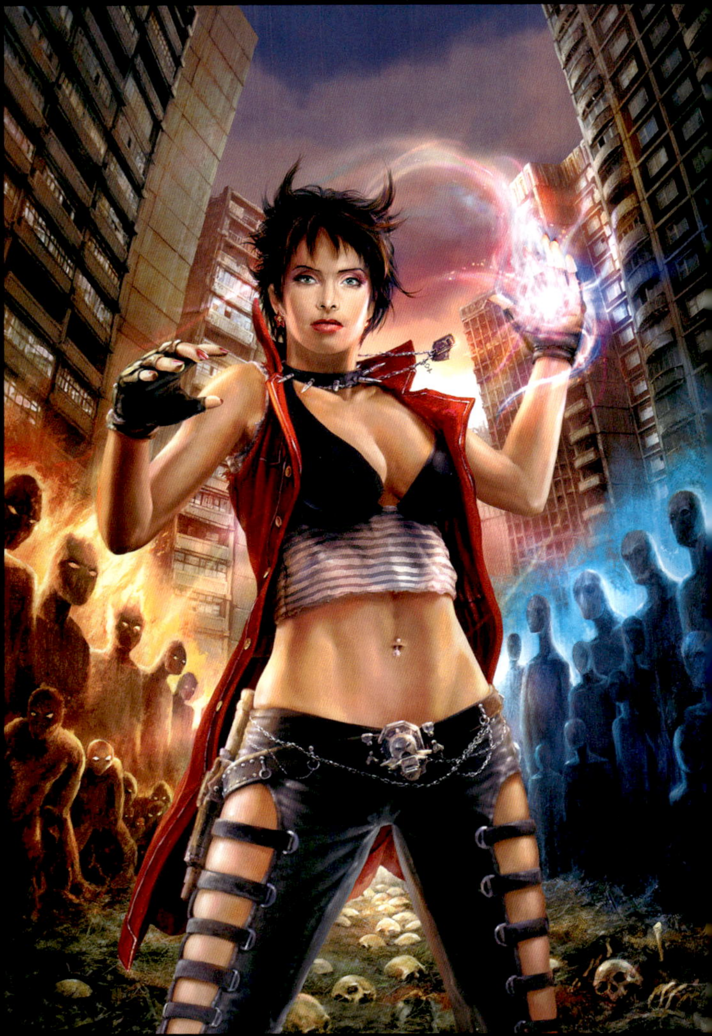

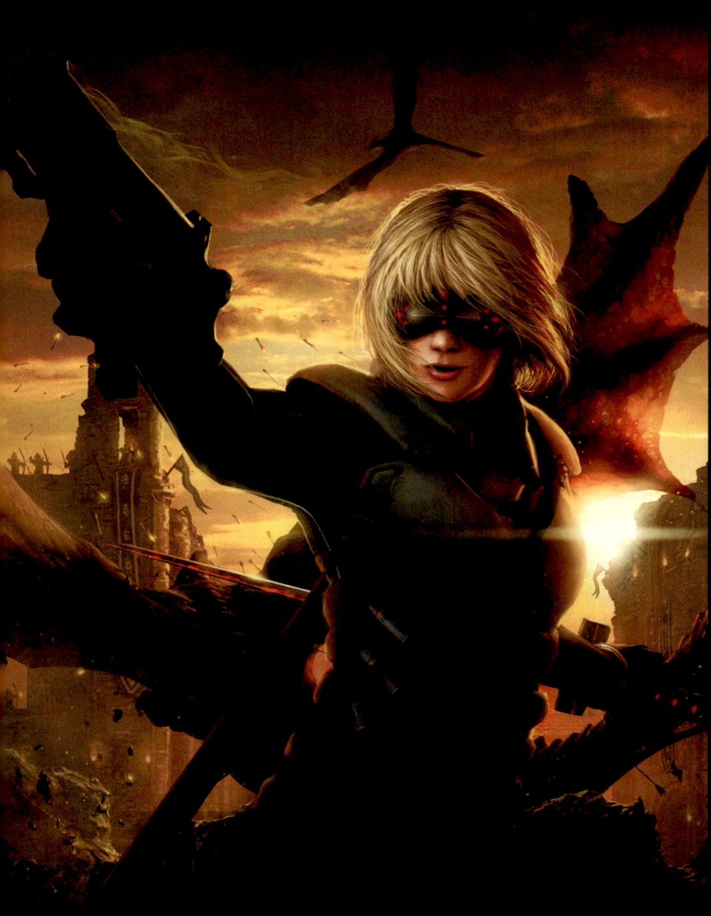

Demon king
Photoshop
Fan Yang, USA
[top left]

Day Watch Cover
Photoshop
Client: Nova Disk Company
Pavel Lagutin, RUSSIA
[above]

Time Crusade
Photoshop
Client: Fabryka Slow
Marek Okon, POLAND
[left]

Stuck after battle
Photoshop
Pavel Lagutin, RUSSIA
[right]

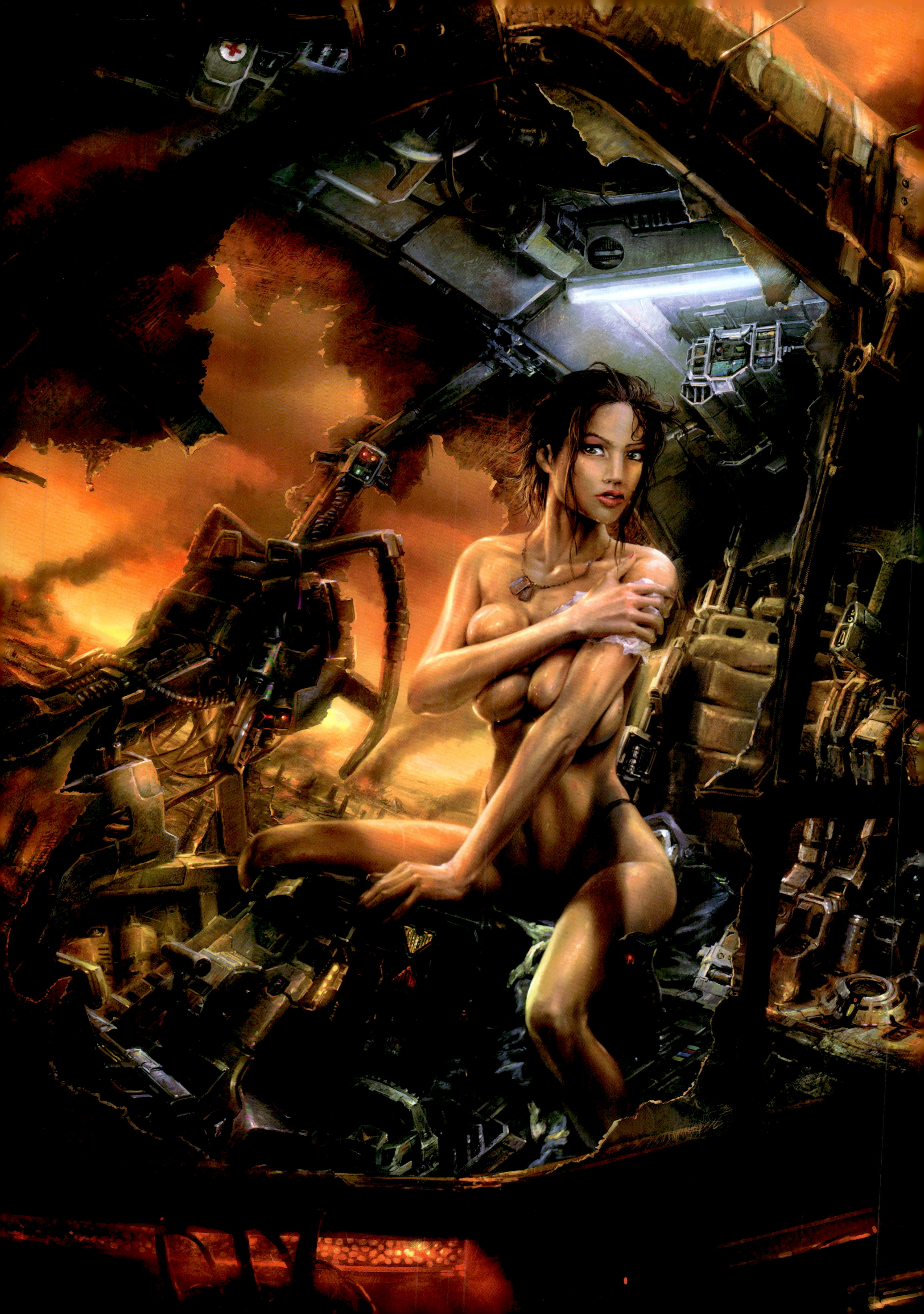

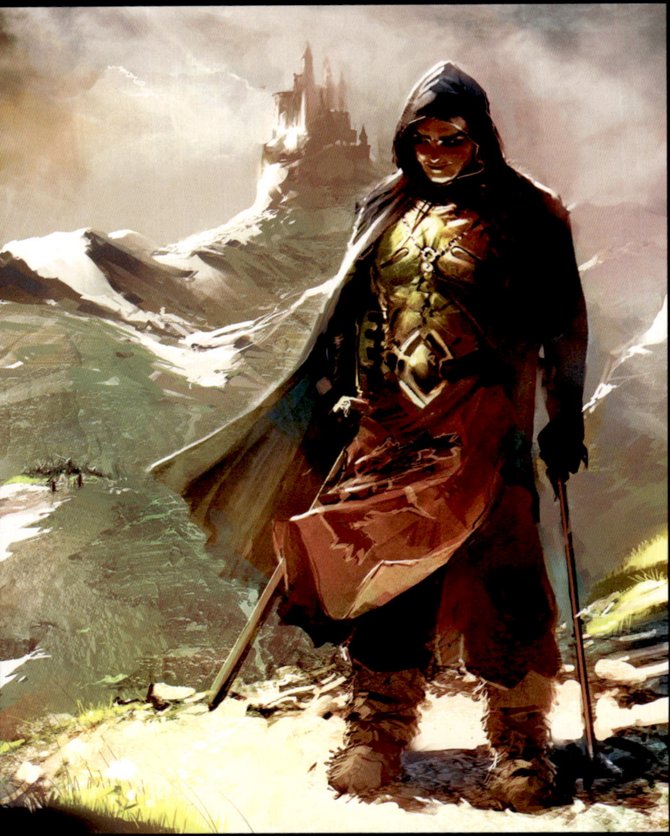

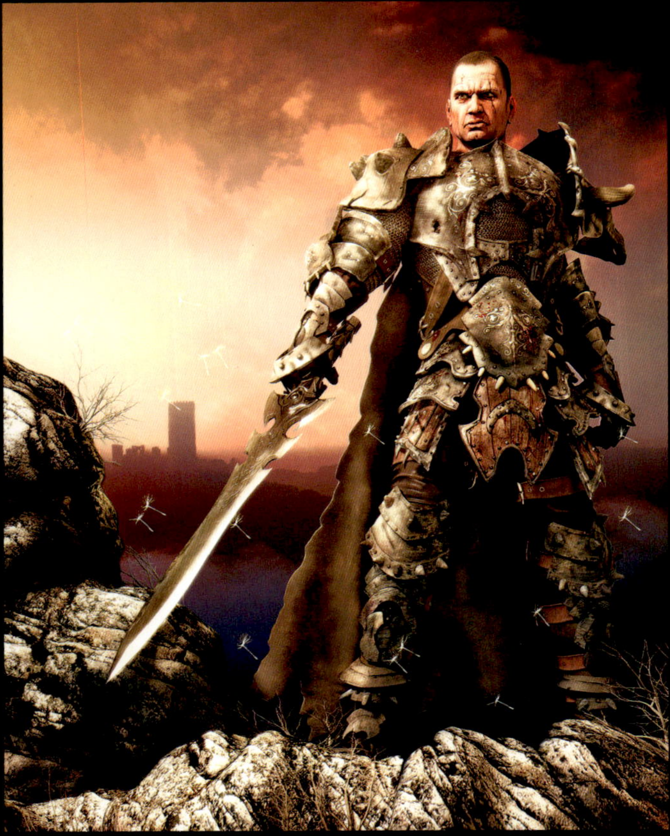

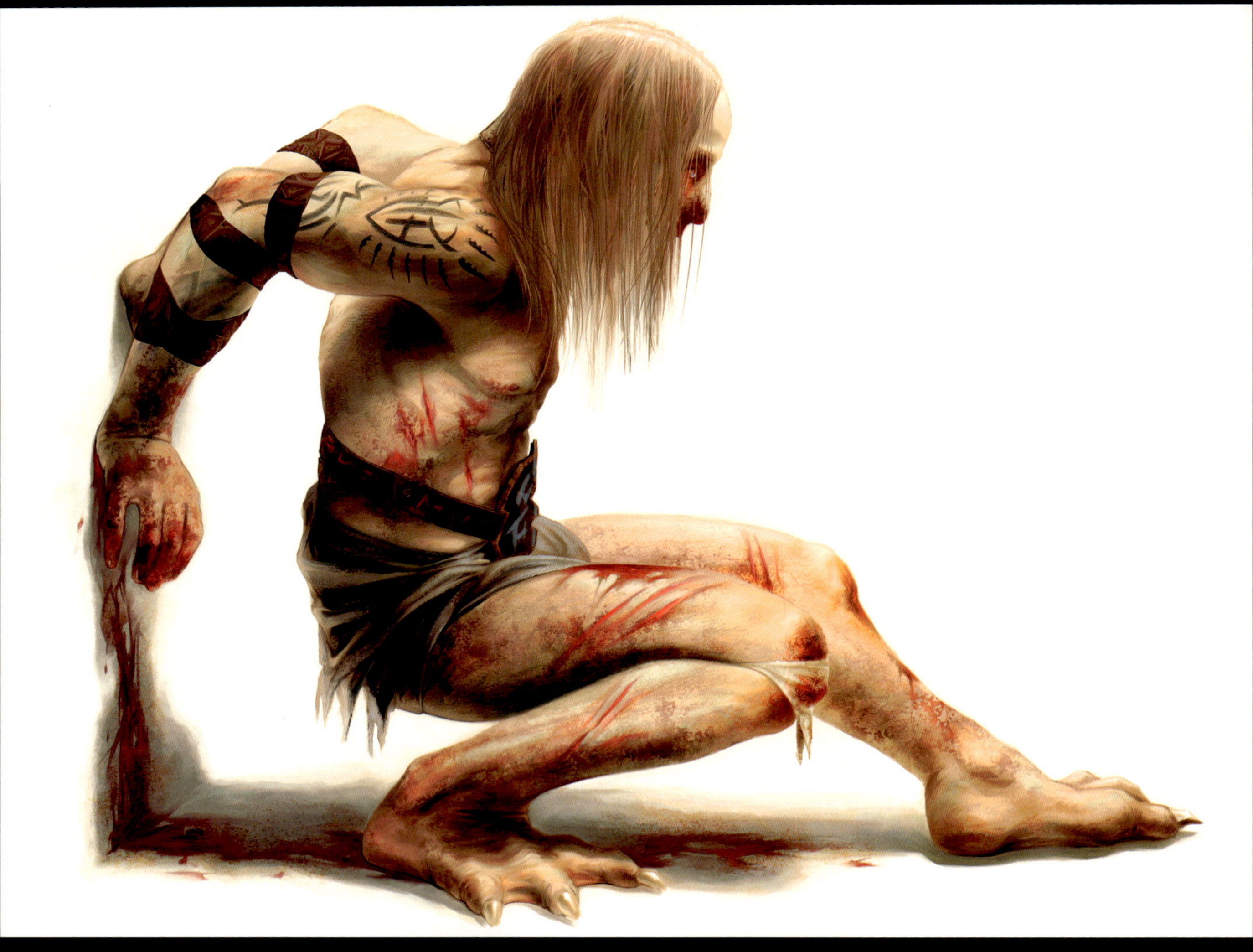

La cuirrasse d'Or
Photoshop

Character 7
Painter, Photoshop

Last Hero
3ds Max, Mudbox, Brazil r/s, Photoshop

Satan
Photoshop

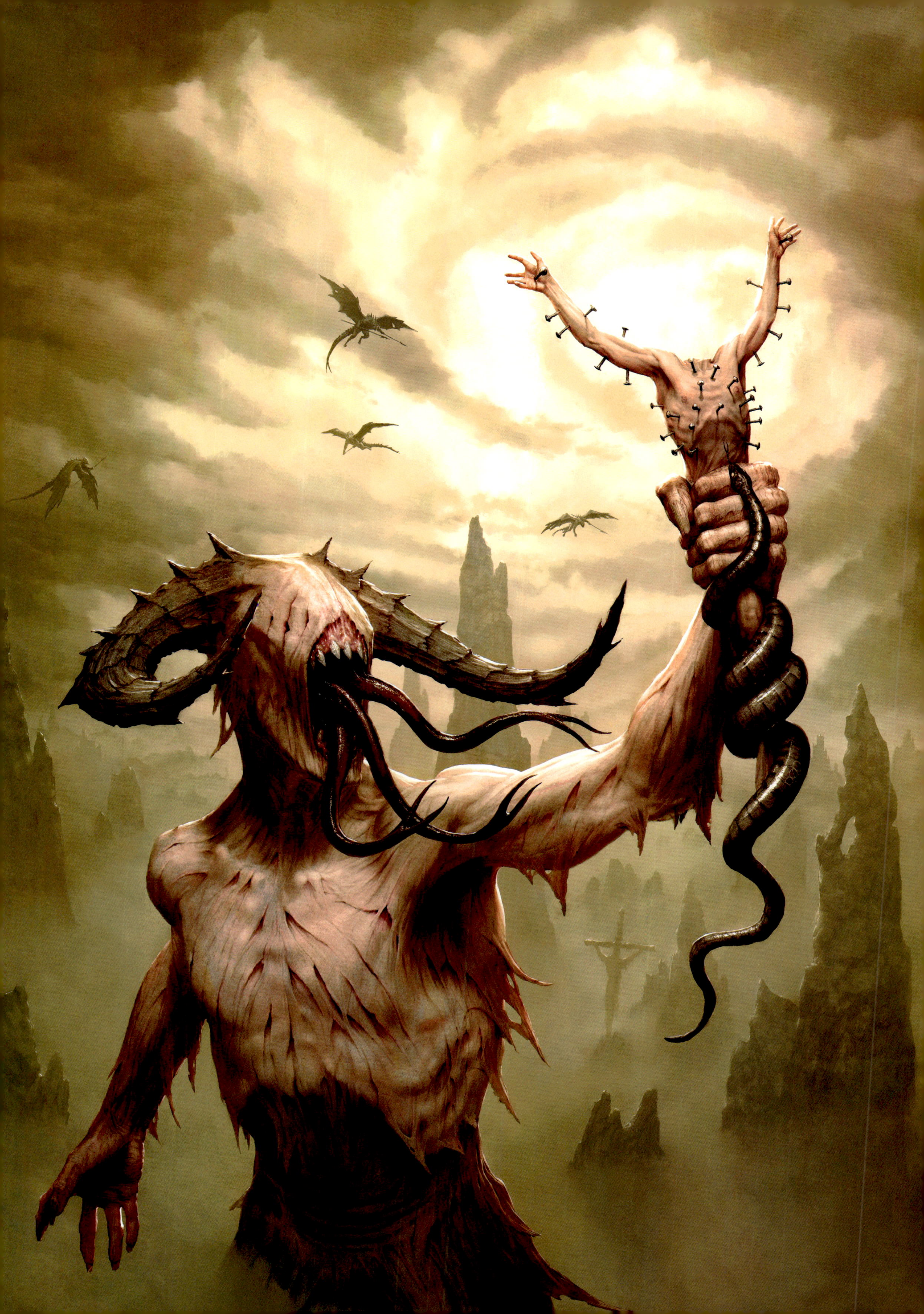

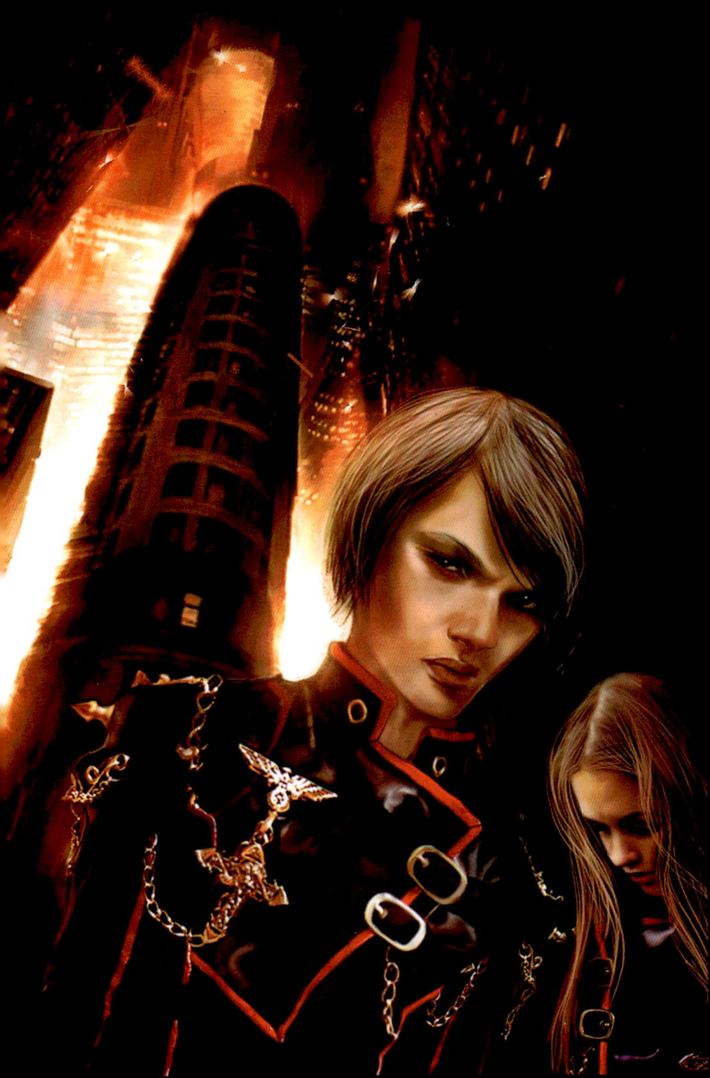

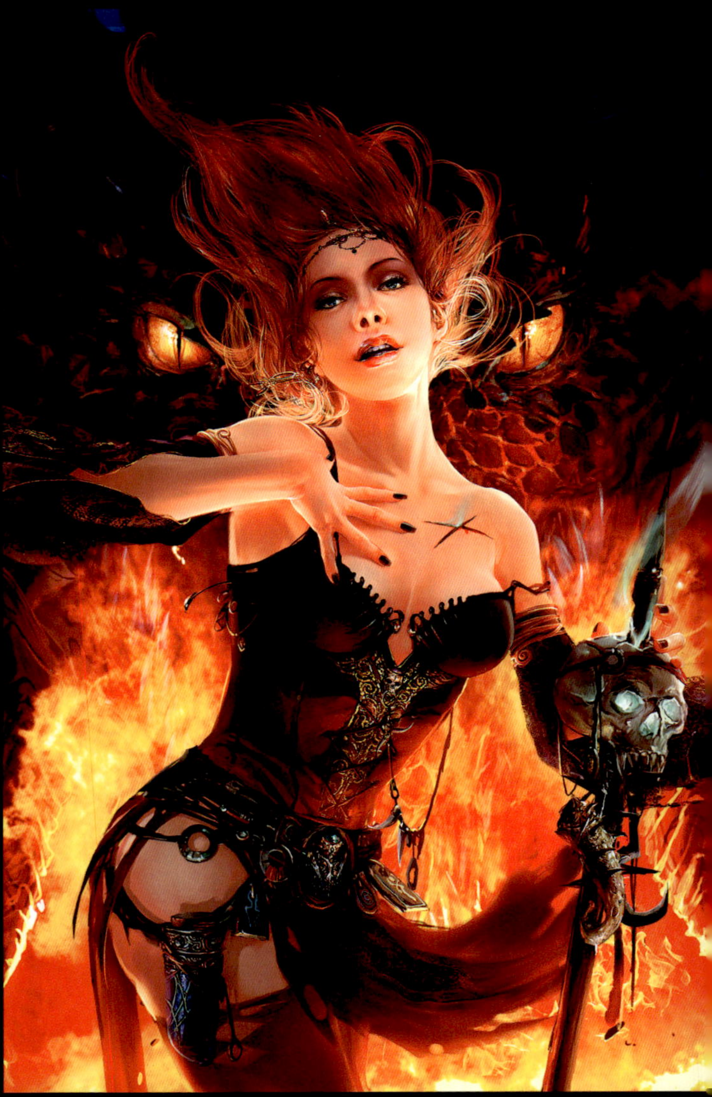

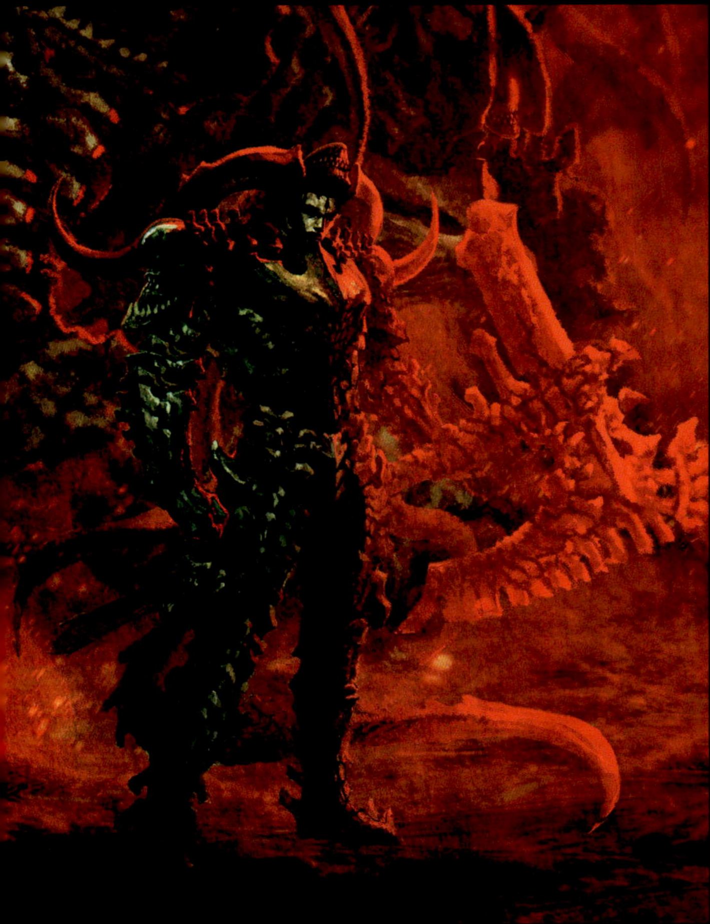

Drop city
Photoshop, Painter
Dawn Austin, austinillustration,
HONG KONG
[top left]

Dragon charmer
Photoshop
Client: ImagineFX magazine
DeHong He, CHINA
[above]

Asreal, the Slayer: KaosWar
Photoshop
Client: Shattered Reality Interactive, Inc.
Thitipon Dicruen, THAILAND
[left]

Dive Skele 1
Photoshop
Andy Park, SCEA, USA
[right]

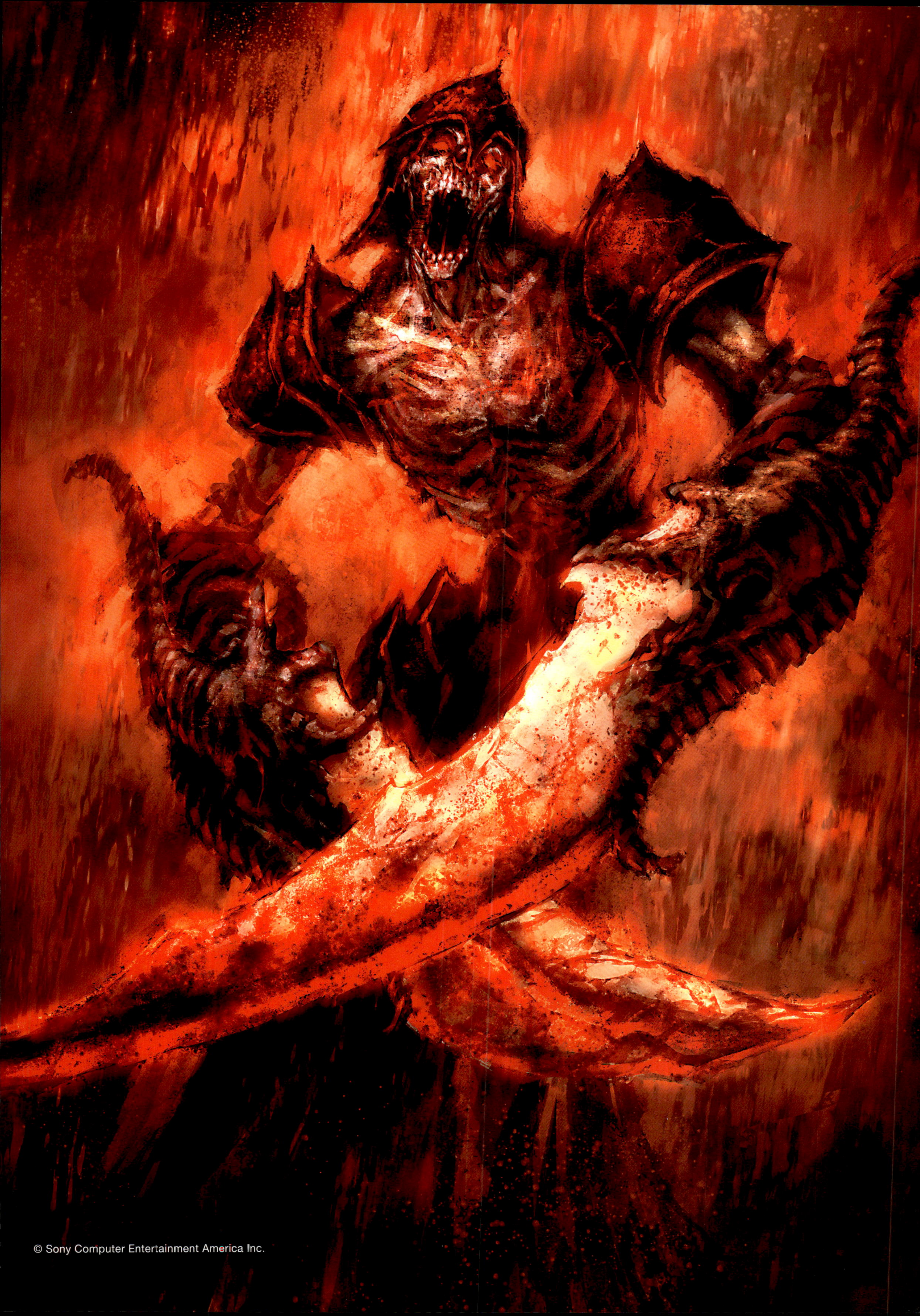

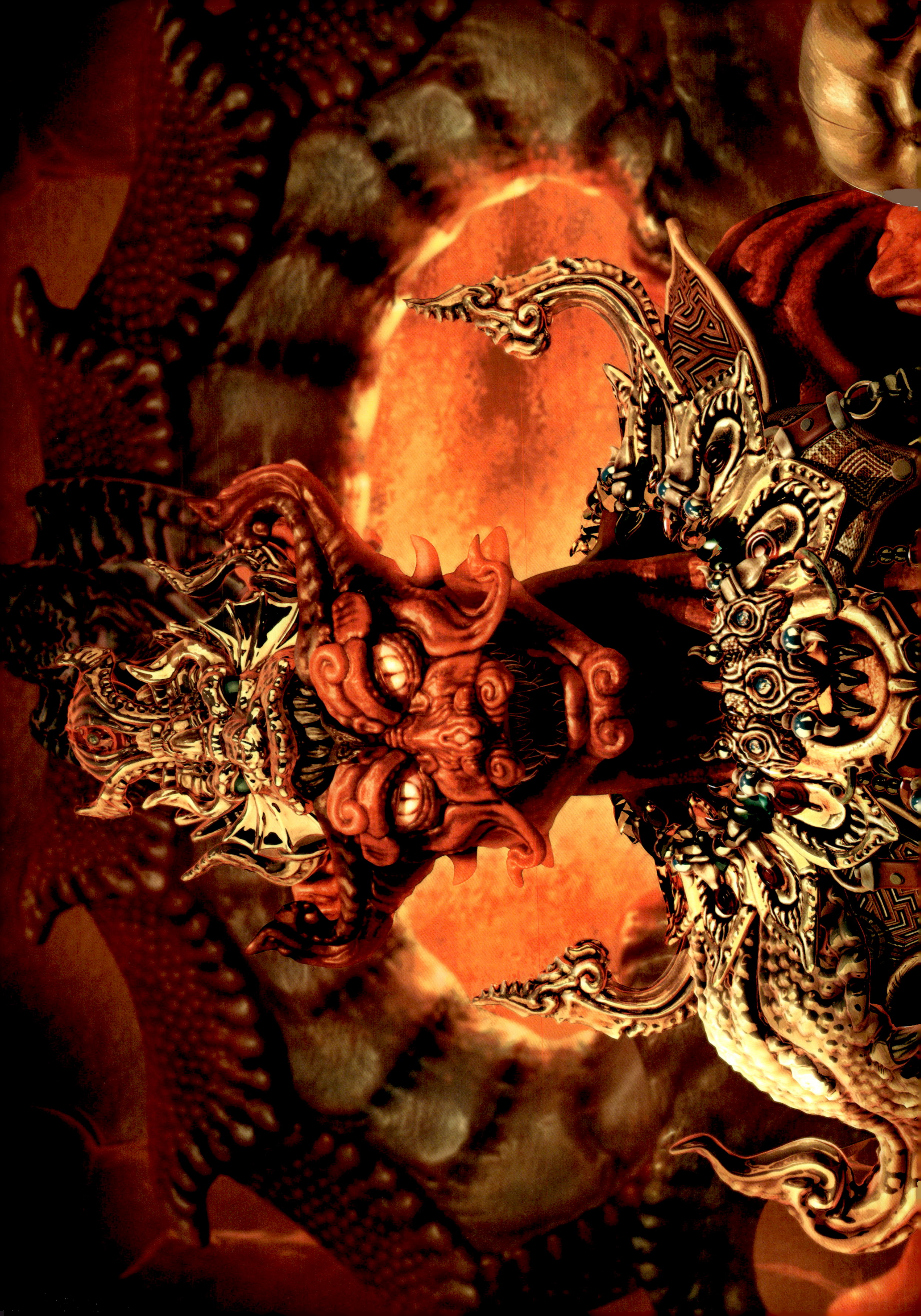

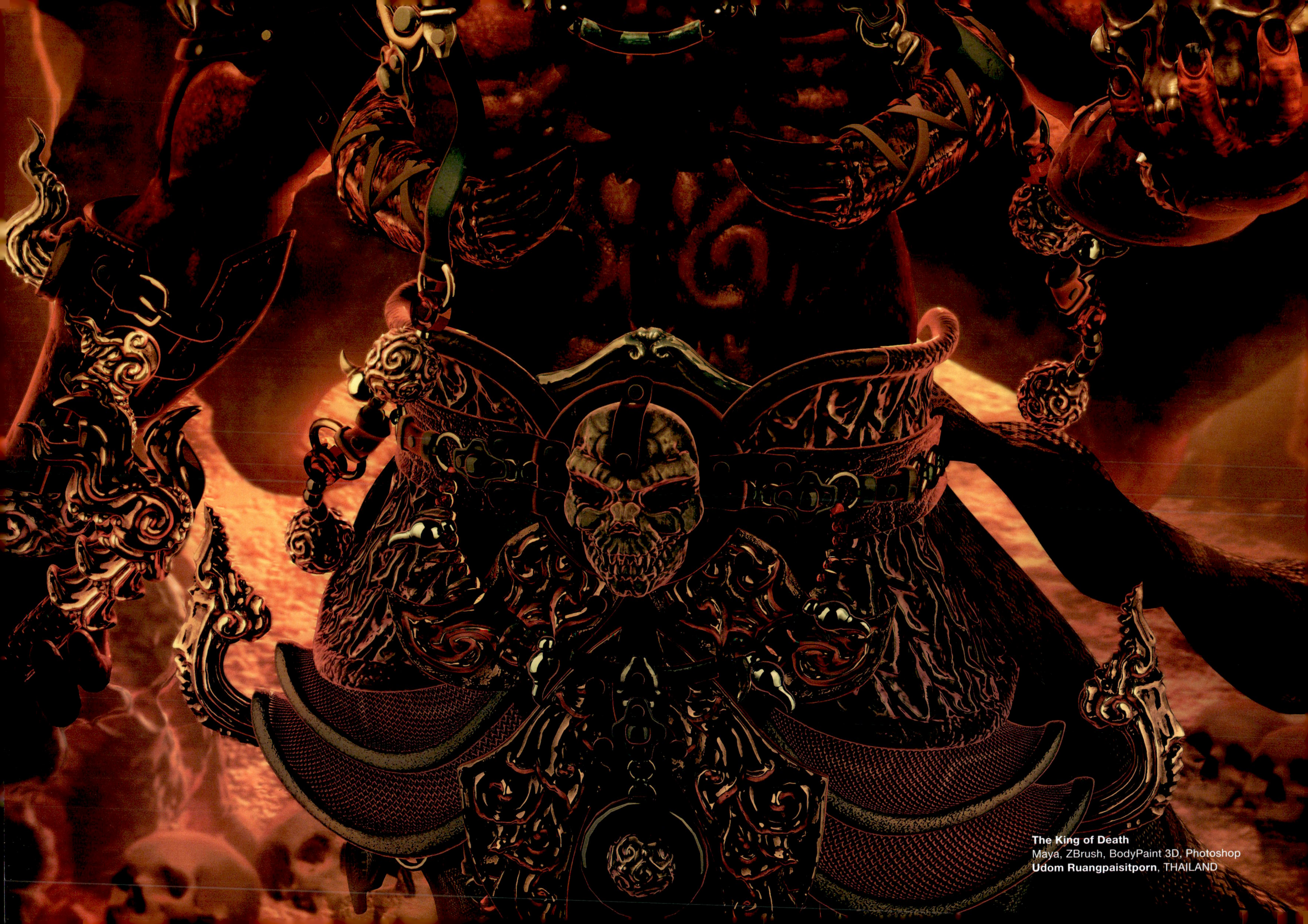

The King of Death
Maya, ZBrush, BodyPaint 3D, Photoshop
Udom Ruangpaisitporn, THAILAND

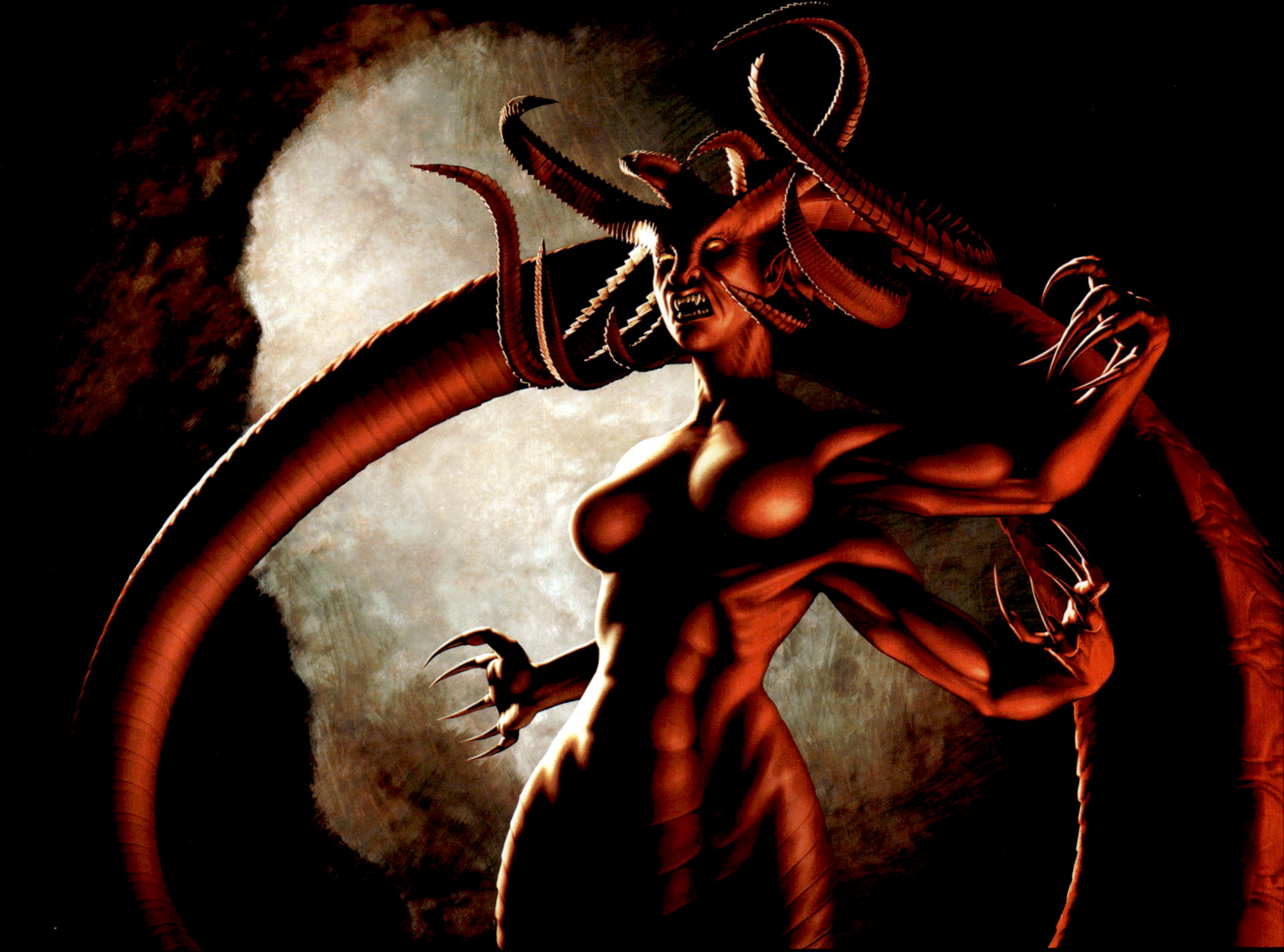

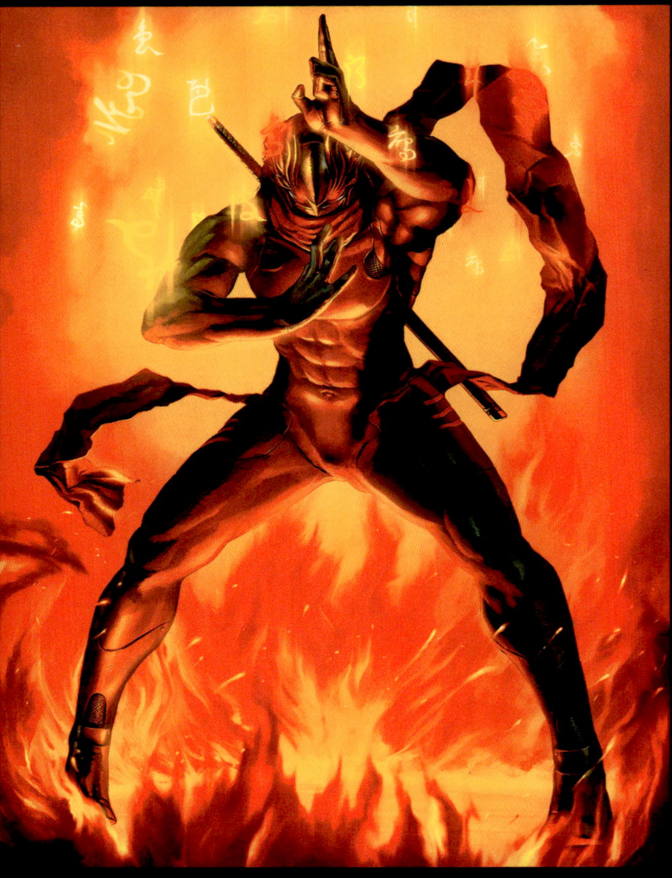

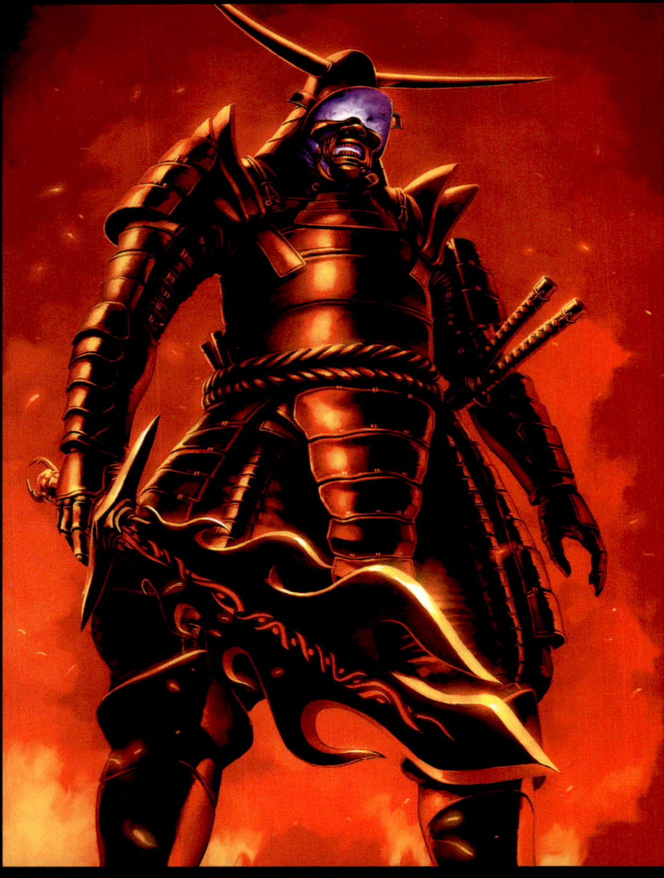

Oni
Photoshop, Maya
Steve Argyle, USA
[top]

Black Inferno
Photoshop
JinJian Xu, CANADA
[above]

Lord of the Greater Fiends
Photoshop
JinJian Xu, CANADA
[above]

Battleground
Photoshop
Alexei Solha, BRAZIL
[right]

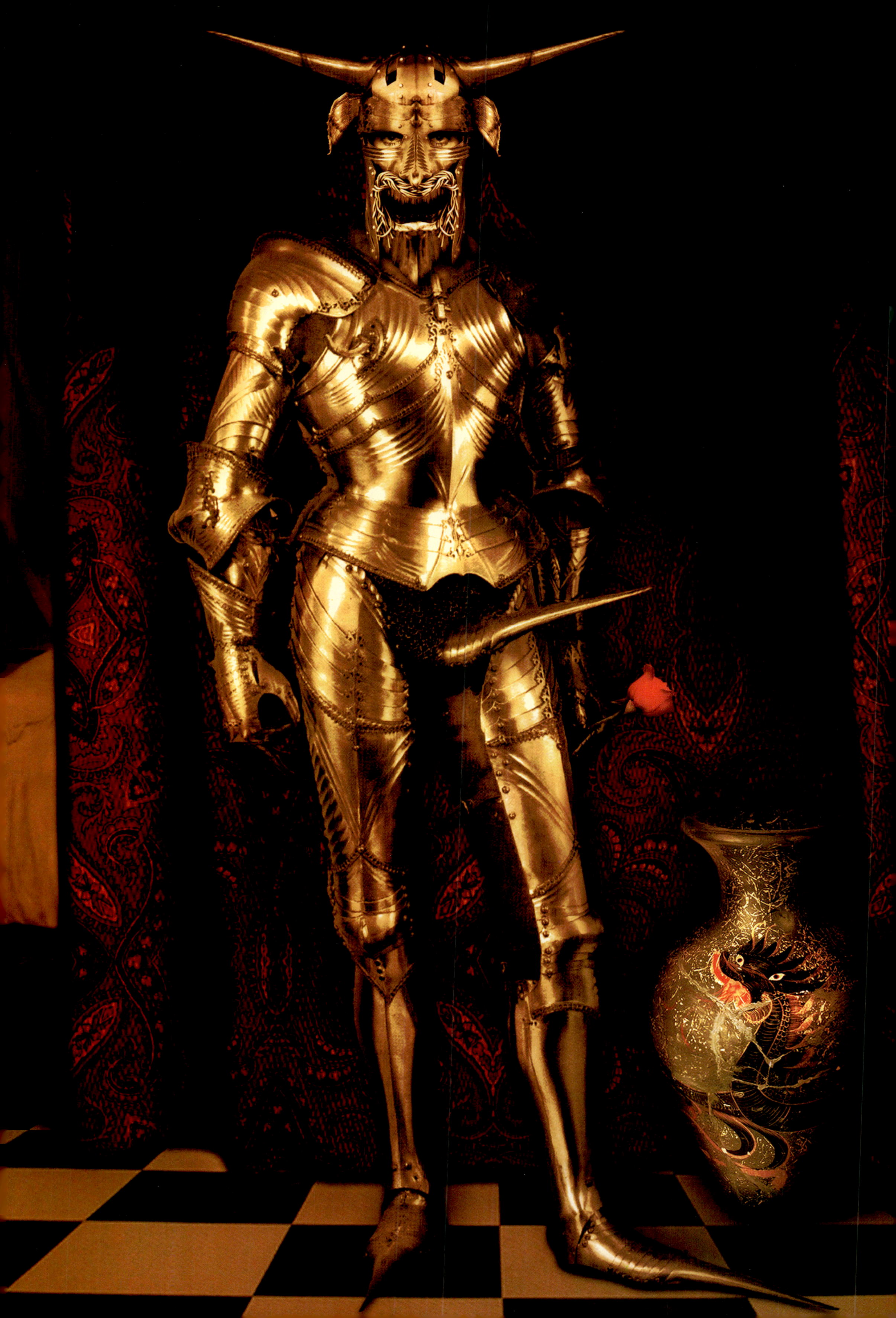

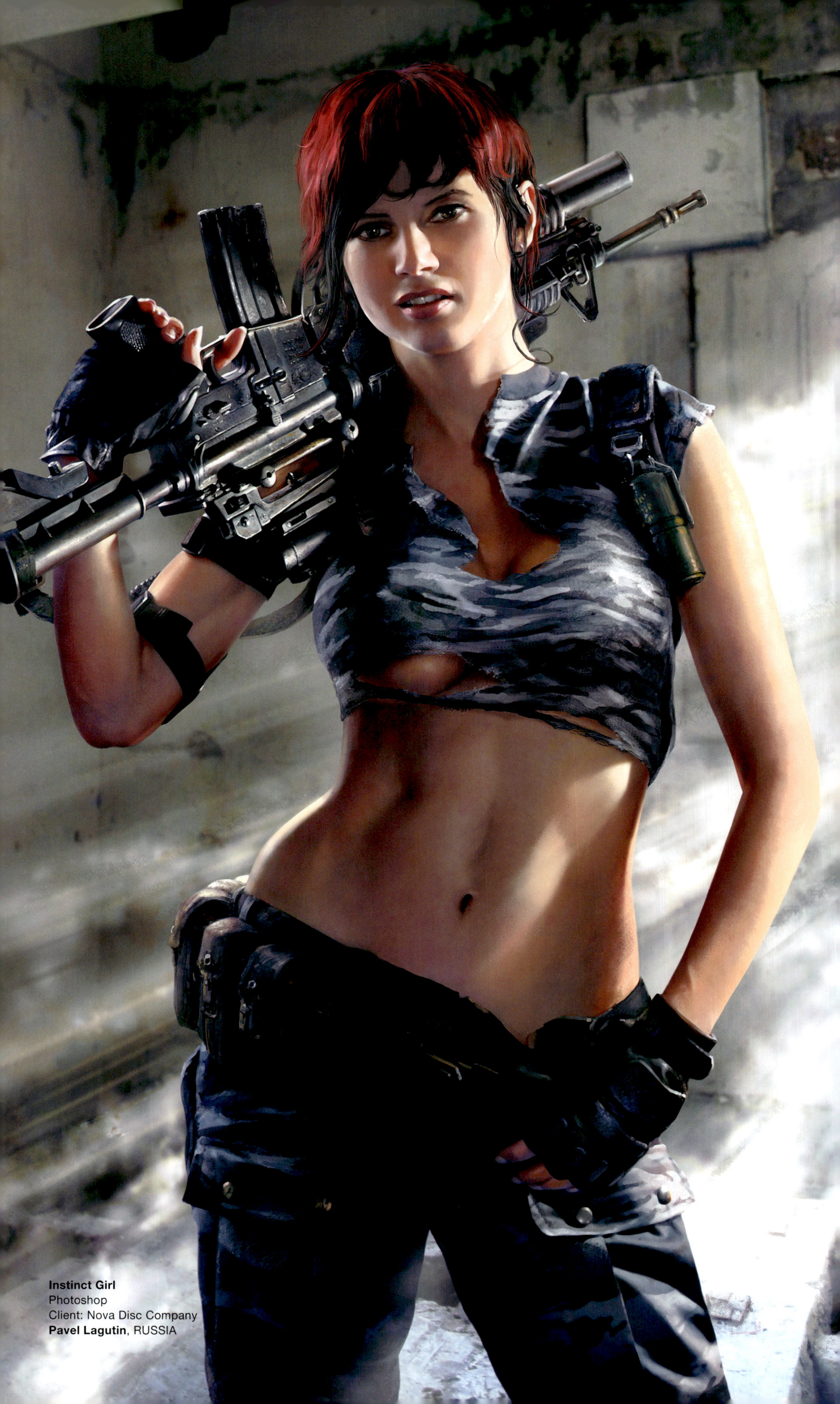

Instinct Girl
Photoshop
Client: Nova Disc Company
Pavel Lagutin, RUSSIA

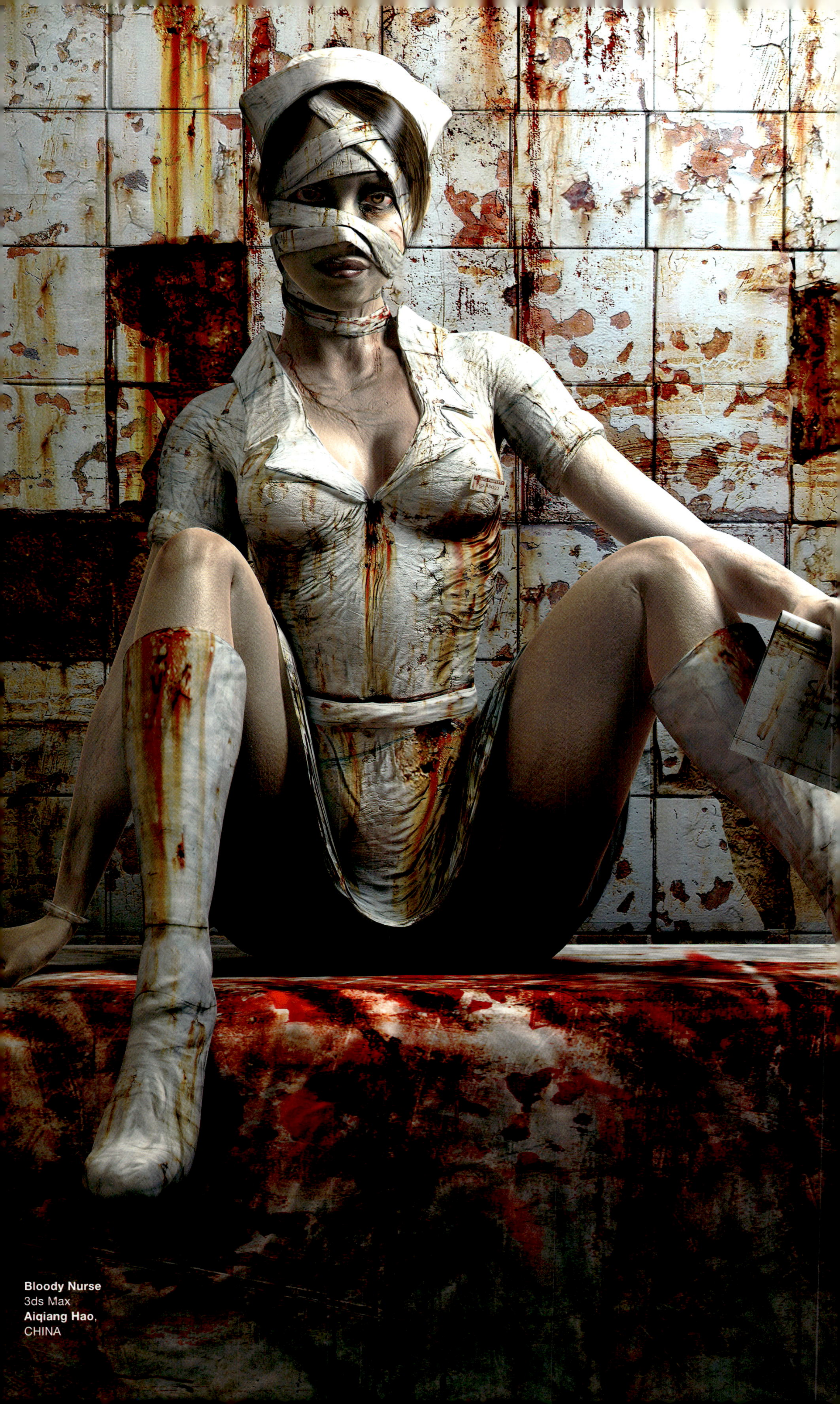

Bloody Nurse
3ds Max
Aiqiang Hao,
CHINA

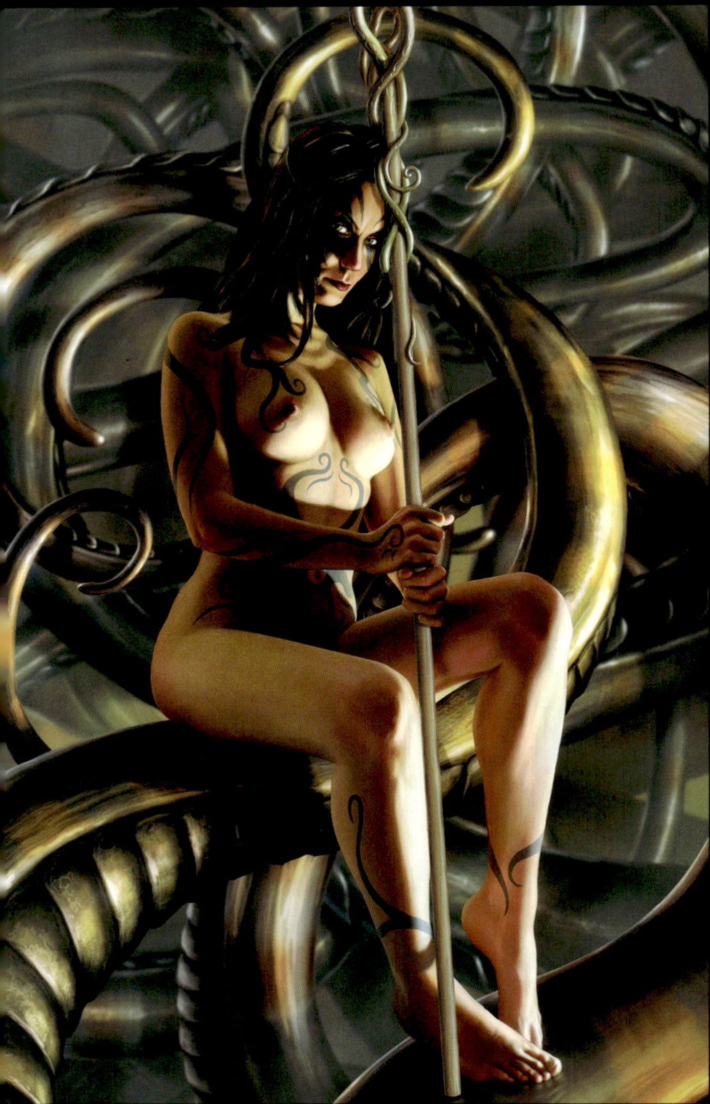

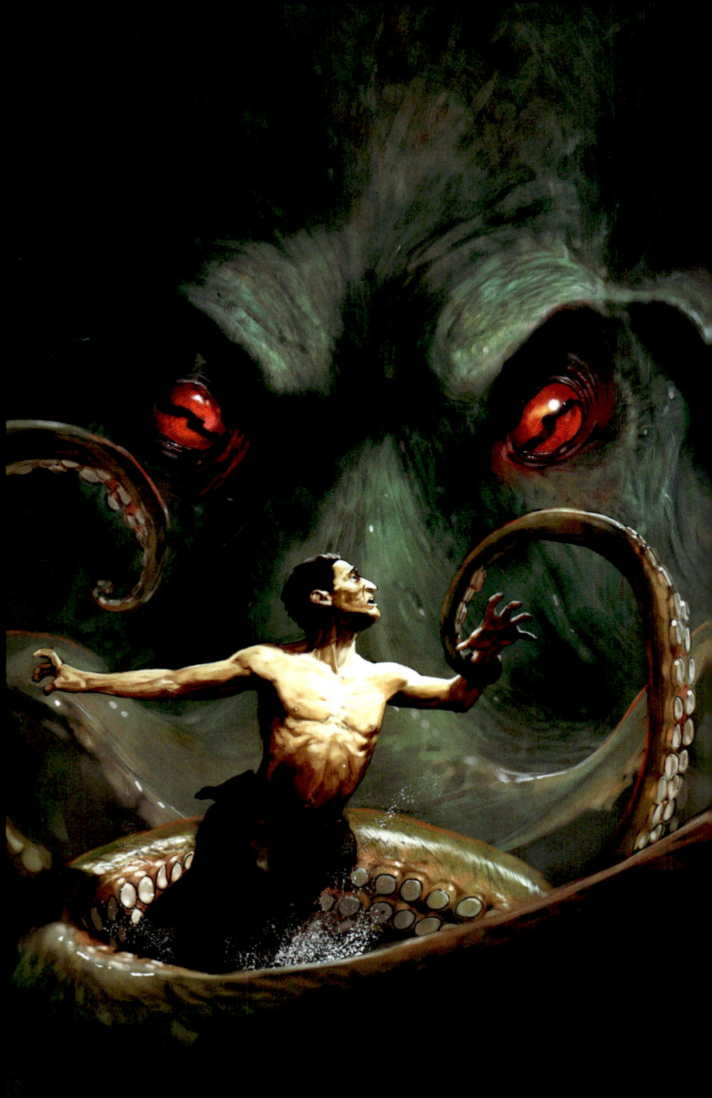

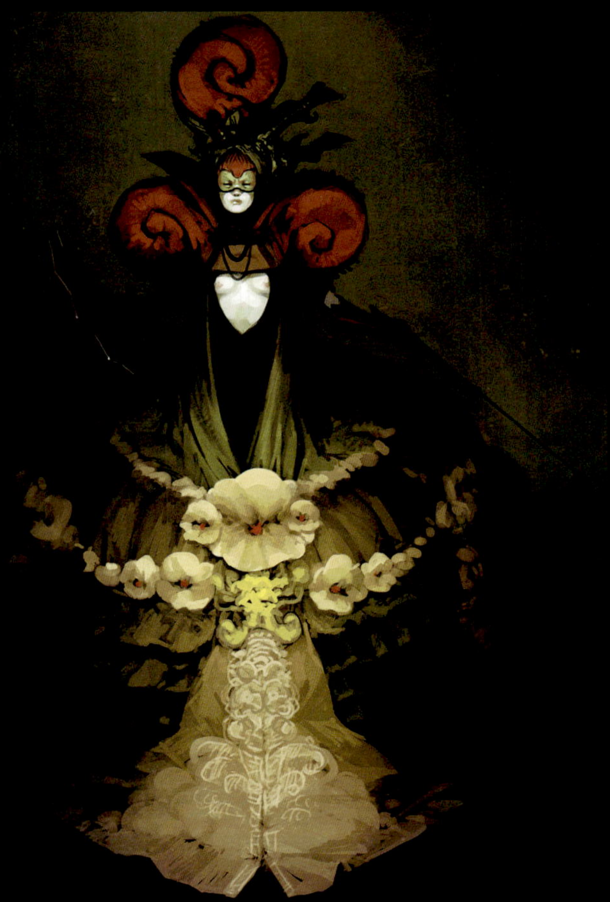

Goh' Cephal
Photoshop
Henning Ludvigsen, NORWAY
[top left]

Call of Cthulhu
Painter, Photoshop
Marc Simonetti, FRANCE
[above]

Orange circles
Photoshop
Whit Brachna, USA
[left]

Swamp Oracle
Photoshop
Sandara Tang, SINGAPORE
[right]

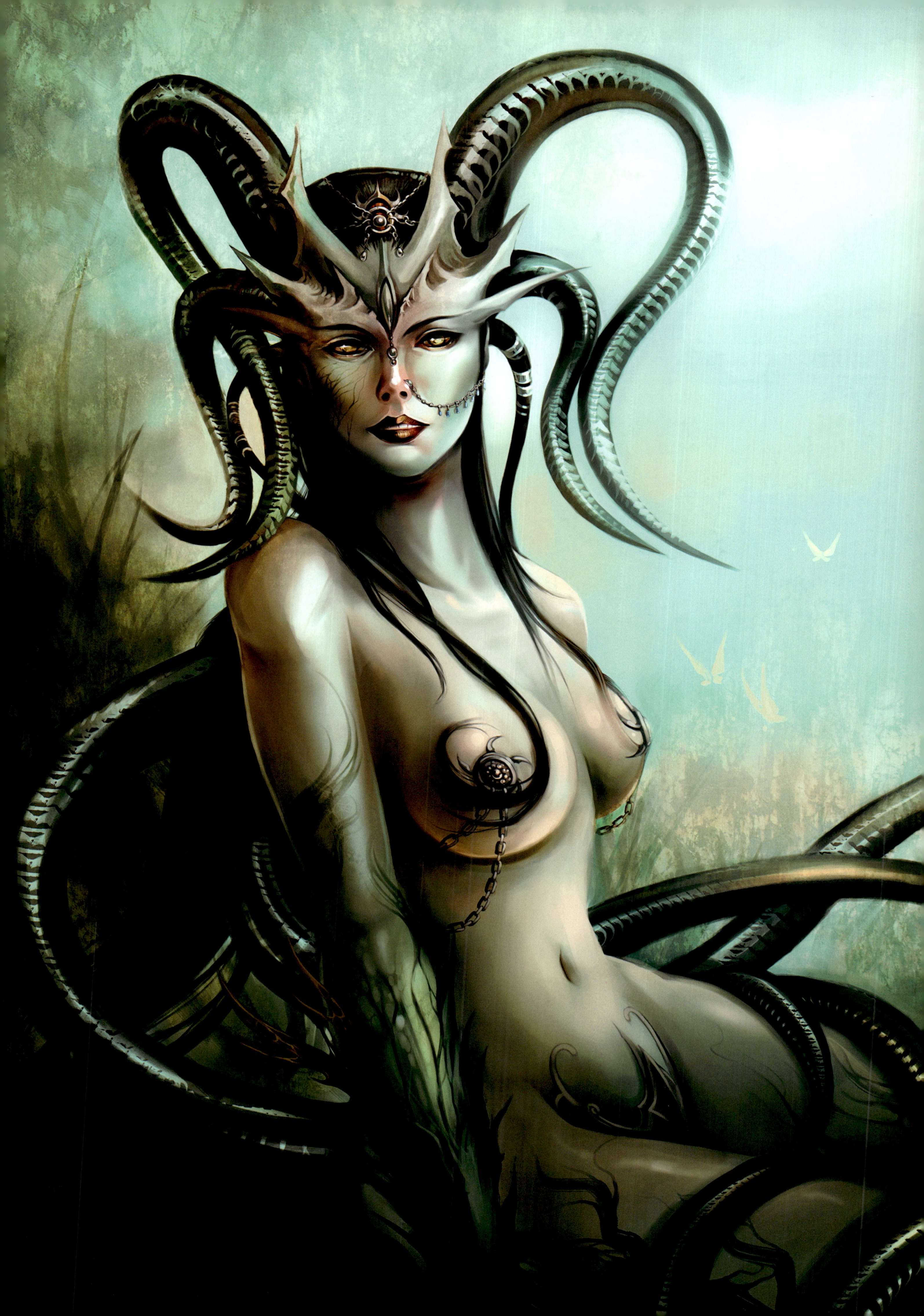

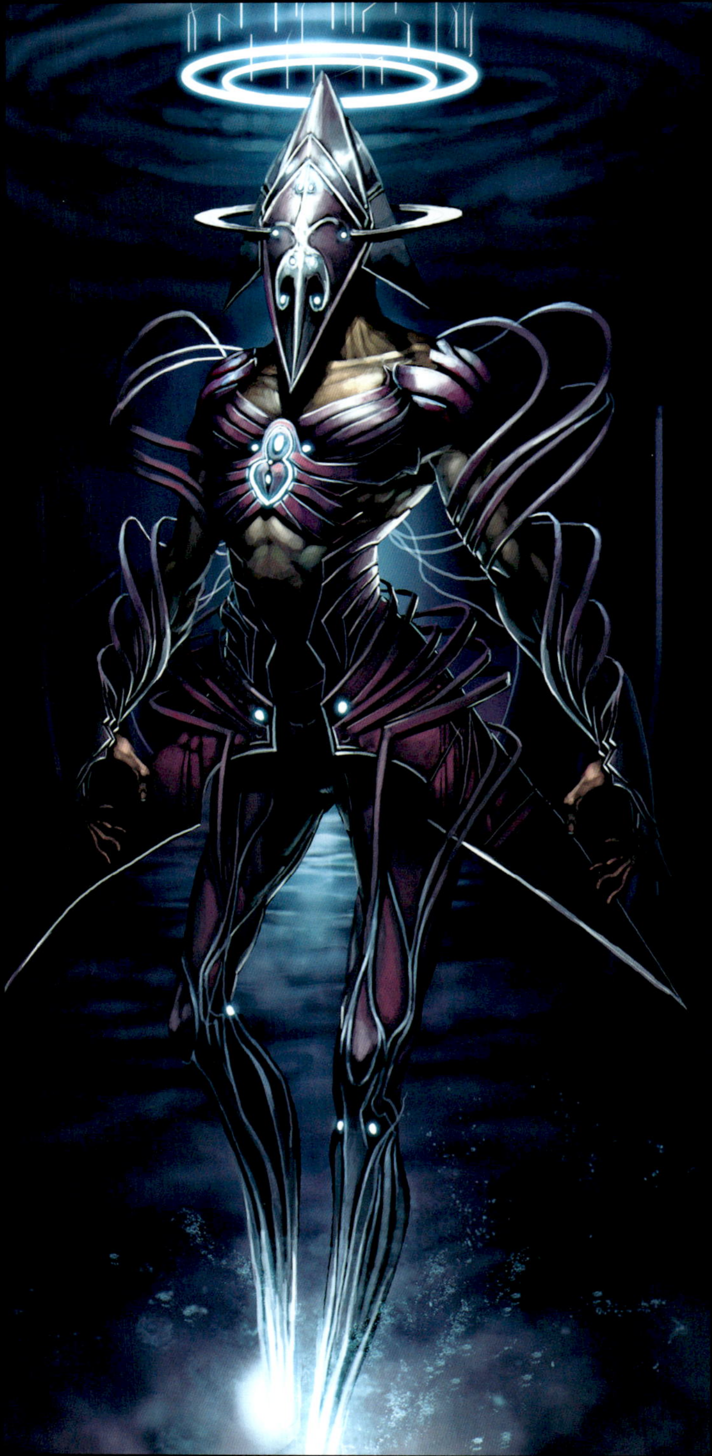

Hasmed
Photoshop
Peter Mohrbacher, USA
[above]

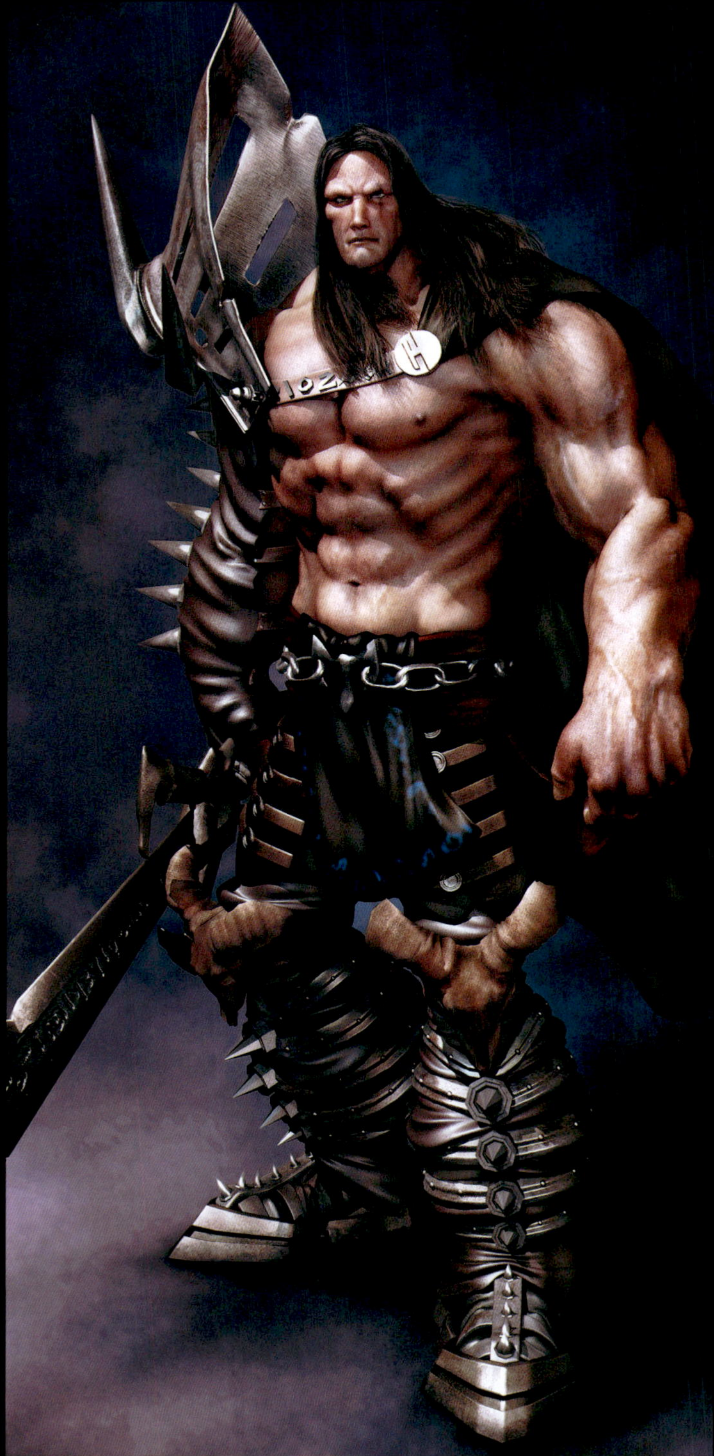

Zerst, Maladan War God
Maya, 3ds Max, Photoshop, mental ray
Vivek Ram, INDIA
[above]

Fallen One
Photoshop, Poser
Gina Pitkänen, FINLAND
[right]

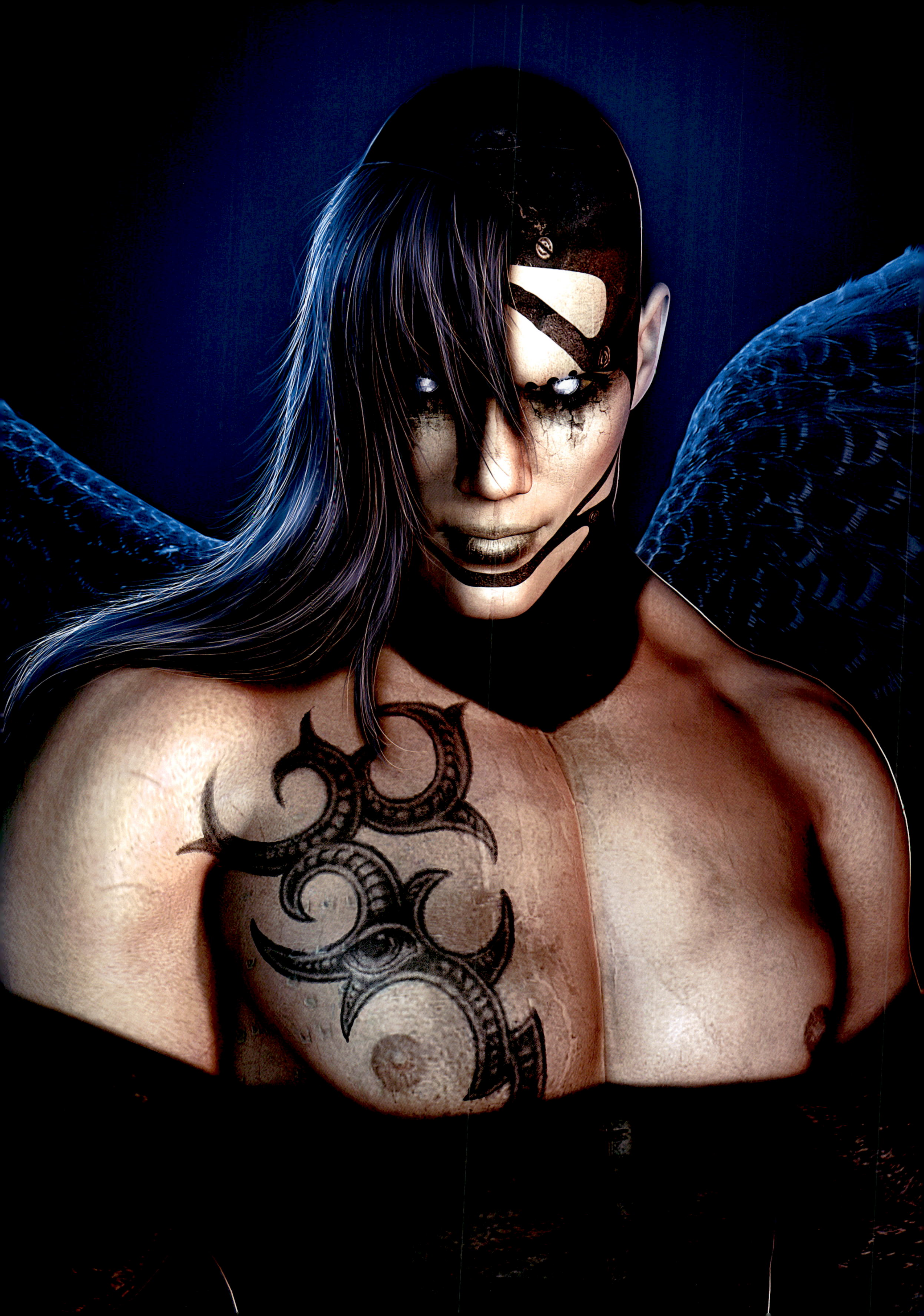

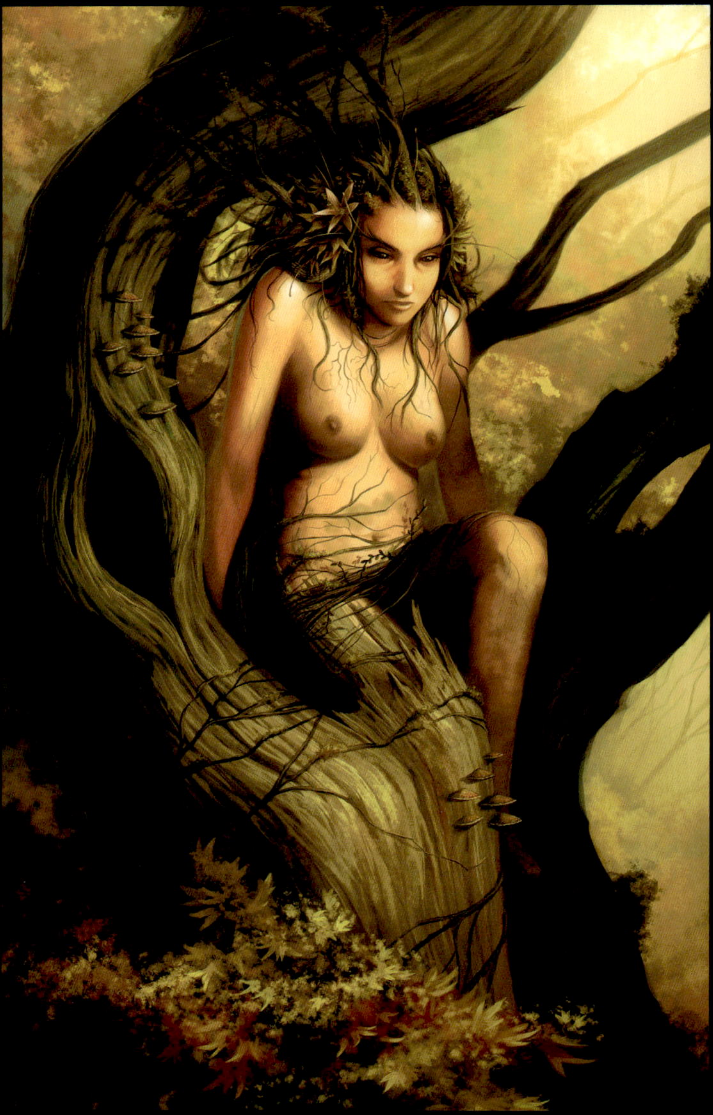

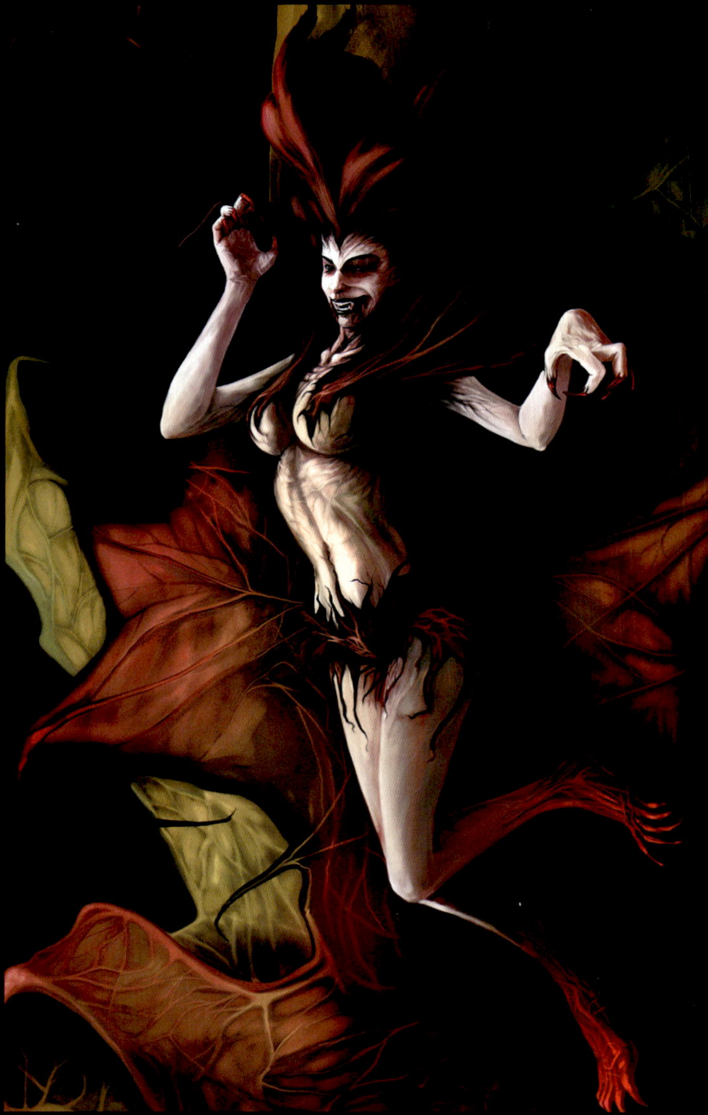

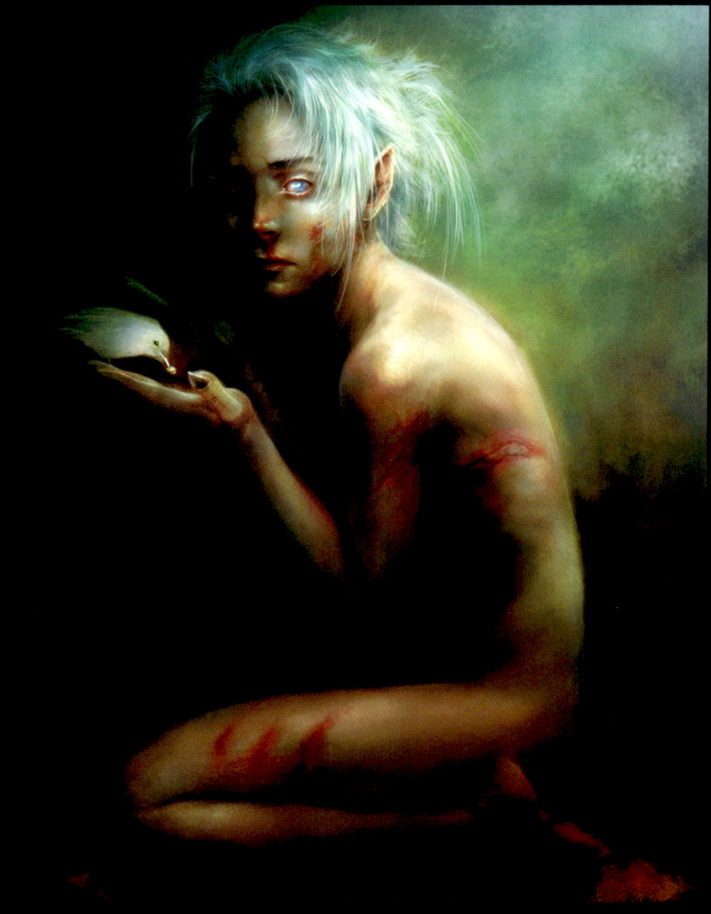

Birth of a Dryad
Photoshop
Xavier Collette, BELGIUM
[top left]

Queen of mosquitos
Painter, Photoshop
Ilker Serdar Yildiz, TURKEY
[above]

You sang to me
Photoshop, Painter
Kirsi Salonen, FINLAND
[left]

Forbidden art
Photoshop
Marc Brunet, CANADA
[right]

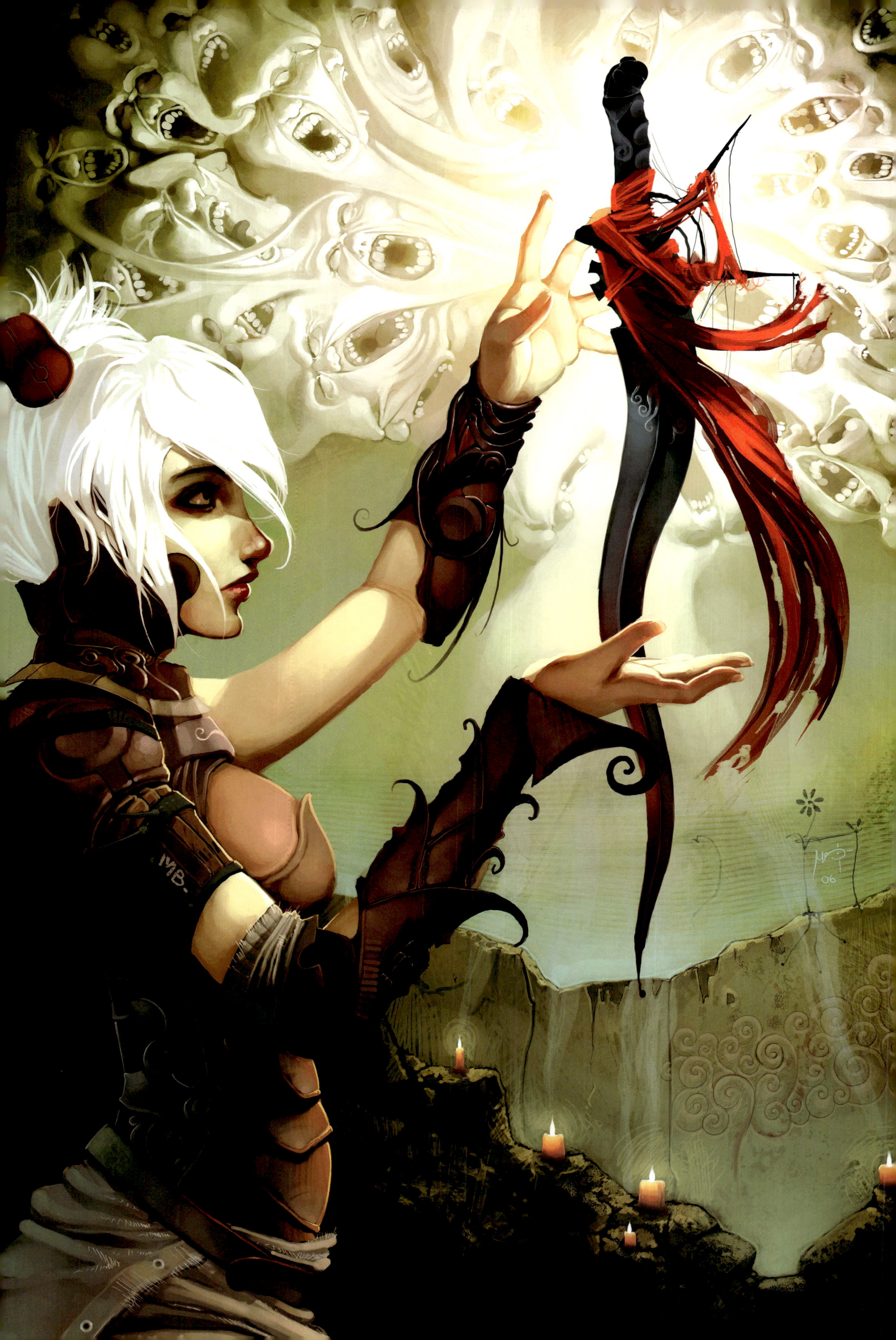

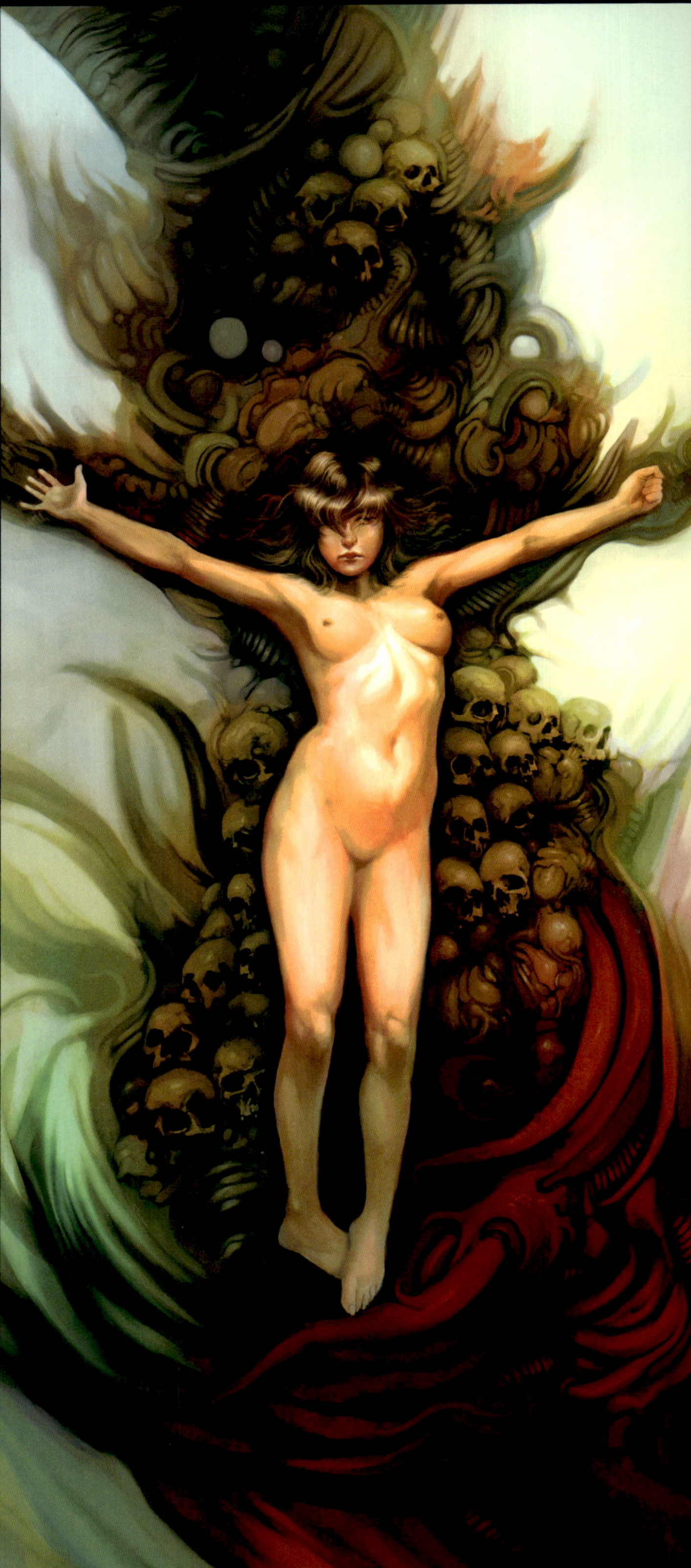

zrk 2
Photoshop
Falk, GERMANY
[above]

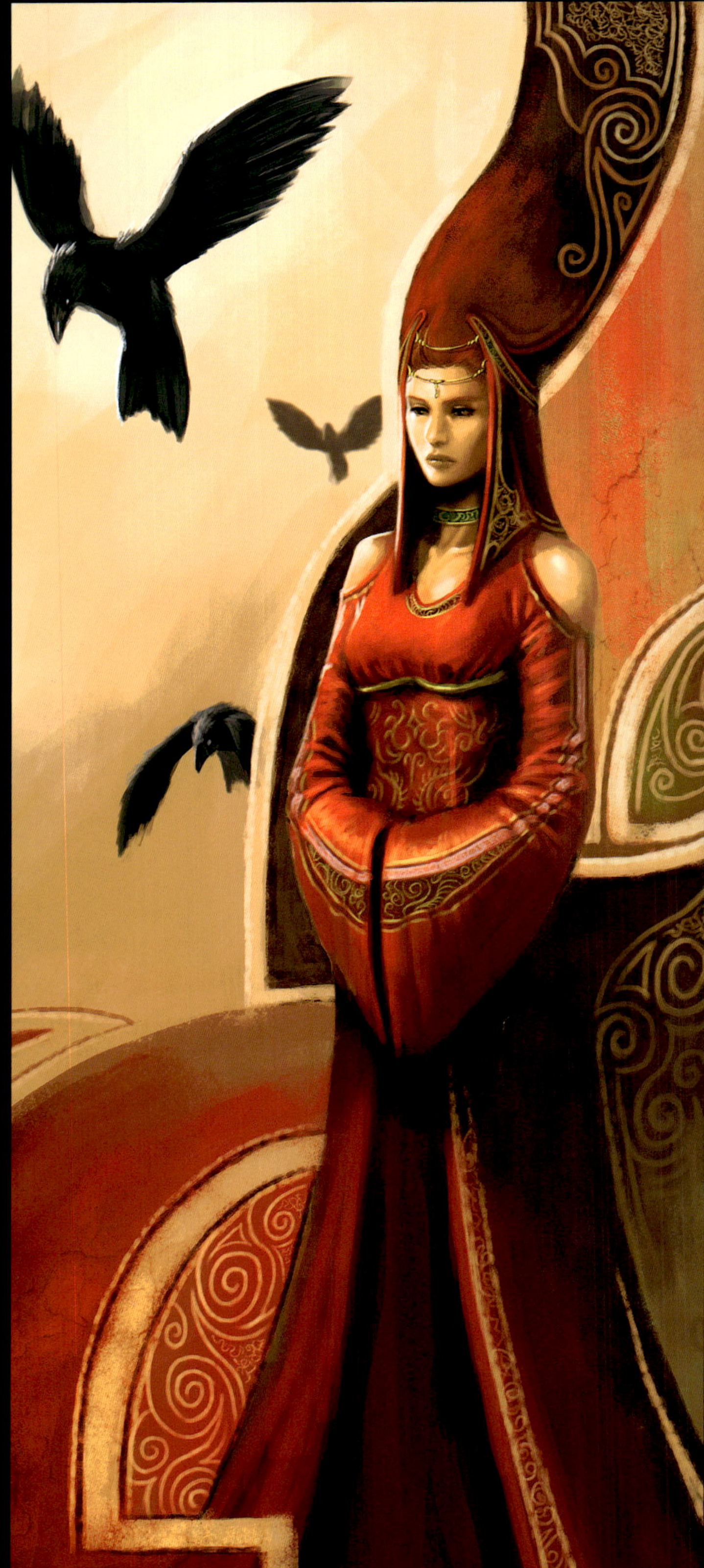

Morrigan
Photoshop
Xavier Collette, BELGIUM
[above]

Marla
Painter, Photoshop
Katarina Sokolova, UKRAINE
[right]

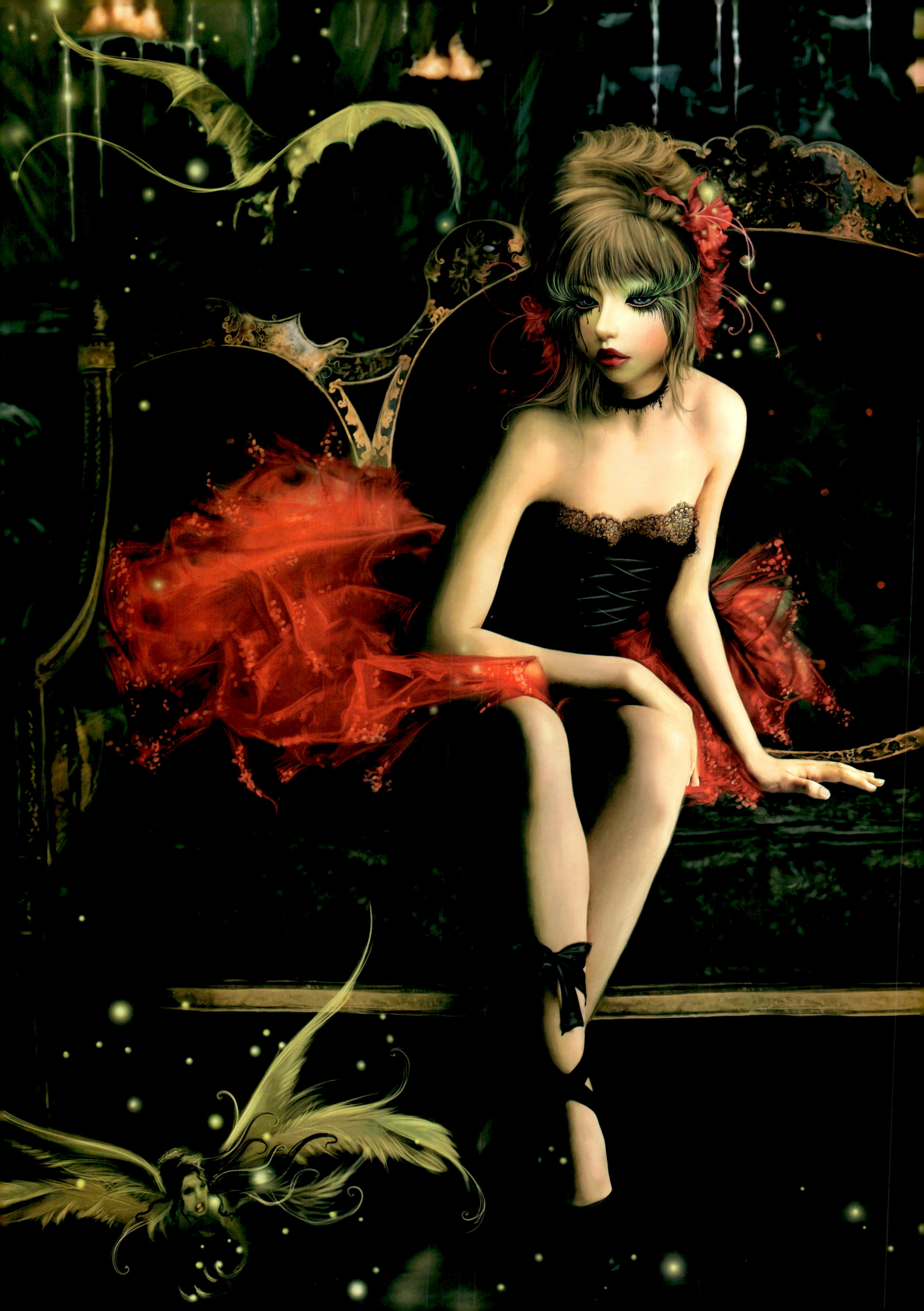

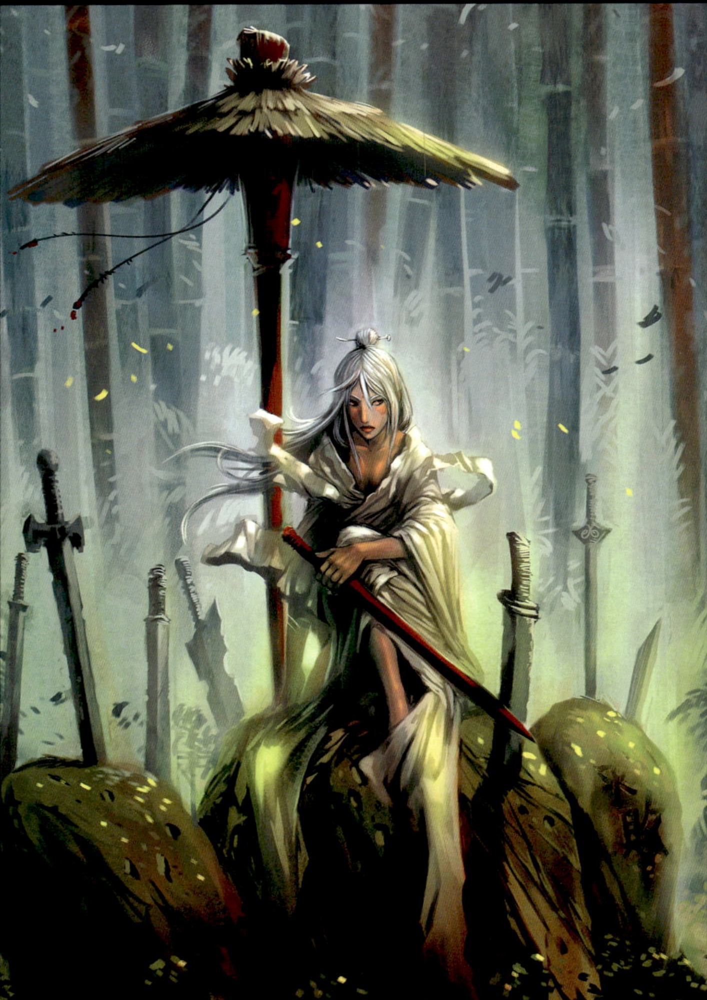

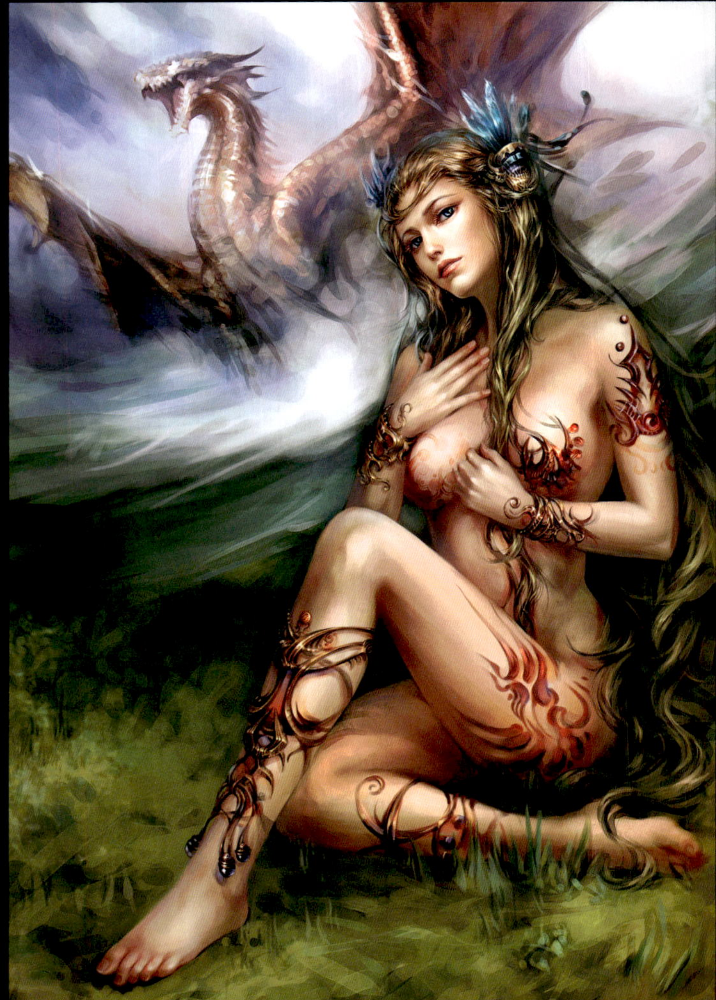

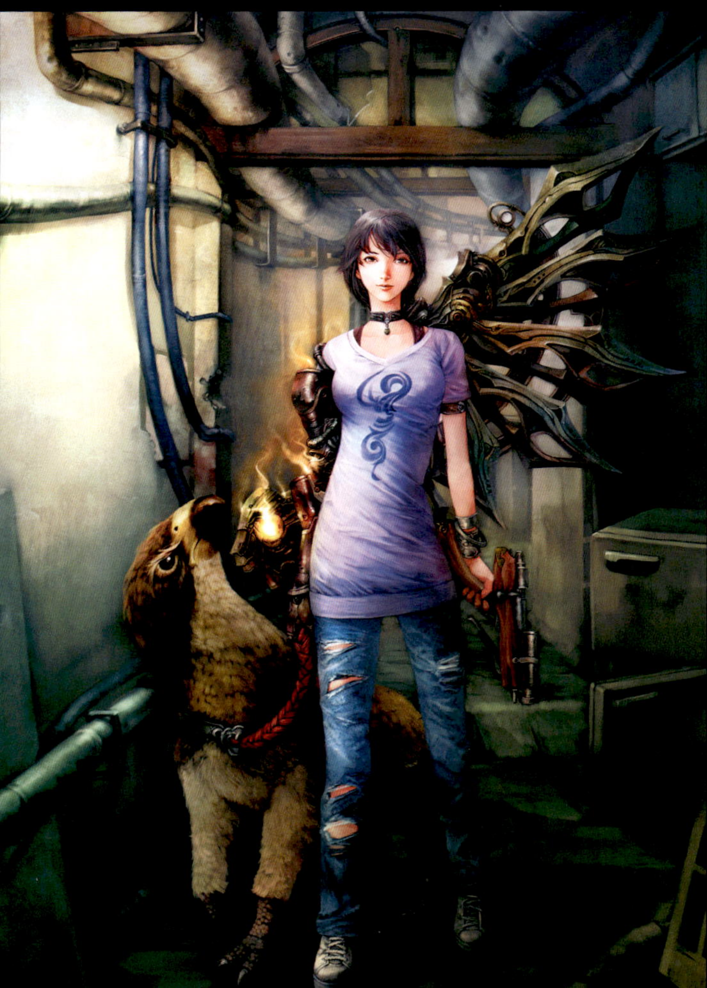

Master of the sword
Painter
Jian Guo, CHINA
[top left]

Goddess
Painter, Photoshop
Na Sun, CHINA
[above]

Exploration of Nine Dragon Castle
Painter
Song Jae Hwon,
SK C&C, KOREA
[left]

Dunhuang flying apsaras
Maya, mental ray, ZBrush,
Photoshop
Jack Qiang, CHINA
[right]

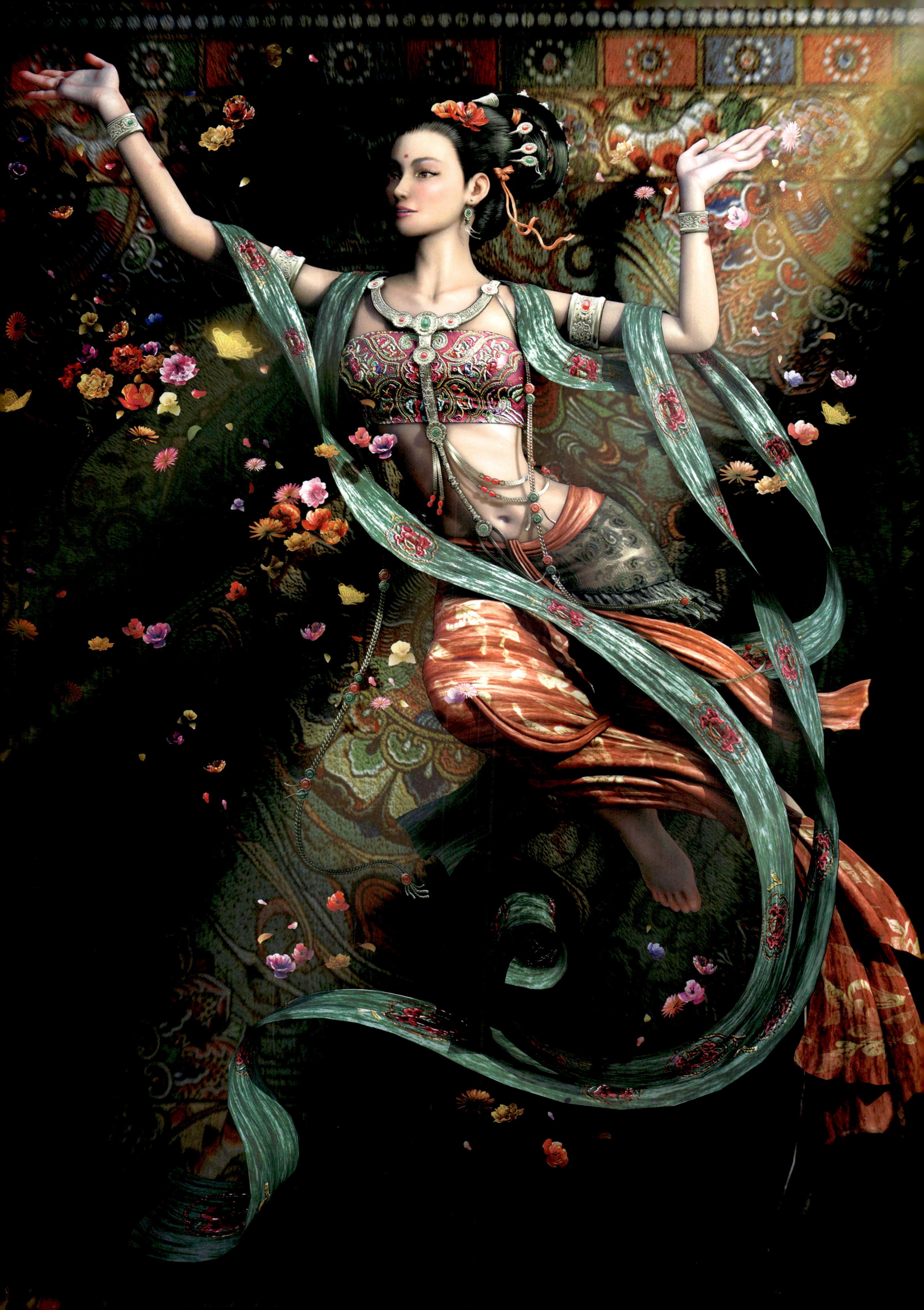

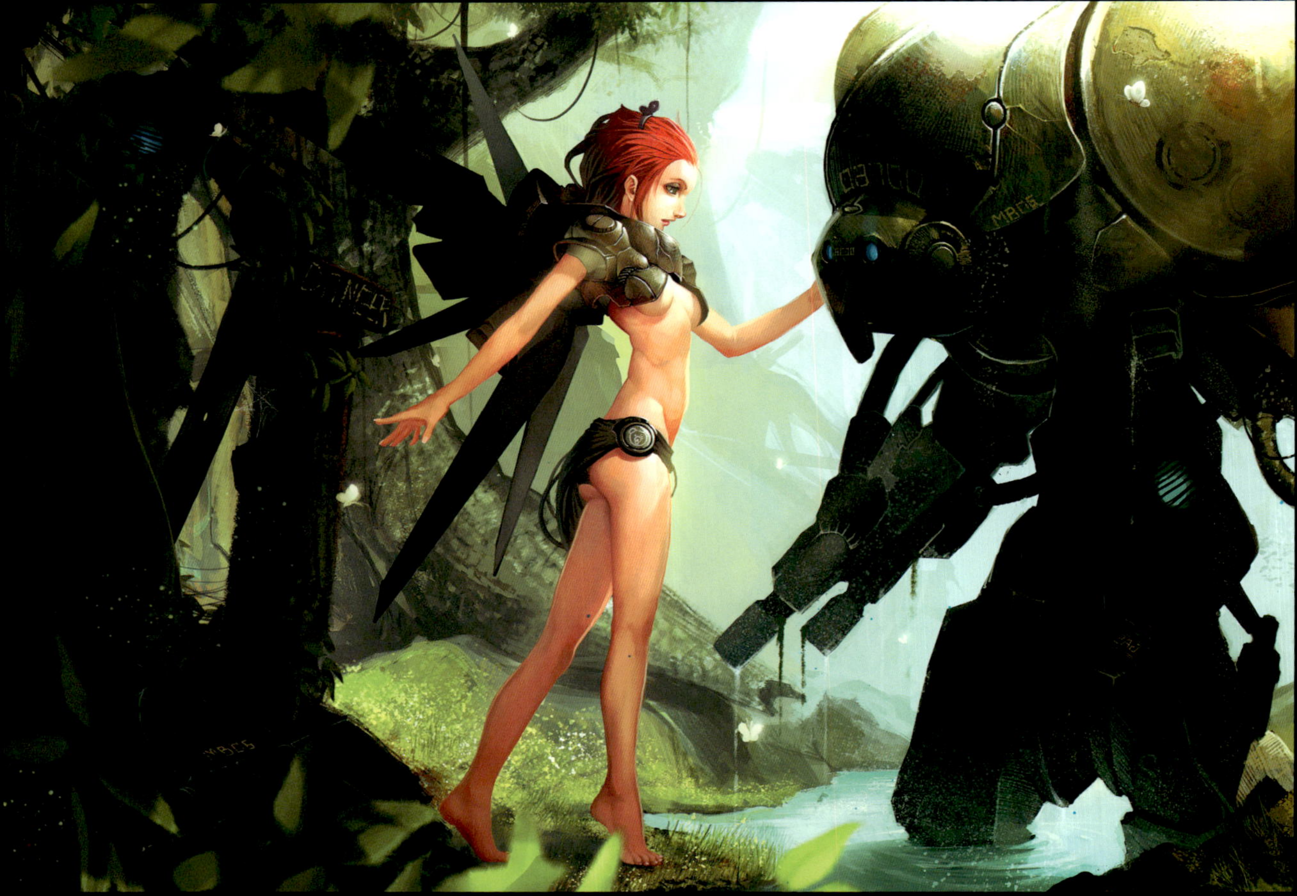

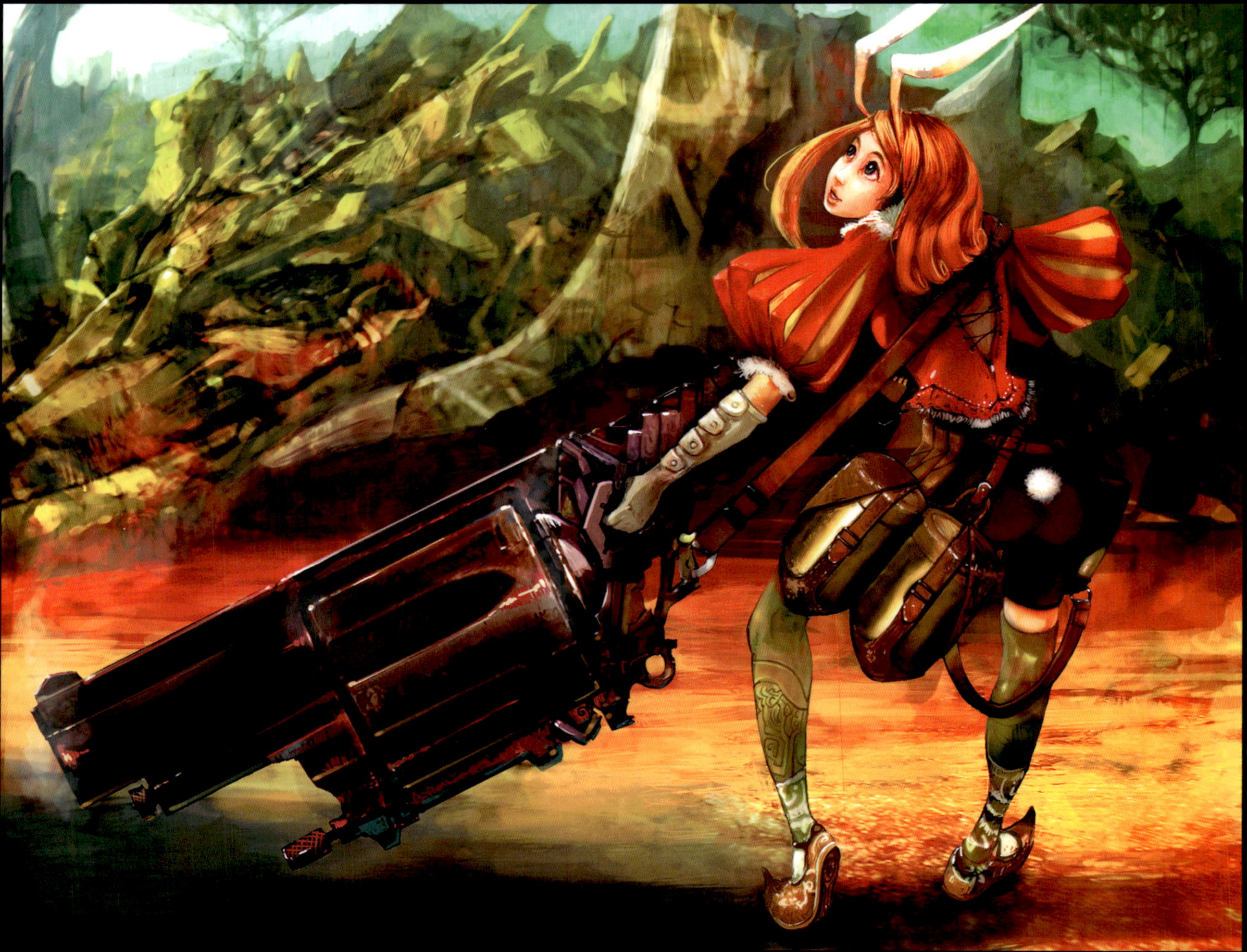

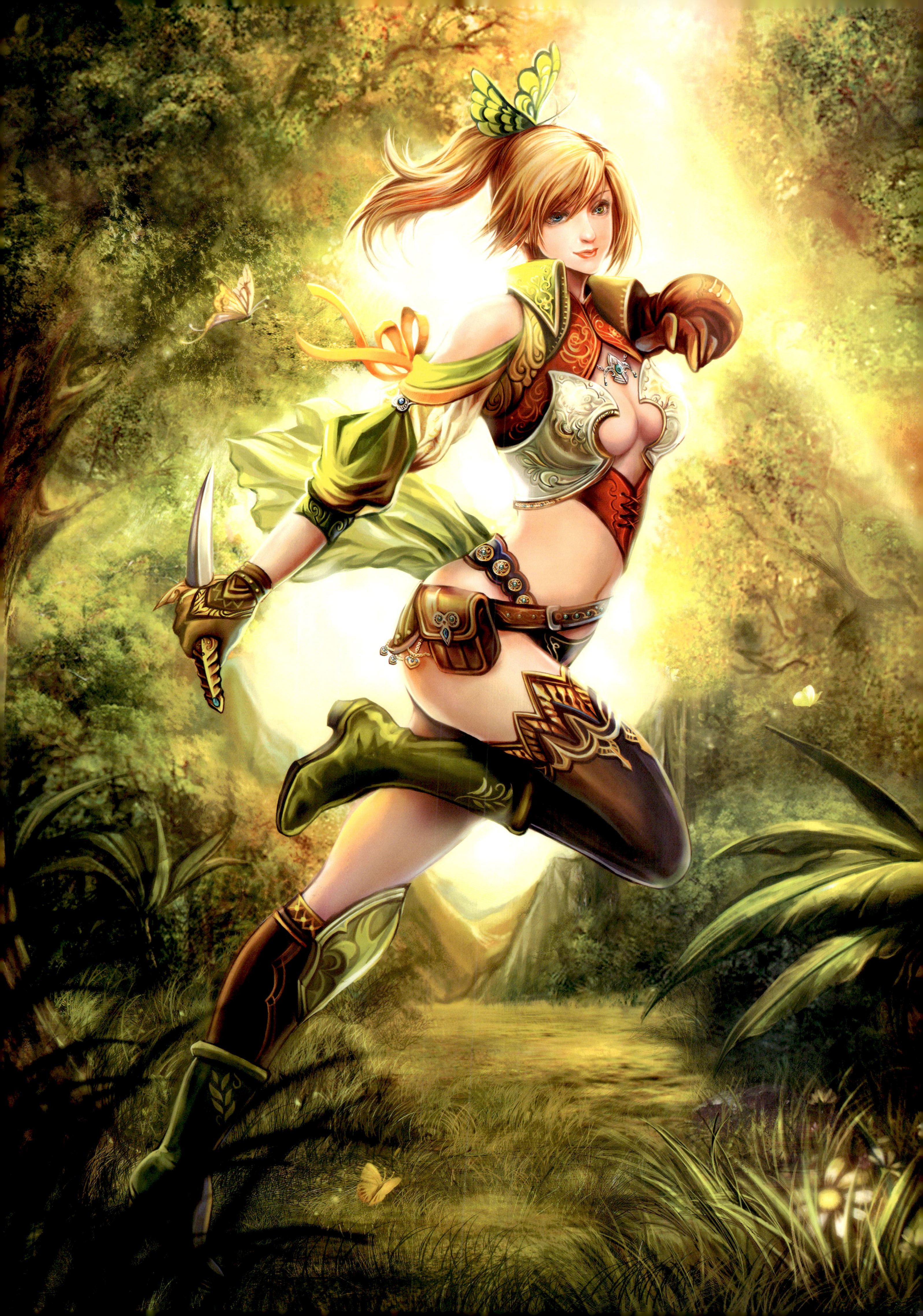

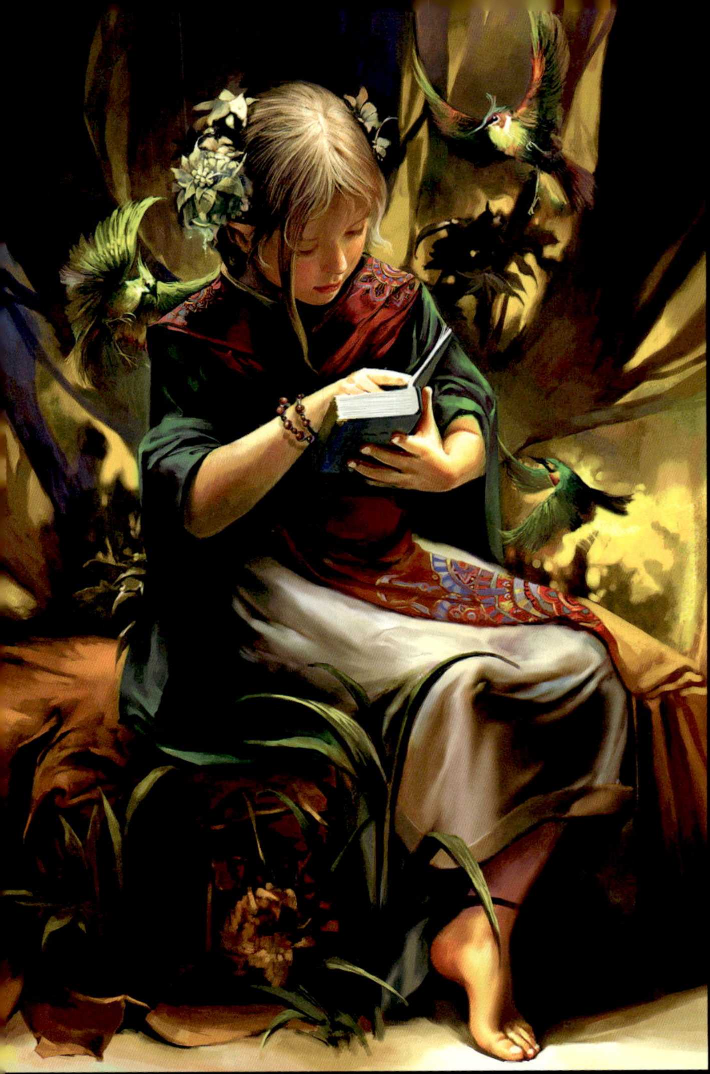

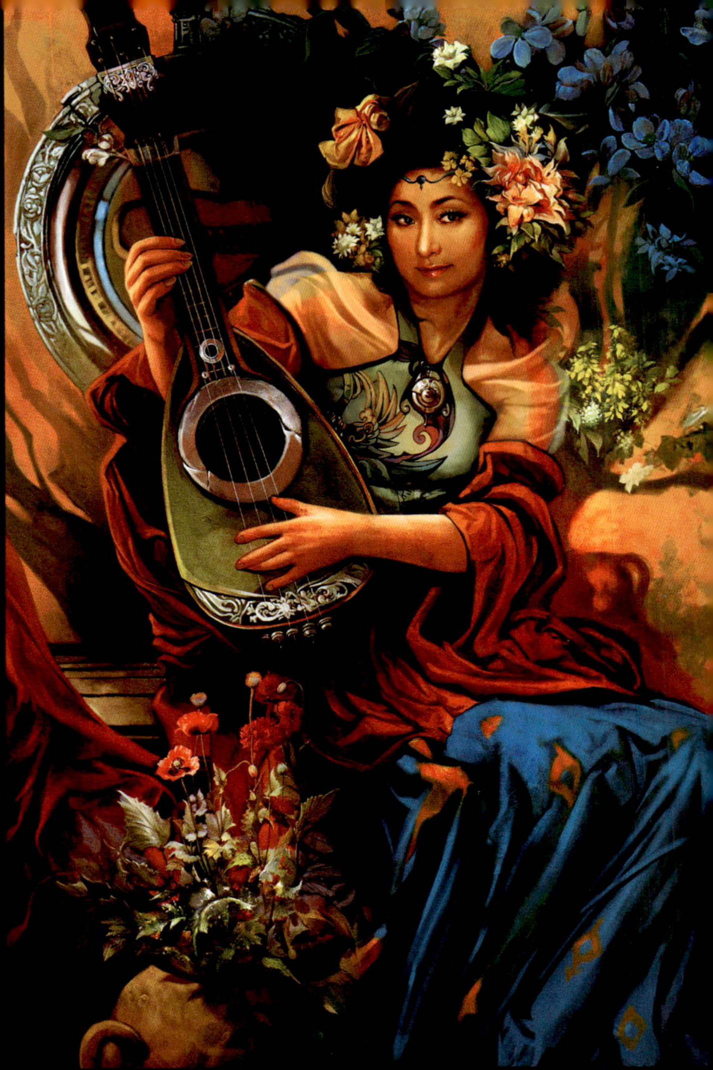

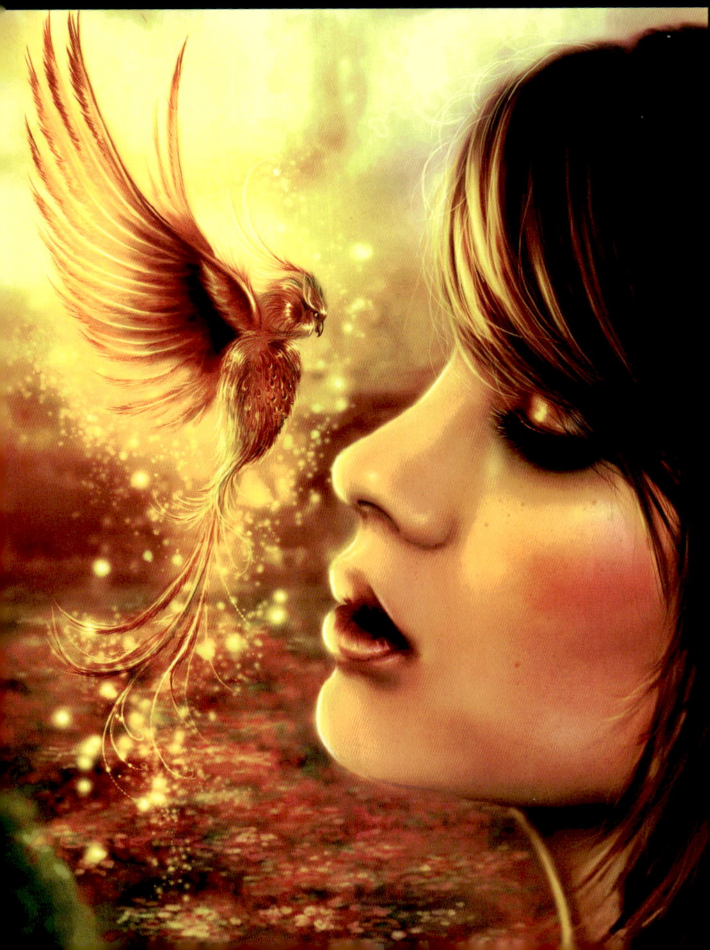

Knowledge and Wisdom
Photoshop
Wei Chen, CHINA
[top left]

The portrait of Shirley
Photoshop, Painter
Wei Chen, CHINA
[above]

Secret Garden
Photoshop
Suzanne van Pelt, NETHERLANDS
[left]

.showering.petals.
Painter
Client: ImagineFX magazine
Hong Kuang, SINGAPORE
[right]

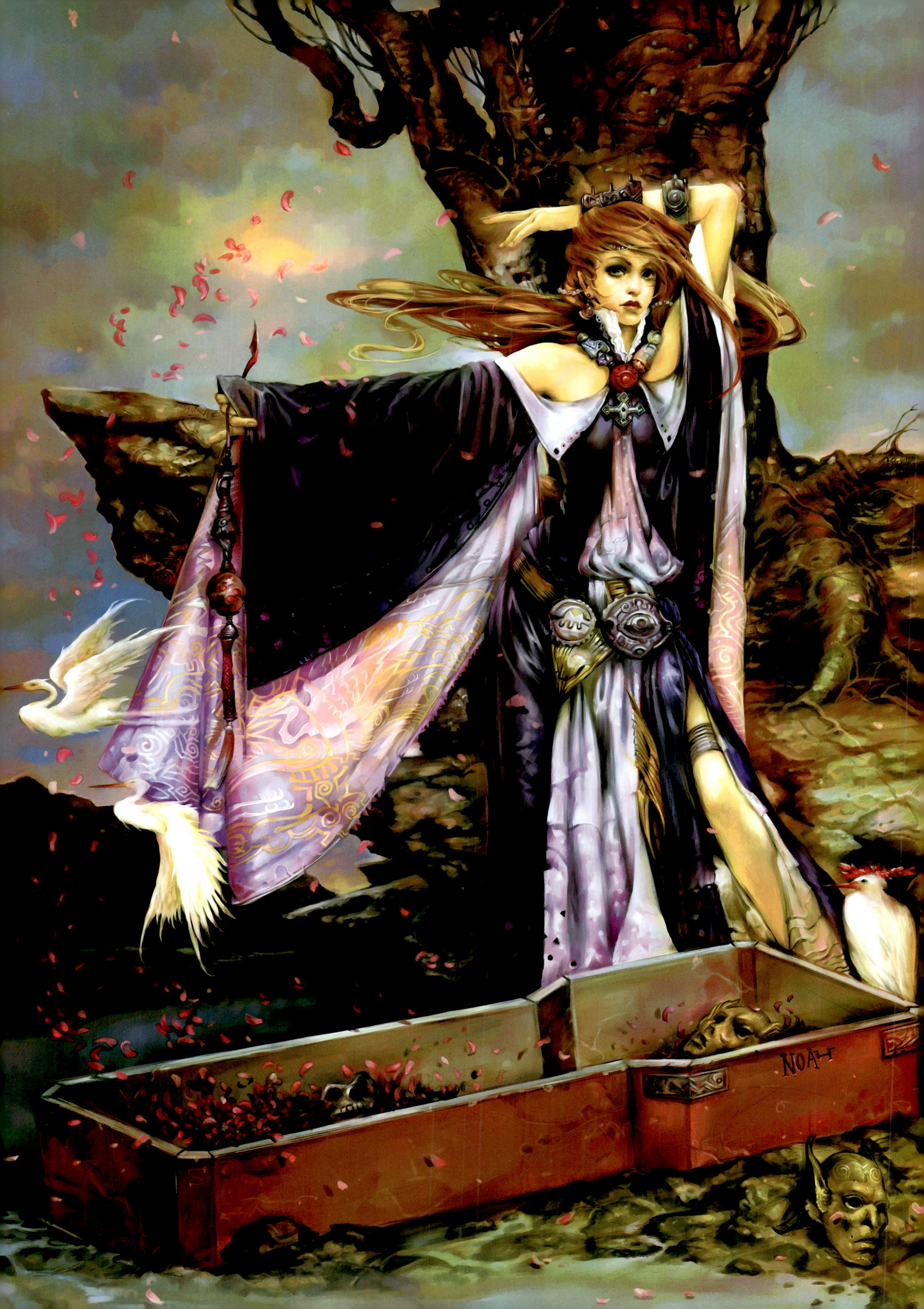
NOAH

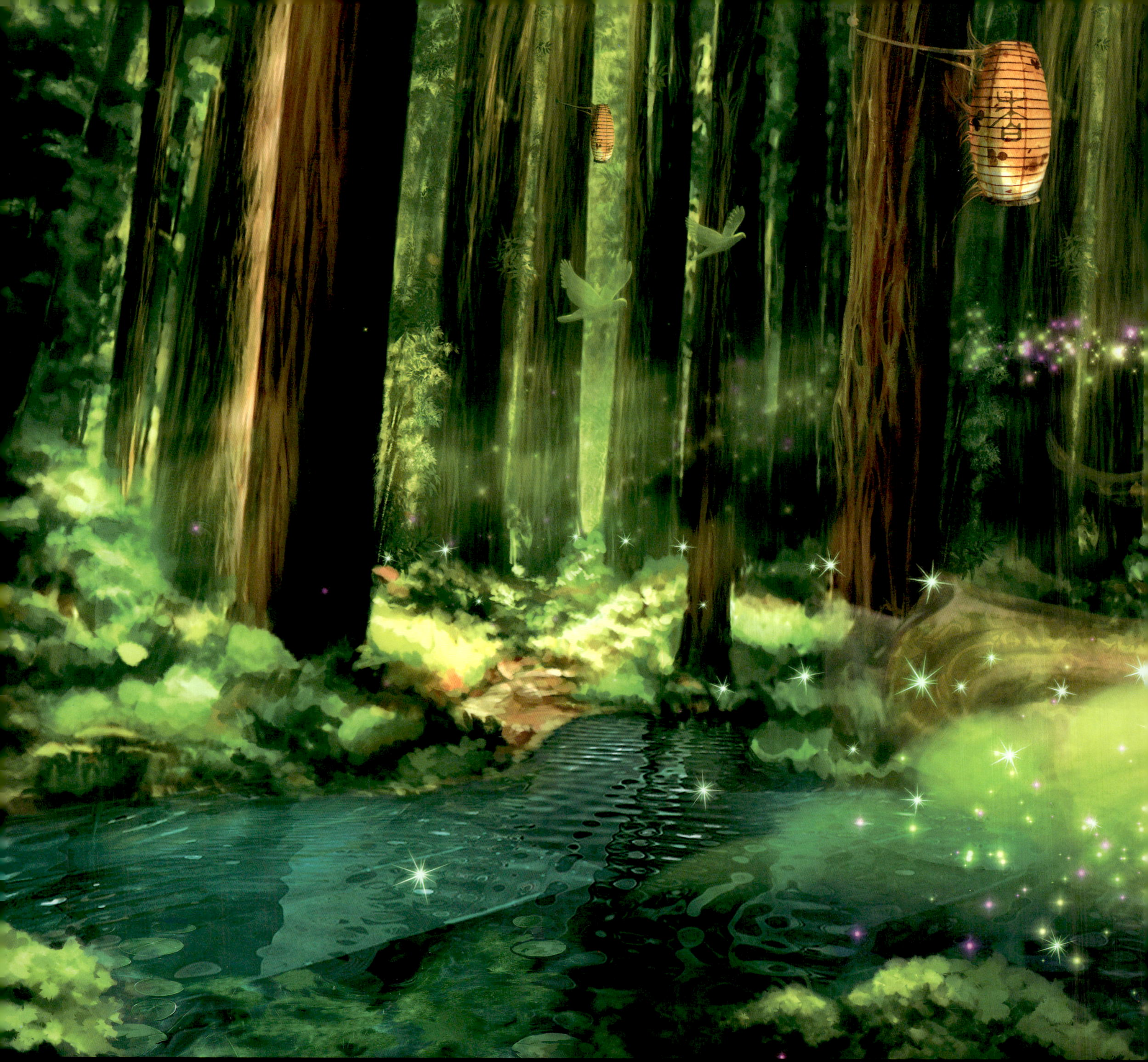

The Wizard of Oz
Photoshop, Painter
Ren Liwei, CHINA

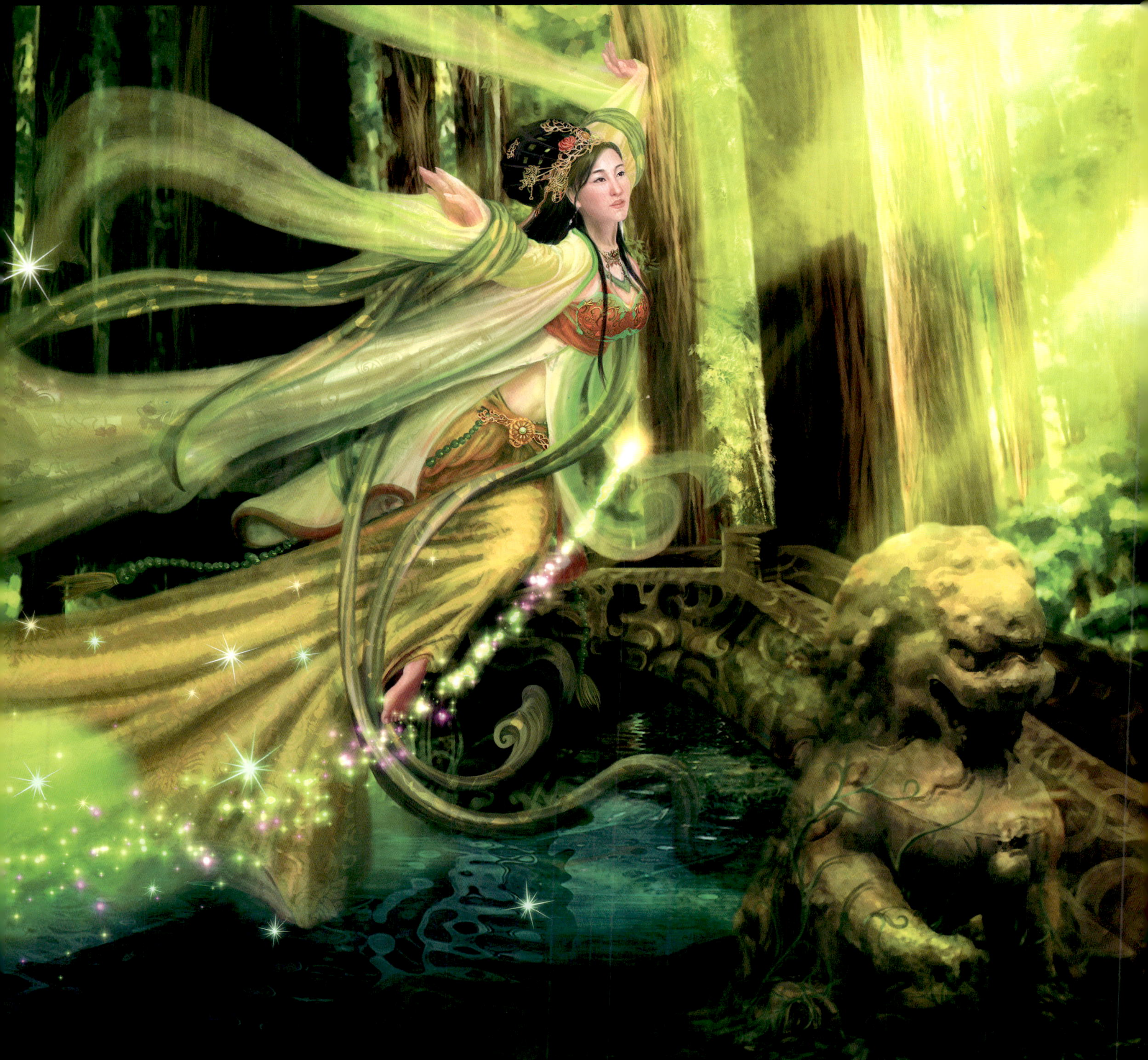

A

Kei Acedera
Toronto, ON
CANADA
kei@imaginismstudios.com
www.imaginismstudios.com
62, 139

Jiri Adamec
Pardubice,
CZECH REPUBLIC
astil@volny.cz
www.a-stil.cz
11

Angelos Agiostratitis
Athens, Glyfada,
GREECE
angel@websight.gr
www.agios.gr
20

Holli Alvarado
San Clemente, CA,
USA
holli@halvaradoart.com
www.halvaradoart.com
134

Glen Angus
Verona, WI,
USA
www.gangus.net
60

Val Aren
Warsaw,
POLAND
info@valaren.eu
valaren.eu
70

Steve Argyle
Orem, UT,
USA
steveargyle@gmail.com
steveargyle.com
168

Daniel Arnold-Mist
Leicestershire,
GREAT BRITAIN
daniel_mist@hotmail.com
152

Marcos Aurelio
Estudio Manga
Jardim Diadema, SP,
BRAZIL
marcos@estudiomanga.com.br
www.estudiomanga.com.br
148

Dawn Austin
austinillustration,
HONG KONG
dawn@austinillustration.net
austinillustration.net
20, 164

B

Sanjana Baijnath
Auckland,
NEW ZEALAND
sanjana@nilut.com
www.sanjanasart.com
6

Marcin Balcerzak
Burnaby, BC,
CANADA
martyb@shaw.ca
90

Alessandro Baldasseroni
Milan,
ITALY
baldasseroni@gmail.com
www.eklettica.com
48-49

John Barry Ballaran
Manila,
PHILIPPINES
johnbarryballaran@gmail.com
98

Leigh Bamforth
GREAT BRITAIN
ljb@wrakedesign.com
111

Tiziano Baracchi
Sona,
ITALY
eginardus@hotmail.com
thaldir.cgsociety.org
82

Patrick Beaulieu
Quebec, QC,
CANADA
squeezestudio@hotmail.com
www.squeezestudio.com
104

Robin Benes
Brno,
CZECH REPUBLIC
tes@tes3d.com
www.tes3d.com
55

Xiao Bing
Shanghai,
CHINA
c_cco@hotmail.com
cabotinecco.cgsociety.org
14

Branko Bistrovic
Toronto, ON,
CANADA
bisvic@gmail.com
42, 144

Whit Brachna
Akron, OH,
USA
alduarouli@hotmail.com
www.brushbook.com
172

Aleksi Briclot
Paris,
FRANCE
aleksi@aneyeoni.com
www.aneyeoni.com
133

Marc Brunet
Montreal, QC,
CANADA
finalxii@msn.com
bluefley.cgsociety.org
31, 177, 182

C

David Cabrera
SPAIN
pefiedolamuette@hotmail.com
34

Krystal Camprubi
FRANCE
contact@krystal-camprubi.com
www.krystal-camprubi.com
112

Damien Canderle
FRANCE
canderled@hotmail.com
www.maddamart.com
106-107, 109

Lauren K. Cannon
Shamong, NJ,
USA
lkcannon@comcast.net
navate.com
30, 66

Antonio Javier Caparó-Salgado
Toronto, ON,
CANADA
ajcaparo@gmail.com
141

Riyahd Cassiem
Johannesburg,
SOUTH AFRICA
riyahd@iburst.co.za
158

Sandra Chang-Adair
Los Angeles, CA,
USA
sandra@sandrachang.net
www.sandrachang.net
32

Jiansong Chen
LusioSoft Entertainment Co.,
Beijing,
CHINA
chain_jane@126.com
www.chainandjane.com
59, 79, 94

Mingjue Chen
San Francisco, CA,
USA
jigokuen@msn.com
jigokuen.deviantart.com
16

Wei Chen
Cheng Du,
CHINA
lorlandchen@hotmail.com
flowercity.ppzz.net
23, 77, 95, 184

Darius Cheong
Singapore,
SINGAPORE
dar2099@hotmail.com
www.aco2099.deviantart.com
78

Kevin Chin
Los Angeles, CA,
USA
chenzan27@yahoo.com
www.kevinchinart.com
27

Bobby Chiu
North York, ON,
CANADA
bobby@imaginismstudios.com
www.imaginismstudios.com
136

Alon Chou
Taipei,
TAIWAN
along.a1120@msa.hinet.net
www.alon.tw
98, 102

Leung Chun wan
HONG KONG
onimask@hotmail.com
www.heretic-family.com
50

Henryca Citra
Medan, North Sumatra,
INDONESIA
henryz_jetsam@yahoo.com
henryz.deviantart.com
45

Xavier Collette
Nandrin,
BELGIUM
acerb@skynet.be
www.acerb.be
176, 178

Francisco A. Cortina
Los Angeles, CA,
USA
francisco@cortinadigital.com
www. cortinadigital.com
115

D

Marta Dahlig
Warsaw,
POLAND
blackeri@poczta.onet.pl
www.marta-dahlig.com
8, 9, 68-69, *[Front cover: EXOTIQUE 3 Softcover edition]*

Antje Darling
Geronimo, OK,
USA
antje@sunnet.net
www.antjesgraphics.com
131

Belinda Day
Brisbane, QLD,
AUSTRALIA
thecityrose@yahoo.com.au
132

Jeffrey M. de Guzman
Makati City,
PHILIPPINES
jeffreymdg@yahoo.com
jeffmd.gfxartist.com
54, 82

Melanie Delon
Paris,
FRANCE
contact@melaniedelon.com
www.melaniedelon.com
Agent: Norma Editorial,
www.normaeditorial.com
7

Raffy Encarnacion Dematawaran
Manila,
PHILIPPINES
shatteredfxraffy@yahoo.com
57

Thitipon Dicruen
Ratchaburi,
THAILAND
xric7@yahoo.com
www.xric7.com
164

E

Eli Effenberger
ISRAEL
marmite_sue@hotmail.com
153

Embrio
DPI Studios
Calgary, AB,
CANADA
jay@dpistudios.net
www.dpistudios.net
35

Neil Eskuri
Electronic Arts Inc.,
Vancouver, BC,
CANADA
www.ea.com
122, 123

F

Rudy Jan Faber
Leeuwarden, Friesland,
NETHERLANDS
rudy@rudyfaber.com
rudeone.cgsociety.org
34

INDEX

SOFTWARE INDEX

Products credited by popular name in this book are listed alphabetically here by company.

Company	Products	Website
Adobe	Illustrator, Photoshop	www.adobe.com
Ambient Design	ArtRage	www.ambientdesign.com
Apple	Shake	www.apple.com
Autodesk	3ds Max, Maya, MotionBuilder, Mudbox, SketchBook Pro	www.autodesk.com
Boris Eyrich	Artweaver	www.artweaver.de
Chaos Group	V-Ray	www.chaosgroup.com
Corel	CorelDRAW, Paint Shop Pro, Painter	www.corel.com
DAZ Productions	Bryce, DAZ Studio	www.daz3d.com
e-frontier	Poser	www.e-frontier.com
Electronic Arts	Renderware	www.ea.com
E-on Software	Vue Esprit	www.e-onsoftware.com
eyeone Software	Fusion	www.eyeonline.com
Luxology	modo	www.luxology.com
MAXON	BodyPaint 3D	www.maxoncomputer.com
mental images	mental ray	www.mentalimages.com
NewTek	LightWave 3D	www.newtek.com
Pixologic	ZBrush	www.pixologic.com
Softimage	Softimage|XSI	www.softimage.com
Splutterfish	Brazil r/s	www.splutterfish.com